CAMBRIDGE LATIN AMERICAN STUDIES

EDITORS

DAVID JOSLIN JOHN STREET

5

PARTIES AND POLITICAL
CHANGE IN BOLIVIA
1880–1952

THE SERIES

PARTIES AND POLITICAL CHANGE IN BOLIVIA
1880-1952

BY

HERBERT S. KLEIN

Associate Professor of History
University of Chicago

CAMBRIDGE
AT THE UNIVERSITY PRESS
1969

Published by the Syndics of the Cambridge University Press
Bentley House, P.O. Box 92, 200 Euston Road, London N.W.1
American Branch: 32 East 57th Street, New York, N.Y.10022

Library of Congress Catalogue Card Number: 77–85722

Standard Book Number: 521 07614 5

Printed in Great Britain
at the University Press
Aberdeen

TO
MY PARENTS

CONTENTS

LIST OF TABLES

PREFACE

Bolivia's political and institutional history conforms in a large degree to the pattern of nineteenth- and twentieth-century political development in Latin America. After a period of severe independence wars, Bolivia went through its age of civil strife and *caudillo* rule. By the latter decades of the nineteenth century it developed its own variant of the liberal-conservative political party system with its characteristic limited political participation and upper class rule. Like the other states of the continent it experienced an influx of foreign political ideologies, beginning in the nineteenth century with European liberalism and positivism, followed by anarchism, fascism and various forms of Marxism in the twentieth. Although these ideologies were expressed in Bolivian idioms and adapted to local needs, the dominant ideas were imported. Even its vital pro-Indian ideology of *indigenismo* acquired a large part of its vocabulary from non-national authors.

Both this imported thought and the political experiences which it shared with many other states of Latin America appeared in Bolivia much later than elsewhere. Bolivia's political growth was often a generation or two behind similar developments in the more advanced states of the continent and its European originated ideologies frequently arrived after being filtered through Chilean or Argentine experience.

But this time lag was dramatically overcome in the middle decades of the twentieth century. In the revolution of April 1952 Bolivia experienced a total breakdown of its traditional political structure and underwent a profound social revolution far in advance of anything which had occurred in any other state in South America. This revolution destroyed a land-tenure and rural labour system that originated in colonial times and nationalized the dominant Bolivian export industry. It saw the adoption of a revolutionary ideology and the effective introduction of the Indian masses into national political life on a scale hitherto unknown except for the Mexican experience.

That such a revolution occurred at all raises of course an important question, but that it occurred in backward Bolivia is even more of a challenge to analysis. Bolivia exhibited the same patterns of exploitation of the masses, harsh inequalities of wealth, feudal agrarian structure and organized radical opposition, as almost all the other republics of the continent. In fact, because of its extreme retardation even by Latin American standards, rapid industrialization and urbanization caused less disruptive tension than in most of the republics. What then brought revolution to this most traditional and backward of states? What was the 'accelerating factor', or catalyst, which set in motion one of the very few social revolutionary processes that Latin America has experienced?

To almost all Bolivians, the key to the understanding of the revolutionary process lies in the disastrous results of the Chaco War of 1932–5. Though all agree that this event is the primary catalyst for the 1952 revolution, few have attempted to present a careful and documented evaluation of its impact, and fewer still have attempted to determine just what mechanisms were set in motion by the bitter defeat at the hands of Paraguay.

While most commentators have assumed that the Chaco War created social discontent and economic dislocation, a careful examination of the post-war period reveals neither of these effects. The Indian peasant masses were easily reabsorbed into the feudal land system after the conflict, and the urban proletariat felt no unusual adverse effects or bitter hostility toward the system. As for the popularly accepted thesis of economic dislocation, this too is a myth. The national economy during and immediately after the war showed surprising resilience, and the immediate post-war years brought full employment, constantly rising imports and exports in a favourable balance of trade, and at first only moderate inflation caused by these booming economic conditions. The impact of the war must rather be seen in terms of political dislocations and basic changes in the political structure of national leadership and ideology.

The aim of this book is to describe the origins and development of the Bolivian political system as it evolved into a stable two-party régime, and to analyse the causes which led to the mutation of this system and the rise of class politics and social revolutionary movements in the third and fourth decades of this century. Finally I have attempted to show how these basic changes had led by the 1940s to such a fracturing of the traditional system, that social revolution was made almost inevitable.

The field research for this study was initially undertaken on a grant from the Henry L. and Grace Doherty Foundation which enabled me to spend a year in Bolivia from December 1960 to December 1961. Further assistance in the form of a Fulbright Travel grant and aid from the Social Science Division of the University of Chicago allowed me to return to Bolivia in 1963 to expand my earlier work, and a final stay in August 1966, was sponsored partly by a Ford Foundation grant.

As in any such research into a foreign culture, I was deeply dependent on others for guidance and support. I wish especially to thank Professor Bernardo Blanco-González, formerly of the Universidad Mayor de San Andrés, and now at the University of Chicago, who was an indispensable friend and mentor throughout all stages of this work. Others who freely aided me with their knowledge were Señor Guillermo Lora of La Paz, Professor Charles Arnade of the University of South Florida, and Professor James Malloy of Pittsburgh. I am especially indebted to Señor Lora for the use of his excellent clipping and manuscript collection and for permission to use many of his own studies on political and labour history which were still in manuscript form. From the several directors and staff of the Biblioteca Municipal Mariscal Andrés Santa Cruz of La Paz I have received only the most courteous assistance and aid in working through their excellent newspaper collection, for which I am deeply grateful. I would also like to thank the several scholars and friends who criticized the work at its various stages, among whom were Professors Robert J. Alexander, Walter Johnson, Stanley M. Elkins, Richard Wortman, Richard Schaedel, and Dr Gunnar Mendoza, of the Archivo Nacional of Bolivia. The journals *The Americas, Inter-American Economic Affairs* and the *Hispanic American Historical Review* have kindly permitted me to use articles of mine which have recently appeared.

Finally, of course, my wife in this, as in all my work, has been my constant assistant, editor and crucial supporter.

H.S.K.

ABBREVIATIONS

AEP	Asociación de Ex-Prisioneros
ANDES	Asociación Nacional de Ex-Combatientes Socialistas
ANPOS	Asociación Nacional Permanente de Organizaciones Sindicales
ASBG	Acción Socialista Beta Gama
CEPAL	Comisión Económica para América Latina
COB	Confederación Obrera Boliviana
COMIBOL	Corporación Minera de Bolivia
CSB	Confederación Socialista Boliviana
CSL	Confederación Sindical Latino Americana
CSR	Célula Socialista Revolucionaria
CSTB	Confederación Sindical de Trabajadores de Bolivia
CTB	Confederación de Trabajadores de Bolivia
EMG	Estado Mayor General
FDA	Frente Democratico Antifascista
FIB	Frente de Izquierda Boliviana
FOI	Federación Obrera Internacional
FOL	Federación Obrera Local
FOT	Federación Obrera del Trabajo
FSB	Falange Socialista Boliviana
FSTMB	Federación Sindical de Trabajadores Mineros de Bolivia
FUB	Federación Universitaria Boliviana
FUS	Frente Unico Socialista
LEC	Legión de Ex-Combatientes
MNR	Movimiento Nacionalista Revolucionario
MNRA	Movimiento Nacionalista Revolucionario Autentico
PCB	Partido Comunista de Bolivia
PIR	Partido de la Izquierda Revolucionaria
POR	Partido Obrero Revolucionario
POS	Partido Obrero Socialista
PRS	Partido Republicano Socialista
PSE	Partido Socialista de Estado
PSI	Partido Socialista Independiente
PSOB	Partido Socialista Obrero Boliviano
PSR	Partido Socialista Revolucionario
PSU	Partido Socialista Unificado
PURS	Partido de la Unión Republicana Socialista
RADEPA	Razón de Patria
YPFB	Yacimientos Petrolíferos Fiscales Bolivianos

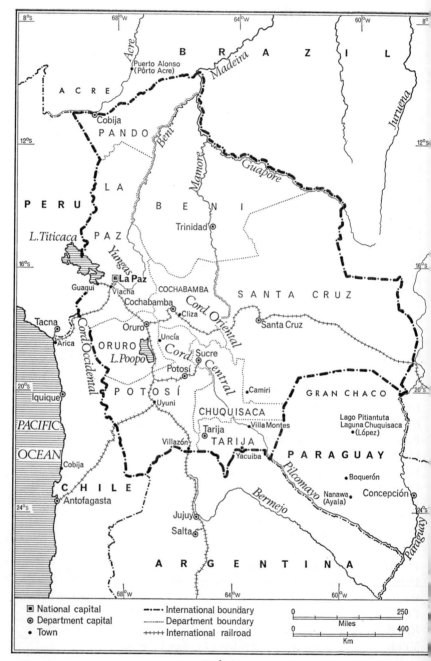

Bolivia

THE ESTABLISHMENT OF THE POLITICAL PARTY SYSTEM

In the last days of the South American wars of independence, a group of delegates gathered in the southern Andean town of Chuquisaca to decide the fate of their region. Bolívar's troops had defeated the last remnants of the royalist forces in the provinces of Lower Peru; and these representatives from Upper Peru decided to declare themselves an independent republic. On 6 August 1825, they solemnly proclaimed, 'before the entire world that their irrevocable will is to govern themselves by themselves . . . and to sustain unalterable their holy Catholic religion, and the sacrosanct rights of honour, life, liberty, equality, property and security'.[1]

With these fine sounding phrases, the Republic of Bolivia was born among the provinces which had made up the old Audiencia of Charcas. But for all the flourish and the bloodshed which preceded it, this declaration of independence was an anti-climatic affair, since the state which emerged was not essentially different from its predecessor. The oligarchy which had ruled before was the one which ruled now, only it was now no longer responsible for its actions to a distant crown.[2]

Unfortunately, the hope of these oligarchic republicans that they could carry on the glories of the past in new republican forms, were to be frustrated. For the nation which emerged after fifteen years of civil war in the Andean highlands was paradoxically an economically retarded area, despite its legendary colonial wealth and prominence.

Although the silver mining region of Potosí had been, in its

[1] Javier Malagón (ed.), *Las actas de independencia de América* (Washington, D.C.: Unión Panamericana, 1955), p. 17.
[2] On the conservative and propertied nature of the Independence Assembly, see Charles W. Arnade, *The Emergence of the Republic of Bolivia* (Gainesville: University of Florida Press, 1957), pp. 183ff.

time, the richest in the world, it was now in complete decay. From its founding in the mid-sixteenth century until the middle of the seventeenth century, Potosí had produced enormous quantities of silver and the city reached a population of over 150,000 persons.[1] Although the region declined in the eighteenth century, it was still the greatest single source of revenue in the viceroyalty of Peru, and was a key area of contention between the Buenos Aires and Lima viceroyalties.[2] But by the last quarter of the eighteenth century this famous mining zone was in decay. The exhaustion of the richest and most accessible veins; the poverty of the miners and their ignorance of advanced technology; and the absorption of new colonial capital into the thriving international commerce of the late eighteenth century all contributed to its decline. This was further accentuated by the collapse of the auxiliary Huancavelica mercury mines after 1800, and by the fifteen years of civil war beginning in 1809 which had a disastrous effect on local miners.[3]

---

[1] According to the admittedly crude calculations made in 1879 by Adolf Soetbeer, Bolivian silver production reached its peak at the end of the sixteenth and first two decades of the seventeenth century. Production thereafter slowly declined until 1700, when it suddenly took a sharp downward plunge, only recovering moderately in the middle decades of the eighteenth century. A new downward plunge occurred after 1800 with the worst years of the new century being the period 1811–30, with a moderate increase in the period 1831–50 and a new severe depression in the period from 1851 to 1865. By the latter years of the 1860s the modern mining era had begun and production began to climb dramatically. Adolf Soetbeer, *Edelmetall-Produktion und Werthverhaltniss zwischen Gold und Silber seit der Entdeckung Amerikas bis zur Gegenwart* (Gotha: Justus Perthes, 1879), pp. 78–9. For the first detailed modern analysis of silver production at Potosí, which covers the period so far only to 1600, see the pioneer study by Alvaro Jara, 'Dans le Pérou du XVIᵉ siècle: La coubre de production des métaux monnayables', *Annales, E.S.C.*, Année 23, No. 3 (Mai–Juin 1967), pp. 590–603. For a summary history of the city see Lewis Hanke, *The Imperial City of Potosí* (The Hague: Martinus Nijhoff, 1956), and the detailed articles accompanying the Hanke and Gunnar Mendoza edition of Bartolomé Arzáns de Orsúa y Vela, *Historia de la Villa Imperial de Potosí* (3 vols.; Providence: Brown University Press, 1965).

[2] In the late seventeenth and early eighteenth centuries, Potosí was the single most important centre for government revenue, producing for the crown between 35 and 44 per cent of the total government income in the viceroyalty. Michel Colin, *Le Cuzco à la fin du XVIIᵉ et au début du XVIIIᵉ siècle* (Caen: Faculté des Lettres et Sciences Humaines de la Université de Caen, 1966), pp. 208–19, tables 10–12.

[3] Guillermo Céspedes del Castillo, *Lima y Buenos Aires, repercusiones económicas y políticas de la creación del virreinato del Plata* (Sevilla: Escuela de Estudios Hispano-Americanos, 1947), pp. 10–11, 77, 80, 165. Also see Arthur P. Whitaker, *The Huancavelica Mercury Mine* (Cambridge: Harvard University Press, 1941), pp. 74ff.

Whereas Potosí still had some forty *ingenios* (or mills) refining silver in 1803, it had only fifteen by the end of the wars of independence, with production declining in this same period by 81 per cent.[1] The depression in silver production was also reflected in the city's population, and in 1835 the famous French naturalist D'Orbigny estimated the population at only some 13,000 and was amazed by the large number of abandoned homes and mines.[2] Nor did the first quarter-century of republican rule bring any major change, for by the first complete national census of 1846 it was estimated that the lack of capital had forced the closing of some 10,000 mines in Bolivia since the late colonial period, and that at least two-thirds of these mines were still capable of being productive, though now abandoned and flooded.[3]

Besides the decadence of this preponderant national industry, the new republic also inherited a poorly integrated national territory, with population disproportionately concentrated. The bulk of the population was located on the inter-mountain Andean highlands known as the *altiplano* and in the tropical valleys of the eastern cordillera escarpment.[4] Over two-thirds of the national population was concentrated in these two regions, according to the 1846 census, while the coastal department of Atacama contained only 0·3 per cent of the population. The fourth major region of Bolivia, the eastern lowlands, known as the *oriente*, and including the departments of the Beni and Santa Cruz, contained only 9·2 per cent of Bolivia's people.[5] Even after adding the lowland provinces of the other departments to the oriente total, it is clear that the overwhelming majority of the Bolivian nation was located in the

[1] Edmond Temple, *Travels in Various Parts of Peru, Including a Year's Residence in Potosí* (2 vols.; London: Henry Colburn and Richard Bentley, 1830), I, pp. 308–10.
[2] Alcides D'Orbigny, *Viaje a la américa meridional*, ed. S. Pastor and trans. A. Cepeda (4 vols.; Buenos Aires: Editorial Futuro, 1945), IV, 1496.
[3] José María Dalence, *Bosquejo estadístico de Bolivia* (Chuquisaca: Imprenta de Sucre, 1851), p. 295.
[4] The valleys included two major groupings, the so-called Yungas of the northeast, and the more open valleys of the Pilcomayo and Rio Grande rivers with the valley of Cochabamba being the richest and most populated of these latter. Oscar Schmeider, *Geografía de América Latina* (Mexico: Fondo de Cultura Económica, 1965), pp. 291–2; Jorge Muñoz Reyes, *Bosquejo de geografía de Bolivia* (No. 215; Rio de Janeiro: Instituto Pan-Americano de Geografía e Historia, 1956), pp. 26–30; Harold Osborne, *Bolivia, A Land Divided* (2nd ed.; London: Royal Institute of International Affairs, 1955), pp. 4–23.
[5] Dalence, *Bosquejo estadístico*, p. 202.

mountain highlands and valleys far from the sea and the neighbouring republics. In this populated core lay the bulk of the
nation's farming and mining and all her important urban
centres.

This core population was several days' journey by mule transport from the nearest seaports; moreover, the republic had only
one serviceable port in the whole Atacama region. This was
Cobija, which in the 1830s had a population of only about 700.[1]
Although Cobija handled something like one-third of Bolivia's
international trade by the 1850s, its own lines of communication
with the interior population were controlled to an extent of over
90 per cent by foreign nationals. And it was the transportation
cost from Cobija to the highland cities which accounted for over
two-thirds of the price of imported goods. As one contemporary
French economist concluded after a detailed study of Bolivia's
trade in the 1850s, its archaic communications system had created
a 'commercial blockade' which was causing 'the growing impoverishment of Bolivia'.[2]

Given these poor communications, it was impossible to export
anything except the most valuable national products, and these of
course were the precious minerals. Bolivia was rich in such metals,
but the years of war and civil strife had drained the nation of capital,
and without capital these resources could not be fully exploited.
Nor was national agricultural production sufficient in either
quality or quantity for exportation. Though close to 90 per
cent of the population was listed as rural in this early period,[3]
Bolivia was not even agriculturally self-sufficient. There were
fertile lands in many parts of the country, but a large part of the
population lived on the impoverished lands of the altiplano, and

[1] [Dr. W. S. W. Rushenberger], *Three Years in the Pacific, Including Notices of
Brazil, Chile, Bolivia and Peru* (Philadelphia: Carey, Lea and Blanchard, 1834),
p. 169.
[2] Adam Dunin Iundzill, *Du commerce bolivien, considérations sur l'avenir des relations
entre l'Europe et la Bolivie* (Paris: G.-A. Pinard, 1856), pp. 10–14. Iundzill estimated that 68 per cent of the final price of European goods in Sucre, the chief highland city served by Cobija, was accounted for by mule transport from the coast.
[3] In the first complete republican census, that of 1846, the eleven cities and
thirty-five towns made up only 11 per cent of the population. But this listing
included many rural centres of a few hundred persons, and the largest single
town, La Paz, contained only some 42,000 persons. Dalence, *Bosquejo estadístico*,
pp. 199–200.

4

the rest were cut off from the national market by poor internal communications. With the single exception of quinine, no agricultural products were exported and few products even left their local regions.[1] As one expert noted in the 1840s, 'cereals are commonly sold and consumed in the same departments in which they are produced'.[2] In fact, Bolivia not only imported cereals, meats, and pack animals from abroad, but even imported from Peru such typical locally produced foodstuffs as potatoes and *chuño*, the famous dried root food indigenous to the Andean highlands.[3] Given this agricultural underdevelopment, and the depression of the mining sector, Bolivia became, for the first time in its post-conquest history, a net importer of goods and ran an unfavourable balance of trade until well into the middle of the century.[4]

This stagnation of the private sector was also reflected quite clearly in the public economy. Whereas the prime sources of government income under the crown had been mining, production, and sales taxes, the republican government obtained the bulk of its funds from a head tax on Indian landowners, and received only a minor income from production, trade, or mining and smelting. Thus in the budget of 1846, the head tax on Indians was the largest single source of government revenue and accounted for 43 per cent of government income. If the tax on coca production, which was a product consumed only by Indians, is added to this figure, then direct taxation on Indians accounted for 50 per cent of all government revenues, while mining and smelting taxes together brought only 11 per cent of government funds.[5] Even as late as 1868, a contemporary observer noted that the

---

[1] Though quinine bark was constantly exported throughout the nineteenth century, it was always a minor export crop. In 1846, for example, it accounted for only 6 per cent of the value of total national exports and contributed but 7 per cent of the government income in taxes. Dalence, *Bosquejo estadístico*, pp. 305–5, and Dr H. A. Weddell, *Voyage dans le nord de la Bolivie* . . . (Paris: P. Bertrand, 1853), pp. 235–46, 249. Despite extreme cycles of prosperity and depression, it still contributed 8 per cent of the value of exports in 1881 (André Bresson, *Bolivia, sept années d'explorations, de voyages et de séjours dans l'Amérique australe* [Paris: Librairie Coloniale, 1886], p. 248), but by 1900 it was only an insignificant export due to the competition of plantation production of the bark in both Colombia and the Far East. Luis Peñaloza, *Historia económica de Bolivia* (2 vols.; La Paz: n.p., 1953–4), II, 3–16.
[2] Dalence, *Bosquejo estadístico*, p. 314.   [3] *Ibid.* pp. 278–9, 309–31, 315–16.
[4] *Ibid.* pp. 302ff.   [5] Dalence, *Bosquejo estadístico*, pp. 361–2.

discriminatory head tax on Indians provided 'the best and most secure source of government income'.[1]

Equally indicative of the backwardness of the government economy was central government expenditure in this early republican period. In a nation desperately in need of a basic communications network, the government in the 1846 budget supplied virtually no funds for national road construction or other major public works. Rather, some 45 per cent of the government's expenditures went to maintain the standing army (a figure astronomical even by the standards of the day), another 10 per cent for funding the public debt, and fully 12 per cent for clerical salaries and church support. This left but 43 per cent of the budget for simply administrative expenses, and virtually nothing for development.[2]

Along with this depressed public and private economy, the new republic also emerged with one of the most backward social systems in the western hemisphere. Its population, which in 1825 was estimated at 1,100,000, was bitterly divided along racial lines between an Indian population estimated at 73 per cent of this total, and a non-Indian minority.[3] Thus Bolivia was probably

[1] Ramón Sotomayor Valdés, *Estudio histórico de Bolivia bajo la administración del Jeneral D. José María de Achá* . . . (Santiago de Chile: Imprenta Andrés Bello, 1874), p. 527. In the budgets published (i.e. 1845, 1847, 1860, and 1864) the Indian head tax income never fell below 37 per cent of the budget and was always the largest single source of income. Casto Rojas, *Historia financiera de Bolivia* (La Paz: Talleres Gráficos 'Marinoni', 1916), pp. 182–3, 222–3, 246–7.

[2] Dalence, *Bosquejo estadístico*, pp. 364–5. As one scholar concluded after a survey of the first fifty years of republican financial history, 'from 1825 to 1879 the development of government incomewas in significant. The country, given over to continuous revolts which sterilized the most important fiscal reforms, did not advance much either in its financial organization or in the development of public or private wealth'. Rojas, *Historia financiera*, p. 412.

[3] This racial breakdown is based on the informed calculations of the Englishman, Joseph Barclay Pentland, who visited Bolivia in 1827 on a scientific mission for the British government. His estimates were 800,000 Indians, 200,000 whites, and 100,000 cholos, giving a total of 1,100,000 which seems to be quite a reasonable guess when compared to the 1,373,896 persons counted in the first complete republican census of 1846. For these figures see R. A. Humphreys (ed.), *British Consular Reports on the Trade and Politics of Latin America, 1824–1826* (Camden 3rd Series, Vol. LXIII; London: Royal Historical Society, 1940), p. 176 n6, p. 208 n4.
It is interesting to compare these 1827 figures with those of the 1900 census, which is the first complete census in Bolivia to give a detailed breakdown of population by racial categories. The breakdown of the whites and Indians in total numbers was almost identical to that of 1827, being 213,088 and 792,850 respectively. The cholo population, however, had more than quadrupled in this half-century to some 484,611. Oficina Nacional de Inmigración, Estadística y Propaganda Geográfica, *Censo nacional de la población de la republica, 1° de setiembre de 1900* (2 vols.; La Paz: José M. Gamarra, 1902–4), I, 31.

the most predominantly Indian of the new American republics,[1] and its stratification along racial lines was unquestionably one of the most rigid. The Bolivian Indians were almost totally unaware of the nation's existence and formed a separate society with their own languages and culture. Their relations with the non-Indian society were confined to the economic sphere, and even here, they were almost exclusively rural, and largely subsistence farmers, leaving the urban centres overwhelmingly to the whites and the mixed Indian-white population known as the *cholos*. These two societies were hierarchically arranged; and the non-Indian minority, the only part of the nation truly aware of national existence, totally exploited the Indian majority, both through the discriminatory taxing system, and even more importantly in its growing control over the land.

In early nineteenth-century Bolivia, the land was divided between an expanding *latifundia* system controlled by the white élite, and a village communal pattern of land ownership used by both the Quechua and Aymara Indians. The Indian communities comprised several categories of land-owning and landless families (*originarios, agregados*, and *forasteros sin tierra*), and in 1846 they accounted for an estimated 621,468 persons. The white *hacendados* and their families made up another 23,107 persons, while the landless estate Indians known as *colonos* or *pongos* numbered some 360,000.[2] Though the 5,000 hacendado families were only 2.3 per cent of the total rural population, they were an aggressive and expanding minority which throughout the nineteenth century utilized the laws of the state to destroy Indian communal property ownership and to exploit the lands for their own ends. Since the republican laws initially conceived of private property as an absolute individual right, all laws denied the legal right of the community to hold land and thus permitted the whites and cholos to use both the courts and the state police power to destroy *comunidad* holdings.

Rapidly absorbing the richest lands in each area, the hacendados

---

[1] For a rough comparison with other nations at this time, see Angel Rosenblat, *La población indígena y el mestizaje en América* (2 vols.; Buenos Aires: Editorial Nova, 1954), I, 199–200.
[2] These estimates are taken from data given in Dalence, *Bosquejo estadístico*, pp. 234–5.

were able to extract free labour from the previous landowning Indians in return for use of usufruct soil on the newly-created estates. In what was unquestionably the most exploitative Indian peasant-hacienda system in the New World in the nineteenth century, the landowners extracted both free farm labour and free personal service (*pongueaje*) from their colonos in return for the simple use of land for their own crops. Often they forced the colonos, when working for the landowner, to provide their own tools, seed, and animals.[1]

Though the majority of the nation's Indians in these early days of the republic were free comunidad Indians, the lack of capital and the primitive level of technology, together with the progressive subdivision of the meagre soil resources where the communities were located, made for a level of existence little better than the landless estate Indians. There were no rural schools, no rights to citizenship—since literacy was the primary qualification[2]—and an exploitative system of local *corregidor* government which retained all the abuses of the royal era and provided none of its benefits. The office of corregidor, usually held by a cholo, was one of the most abused in nineteenth-century American government. The corregidor was in charge of collecting the onerous discriminatory head tax on comunidad Indians, as well as *corvée* labour for public works and even for private exploitation. The corregidores at times even controlled the price of such basic imported commodities as salt and coca.

Faced by a diminishing supply of land and a near starvation level of subsistence agriculture which often resulted in famine cycles, it was the comunidad Indians who, from the first days

---

[1] A good survey of the relations of nineteenth-century Indians with non-Indians is contained in the pioneering study by Ramiro Condarco Morales, *Zarete, el 'Temible' Willka, historia de la rebelión indígena de 1899* (La Paz: Talleres Gráficos Bolivianos, 1966), pp. 23–59; also see Arturo Urquidi Morales, *La comunidad indígena, precedentes sociológicos, vicisitudes históricos* (Cochabamba: Imprenta Universitaria, 1941), pp. 79ff. For a more detailed analysis of the colono and the hacienda system, see below, ch. 6.

[2] In 1846, 100,000 persons, or only 7 per cent of the population, were considered literate (Dalence, *Bosquejo estadístico*, p. 242). By 1900 the percentage of literates had only risen to 17 per cent of the total population (*Censo nacional de 1900*, II, Primera Parte, p. 33), and by 1950 it was 31 per cent. Dirección General de Estadística y Censos, *Censo demográfico 1950* (La Paz: Editorial 'Argote', 1955), p. 112.

of the republic until the middle decades of the twentieth century, provided labour for the mines of the Oruro and Potosí regions. But exporting labour was not always a successful means of relieving the harsh exploitation of government and a diminishing supply of land; and in almost every decade of republican history local comunidad Indians rose up in senseless and brutal caste wars of extermination against the oppression of the corregidores and clerics and the expansion of the white élite. Every time they rebelled, they were violently suppressed by government troops.

This harsh world of the comunidad Indians, as well as that of the hacienda colonos, was a world apart from the national life of Bolivia. The only avenue of mobility open to the Indian across this social and almost caste-like barrier was through rejection of his rural and/or communal life and migration to the cities, where he could learn an urban trade or skill and the Spanish language. These transplanted and re-educated Indians became in effect a new 'racial' group, the so-called cholos or mestizos. While the cholos formed the lower class urban proletariat, and became a conscious part of national life, they nevertheless remained, under the oligarchic governments of the nineteenth century, a disenfranchised group which was denied access to power or even a voice in its own destiny. Forming the lower ranks of the armies and of the unskilled and artisan workers, they often served as political instruments in mob action for the various factions of the oligarchy. Though a few demagogic governments, such as that of Belzu, made appeals for their support, and others permitted talented individuals to rise into the oligarchy, the cholo masses were in general denied access to office, to power, and to the vote. But the number of these urban cholos in the early part of the century was relatively small, probably no more than 100,000 to 200,000, and this inhibited their ability to find self-expression in political terms. However, their constant increase in numbers throughout the nineteenth and early twentieth centuries, and the new economic opportunities which developed with the rebirth of mining, created by the third decade of the twentieth century a pivotal, self-conscious and powerful middle group, between the inarticulate and non-participating Indian masses and the formerly all-powerful white oligarchy.

But until then, national political life was the exclusive monopoly of the small and relatively stable number (approximately 200,000) of racially and culturally defined whites. This European-dressed, Spanish-speaking, literate élite based its intellectual leadership on the almost exclusive possession of literacy and European culture, and its economic power on the latifundia system. Despite its firm economic base in agriculture, this white oligarchy was overwhelmingly an urban group, for except in the Cochabamba valley, absentee ownership was the prevailing rule of the latifundias, and almost every white hacendado had an urban residence and a liberal profession.[1] But so long as the nation was barely self-supporting in agriculture, and the principal export and capital-obtaining industry of mining was completely disorganized, the economic strength of this élite was severely limited. Throughout most of the nineteenth century, in fact, the government itself was one of the most lucrative sources of income in the nation. Thus, despite its social and economic leadership in regard to the other classes and *castas* of the nation, the Bolivian oligarchy lacked the economic strength and independence to control its own destiny.

Although the white creoles had succeeded in suppressing cholo and Indian uprisings during the wars of independence, and emerged by 1825 with exclusive control over the new government, they were incapable of maintaining that control and creating instruments of power which would guarantee their peaceful dominance. The long years of civil wars which led to independence left the nation and the oligarchy in an economically depressed condition and sapped the vital reconstructive energies of the creole élite, leaving it a passive and essentially parasitic class. Because of the population settlement pattern and the difficult terrain, the republic also inherited a major problem of extreme localism, with provincial élites more interested in the *patria chica* than in the problems of the entire nation. Finally, the new republic unfortunately inherited a strong tradition of militarism and

[1] The 1900 census listed 49,647 persons engaged in liberal professions, or only 4 per cent of the labour force (*Censo nacional de 1900*, II, Primera Parte, p. 46). This percentage hardly changed in the next fifty years for by 1950, when the category was also made to include personal servants, the liberal professions made up only 5 per cent of the work force. *Censo demográfico 1950*, p. 142. The number of lawyers actually declined in this period from 1,546 to 1,103. There had been only 449 lawyers in 1846. Dalence, *Bosquejo estadístico*, p. 230.

political violence as a result of the wars of independence, along with a host of newly risen military chieftains who were soon vying with each other for control of the government and its limited fiscal resources. All of these factors created in Bolivia the classic Latin American era of *caudillismo*, which was to last until the last quarter of the nineteenth century. A period of constant military coups and illegal successions, the rule of caudillos was an age of anarchy without political parties and ideologies and only moderately affected by civilian constitutional forms of government.[1]

A final factor which aided the breakdown of orderly constitutional government was the problem of foreign intervention. The inability of Bolivia to develop or even control her vast unexploited territories in the littoral and the oriente was a major cause of the prolonged internal instability in these early years. A strong and progressive state such as Chile soon found the rich territories of Bolivia which fronted on her own borders an irresistible temptation. Unencumbered by political and social disunity, Chile by the 1830s had a stable civilian government dominated by a powerful and developing commercial oligarchy which turned its full attention to Bolivia's Atacama desert and began active expansion northward.

Another foreign power which soon intervened in Bolivian affairs was Peru, culturally, economically, and geographically a natural part of the Bolivian republic. It was inevitable that a strong sentiment toward amalgamation would exist in both countries in these early republican years. From 1825 until well into the middle of the century there was a constant succession of interventions in each other's internal affairs by both nations. The first to initiate an attempt towards unification was Marshal Andrés Santa Cruz, a leader in the independence wars and one of Bolivia's greatest presidents. Facing the threat of Chilean expansion, Santa Cruz attempted to compensate for Bolivia's weakness by uniting with the more powerful Peru in a close-knit political

---

[1] Gino Germani has elaborated a rough typology for the development of Latin American republican governments, which fits the Bolivian pattern, with some variations, quite well. This typology has a progression from civil wars, through limited participation parliamentary governments for the nineteenth century. See Gino Germani, *Política y sociedad en una época de transición, de la sociedad tradicional a la sociedad de masas* (Buenos Aires: Editorial Paidos, 1962), pp. 147ff.

and economic confederation. This short-lived confederation was thwarted by Chile, which clearly saw it as the greatest threat to its own dominance on the Pacific coast; and in 1838–9 Chilean arms ended the experiment.[1] Nevertheless, for several years thereafter amalgamation and annexation movements continued to create internal chaos in both republics.

The defeat of Santa Cruz and the confederation ended Bolivia's ephemeral attempt at leadership on the Pacific coast, and, in the years that followed, economic and political stagnation continued to plague the nation, inviting intervention and aggression from its neighbours. Intervention became even more frequent after the 1830s as rich guano fields were discovered in the Atacama desert. While Bolivians remained indifferent, Chilean entrepreneurs with Anglo-Chilean capital began exclusively to develop these deposits, along with the extremely rich nitrate fields that were discovered in the same area in the 1860s. The Chilean capitalists were easily able to obtain vast concessions from the weak and uninterested altiplano government, and were soon advocating direct Chilean territorial expansion into the Bolivian department.[2] The Chilean government proved receptive to this desire for expansion and the flag soon began to follow trade. From the 1830s onward, therefore, Bolivia found itself hard pressed to defend its borders against Chilean aggression, and survival on the coast became one of the major problems facing the republic.

But the economic depression which Bolivia experienced in the first decades of independence was matched by an intellectual and political stagnation which prevented her from meeting this or any other serious challenge. Bolivia produced individual leaders of some quality after Santa Cruz, but the pattern of political development after the destruction of the confederation was that of a steady succession of caudillos and palace revolts, in the classic tradition of most newly emergent states of Latin America. Bolivia even suffered an extreme instance, in the person of Mariano

---

[1] Alfonso Crespo, *Santa Cruz, el condor indio* (Mexico: Fondo de Cultura Económica, 1944), pp. 120ff; Jorge Basadre, *Chile, Perú y Bolivia independientes* (Barcelona: Salvat Editores, 1948), Parte Segunda, chs. I, III, IV; Robert N. Burr, *By Reason or Force, Chile and the Balance of Power in South America, 1830–1905* (Berkeley: University of California Press, 1965), pp. 24ff.

[2] Peñaloza, *Historia económica de Bolivia*, I, 257–8; II, 98–9, 122–9.

Melgarejo, a caudillo who was not above selling vast amounts of national territory to foreign powers for personal profit. Although civilians of the white aristocracy succeeded in gaining control of the government from time to time, especially under Ballivián and Frías, they were unable to establish orderly constitutional government or remove the army and its caudillos from politics. Nor could they establish viable political parties or other institutional alternatives to the use of force, the dominance of irresponsible leaders, and the rule of factions based on personal loyalties.[1]

This pattern of caudillismo was finally broken in the 1870s with the resurgence of the altiplano mining industry and the rise of a new mining élite within the traditional oligarchy. This new élite proved a dynamic and progressive force and soon began to work for a fundamental change in the political structure which would produce the political stability necessary to guarantee the continued growth of the private sector of the economy. Fortunately for this group, both the military and the caudillismo pattern of government were totally discredited in 1879 with the great disaster of the War of the Pacific, a war which also finally resolved Bolivia's border disputes with Chile and Peru.

The War of the Pacific was the inevitable outcome of Chile's expansive territorial drive on Bolivia's Pacific coast and her desire for domination over the states along the Pacific. Long anticipated by all observers, including the Peruvians, the war caught Bolivia completely by surprise. Faced by constant Chilean pressure on Bolivia's rich littoral territories, the altiplano politicians continued to ignore this threat until the very last minute, when there could no longer be any hope of successful opposition. While Peruvian capitalists with the aid of United States funds had attempted to counteract Chilean development of the Bolivian littoral, and Peru had prepared militarily and diplomatically for the inevitable test of strength, Bolivia had merely fumbled along, concentrating all her energies on the Andean highlands. As a result, when war came, Bolivia could offer little aid to her

---

[1] For the best general survey of this period see Enrique Finot, *Nueva historia de Bolivia (ensayo de interpretación sociológica)* (2nd ed.; La Paz: Gisbert y Cía., 1954), pp. 205ff.

Peruvian ally. The war also occurred during one of the usual reactionary caudillo periods. After a short spell of civilian government following the overthrow of the Melgarejo tyranny, General Hilarión Daza had re-established a military rule based on his leadership of the élite 'colorado' army battalion. But he was a typical military politician of the period, with no real technical training, and he proved incapable of leading the initially nationalistic and optimistic nation in the war. Defeat, mismanagement and delays soon turned the jingoistic public into a bitter and defeatist one, and the civilian leadership of the nation was able to oust the barracks' caudillo with the aid of a chastened and subservient army command.[1]

In December 1879, under the direction of Colonel Eliodoro Camacho and with the full support of civilian leaders, Daza was overthrown and the popular General Narciso Campero took his place. A man of much political experience, Campero was also one of the very few European-trained officers in the army and a highly respected national figure.[2] Once provisional president, Campero immediately called together a national assembly, and at the same time gave new life to the Bolivian war effort.[3] The national assembly was organized in May 1880, after a general election, and contained the leading civilians of Bolivia. Endorsing Campero's renewed military efforts, it officially elected him to a four-year term with two leading civilians as his vice-presidents. But internal political harmony was short-lived, for during the deliberations of this assembly news came of the crucial allied defeat at the battle of Tacna, which in reality meant the end of Bolivian resistance and the complete loss of the littoral territory. But President Campero refused to accept this seemingly final overthrow of allied arms, and not only proposed to continue the war with Chile on a greater scale, but even signed a preliminary protocol of federal union with Peru.[4]

With continued opposition useless and with powerful economic groups demanding peace, the action of Campero in prolonging the war caused a major schism in national political life. A clear division soon became apparent between those who wanted to

---

[1] Basadre, *Chile, Perú y Bolivia*, pp. 387, 389–91; Alcides Argüedas, *Historia general de Bolivia (el proceso de la nacionalidad), 1809–1921* (La Paz: Arno Hermanos, 1922), libro sexto. [2] Argüedas, *Historia general*, pp. 397–8.
[3] Basadre, *Chile, Perú y Bolivia*, p. 483. [4] *Ibid.* pp. 575–6.

come to terms with Chile and end the war and those who were for following Campero to the utmost in a continuation of the war-effort. The anti-war, and thus anti-Peruvian, faction was led by Campero's first vice-president, Aniceto Arce, and by the leading parliamentarian of the day, Mariano Baptista. This group was soon in bitter opposition to the policies of the régime. So hostile was Arce's reaction to the Peruvian unification protocol that at the beginning of 1881 he was exiled by the Campero government. But Campero's toleration of free debate permitted Baptista to mobilize public opinion for the pacifist position, especially as the war continued its calamitous course. The acknowledgement of the victory of this position came in 1883 when the senate called upon Arce to return to his position in the government and to preside over its sessions as vice-president of the republic. This recall also signified that Campero finally admitted the impossibility of reversing the Chilean victory.[1]

While it would seem that the resolution of the war and the recognition by all Bolivians of ultimate defeat should have ended the incipient growth of these two clearly defined political groupings, this did not occur. For Bolivia in 1883 had reached a state of economic growth and stability in which the establishment of a government more politically responsive and secure than the petty caudillo military régimes which it had experienced up to that time was a fundamental necessity. Thus while the immediate causes for two clearly defined political formations no longer existed, both groupings sensed the need for the establishment of organized and disciplined political parties, so that an orderly civilian-dominated government could be arranged.[2] That one group would soon call itself conservative and the other liberal was of less importance than that they both acknowledged the need for a government sensitive to civilian leadership which would promote the economic development of the nation. This was clearly reflected in the fact that, whatever their differences in platforms or even professed philosophies, both liberals and conservatives held firmly to the idea of the role of the government as

[1] Finot, *Nueva historia*, pp. 308–11.
[2] This idea was cogently expressed by one of the political leaders of the new era in the slogan, *¡viva el orden y abajo las revoluciones!* Basadre, *Chile, Perú y Bolivia*, p. 579.

economic developer of the nation.[1] Bolivia, in short, had finally matured into the nineteenth-century Latin American pattern of rule by a civilian oligarchy divided along conservative-liberal lines. It was certainly not accidental that the new age of political parties was called the 'era of silver' and later the 'century of tin', for before Bolivia could emerge on to this more advanced political plateau it had to rise out of the economic decadence in which it had remained since the late colonial period.

Although Bolivia always devoted its greatest effort to agriculture, which absorbed around two-thirds of the labour force, national agricultural production was barely sufficient for even internal needs, and the mining industry, even in its most depressed state, always dominated the export trade and provided Bolivia with most of her foreign earnings. Yet by any standards the mining industry in the early republican period was in a very backward condition and lacked the capital to develop the new technology needed to improve production. But from the middle decades of the century Bolivian and foreign entrepreneurs were able to draw on the capital being generated by the English and the Chileans in the copper, nitrate, and guano mines along the coast. By the late 1860s capital began pouring into the altiplano and almost overnight production began to climb dramatically. Annual production, which had averaged only some 72,000 kilos of silver in the depression years of 1851–65, suddenly rose to some 90,000 kilos in the last years of the decade, and to the astronomic figure of 222,500 kilos in the period 1871–5,[2] a rate which was maintained until the depression of 1890.[3]

This sudden burgeoning of the silver industry had an immediate impact on the entire Bolivian economy as well as on government

---

[1] Thus the first conservative presidential candidate announced as his programme the 'creation of national industry through free development of the spirit of association; expansion of commercial relations through the realization, by national endeavour, of a rail link which . . . will put us into immediate contact with the world'. He also promised to promote the creation of new jobs, the investment of capital and the expansion of credit in order to create 'the great evolution which must be initiated in Bolivia'. Quoted in Ignacio Prudencio Bustillo, *La vida y la obra de Aniceto Arce* (2nd ed.; La Paz: Fundación Universitaria 'Simón I. Patiño', 1951), p. 111.

[2] Soetbeer, *Edelmetall-Produktion*, pp. 78–9.

[3] Bureau of the American Republics, *Bolivia* (Bulletin No. 55; Washington D.C., 1892), p. 60.

income. Bolivia's trade deficit rapidly turned into a surplus, and by 1886, she was exporting in total value of goods more than twice as much as she imported.[1] At the same time, though taxes on Indian landowners still remained the second major source of government income, their importance as a percentage of the total fell dramatically, and import and export taxes took their place as the key source of government revenue. By 1881 the Indian tax provided only 24 per cent of government income, with taxes on international trade and mining accounting for 47 per cent.[2]

Thus, in both the private and public sectors, Bolivia by the 1870s had finally broken out of its stagnating economic condition and had become firmly oriented toward international markets. The new mining industry also produced an economic leadership with a new outlook on national politics and development. Utterly dependent on foreign markets, capital and technology, and desperately in need of reasonable communications and stable political conditions, these new leaders formed, for the first time, a powerful pressure group capable of influencing government action. Forced to expend vast sums on maintaining and opening new communications networks, these men began to demand serious government attention to their most basic needs.

This new breed of entrepreneur arose from the white upper class of Bolivia, but its interests and needs were entirely different from the tradition-bound landed oligarchy which until then had dominated national economic and social life. These new economic leaders included such men as José Avelino Aramayo, who had begun investing in the mines and in all other parts of the Bolivian economy, as early as the 1850s. Aniceto Arce, the developer of the world famous Huanchaca mine, was typical of this group. He first began operating at Huanchaca in 1865 and after innumerable reorganizations and with the influx of liberal sums of Chilean capital, he turned his mine into the largest in Bolivia and one of the greatest sources of silver in the world. By 1877 Compañía Huanchaca de Bolivia was employing over 1,500 workers and producing about 35,000 kilos of silver, a figure which rose to over

---

[1] Bureau of the American Republics, *Bolivia* (Bulletin No. 55; Washington D.C. 1892), pp. 87, 91.   [2] Bresson, *Bolivia*, p. 247.

113,000 kilos by 1882 and represented something like 45 per cent of national silver production.[1] Men like Arce, and Gregorio Pacheco, who developed the rich Guadalupe mines,[2] were active propagandists for railroads, government investment policies in public works, and a full commitment to economic development. To these men, the traditional pattern of civil strife, of government corruption, inefficiency, and essential indifference to economic growth was absolute anathema, and once they were able to establish their own economic position firmly within the volatile mining industry, they all turned their attention toward the national government to secure the necessary prerequisites for the continued development of their industry.

The war with Chile badly disrupted the economic relations of this group and their own productive activity, but the defeat of Bolivia provided them with a valuable excuse for establishing themselves in national political life. The fact that Pacheco, Arce, and Alonso, all silver potentates, all became president of Bolivia in the years immediately following the war is proof of the vital interest which these men of wealth took in transforming the political structure of their nation.

In searching for an institutional base which would provide a structure for stability, the convention of 1880 reviewed the constitutional history of the nation and, as Mariano Baptista noted for the Constitutional Commission of the convention, upon 'examining the diverse constitutions, it had found that the constitution of 1878 filled not only the necessities and aspirations of Bolivia, but of any other country more advanced'.

The 1878 charter had been written, surprisingly, under the Daza government. Daza wanted to give legality to his military usurpation, and had called together a constituent assembly in 1877 to write a new charter and, more important, to formally elect him president. Having achieved this, he permitted the convention freedom of action in writing the constitution, which was done by some of the more advanced thinkers of the day, men who were also extremely sensitive to the workings of the Bolivian

---

[1] Bresson, *Bolivia*, pp. 248, 266–71; Prudencio Bustillo, *La vida de Arce*, pp. 67–83; Peñaloza, *Historia económica*, II, 179–88.

[2] Peñaloza, *Historia económica*, II, 183. General Narciso Campero, a relative of Pacheco, was a partner in the enterprise.

political order. Providing for a unitary republic with a far stronger parliamentary government than ever before in Bolivian constitutional history, the constitution established a bicameral legislature with the right of interpellation of the executive branch of government. Senators and deputies were elected by direct suffrage, and the congress in turn elected the members of the supreme court. An attempt was also made to control illegal use of force by defining constitutionally the limits of the state of siege. Taking the advice of its commission, the 1880 convention adopted the two-year-old charter as its own, adding only a few minor modifications. That this charter satisfied the needs of the new era of political parties can be seen in the fact that it survived with but minor changes until 1938, the longest reign of any constitution in the history of the republic.[1]

In the congresses of 1882 and 1883 the two political tendencies became more sharply defined, especially as the presidential elections of 1884 approached. The peace or constitutionalist faction, as it was first called, turned toward Mariano Baptista for leadership, especially after his famous advocacy of a treaty of peace with Chile in the legislative sessions of 1883. Meanwhile, Colonel Eliodoro Camacho, the leader of the anti-Daza revolt, upon his return from Chilean imprisonment in 1883, formed a group of adherents around his banner of liberalism.[2] His supporters were anti-Chilean and anti-peace settlement; and under the able direction of Camacho they also sought to found a party on the classic liberal doctrines of the nineteenth century, with a healthy intake of positivist ideology, a philosophy which was then gaining wide acceptance throughout Latin America.[3] As early as June 1883, in an Oruro newspaper, Camacho outlined the basis for a Liberal party. Attacking the classic pattern of Bolivian politics in the early national period as one of personalism without ideology, he maintained that a truly ideological party structure could be established. For, he declared, 'there exist in Bolivian political life, as in that of all peoples, the standard conservative, authoritarian

---

[1] Ciro Félix Trigo, *Las constituciones de Bolivia* (Madrid: Instituto de Estudios Políticos, 1958), pp. 112–17.

[2] Finot, *Nueva historia*, pp. 311–13; Argüedas, *Historia general*, pp. 418–19, 422.

[3] Guillermo Francovich, *El pensamiento boliviano en el siglo xx* (Mexico: Fondo de Cultura Económica, 1956), pp. 13–17.

and dictatorial tendencies as opposed to the progressive, liberal and legalist ones . . .'. It was only necessary for 'each party to inscribe on its banner the name of its aims, and adapt its conduct to the label which it carries' for a truly ideological system to be created. Camacho claimed that he and his followers were devotees of liberty, and that with this sacred ideal they proposed to found an ideological party.[1]

Baptista took up this challenge and sought to mould an ideology around the political groupings of the pacifists. He quickly charged the liberals with revolutionary aims and with attacking the basic institutions of the republic. However, it was not until the late 1880s that the church issue became prominent enough for Baptista to adopt the standard of defender of the faith against what he would call the assault of the atheist, positivist, anti-clerical, and masonic liberals. The success of Baptista's attack was admitted officially by Camacho in his famous 1885 *Programa* for the Liberal party, a document which has served as the basis of the official party programme since that time. Liberalism, he wrote:

does not consist in breaking brusquely with the traditions of the past, as those who attack it claim, nor in leaping into violent innovations or adopting indiscriminately all the reforms imaginable. Nor does liberalism consist in glorifying licentious ideas, coarse language, or immoral manners. Neither does it boast indifference and religious disbelief nor contempt for the faith. Rather the liberalism which we proclaim is that which gave glorious existence to the Great American Republic, not that aberration which produced the bloody catastrophes of the French Revolution or the repugnant excesses of European socialism; this latter being the enemy of liberty.[2]

As the elections of 1884 approached, General Campero, although a partisan of the liberal pro-war group headed by

---

[1] Partido Liberal, *La Política Liberal, formulado por el jefe del partido, General Elio-doro Camacho* (Nueva edición; La Paz: Imprenta Andina, 1916), pp. 8–9.

[2] Partido Liberal, *La Política Liberal*, p. 13. The positive programme of the new party, according to this same document was enunciated as follows: 'The principles which the liberal school sustains, are based on the individual rights which protect the life, liberty, honour and property of man, in the sovereignty of the people, popular suffrage . . . administrative and municipal decentralization, political concentration and unity, tolerance of opinions, obligatory and free state education, freedom of speech, freedom of the press, freedom of association, freedom of work, the inviolability of the conscience, etc., etc.' *Ibid.* pp. 13–14.

Camacho, nevertheless promised to refrain from interfering in any way in the elections and kept his promise faithfully. In this uniquely free atmosphere, the two groups coalesced around the candidatures of Camacho and Baptista. However, the silver magnate Gregorio Pacheco suddenly emerged, to everyone's surprise, with a nondescript coalition of old displaced *politiqueros* and political novices in a newly organized Partido Democrático which proclaimed itself the party of national reconciliation. Baptista reacted to this challenge by stepping down from the nomination and putting his chief supporter, the millionaire Aniceto Arce, as a candidate for his party. Suddenly the campaign was transformed into something new for Bolivia, a political struggle between civilian capitalists instead of barracks officers, and it presaged a whole new political era when the prestige of money would replace the old praetorianism.

When Pacheco entered the race, Arce is supposed to have remarked that he would oppose his fellow magnate 'cheque against cheque and banknote against banknote'.[1] Newspapermen and voters were bribed in the most open electoral campaign Bolivia had experienced. Men changed sides as often as money changed hands, and when all was through Pacheco won by a plurality, followed by Arce and then Camacho.[2] Because of this lack of a clear majority the election went to congress, where the Liberal party had the largest, though not the majority, block of votes. In this atmosphere of bargaining, the Liberals proved to be too unbending, and Baptista was able to reconcile the two formerly hostile magnates. In the Democratic-Constitutionalist compromise, Pacheco accepted the presidency with a promise to support Arce as his successor. As a guarantee of this pact Mariano Baptista was to be appointed vice-president in the Pacheco government.[3]

With the government of Pacheco begins the rule of the so-called 'Conservative Oligarchy'—a term quickly adopted by the opposition Liberals and later historians to define this new political era. Pacheco himself was not a dynamic leader, and his party of opportunists and old-style politicians seeking to maintain themselves against the onslaught of the new parties did not

[1] Finot, *Nueva historia*, pp. 314–15.   [2] Argüedas, *Historia general*, pp. 422–7.
[3] Finot, *Nueva historia*, p. 316.

hold together for long, but he nevertheless governed an unusually tranquil republic. This internal political peace was firmly based on the promise of respect for the electoral results which Camacho had given to Baptista on the eve of the 1884 campaign. However, the party battles were, if anything, intensified during the Pacheco period of government, even though the original cause for party development, the peace issue, had been resolved. Under Pacheco, Bolivia finally signed the long delayed truce with Chile, but new issues quickly arose to replace the debate over foreign policy. Baptista and the co-founder of the true Partido Conservador, Monseñor Taborga, took full political advantage of the more open adoption of anticlerical and positivist attitudes by the advanced forces of liberalism, and deepened and maintained divisions by concentrating on the church-state issue. Claiming that his group was the true defender of the faith and champion of the beliefs of the Bolivian people, Baptista proudly adopted the party label of Conservative.[1] The principles of this party, according to Baptista, were also based on liberty. But this was a liberty 'founded on the social law of Christianity'. It was an individual and highly responsible liberty, and was sharply opposed to the excesses known under the name of 'Jacobinism, which is a fickle and anonymous collective tyranny which has proved more bloody and inconsistent in a few months of domination than the tyranny of the kings in a century of empire. And because we want to maintain the [true] liberties, pure of sophisms and free of violence, they call us conservatives.'[2]

But for all the complaints about labels, Baptista actually delighted in the conservative tag, for it brought into his party new sources of strength to overcome the obviously more popular Liberal party. It also gave to his group an ideological tint which it had previously lacked, and which seemed to distinguish it from its opponents. Yet for all the talk of religion on both sides, there was fundamental agreement in both parties on the need for civilian-dominated government and a government responsive to the economic needs of the country. Both groups came from

---

[1] Finot, *Nueva historia*, pp. 319–20.
[2] Quoted in Guillermo Francovich, *La filosofía en Bolivia* (Buenos Aires: Editorial Losada, 1945), pp. 118–19.

the white upper classes, which sought to lead the nation into a new era of peace and prosperity through constitutional government, and the aims of both were stability, national unification, and the stimulation of economic development.

Although the Conservative party played an important role in the Pacheco government, even absorbing much of his Democratic party, Pacheco attempted to remain impartial in the coming conflict between the two parties as the election of 1888 approached. But compromise between the two groups proved impossible, for the Conservatives refused to abstain from openly attempting to bribe the electorate away from the obviously more popular Liberals, and also refused any plan for alternation in the presidency. As a result the election of 1888 became a violent and bloody affair with the embittered Liberals finally abstaining in a defiant gesture against electoral fraud.[1]

Thus there was a return to violence in politics before the decade was out. The new era of modern party government did not eliminate violence from national politics, though it dramatically reduced its incidence, and brought it within the framework of the party system. The resort to violence was made inevitable by the refusal of all governments to accept total electoral defeat. For once in office and close to the only major source of wealth in the nation—except for mining—politicians refused to relinquish their spoils, and no tradition of political compromise existed to force them to do so on moral or practical political grounds. Voting was open and readily controlled by central government appointees in all the local districts, and presidential elections and congressional seats were easily secured. But while the government party made sure of its majority in congress, it invariably permitted a substantial representation of all the opposition parties, as an easily supportable escape valve which did not seriously threaten its control over the spoils of office, all of which sprang from the executive. This refusal to allow free elections for the presidency soon made even the pacific Camacho, whose slogan had been 'Up with order and down with revolutions', resort to violence as the only means of gaining control over the government, a conclusion to which all opposition politicians

[1] Argüedas, *Historia general*, pp. 456–60.

who followed him were drawn in the end. Although resort to elections to gain the executive office was soon given up as hopeless, the two-party system continued to flourish, for congressional victory was always a faint possibility and congress itself always offered an excellent forum for the dissemination of party propaganda, the development of leadership, and the organization of an anti-government opposition.

Both Camacho and Baptista had fully sensed the needs of the nation; for while both were undoubtedly dominating personalities who impressed their image on the fledgling parties, the parties they created and the two-party system they developed survived them. Thus the great political development of the last quarter of the nineteenth century in Bolivian history was the creation of a viable civilian political party system which was to rule unchallenged in the subsequent life of the nation. Given the similar socio-economic base of all politicians in that period, and the small number who were politically active, it was of course inevitable that the system was not fully mature and that charismatic leaders arose from time to time who completely dominated their followers, created strictly personal factions within the old parties, or broke off to form new ones. But despite the dominance of personalities over issues and ideologies in these early years,[1] the pattern of political party government was firmly established, and endured until well into the twentieth century. The effectiveness of this two-party system in bringing order out of the pre-Pacific War chaos can be seen from the sharp drop in the incidence of revolutionary activity which is clearly revealed in Fig. 1.

Nor were Bolivian politicians unaware of these developments, for all marked the 1880s as a turning-point in the nation's history. As the great twentieth-century political leader Bautista Saavedra said, before 1880

[1] Finot, *Nueva historia*, pp. 321–6; Basadre, *Chile, Perú y Bolivia*, pp. 582–5. As Carlos Montenegro has rightly pointed out, the terms liberal and conservative applied to the two parties which ruled Bolivia from 1884–1920 'certainly do not signify any ideological opposition between them. The two parties rendered identical devotion to liberal, individualistic and constitutionalist thought. Their alternation in power is similar to that of the Democrats and Republicans in the United States, or to the Liberals and Conservatives in England, producing only ... a change of one branch of the privileged class for the other, in the exercise of the government.' Carlos Montenegro, *Nacionalismo y coloniaje* (3rd ed.; La Paz: Biblioteca Paceña-Alcaldía Municipal, 1953), p. 179.

there were no political parties with clearly defined programmes . . . Instead of parties, there were only political groups more or less based on a common interest or popular reactions against tyrannical governments . . . Not distinguishing themselves by differences in political doctrine or conceptions of managing national interests, these parties or political groups took the name of their caudillos . . . [and] thus called themselves: crucistas, ballivianistas, belcistas, melgarejistas, dacistas, corralistas, or else they took the date of their best deeds, being: septembristas, marcistas, octubristas.[1]

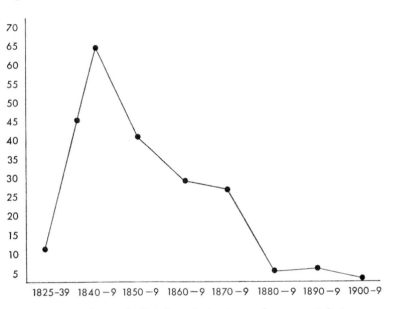

Fig. I. Incidence of political revolts in nineteenth-century Bolivia.
Source: Nicanor Aranzaes, *Las revoluciones de Bolivia* (La Paz: Casa Editora 'La Prensa', 1918).

Before 1880 only one of these groupings dominated the political scene at any given time, and no conception whatsoever of a viable two-party system was developed. Probably the most important and self-conscious of these pre-1880 'parties' was the famous *rojo* group of intellectuals which supported the régime of Linares (1857–61). But these intellectuals, though recognizing the need for non-revolutionary governments, were themselves unable

[1] Bautista Saavedra, *La democracia en nuestra historia* (La Paz: González y Media, 1921), pp. 90–2.

to create a normal political party with even minimal popular support, and tended in the end to be simple followers of a caudillo. As Alcides Argüedas noted of the 'partido' rojo, 'the word partido was only a title, for they were essentially a group of persons gathering around the defence of the Dictator (Linares).'[1] Although there were brilliant civilian leaders and intellectuals within the group, many of whom played a part in the new post-1880 era, the rojos had no coherent programme nor followers and finally disintegrated after the death of their last leader Ballivián, and the overthrow of the Frías government.

The effective creation of a two-party system after 1880 eliminated the disorganized pattern of caudillo uprisings and concentrated political violence under civilian leadership. Violence now tended to coalesce around party banners, with the 'out' party absorbing all anti-government movements. It also became the inevitable tool for forcing an alternation of parties in power and eventually all 'out' parties sought a revolutionary solution. Thus after the election of Arce in 1888, the Liberal party finally resorted to armed insurrection to capture a presidency which it felt had been denied to it by fraudulent elections. No sooner had Arce taken office than he was forced to lead an army in several weeks of hard campaigning to dominate a powerful Liberal uprising. Although he treated the Liberals harshly and suppressed political liberties, his government was nevertheless one of the most constructive in the history of the republic. With scant resources he carried out the most ambitious public works programme ever attempted. Obsessed with the ambition to connect Bolivia with the outside world by railroads and to end the internal isolation of her provincial cities, Arce had begun to devote his own money and energies to this end when he was still a private individual. Despite political unrest, charges of opening up the country to easy Chilean invasion, and stubborn isolationist conservatism, he succeeded in constructing the railroad from the Chilean port of Antofagasta to the altiplano. He also put into operation a major road-building development plan, connecting the various departmental capitals for the first time by modern

---

[1] Alcides Argüedas, *La dictadura y la anarquía, 1857–1864* (Barcelona: López Roberto y Cía., 1926), p. 272.

roads. Arce was also instrumental in establishing military academies and other innovations designed to modernize and pro-fessionalize the archaic Bolivian army. He accomplished all of this while increasing government revenues and without recourse to foreign loans. Although Arce's enemies mercilessly attacked him and his visions, they themselves brought many of his extra-ordinary initiatives to their fruition in the years which followed.[1]

Before he completed his term, Arce once again had to put down a major Liberal uprising, this time led by the mercurial Colonel José Manuel Pando in 1890. In the election of 1892 Mariano Baptista, the old 'magician' as his political enemies called him, finally stood for his party's presidential nomination and became the official government candidate. In a violent election the popular Liberal party allied with the remnants of Pacheco's Democratic party gained control of congress, thus threatening Baptista's precarious minority victory since the presidential selection was decided by the new parliament. Baptista offered a half-hearted compromise proposal to the Liberals with the promise of two cabinet ministries, but Camacho countered by demanding that all Liberals elected to congress should take their seats there, and the government should promise to respect the decisions of that congressional majority and to expel officials accused of attempting to fix the elections. Baptista refused, and the day after the conferences broke down the Arce government proceeded to exile the leading Liberals and unseat their congres-sional representatives, thus ensuring the congressional approval of Baptista.

Although he had grown even more ultramontane in his old age, Baptista continued the progressive government stimulation of the economic development of the nation. Much pioneering work was carried out under his leadership in education, and in the exploration and penetration of the Beni rubber regions, while the Antofagasta railroad was completed as far as Oruro. He also signed several demarcation treaties with Bolivia's neighbours and a preliminary peace protocol with Chile in 1895, which implied an outlet to the sea for Bolivia, a promise which was to be upset

[1] Prudencio Bustillo, *La vida de Arce*, pp. 187–215.

by Bolivian internal opposition and by Chile's later rapprochement with Peru and Argentina.[1]

The final president of the Conservative party was Sergio Fernández Alonso, a lawyer and mine owner like his predecessors Pacheco and Arce. However, Alonso lacked their dynamic vision and forceful character, and the embittered Liberal opposition took full advantage of this. In 1894 the Liberal party at its national convention and under the leadership of its old chief Eliodoro Camacho selected as its new presidential candidate and party leader Colonel José Manuel Pando. Pando, an artillery expert and hero of the Pacific War, leader of several Liberal uprisings, and a renowned explorer of the Beni region under several Conservative administrations, was a popular personality and was to be a key political figure in the coming years. In a closely fought election he lost to Alonso by only some 3,000 votes out of some 36,000 cast.[2]

Alonso talked of a coalition government and even sent Pando out on more geographic expeditions to the oriente, but he was incapable of reconciling the Liberal opposition. In much the same way as his predecessors, he encouraged the opening up of the rich Beni rubber lands and the expansion of the rail network, initiating preliminary studies on an Argentine-Bolivian railroad link.[3] Yet despite the intended unification of the nation by all these developments in the national communication system, the Alonso period witnessed the temporary rise of a marked regionalist sentiment. Possibly because of the growing importance of La Paz in this new economic and communications development, the old struggle between the *paceños* and *chuquisaceños* over the capital of the nation reached a virulent stage.[4]

Before 1898 the government had always recognized Sucre as the capital, though that city had never been the permanent home of either Bolivia's president or its congresses. The latter had

---

[1] Basadre, *Chile, Perú y Bolivia*, pp. 585–8; Augusto Guzmán, *Baptista, biografía de un orador político* (2nd ed.; La Paz: Editorial 'Juventud', 1957), pp. 135–44.
[2] Rodolfo Soria Galvamo, *Ultimos días del gobierno Alonso* (2nd ed.; Potosí: Imprenta Angel Santelices, 1920), p. 140.   [3] Guzmán, *Baptista*, pp. 588–9.
[4] La Paz from the beginning of republican rule had always had a greater population than Sucre, and in the latter half of the nineteenth century had about double the number of inhabitants. By 1900 the populations stood at 52,000 and 20,000 respectively. Asthenio Averanga Mollinedo, *Aspectos generales de la población boliviana* (La Paz: Editorial 'Argote', 1956), pp. 30, 44; *Censo nacional de 1900*, II, 17.

28

always been rather migratory, the actual seat of government alternating principally between La Paz and Sucre. In 1898, however, Sucre leaders, crossing party lines, forced through congress legislation requiring the president and the legislature to fix their residence permanently in that city. Delighted with an issue which created such deep feeling, the normally unitarian Liberals capitalized on the issue and stood behind the growing fury of La Paz.[1] Alonso, caught in the middle, tried to temporize, but both sides demanded unqualified support for their positions, and he finally put his signature to the congressional enactment. Immediately the federalist banner of rebellion was raised in La Paz, with heavy Liberal party overtones and with a healthy amount of Indian unrest on the altiplano.[2] From December 1898 to April 1899 the battles raged, with a heavy loss of life on both sides, and the generalship of Pando finally overcame the government's early advantage. In the second battle of Los Cruceros, on the plains outside of Oruro, the domination of the Conservative party was ended, and the Liberal party came to power.[3]

The year 1899 marked the end of Conservative party rule, and of the party itself, which died a short time later. The era of the 'Conservative Oligarchy' had been a uniquely fruitful one for Bolivia. Under the rule of the Conservatives the nation had witnessed the establishment of the first modern means of communication, the major expansion of its economy, and the first long-term period of civilian rule in its history. Most importantly, it saw the foundation of a modern political party system and constitutional form of government which would survive intact for the next thirty years. Along with the political and economic stability had come an intellectual flowering, and Bolivia in the last quarter of the nineteenth century for the first time began to develop a distinctive national culture and an intelligentsia committed to exploring national themes

[1] It is interesting to note that Pando, senator for Sucre, originally voted for the residence law, while Alonso's minister of government, a Conservative, but also a paceño, resigned to join the rebellion.

[2] For an excellent account of this Indian unrest, based on unique original research, see Condarco Morales, *Zarate, el 'Temible' Willka*, pp. 60ff.

[3] Alipio Valencia Vega, *Desarrollo del pensamiento político en Bolivia (bosquejo)* (La Paz: Editorial 'Trabajo', 1953), pp. 76–8; Basadre, *Chile, Perú y Bolivia*, pp. 588–90.

and problems.[1] In all respects, then, the Conservative period was to prove a 'classic' epoch in Bolivian history and was to set the foundations for the developments of the twentieth century.

[1] Fernando Díez de Medina, *Literatura boliviana* (Madrid: Aguilar, 1954), ch. X.

2

THE LIBERAL PARTY IN POWER

The end of the nineteenth century and the beginning of the twentieth was a period of major change for Bolivia, both politically, and even more importantly, in terms of economic reorganization. For in the late 1890s silver mining had declined steadily and its pre-eminent place in the Bolivian economy had been taken by tin. This change in the economic base was so profound that tin quickly became the dominant product of the nation and the new century came to be known as the *siglo de estaño* (century of tin).

Tin had been an important byproduct in the production of silver from the earliest times. In the general mining renaissance of the last quarter of the nineteenth century tin had even been shipped in crude bulk form to Europe. This minor trade, however, suddenly took on a new importance and value with the change in industrial technology in Europe and North America at the end of the century. Tin became a basic metal in both consumer and heavy industry, and was suddenly one of the most sought-after metals. Almost overnight demand began to expand at a fantastic rate. As traditional European sources were either on the point of exhaustion or incapable of expansion, demand exceeded supply and the price of tin rose astronomically. Taking advantage of its rich deposits and the rail network which had been elaborated for the silver industry, Bolivia was soon able to meet this growing demand and feverishly turned its full attention to the virtually untapped tin resources of the nation.[1] From the annual production in the 1,000 ton range at the beginning of the 1890s, tin production was up to 3,500 tons in 1899, 9,000 tons in 1900, and by

[1] Paul Walle, *Bolivia, Its People and Its Resources*, trans. B. Miall (New York: Charles Scribner's Sons, 1914), pp. 327–8. In 1890 world tin production stood at 55,000 English tons per annum, by 1904 it had risen to 100,000 tons. Meanwhile prices rose from £85 per ton in 1893 to £126 per ton in 1904. Peñaloza, *Historia económica*, II, 209, 235.

1905 the figure was over 15,000 tons per annum.[1] Very rapidly Bolivia became one of the leading producers in the world, and by 1904 the British vice-consul at Oruro was noting that the Oruro mining district alone, exclusive of the other tin producing areas of Bolivia, was mining 'over 10 per cent of the world's production'.[2]

The rise of tin came at an extremely opportune time for Bolivia, for it has just begun to experience the effects of a major depression in the silver mining industry. In the late 1890s the world price of silver was severely shaken, and, although more modern methods were introduced into the Bolivian mines at this time, the economic future of the industry looked bleak. The value of silver exports declined from an annual average production of Bs. 15·4 million in the period 1895–9 to Bs. 10·2 million annual average in 1900–4, and continued its steady decline until the outbreak of World War I, reaching Bs. 3·8 million in the period 1910–14.[3] Meanwhile, as is shown in table 1, the value of

Table 1. *Average annual Bolivian tin exports and
total exports, 1900–19*
(*in bolivianos*)

Period	Average annual tin exports	Average annual total exports	Tin as % of total exports
1900–4	16,918,556	31,652,923	53·4
1905–9	30,794,706	51,019,522	60·3
1910–14	52,029,712	81,979,794	63·4
1915–19	80,466,354	136,261,516	59·0

Source: Eduardo López Rivas, *Esquema de la historia económica de Bolivia* (Oruro: Universidad Técnica de Oruro, 1955), pp. 13ff.

[1] Peñaloza, *Historia económica*, II, 207–8, 221.
[2] Great Britain, Foreign Office, *Trade of Bolivia for the Year 1904* (Diplomatic and Consular Reports, Annual Series, No. 3388; London: His Majesty's Stationery Office, June 1905), p. 25. By 1905 total Bolivian production accounted for 17 per cent of world production, and by 1927 the figure had reached 24 per cent. Comisión Económica para América Latina, *El desarrollo económico de Bolivia* ('Análisis y proyecciones del desarrollo económico', Vol. IV, México: Naciones Unidas, Departamento de Asuntos Económicos y Sociales, 1958), cuadro 3, p. 8. This work is hereafter cited as CEPAL, with title given.
[3] Pedro Aniceto Blanco, *Monografía de la industria minera en Bolivia* (La Paz: J. Miguel Gamarra, 1910), p. 344; W. L. Schurz, *Bolivia, A Commercial and Industrial Handbook* (Department of Commerce, Special Agents Series, No. 208 Washington: Government Printing Office, 1921), p. 112.

tin exports rose sharply. The impact of tin in the national economy exceeded even that of the republican silver boom. This can be seen in the expansion of total Bolivian exports which rose astronomically by 330 per cent between 1900–4 and 1915–19, an amount just short of the 374 per cent increase in the value of tin exports in the same period. Thus tin, along with the pre-Acre War rubber boom of the 1890s,[1] not only helped to tide the nation over a serious depression caused by the decline in silver prices, but also ushered in a totally new era of previously undreamed of prosperity.

Although initially silver capital largely provided the base for the development of the new tin mines, the tin-mining industry eventually produced a substantially new capitalist class. Following the early mergers and reorganizations in the booming industry, a new mining élite arose in Bolivia, an élite which differed from the old silver magnates, not only in social background, but in outlook as well. To these new miners, with their vastly increased production and technology and their complex relations with the industrial and finance capital of the outside world, direct involvement in national politics became an impossible and even distasteful goal. Given the depersonalization and extensive foreign management of these new companies, the so-called tin barons refused to participate in Bolivian life to the same extent as their silver magnate predecessors. Although the nineteenth-century silver magnates had resorted to the creation of joint-stock companies, they always maintained direct control over their mines and actively participated in their administration. But the new multi-million dollar tin mining complexes were soon to be run by foreign engineers and administrators, with the more general control often placed in boards of directors residing in foreign capitals. In contrast to the intimate involvement of the nineteenth-century silver miners in national political life—four of

---

[1] From representing 2 per cent of government income in 1890, rubber taxes by 1902 accounted for 38 per cent. In its best export year, 1898, the value of rubber exports represented 49 per cent of the value of total national exports. Oficina Nacional de Inmigración, Estadística y Propaganda Geográfica, *Geografía de la República de Bolivia* (La Paz: Ismael Argote, 1905), p. 290; Oficina Nacional de Inmigración, Estadística y Propaganda Geográfica, *Sinopsis estadística y geográfica de la República de Bolivia* (2 vols.; La Paz: J. M. Gamarra, 1903), II, 171, 294.

them being party leaders and presidents and others being fully committed to the contemporary political parties—the tin magnates of the twentieth century by and large isolated themselves from so direct a participation in the political life of their times. Rather than participate themselves, these new capitalists left the defence of their interests to the developing pressure groups of native lawyers, economists, and advisers with whom they surrounded themselves and whom the Bolivian public soon gave the label *Rosca*.[1]

The dissociation of the dominant figures of the Bolivian economy from commitment to the national existence became an important factor in defining national politics in the first half of the twentieth century. It represented the initial development of interest group politics, the major tin miners now leaving politics to full-time specialists recruited from the hacendado and urban middle classes. It thus indicated a new stage of sophistication in the Bolivian political structure, for now leading entrepreneurs no longer needed to intervene directly in the political process to protect or promote their interests, since full time political specialists, effectively did this for them. These entrepreneurs also had their own retinue of advisers, lawyers and retainers, who became an extremely effective pressure group capable of guaranteeing that the tin interests were always properly served.

Unquestionably the leading example of this new type of mining entrepreneur was Simón Iturri Patiño. Born in the Cochabamba valley in 1860, Patiño was apparently of an artisan and part cholo background. Though of modest origins, he received a secondary education, and in early adulthood he spent a

---

[1] Augusto Céspedes, *El dictador suicida, 40 años de Bolivia* (Santiago de Chile: Editorial Universitaria, 1956), pp. 13, 21. The only partial exception to the above generalizations was the Aramayo family. While grandfather José Avelino Aramayo had begun the fortune in silver mining in the 1850s, his son Félix and grandson Carlos Víctor were to move easily into the age of tin, with the aid of foreign capital. Both Félix and Carlos Víctor had semi-active careers in the national foreign service, with Félix constantly pressing his advisory services on the Liberal governments and his son actively influencing public opinion through the family purchase in the 1920s of *La Razón*. Both men, however, played rather independent political roles and neither held elective office or dominated the leadership of any of the major political parties. See A. Costa du Rels, *Félix Avelino Aramayo y su época, 1846–1929* (Buenos Aires: Domingo Via y Cía., 1942).

long apprenticeship in the mining industry, first as a clerk in the famous Huanchaca silver mining company at Pulacayo, and later in the metal-buying firm of Germán Fricke of Oruro. He arrived in Oruro at the beginning of the tin boom in the late 1880s, and by 1894 he had succeeded in purchasing a half-interest in the tiny La Salvadora tin mine located in the rich tin zone near Oruro known as the cantón of Uncía in the northwestern corner of the department of Potosí. By 1897 Patiño purchased full control of the mine, and three years later, after heavy personal investments of labour and capital, he uncovered an enormously rich vein. He immediately introduced foreign engineers and the latest refining equipment and by 1905 La Salvadora had become the largest single tin mine in Bolivia. From this initial investment, Patiño rapidly expanded his holdings both vertically and horizontally. In 1910 he purchased the neighbouring English-owned Uncía mining company and before World War I had already begun his investments in European smelters which culminated in 1916 with his takeover of the English smelting firm of Williams, Harvey & Co. Ltd. By 1924 he had completed his major Bolivian tin holdings with the purchase of the Chilean Llallagua company and by this time his companies were producing around 50 per cent of national tin production and employed over 10,000 workers.

Through Patiño's activities the tiny village of Uncía developed a population of 10,000 and along with the neighbouring town of Llallagua was soon connected to Oruro by Patiño-built roads and rails. In 1905 Patiño had enough capital to organize his own bank, the Banco Mercantil, while his excellent political connections were revealed in the late 1910s when he was aided by such men as Ismael Montes and Luis Paz in his successful efforts to destroy all challenging claims to his proprietorship rights over La Salvadora. From tin, Patiño expanded into other minerals such as silver, wolfram, and tungsten and began to expand vertically into the international tin industry.

By the early 1920s Patiño lived permanently abroad and, considering his extraordinary non-Bolivian interests, could by then be more accurately classified as a European than as a Bolivian capitalist. He even resorted in the early 1920s to registering the majority of his Bolivian holdings under foreign-based companies. Thus, while Bolivia soon became only a minor part of Patiño's far-flung empire, he remained Bolivia's greatest capitalist, who always controlled a minimum 50 per cent of the national tin industry and at the same time was its largest banker.[1]

This withdrawal of Patiño and the other new tin magnates from direct involvement in national affairs left the operation of Bolivian politics in the hands of a rising urban professional upper middle class and the local provincial landed élite (men of modest landholding wealth and solid social position). Almost all of these political leaders, whether from the former or latter categories, were men trained in the law and deeply imbued with the liberal and positivist ideologies of their day. Steeped in the classical economics of *laissez faire*, they nevertheless had a strong commitment to the government's role as an originator of development. Although they were also committed to a belief in democratic symbols and constitutional government, they believed strongly in a caste system and oligarchical rule by the élite.

Benefiting from the rising economic prosperity of the nation, this expanding oligarchy felt in itself powerful energies which it applied to the political and intellectual life of the nation. While the old conservative oligarchy had done much to further national development, they had lacked the resources which the new leadership now found easily at hand, and in a sense they lacked the complete commitment to that positivist conception of progress which was the hallmark of the Bolivian liberal. Condemning the conservative rule and ignoring the important beginnings made by their predecessors and the fortuitous developments outside Bolivia which prompted national expansion, these new men of government believed in their divine right to rule and in their unalterable pursuit of progress.[2]

[1] For a more detailed study of the Bolivian mining career of Patiño, see Herbert S. Klein, 'The Creation of the Patiño Tin Empire', *Inter-American Economic Affairs*, XIX, No. 2 (Autumn, 1965), 3–23. Also see the reminiscent study by his business associate, Manuel Carrasco, *Simón I. Patiño, un prócer industrial* (Paris: Jean Grassin Editeur, 1960).

[2] 'Not only . . . did positivism give to the political activity of that time a progressive vigour and an ideology which filled it with confidence in itself and permitted it to act with the security of pursuing the lines of human progress, but it also furnished the theoretical justification for many of the reforms and plans

Given this intellectual milieu and the concrete results which were obtained from their policy, the leadership of the Liberal party was capable of cynical disregard for practically all the symbols and positions for which they had fought so valiantly while in opposition. Government control over the electoral machinery continued, toleration of political opposition was nil, and opposition was in fact considered close to heresy. The executive power was strengthened and the party majorities in congress slavishly followed presidential leadership. Even on such highly-charged issues as reintegration of national territory there were complete reversals of opinion. The dominating figure of the era, Ismael Montes, summed up much of this attitude when he stated: 'I am a positivist in politics, economic questions, and spirit. Give me only realities'; and to opposition charges that he was transgressing sacred rights he remarked, 'While they are talking, we are acting.'[1]

One of the very first acts of the victorious Liberals was to divest themselves of the cumbersome federalist philosophy which they had temporarily adopted as a weapon in the struggle for power with the Conservatives. Despite the very strong federalist movement in the country and the large amount of blood which had just been shed in its name, Montes, Pando's chief assistant, soon began a newspaper campaign against federalism. He argued that 'Bolivia needs to reconstruct its forces before carrying out such radical innovation', and that 'a question [such as federalism] which can compromise the future of the country and deter its

of reorganization which were then adopted in the country . . . The men who governed the country from the most important posts of the administration were positivists and the ideological directors of the party were convinced that it was necessary to substitute for the traditional order new forms of life inspired by science, for which they then felt a kind of veneration.' Derivative of this ideology was 'that confident security in the national and human future [which] was common in Bolivia to all men at the beginning of the twentieth century . . . An unlimited faith in Europe, as the expression of progress and civilization, was another attitude peculiar to the Bolivian positivists. They felt a sincere and spontaneous admiration for the achievements of European culture, especially French . . . Bolivia, like Latin America in general, felt itself shamed by its history, its despots and its tyrannies [and one might add, its Indians] encountering in Europe of the late nineteenth and early twentieth century the ideal of political equilibrium and social order.' Francovich, *El pensamiento boliviano en el siglo xx*, pp. 17, 18–19.
[1] Quoted in Díez de Medina, *Literatura boliviana*, pp. 263, 264.

37

development should be eliminated from debate'.[1] The federalist movement, however, was not so easy to suppress. It took a hard-fought electoral campaign and a split constitutional convention in October 1899, for the Liberals finally to overcome the federalist position and prevent the overthrow of the 1880 centralist constitution. After 1899, the federalist wing of the party declined dramatically and by the early part of the first decade of the new century had disappeared from the political scene.[2] That federalism was not a more potent force in Bolivian politics, given the economic and geographic disunity of the nation, can probably be explained by the overwhelming concentration of the national population in the core inter-Andean area and the sensitivity of politicians of that region to the potential destructiveness of the doctrine in the underpopulated outlying frontier areas.

In October 1899, Pando took over the presidency and in 1900 the Liberals elected their first ordinary congress under the new régime. But before the new government could turn to internal issues of importance, it was faced by a major international crisis. In the late 1890s, Bolivia's rich rubber zone in the northeast oriente, known as the Acre region, became a hotbed of separatist rebellion. Located on the Brazilian border, Acre had drawn large numbers of Brazilian rubber collectors as well as Bolivian colonists as a result of the boom in wild rubber which had started in the late 1880s. Despite the sudden importance of Acre, it was not until the middle of the 1890s that the Bolivian government attempted to establish its own control more firmly in the area. When the last Conservative government finally succeeded in creating a customs house at a key river outlet (Puerto Alonso on the Acre river) and began collecting an unexpected deluge of revenue from the rubber trade, the previously untaxed independent producers, encouraged by nearby Brazilian authorities, were quick to react and before long the rubber region was the centre of several filibustering expeditions. Although Brazilian support to the rebels was at first covert because of undoubted

---

[1] Finot, *Nueva historia*, p. 338.
[2] Trigo, *Las constituciones de Bolivia*, pp. 115–24; David Alvéstegui, *Salamanca, su gravitación sobre el destino de Bolivia* (3 vols.; La Paz: Talleres Gráficos Bolivianos, 1957–62), I, 155–7.

Bolivian title to the territory, Bolivia's inability to control the area led to open support of the annexation movement by Brazil. After several campaigns, in which Pando organized an Andean army under his own direction to crush the rebellions, the Bolivian government finally conceded the impossibility of destroying the rebel movement in the face of strong Brazilian opposition, and by the Treaty of Petropolis in 1903 it sold the vast Acre rubber territory to Brazil for two and a half million pounds sterling.[1]

With the Acre question resolved, the nation again began turning inward to deal with pressing political and economic problems. Having absorbed most of its energies in recovering from the federal revolution and the Acre War, the Pando government completed its term of office and prepared to hand the régime over to a Liberal party successor. But the party had temporarily split into two factions, one supporting Ismael Montes, and the other the first vice-president, Lucio Pérez Velasco. When Pando began using direct government pressure to support Montes, many purists of the party, who firmly opposed the idea of government interference in the elections, rebelled. Joining forces with the few intransigent federalists who were still left, they formed an opposition grouping which soon took the apt label of *puritanos*.[2]

Despite strong puritano opposition, government intervention produced a landslide victory for Ismael Montes, and this bitter defeat at the polls marked the end of the puritano grouping. The Congress of 1904 quietly accepted the election returns and thereafter the Liberal party found itself unopposed by any formal opposition party on the national scene until the outbreak of World War I, a situation unique in the political history of the republic and particularly unusual in the period of the political parties. Not only did the Liberal party rule for so long a period undisturbed by any organized opposition, but the nation itself did not experience a single revolutionary attempt at overthrowing the government from 1899 to 1920, a record never equalled before or since!

[1] Basadre, *Chile, Perú y Bolivia*, pp. 594–600; Finot, *Nueva historia*, pp. 339–46.
[2] Alvéstegui, *Salamanca*, I, 171–80.

Without question the dominant figure in this extraordinary period of constitutional government was that vibrant caudillo Ismael Montes. Montes was born in La Paz in 1861, and came from a professional military family. In his youth he entered the army during the War of the Pacific, eventually rising to the rank of captain. But with the end of the war, Montes returned to civilian life and proceeded to make his fortune as an able lawyer, obtaining a professorship in civil law at the University of La Paz.

Montes was an early and vociferous leader of the Liberal party, and played a leading part in the federalist revolution, being second in military command to Pando and forming with Pando and Fernando Gauchalla the dominant leadership of the rebel government. He was raised to the rank of general by the national convention of 1899 and was appointed by Pando to be his minister of war. In his cabinet post he worked hard at re-organizing the national army after the civil war, but he also astutely used his new position to build up a solid following for himself within the party ranks.

An able man who tended to commit himself totally to immediate action and rapid decisions, Montes was extremely intolerant of any opposition. He therefore surrounded himself with a hard core of loyal followers, who were essentially secondary supporting figures, though often able administrators. His intolerance of all opposition and his conviction of the righteousness of his cause allowed Montes deliberately to ignore every one of the moral positions on democratic and free government which the Liberal party had fought for in their long years of opposition to Conservative party rule. Fixing elections, silencing opposition papers, packing congress, and ignoring its censures, Montes proceeded along his own predetermined path oblivious to cries for morality. Much like Arce in his determination to achieve national development, he was ruthless in his means and oblivious even to personal ethics.[1]

Yet for all his faults, he gave a unique dynamism to the national government. He carried out a vast programme of railway

---

[1] Montes was not above taking retainer fees from Patiño when he was out of office, nor seizing private property for his own use when he was in power. See Céspedes, *El dictador suicida*, p. 35; also see below, pp. 164–5.

construction and urban development. He built schools, roads, and public works, professionalized the military and finally created a viable governmental economy and a rational banking system. No doubt the fortuitous development of tin, the favourable international credit of the nation due to the work of his predecessors, and the funds made available by the various international indemnities for loss of territory were crucial determinants without which his leadership would have been ineffective, yet there is no denying his own individual contributions.[1]

The first major problem the Montes administration faced in 1904 was the long-standing issue of the littoral. Following the initiative of Pando, Montes completely reversed the position of the Liberal party which for so long had stood for the full-scale reintegration of the Pacific coast territory and proceeded to negotiate a definitive peace treaty with Chile. By the terms of the treaty, Bolivia not only gave up all of its former coastal territory, but even abandoned the minimum conservative position of a port outlet on the Pacific. Justifying himself on the grounds that Bolivia's rising commerce was threatened by the old treaties which gave Chile control over Bolivian tariffs, Montes held to the position that any treaty, no matter how onerous, was worthwhile in order to restore Bolivia's control over her economy.

It is obvious from the negotiating process that both Pando and Montes, though not their opponents, were driven by a great sense of urgency. Initiating the conferences when Chile had resolved all her disputes with Peru and Argentina, Bolivia could not possibly use the threat of an alliance with either of these two powers as a bargaining lever with Chile. Nor was Chile particularly sensitive to Bolivian demands as the famous Koning memorandum indicates. Claiming that the great law of the right of conquest made Chile absolute master of the Bolivian littoral, Chilean Ambassador Koning denied Bolivia even the right to ask for compensation, let alone a port, and declared that if Chile decided to compensate Bolivia for the territory it would be out of charity. Insulting as this memorandum was, Pando and Montes

---

[1] For an interesting discussion of Montes' character, see Alvéstegui, *Salamanca*, I, 251–7. Also, Humberto Vázquez Machicado, José de Mesa y Teresa Gisbert, *Manual de historia de Bolivia* (La Paz: Gisbert y Cía., 1958), p. 408.

swallowed their pride and continued to negotiate. The negotiations were begun in 1902 and ended with the signing of the peace treaty in October 1904.[1] The major terms of the treaty provided for the recognition of Chile's perpetual domination of the littoral, in return for which Bolivia received £300,000 outright, a railroad from Arica to La Paz, and an agreement by the Chilean government to guarantee capital investments in internal railroad construction on the Bolivian altiplano. The old trade barriers were re-established, and finally Bolivia was given the right of free transit through Chilean ports.[2]

When the terms were made public, national opinion was shocked. But Montes was not unduly perturbed by this reaction and in secret sessions of congress, after long and arduous debate, succeeded in securing approval of the treaty. Surprisingly, with approval of the treaty, passions calmed down considerably and the nation, though not later political leaders, seemed to accept the results. Instead of debating the terms, everyone discussed the fabulous sums available to the Bolivian government for the first time in its history, sums which would finally bring to reality the railroad dreams of such long standing. Thus in the 1905 congress, there arose great discussions on how to spend the two and a half million pounds sterling just deposited to Bolivia's account in London by Brazil for the Acre territory, as well as the sums to be expected from Chile, and soon an intense game of political negotiating began with every provincial congressman proposing a new rail line for his own district.

Though a modest scheme calling for seven lines and for open bidding eventually passed congress, Montes in his usual manner had proceeded to negotiate his own scheme in a closed contract with a consortium of New York bankers—the First National City Bank and Speyer and Company. Again Montes caught his opponents by surprise, and though they put up a hard struggle in the sessions of 1906, charging that there were no real guarantees

---

[1] For the background and terms of the treaty see Domingo Flores, 'Estudio y comentario del tratado de 1904', in Instituto de Investigaciones Históricas y Culturales de La Paz, *Mesa redonda sobre el problema del litoral boliviano* (La Paz: Municipalidad de La Paz, 1966), pp. 161–202; also Alvéstegui, *Salamanca*, I, 214–24.

[2] Basadre, *Chile, Perú y Bolivia*, p. 601.

for Bolivia in the contract and that it meant handing the lines over to private control, his loyal adherents successfully provided the usual endorsement.[1]

The Speyer contract was unquestionably an inadequate and expensive scheme, as Montes' opponents charged, and it did eventually permit Bolivia's key railroads to come under control of the English Antofagasta and Chile Railroad Company.[2] Nevertheless, the contract was fulfilled and the railroad network was created, connecting the key cities of Potosí, Sucre, Cochabamba, Oruro, and La Paz with each other by rail lines, and with the ports of Arica and Antofagasta. Montes also initiated a railroad to Guaqui, on Lake Titicaca, connecting up with the Peruvian railroad system, and together these new rail systems finally began to destroy the destructive isolation and regionalism of Bolivia and open up her internal markets as never before.

Having overcome the opposition to the two great acts of his government, the signing of the peace treaty and the Speyer contract, Montes completed his first presidential term in triumph. But the anti-*montista* forces were given their opportunity when Montes was forced to name Guachalla, the last of the triumvirate of the federal revolution, as the official candidate of the Liberal party. Guachalla was an independent political figure with his own following, and his candidacy in 1908 represented a threat to the now thoroughly entrenched montistas. But Guachalla's sudden death on the eve of inauguration permitted Montes and his followers to regain control of the situation and, invalidating the election, they continued themselves in office under a docile montista. Now known to their opponents by the name of *doctrinarios*, the montista stalwarts made Eliodoro Villazón president for the 1909–12 term—an obvious caretaker administration until Montes could be constitutionally re-elected.[3] In all respects, the Villazón government was a smooth transition between the two Montes periods, differing from the latter's administrations only in its lack of vitality and controversy and the relative calm of the

[1] Alvéstegui, *Salamanca*, I, 225–35.
[2] Margaret A. Marsh, *The Bankers in Bolivia, A Study in American Foreign Invest-ment* (New York: Vanguard Press, 1928), pp. 73–9.
[3] Alvéstegui, *Salamanca*, I, 261–70.

opposition. The administration did make some advances, however, and building upon the monetary and banking initiatives of
the Montes period, it created Bolivia's first national bank.[1]

In 1910 Villazón obtained a £1,000,000 French loan and with
the aid of another £1,000,000 in private subscriptions, the Banco
de la Nación Boliviana was created in February 1911. A mixed
state-private enterprise, the bank absorbed several Bolivian banks
and proved such a success that it doubled its capital by the end of
the Villazón administration. While the new bank was largely run
by private bankers and obtained several general controls over the
banking houses of the nation, the Villazón government was not
strong enough to force the private banks to give up their
currency issuing rights, and this reform was temporarily
dropped.[2]

In other ways, the Villazón period was one of economic
prosperity. Recovering from the rather harsh depression of 1908,
which temporarily put a halt to the early boom of the decade,
exports rose from Bs. 63 million in 1909 to Bs. 93 million in
1913, while government income in the same period rose from
Bs. 10·3 million to Bs. 22 million. This fortuitous rise in government income reflected to a marked degree the increased tempo of
the entire national economy, for government revenues were
derived chiefly from internal sales taxes, and import and export
duties, with the light taxes on the tin industry and its exports
providing only a minor source of income, something like 17 per
cent of government revenues in the 1913 budget. So prosperous
were the times, in fact, that Villazón, despite his continuation of
the ambitious public works programme of his predecessor, was
still able in 1912 to produce the first and only government budget
surplus in Liberal government history.[3]

When Villazón handed the government back to Montes in
1913, he presented him with a thriving economy and a peaceful

[1] Moisés Ascarrunz, *El Partido Liberal en el poder, a través de los mensajes presidenciales* (2 vols.; La Paz: Arno Hermanos, 1917), II, 180ff.
[2] Peñaloza, *Historia económica*, II, 47–51; Víctor Paz Estenssoro, 'El pensamiento
ecónomico en Bolivia', in *El pensamiento ecónomico latinoamericano* (Mexico:
Fondo de Cultura Económica, 1945), pp. 57–8; Céspedes, *El dictador suicida*,
pp. 36–9.
[3] Eduardo López Rivas, *Esquema de la historia económica de Bolivia* (Oruro: Universidad Técnica de Oruro, 1955), tables on pp. 21, 28, 33, 36–7.

internal political scene. But neither of these lasted under the new Montes administration. After his return from his European travels with a host of new projects for greater reforms, Montes soon created a hostile political climate and at the same time faced an economy badly shaken by a world depression. Assuming the presidency in August 1913, Montes presented a plan of major financial reorganization. The essence of this plan involved the granting of a monopoly on currency issue to the state-controlled Banco de la Nación Boliviana thereby giving the government greater control over the circulation of paper currency.

This move had been long expected, and had been part of the 1911 plans to create the national bank, but its timing was badly managed. The private bankers were opposed to the idea, and as a reaction to the government plan they began severely to restrict bank credit. This sudden credit restriction occurred just as the nation was experiencing the first effects of the pre-World War drop in rubber and tin prices, and the combined developments badly upset the national economy.[1]

As a result of the pre-war depression, the value of total exports declined 32 per cent between 1913 and 1914 reflecting a 31 per cent decline in tin production for this same period.[2] Along with this decline in the export market, there was a severe decline in agricultural production throughout the republic in 1913–14 due to adverse weather conditions.

The widening economic crisis created a tense political climate and Montes suddenly found himself faced by an extremely hostile public. This opposition was led by the bankers who defended their position in congress, in the press, and to the public at large. As a more dramatic gesture, two of the three foreign banks with branches in Bolivia terminated operations, claiming as their reason for leaving the restrictive Montes reforms.[3]

This economic opposition also sought to express itself more powerfully in the creation of a coherent political party grouping

---

[1] Alvéstegui, *Salamanca*, I, 297–300; Peñaloza, *Historia ecónomica*, II, 51–60; Julio Benavides M., *Historia bancaria de Bolivia* (La Paz: Ediciones 'Arrieta', 1955), pp. 93–104.

[2] López Rivas, *Esquema de la historia económica*, pp. 33, 35.

[3] Charles A. McQueen, *Bolivian Public Finance* (Trade Promotion Series, No. 6; Washington: Department of Commerce, 1925), p. 8.

together all the anti-montista factions. With strong support from the private bankers, various dissident politicians began meeting together to map out plans for a formal political opposition. Under the leadership of the aggressive young ex-diplomat, Bautista Saavedra, contact was made with leading opposition figures of the old conservative and puritano groupings and Daniel Salamanca, the most powerful anti-Montes senator, was asked to head this new coalition. Salamanca, an independently wealthy landowner from Cochabamba, had been a leading parliamentarian since 1900. Although he had initially been affiliated with the Liberal party, he had joined neither the montistas nor the puritanos and had been a leader of the congressional opposition to the treaty of 1904 with Chile and the 1905 Speyer contract. Morally austere and socially introverted, Salamanca was considered the outstanding parliamentary orator of his day, and was famous for his insistence on strict constitutionality of government and support for the original principles of the Liberal party as expressed by Camacho. In 1913, at the beginning of this major agitation, Salamanca was abroad undergoing treatment for his chronic severe stomach ailment. Accepting the overtures of Saavedra and other paceño leaders, including the ageing General José Manuel Pando, now in opposition to his party, Salamanca initiated final pre-organization conferences in April 1914, on his return from Europe. On 22 April he issued under his name a call to local leaders to organize a new party. The response was strong and overnight local assemblies were meeting and creating directories, forming programmes, and adopting the name *Unión Republicana*.[1]

The strong response to his call, according to Salamanca, could be traced directly to the banking issue, and he explained the origins of the whole movement, in the following manner:

The present head of the republic [Montes] returned from Europe and was received in the country without any resistance. His friends gave him ample support, his enemies were discouraged and the country remained indifferent. This situation would probably have lasted a long time, if tact and prudence had inspired the acts of his government. But, poorly advised, he resolved to develop a complex and extensive

[1] Alvéstegui, *Salamanca*, I, 300ff.

economic policy out of all proportion to the resources of the nation. In this he showed an error of judgement, or at least a lack of sensitivity in its applications; all things which could have been easily remedied, if the government had renounced its habitual self-sufficiency, and if it had shown itself capable of listening to the councils of public opinion. The first measures of this policy upset the economic life of Bolivia.

The national economic life is a solid linking of interdependent phenomena. In this interdependence, the provision of bank credit can be considered as an initial point of the movement. The government struck at this point and created an almost unforeseen suppression of the normal service of credit. The Banco de la Nación which should have resolved this deficiency was incapable of doing so. Thus business was paralyzed and a violent malaise spread everywhere. Other adverse forces came to add to these . . . The people felt themselves maltreated in their interests and vexed in their dignity. It was not so long ago that the president had been touted by influential officials and passively accepted by the country as the man most capable of administering its commercial affairs. The nation which had suffered with resignation the usurpation of all its sovereign rights and which contemplated with indifference the corruption of its institutions, could not suffer with the same patience the damage done to its economic interests. The indignation and protest spread throughout the republic. Such was the causal origin of our party.[1]

The difficulty of forming this protest into a cohesive party was clearly recognized by Salamanca, who carefully worked to smooth out all potential conflict and orient the new party into unified opposition to the Liberal government. 'Defensa nacional contra los avances del poder' became his rallying cry, so that puritanos and conservatives might easily sit together.[2] The rapid organization of republican committees in all the centres of the

[1] Alvéstegui, *Salamanca*, 305.

[2] In a letter to Pando on 2 May 1914, Salamanca stated that: 'Given present conditions this movement is adopting a defensive position, that is to protect the institutions and the national interest . . . The principal obstacle to our political organization has been the suspicions which arise between Liberals and Constitutionals (i.e. Conservatives), who are the elements who must inevitably compose the opposition. In order to avoid these obstacles, I resorted to . . . a programme which stresses the unity of the aspirations of the opposition group. However, I have the hope . . . that the definitive programme of the party will be formulated upon liberal foundations which are generally accepted.' *Ibid.* p. 306. Interestingly Montes also charged that the new party was nothing more than 'a conglomeration of apostates, without civic conscience and without doctrine'. Quoted in Céspedes, *El dictador suicida*, p. 39.

nation showed that his ideas were well conceived and bore fruit. By the end of June 1914, Salamanca felt that the party was sufficiently organized to call for a national founding convention, which was to be held in early August in La Paz.

The rapid development of an opposition party of major proportions for the first time in its fifteen peaceful years of rule badly disturbed the Liberal party. Added to the fear of the party regulars for their government positions was the wilful character of Montes, who saw any opposition as an insult to himself and something which had no right to exist. In this atmosphere, a viable two-party system was not welcomed by the party in power and almost immediately local officials began interfering with the new organization. This was soon followed by a more vigorous central reaction, and on 7 August 1914, the eve of the national Republican party convention, Montes declared a state of siege, exiled leading opposition leaders—some forty in number—and closed down thirteen newspapers which had sprung up to defend the new political movement. Over Salamanca's minority opposition in congress, the Liberal deputies proceeded to give full endorsement to their government.

Despite Montes' pious hope of having effectively crushed the opposition by this action, the Republican party was not stillborn. When they had recovered from the initial shock, the local committees gave renewed support to their leaders, and with the lifting of the state of siege in December 1914, the party under Salamanca's leadership again organized a national convention, this time for Oruro in January 1915. With almost exactly the same membership which had assembled the year before in La Paz, this Oruro assembly proceeded to establish the *Partido Unión Republicana* and issued a formal manifesto to the nation, outlining its programme.[1]

As was to be expected, this party programme called for free elections, an independent parliament and a judiciary free from executive influence. The usual statements about local autonomy and governmental decentralization were included, but the key issue was free elections for, according to the programme, 'If you had the security of a free election, the complexion of things would

[1] Alvéstegui, *Salamanca*, I, 309ff; II, 7–8.

change radically, for then the majorities would have access to power and the government would always sustain itself upon a democratic base. Therefore, the freedom of suffrage is nothing less than the key to our institutional renovation.'[1] The Montes government was attacked for absolutism and personalism, and for increasing the public debt despite increases in national income. Constitutional amendments were also proposed to restrict the state of siege, to guarantee individual civil liberties, and finally to protect the other two branches of government from excessive executive power.

Aside from these political issues, the government was attacked for dangerously wrecking the economy with its recent monetary and credit reforms. It was also charged with granting industrial monopolies and a heavy system of taxation. Finally, the manifesto included a short paragraph calling for mild legislative reforms on social issues, and a nationalist call for the encouragement of the growth of national as opposed to foreign capital.[2] Essentially a reworking of the famous Camacho Liberal party programme, the Republican manifesto nevertheless contained an important foretaste of things to come in these last two positions.

But as yet the new ideas were well submerged in classical liberal and *laissez faire* statements and, as the articulate Salamanca noted, this new party was 'a party which had sprung from the necessity of things and not from preconceived theories'.[3] By this 'necessity of things' Salamanca meant the inevitability of opposition political formations. In the long period of montista rule, a large body of professional politicians, ambitious for office, had developed. Thus the classic pattern of 'ins' versus 'outs' set the stage for the growth of a large opposition party, and the traditional personalismo pattern of nineteenth- and early twentieth-century politics only exacerbated the climate. So long as Montes seemed to be producing economic miracles, these combinations

[1] Alberto Cornejo S., *Programas políticos de Bolivia* (Cochabamba: Imprenta Universitaria, 1949), pp. 73–4.
[2] *Ibid.* pp. 71–81, for entire text. As for the social legislation, it proposed 'Laws on salaries, hours and work accidents. Laws for the protection of infancy. Special protection for the indigenous race and protection of its territorial ownership. Reform of the legal codes, adopting them to the social, moral and intellectual state of the Republic.' *Ibid.* p. 80.
[3] Alvéstegui, *Salamanca*, II, 9.

5   49

of patterns could be prevented from coalescing. But once this thrust of progress was stopped, then splintering was the inevitable result, as Salamanca so clearly recognized.

Nor did the new political grouping differ in any fundamental respect either structurally or ideologically from the Liberal party. So long as all politically active leadership came from the same socio-economic background, the dominance of personality over ideology was inevitable, and the new party revealed the same personalist fissures as the old Liberal grouping. It was also inevitable that given the agreement on fundamental principles, the major platform of the new party would be legality and honesty in government, a slogan which it would abandon just as quickly as had the Liberals when they finally achieved office. For the gaining of office was the only real goal of the new party, and once this was achieved, the office was to be held at all costs. Thus time and again all the great defenders of constitutionality became severe tyrants in their own right when they took office, and with the reintroduction of a viable two-party system in Bolivian politics, there was also reintroduced the practice of governmental change through revolution rather than the ballot, though the result never basically affected fundamental economic and social institutions. It is true that in this period of Bolivian political history there were some overtones of ideological commitment—either to regionalism, anti-clericalism, or commercial versus mining interests— but these overtones were found in both parties, and in comparison with later periods, when new socio-economic groups rose to power and expressed themselves in the classic patterns of European ideological thought along with American radicalism and *indigenismo*, these earlier distinctions were comparatively superficial.

With the return of a two-party system to Bolivia in late 1914 and early 1915, a pattern of structural electoral violence unique in Bolivian history developed. As Bolivia had still not adopted the secret ballot, elections were carried out in the central plaza of each city, where voters brought their tickets openly to the electoral urns. Therefore if a party could keep voters from entering the plaza to cast their ballots, or prevent the opposition members from sitting on the election boards, they could conveniently carry the elections for themselves. Given this possibility and the limited manhood suffrage which kept the voters to a small number of upper and middle-class whites and the more advanced cholo artisans and tradesmen, violence and intimidation became a useful tool to which everyone resorted. Both Liberals and Republicans organized their own gangs or 'clubs' made up of lower-class urban cholos and financed by the local party leader. These 'clubs' had their headquarters at the local *chicherías* or small taverns, and their sole task was to form mass demonstrations on days of campaigning and physically to prevent the opposition from reaching the polls on the day of election. Violent battles were fought between these groups and their opponents, and between Republicans and the local police, and every election from 1914 on had its full complement of death and bloody mob scenes. Of all the cities of the nation, only La Paz was relatively immune from this pattern, due to the greater number of voters involved and the presence of the diplomatic corps, but even here local clubs or 'workers' sections' of the two parties were carefully maintained for use in popular demonstrations. Despite all their congressional talk of constitutionality and peaceful elections, the Republicans had full recourse to this system, and even Daniel Salamanca, supposedly the most honest and upright of politicians, is said to have maintained at his own expense such a 'club' in Cochabamba.[1]

This system of electoral violence grew in importance with the increasing security of the Liberal régime, which now was willing under the reviving Montes administration to challenge the opposition through electoral contests. For the Montes administration, after unsuccessfully attempting to destroy the Republican party, had come minimally to accept its existence and to turn to control over elections as a means of preserving its position. Montes also attempted to destroy the initial impetus behind the opposition formation by resolving the crisis caused by his economic policies. Faced by the increasing tempo of political opposition which he could not control and by the rapid development of a serious depression as the result of his credit war and the impact of the trade restrictions resulting from the opening of European

---

[1] Céspedes, *El dictador suicida*, pp. 42–3.

hostilities, Montes had decided to withdraw his ambitious economic programme. He postponed the date when restrictions on the outflow of private bank currency would come into effect for several more years, and also declared a national moratorium and the temporary suspension of gold payments by the banks to prevent the flight of gold.

Fortunately for Montes the initial disruption of world trade as a result of the Great War in Europe was followed by a rapid expansion of Bolivian mineral exports to England and the United States as each nation began fully to commit itself to a war mobilization programme. Tin production, now the prime determinant of Bolivian prosperity, rose to new heights with prices rapidly following. By late 1916 Montes was again at the head of a prosperous régime and economy and was able to carry through to completion his entire programme of currency and banking reform. And by 1917 he was able joyfully to announce to congress that Bolivia in the previous year had for the first time passed the 100 million boliviano mark in her national exports.[1] Thus Montes succeeded in eliminating the key economic factor which initially had given rise to the Republican party and was able to maintain his government in power with considerable ease despite some successes of the Republicans in the municipal elections of 1915, 1916, and 1917 and the seating of some of their leaders in congress.

Opposed by a ruthless president who grudgingly accepted their existence, and with the return of prosperity, 1916 was a difficult year for the new party. In the congressional elections of May 1916, only three Republicans were elected to the chamber of deputies and none to the senate. Even Salamanca had to give up his race for senator from Cochabamba, his traditional post, and run as an ordinary deputy from La Paz to gain office.[2] Yet despite this slow beginning and the removal of some of the key propaganda weapons of the party with the new economic conditions, 1916 was an important organizational year. For in February the Republican party, under the financial leadership of Bautista Saavedra, succeeded in establishing its own official party newspaper, *La Razón*, under the able editorship of one of the energetic

[1] Peñaloza, *Historia económica*, II, 62–3; Ascarrunz, *El Partido Liberal*, II, 344.
[2] Alvéstegui, *Salamanca*, II, 73–5.

young party men, David Alvéstegui. Set up in opposition to the dominant Liberal daily newspaper, *El Diario* (founded in June 1904, by the montista and former cabinet minister, José Carrasco), *La Razón* soon became an influential manipulator of public opinion and the chief sustainer of the Republican party in season and out.[1] Also at the second party congress held in La Paz in October of that year, some 124 delegates attended from all the regions of the republic, and the party gained at this time the support of several influential political personalities.[2]

The dominant theme of the convention as well as of national politics was the presidential succession. Montes was unwilling to give up his iron-like control, and hesitated long before choosing a successor. He finally ended by naming a leading banker and relatively new and unknown political figure, José Gutiérrez Guerra, as his party's candidate.[3] For their part the Republicans chose a leading southern landowner and doctor, José María Escalier. A practising physician in Buenos Aires, Escalier had important social connections throughout the republic and was chosen by the Republicans as an independent who could attract a broad spectrum of respectable votes. But the outcome of the election, despite the tremendous effort of the Republicans in this, their first presidential contest, was a foregone conclusion. In a violent May election, Escalier was defeated by 73,000 to 9,000.[4]

With the Liberals easily controlling the presidency and taking full advantage of the issues of peace and prosperity, the Republicans began to look desperately for a new cause with which to arouse the nation. Because of this, they hastily seized on the assassination of General José Manuel Pando, who was murdered in June 1917 outside La Paz, as a major political issue. Though the murder of Pando was most likely a local criminal incident, the mishandling of the whole investigation by the Montes régime, and its marked hostility to Pando after his death, soon encouraged the charge of political assassination by the opposition. Given the popularity of the ex-president, a Pacific and Acre War hero, it

---

[1] Alvéstegui, *Salamanca*, II, p. 157.
[2] *Ibid.* pp. 103–5.
[3] On the career of Gutiérrez Guerra see Paz Estenssoro, 'El pensamiento económico', pp. 59–60; Alvéstegui, *Salamanca*, II, 97–102.
[4] Alvéstegui, *Salamanca*, II, 103–11, 113–29.

seemed a promising issue, and the Republicans used it heavily, especially after their harsh treatment in the recent elections. In August 1917, when the new congress assembled, the Republicans, in a surprise move, charged Montes with the crime. On 5 December, just before he left for Europe, Montes presented himself before congress and in a tense atmosphere defended himself and his actions. Meanwhile, outside the *palacio legislativo*, scores of people were killed and wounded, as troops and Republican mobs clashed, and gunfire constantly interrupted the speech of the old caudillo. The government reacted to the mob violence by exiling Saavedra along with Alvéstegui and his editorial staff in an obvious attempt to silence *La Razón*. With this act the parliamentary minority withdrew, and in the final vote on the accusation, only four votes were registered against Montes—these four being Liberal ones.[1]

After this episode, Montes finally departed from the national political scene, and under the new administration of José Gutiérrez Guerra, some concessions were made to Republican demands. In early 1918 the administration signed a series of inter-party pacts whereby it agreed to carry out free elections. These pacts were carried out by the Liberals and the May 1918 congressional elections were the freest ever participated in by the Republican party. But the party with its moderate programme and its lack of decisive issues did poorly and only obtained ten seats in congress.[2] Thus while it appeared that the Republicans could hold their own under the divided leadership of Escalier, Salamanca, and Bautista Saavedra, they seemed incapable of becoming a majority party. Neither the banking issue nor the Pando affair was enough to break the power of the Liberals, and even with a strong press and important national leaders behind it, the new party was finding it difficult to obtain power, and desertions from its ranks grew every year that it remained out of office.

An attempt was made in late 1918 to revive the perennial issue of the old littoral, with all its emotional overtones. Appealing to the League to guarantee Bolivia's right to the sea, which

---

[1] Alvéstegui, *Salamanca*, II, 141–56; Moisés Alcázar, *Crónicas parlamentarias* (2nd ed.; La Paz: Talleres Gráficos Bolivianos, 1957), pp. 100–7.

[2] Alvéstegui, *Salamanca*, II, 171–6.

was an important part of Wilson's fourteen-point programme, the Republicans demanded that the government obtain complete reintegration of all coastal territory lost to Chile.[1] The Gutiérrez Guerra administration was slow to respond to these attacks, and the public became deeply stirred over this emotionally charged issue and demanded immediate negotiation with the Wilson government. Finally giving in to the pressure Gutiérrez Guerra invited the Republican and Radical parties to join the Liberals in a cabinet of 'National concentration' (i.e. all-party cabinet).[2]

With this gesture and the development of an active diplomatic campaign the issue lost most of its potency, and before long the Republicans found that many of their important leaders refused to support the extreme irredentist position of *reivindicacionalismo*, as it was called. By March 1919 the issue had subsided to such an extent that Gutiérrez Guerra was able to dissolve the national concentration cabinet and return to an exclusively Liberal party government.[3]

While the government found it easy to circumvent Republican opposition on practically every major issue, the new tone of moderation of the Gutiérrez Guerra administration began to cause deep schisms within the previously monolithic and montista dominated Liberal party. The government also became seriously embroiled at this point with Simón I. Patiño, and the two issues deeply divided the party. In 1912 Patiño had bought the alcohol import monopoly from the government and in 1918 asked for a reduction of his annual annuity to the government for this privilege. In the midst of these negotiations, the concession ran out and Patiño introduced some 80,000 containers of this product after the expiration date had passed. The government attacked this move as being an act of contrabandage, and after

---

[1] Alvéstegui, *Salamanca*, II, pp. 179–86.

[2] The Radical party was primarily a group of La Paz intellectuals with only tenuous support elsewhere in the nation, which was founded in the early 1910s by Franz Tamayo, Tomás Manuel Elío, and Daniel Sánchez Bustamante. By 1918 only Bustamante remained in the party, giving it leadership, prestige, and his own uniquely flavoured style of progressive liberal programme. See, e.g. Daniel Sánchez Bustamante, *Programa político. Problemas de Bolivia en 1918* (La Paz: Imprenta Velarde, 1918); also Francovich, *El pensamiento boliviano en el siglo xx*, p. 31.

[3] Alvéstegui, *Salamanca*, II, 186–92.

long litigation fined Patiño the significant sum of Bs. 1·5 million. Although Patiño eventually won a retraction of the fine in the supreme court, he seems to have developed an extreme antipathy toward the formerly friendly government. This was clearly indicated in the actions of his chief Bolivian aid, Arturo Loayza. For in the late 1918 congressional sessions an opposition group appeared within the Liberal ranks, which the popular press began to call the *patiñista* group. With no clearly defined ideology, this group of senators led by José Antezana claimed for itself the purity of liberal principles, but in practice seemed intent on destroying congressional support for the Gutiérrez Guerra government. In early 1919 they attempted to replace the first vice-president, Ismael Vásquez, as senate president when he took up the post of minister of government. But Vásquez' rejection of the cabinet appointment and immediate reincorporation into congress prevented this takeover move. They next demanded that the senate recess altogether for alleged attacks on its members by *La Razón*, but a coalition of Republicans and pro-government Liberals prevented this. Frustrated in these attempts, by late 1919 the patiñistas were finally strong enough to call for an interpellation of the Liberal cabinet and, after tough debate, succeeded in censuring the cabinet and bringing about its downfall—the first such incident in the twenty-year history of Liberal government. According to the minister of finance, José Luis Tejada Sorzano, the cabinet's chief defender in this debate, the fall of the cabinet did not occur 'for having offended the constitution or the laws. It will fall to the clangour of 80,000 cans of alcohol, introduced as contraband by a great mining enterprise.' He also charged the patiñista faction with planning to place Arturo Loayza, administrator of the Patiño empire, in the lists as Liberal presidential candidate for the elections of 1921.[1]

While this dissension was occurring within the ranks of the Liberal party, the Republican party was experiencing sharp divisions among its leadership. Hostile to the party's actions on the littoral issue and irked by Escalier's often unconscious usurpation of his own authority, Salamanca in late 1919 resigned his post as party head and supposedly retired to private life. After a period

[1] Alvéstegui, *Salamanca*, II, 244–8; Céspedes, *El dictador suicida*, pp. 61–4.

of indecision a compromise leadership plan was worked out whereby Escalier became chief of the party and Saavedra became its director in the latter's annual absences in Argentina.

Along with this change of active leadership, there was also a shift within Republican ranks to a commitment to revolutionary action as the only road to power. For despite Liberal party divisions, the government easily kept its supporters in office in election after election, and despite its revocation of electoral freedom for the Republican opposition, its bloody repressions were not engendering any reaction from the largely apathetic public. In the December 1919 municipal elections the Republicans put up a full slate of candidates only to see the government forcibly dominate the results with much bloodshed, especially in Oruro. Although party practice throughout the period so far had been to run in every election no matter what the results, this policy seemed to be leading nowhere and the more radical members called for a new approach. The dominance of this new trend of thought was revealed when after this last election, Saavedra charged the government with brutality. Even the usually pacific Salamanca, in his retiring parliamentary speech, warned the government that the opposition could no longer accept this policy of suppression and would have to turn toward non-legal means for changing the *status quo*.

In February 1920 Escalier and Saavedra met in Oruro to decide the future strategy of the party, and it was there agreed to have one last try at a national election, while at the same time plans were laid for the creation of small revolutionary committees in the major cities. To Saavedra and other key leaders the choice had come to be either revolution or dissolution of the party and they convinced Escalier that action was necessary. Meanwhile the government furthered the argument of the revolutionary faction when in March 1920 the party's paper *La Razón* was completely destroyed by Liberal mobs with the tacit support of the Gutiérrez Guerra government. In reaction to this act, the party declared that it would abstain from the congressional election in May 1920, which was an open statement of revolutionary intent. The strong Salamanca faction of the party, however, refused to accept this decision and the Oruro and Potosí committees put up full slates of candidates, including the name of Salamanca on the Oruro one. This internal upheaval embittered Escalier who threatened to resign and destroy the party with him. Nevertheless the conspiracy developed rapidly under the leadership of Saavedra who now became in fact the active leader of the party.[1]

Despite all this rather heavy-handed plotting, the government seemed indifferent to the conspirators and was firmly convinced that the Republican party could never carry such a scheme to completion. The Liberals believed in their own invincibility after twenty years in power, despite recent obvious signs of disunity, and they were thoroughly convinced of the stability and disinterest of the army, which Montes and his successors had so carefully trained and which they believed was psychologically incapable of subverting a constitutional government. Also it appeared to government observers that the disunity exhibited by the Republican party, especially the Oruro-Potosí disobedience, indicated the beginnings of a major split in their opponents' camp.[2]

While Saavedra's plotting successfully proceeded, the economic condition of the nation was creating serious strains. For the very economic attainments of the twenty years of Liberal rule were beginning to create a whole new set of economic and social forces which had not existed in the less sophisticated days of the Conservative oligarchy. As early as 1910 Bolivia had achieved its position as the second largest tin producer of the world, with something like 20 per cent of world production.[3] And this was a constantly expanding export, the value of which rose from

[1] Alvéstegui, *Salamanca*, II, 193ff. So important had Saavedra now become in this plotting period, that the Oruro committee, loyal to Salamanca, sent a representative to La Paz to ask Saavedra to withdraw from active leadership, claiming the army was hostile to him and would therefore not participate in the revolt. As could be expected, Saavedra was not about to divest himself of his newly dominant position and the plotting continued smoothly under his direction. Benigno Carrasco, *Hernando Siles* (La Paz: Editorial del Estado, 1961), pp. 125–6.

[2] Alvéstegui, an important plotter, recounts an episode in which he encountered the minister of government, Julio Zamora, on a trip to Buenos Aires, and the minister not only knew that the purpose of his trip was to buy arms, but informed him that 'I can give the Republicans all the arms they want, in the security that they could never carry through a revolution against us'. Alvéstegui, *Salamanca*, II, 255.

[3] López Rivas, *Esquema de la historia económica*, p. 23.

Bs. 14·6 million to Bs. 122·2 million, or by 743 per cent, between 1900 and 1920,[1] while at the same time the boliviano held firmly.[2] Comparable to this growth in the value of tin exports was the growth in the total value of all national exports which went from Bs. 35 million to Bs. 156 million, a rise of 431 per cent, in these same twenty years.[3] Together with the development of the tin industry, and the spreading of prosperity to the urban centres, there even occurred a small growth of light industry in such cities as La Paz, Oruro, and Cochabamba.[4]

The result of this growth in the private sector of the economy was a rise in population and a great increase in urbanization. Whereas La Paz had an estimated population of 70,000 in 1900, by 1920 the city had grown to 115,000,[5] and a proportionate growth was experienced in all the major cities. With the twenty years of Liberal peace and progress came the modernization of the cities. The first paved roads, sewerage and drinking water facilities were laid down, and a whole range of public works was carried out to bring the Bolivian cities up to twentieth-century standards of hygiene and organization. Throughout the nation, telephones, telegraph, roads, and railroads were constructed, and by 1920 the Liberals had almost completed the altiplano rail network which had begun with Arce. Finally, a free primary

---

[1] López Rivas, *Esquema de la historia económica*, pp. 12, 49. These and subsequent figures have been taken to the nearest hundred.

[2] Peñaloza, *Historia económica*, II, 233–4. This twenty-year record of monetary stability was another of the records never again equalled in the twentieth century.

[3] López Rivas, *Esquema de la historia económica*, pp. 10, 45. Though a favourable balance of trade was always maintained, Bolivian imports between 1900 and 1920 also rose steadily, from Bs. 13,300,000 to Bs. 65,300,000.

[4] By 1920, some moderate light industry had begun to develop, though still on a primitive scale. At this time the country still had only one textile factory, and the major manufacturing plants were breweries, tanneries, printing establishments, and cigarette factories. There was also an important shoe, match, and nail factory and several flour mills. Schurz, *Bolivia*, pp. 180ff; Carlos Harms Espejo, *Bolivia en sus diversas fases, principalmente económica* (Santiago: Talleres, 1922), pp. 117ff. Major manufacturing concerns did not really begin on an important scale until the 1930s under the impact of the Depression. Although increasing in importance throughout the next decade, by the census of 1950, persons engaged in manufacturing accounted for only 8 per cent of the actively employed work force, and some 50 per cent of these manufacturing workers were listed as artisans. CEPAL, *El desarrollo económico de Bolivia*, pp. 114–19.

[5] In the sixty-four years up to 1900, La Paz had increased in population by only 22 per cent, whereas in the period 1900–20, it grew by 64 per cent. Averanga Mollinedo, *Aspectos generales de la población*, p. 33.

education system was for the first time effectively established in Bolivia, though exclusively confined to the urban areas, giving the urban masses their first real opportunity to obtain an education. As a result of these new educational and economic opportunities, there now arose a fairly self-conscious middle class within Bolivian society, which was both literate and westernized, and considerably superior to the old cholo masses.

But this partial replacing of the caste system by a developing class system in Bolivia's cities was not an unmixed blessing. With the development of the middle class there also emerged an urban proletariat, many of whom were literate and fully absorbed into the national system. With the rise of light industry and heavy mining, the growth of government service and, most important, with the development of the communications and transportation network, a new type of industrial wage worker came into existence. And with his emergence, almost exclusively confined to the urban and mining areas, there now appeared on the Bolivian scene a modern labour movement.

Unlike its more advanced neighbours, Bolivia had experienced a slow and retarded evolution of its labour movement. Before 1900 there had been very few industrial workers, and even the overwhelming majority of artisans had been unorganized. The few labour organizations which had existed were either artisan guilds or mutual aid societies, which had little impact beyond the few workers involved.[1] But with the rise of the tin industry, and the twenty years of peace and prosperity under the Liberals, this simple pre-industrial pattern began to change and there arose a small but important urban industrial working force. It was inevitable that these new workers, with their greater participation in society and more technical ability, would prove a fertile ground for radical political and social philosophy.

Long delayed, as were all ideas coming from abroad, socialist, anarchist, and syndicalist concepts finally began to reach Bolivia in the first decade of the twentieth century. In this period the first ephemeral radical and labour newspapers appeared, which, though limited in circulation and irregular in publication,

---

[1] Guillermo Lora, 'Historia del movimiento sindical boliviano (sus tendencias políticas)' (La Paz, unpublished manuscript, 1963), capítulo I.

nevertheless initiated the long history of radical education of the Bolivian working classes.[1]

The first concrete result of this new awareness was the creation in 1905 of the first modern style union, or *sindicato*, in Bolivia, which was organized among the printers of La Paz.[2] In 1906 and 1907, after a series of severe mining disasters,[3] the first tentative attempts were made at miner unionization in the mines of Tupiza and Potosí. But powerful company opposition and the fact that the majority of the miners were seasonally employed free comunidad Indians who were easily reincorporated onto the land, made permanent organization on a large scale impossible. And it was not until almost thirty-five years later, when the bulk of the non-mining workers had been organized, that the mine fields were finally unionized.

The leadership of the embryonic labour movement was thus left to the urban unions allied with the vitally important railroad brotherhoods. The first attempts at inter-union activity came in 1908 with the short-lived La Paz Labour Federation (*Federación Obrera de La Paz*). The federation, largely controlled by artisans, received the temporary support of the Liberal government, which hoped to use its influence among the workers, and even elected a deputy to congress. But when the federation and its deputy demanded a working men's accident compensation law from the government, the Liberals withdrew their support. The deputy was not re-elected to congress, and with the removal of Liberal party backing, the federation fell apart, leaving the labour movement temporarily without central direction.[4]

But with the end of the first Montes administration and the impact of increased prosperity under the Villazón government, the labour movement took on new life. On 1 May 1912, the labour unions and artisan guilds of La Paz successfully organized Bolivia's first May Day parade, and a short time later they

---

[1] Augustin Barcelli S., *Medio siglo de luchas sindicales revolucionarias en Bolivia, 1905–1955* (La Paz: Editorial del Estado, 1956), pp. 47–57; René Canelas L., 'El sindicalismo y los sindicatos en Bolivia', *Revista Jurídica* (Cochabamba), Año VIII, no. 35 (June 1946), pp. 69–70.

[2] Barcelli, *Medio siglo de luchas sindicales*, pp. 60–1; [Waldo Álvarez], 'Fundación de la Federación Gráfica Boliviana', *Primer Congreso Nacional de Trabajadores Gráficos* (La Paz: Federación Gráfica Boliviana, 1952), p. 95.

[3] Barcelli, *Medio siglo de luchas sindicales*, pp. 61–3.   [4] *Ibid.* pp. 64–6.

replaced the defunct Labour Federation of La Paz with the *Federación Obrera Internacional*. This new La Paz federation, unlike its predecessor, was primarily composed of the new type of modern syndicalist unions, and as a consequence took on a decidedly class conscious tone and completely eschewed political involvement with the existing parties.[1] The FOI even founded Bolivia's first avowedly labour newspaper, *Defensa Obrera*, which was soon leading a campaign for the eight-hour day, and for a while even attracted to its columns such upper-class intellectuals as Franz Tamayo and Tomás Manuel Elío.[2] Finally in 1912, the extremely important railroad workers organized their first successful union local, the *Sociedad Mutualista Ferroviaria de Oruro* (Mutualist Society of Railroad Workers of Oruro).[3]

A new stage of development in these early years came with the impact of World War I. The new generation of union leaders began to have intimate contact with the more advanced labour movements in other countries, primarily Chile, from whom they received an important new intake of ideological and organizational skills which they soon began applying at home.[4] In 1914, the railroad, graphics, and other urban workers organized the first all-city labour federations in the departmental capitals, first in Oruro, then in Potosí in 1916, and in Cochabamba in 1917. In 1918 the largely ineffective La Paz federation, the FOI, was replaced by the *Federación Obrera del Trabajo* (FOT)—Workers' Federation of Labour. This La Paz federation, unlike its two predecessors, took on a permanent character after its founding, and was a major force within the Bolivian labour movement from the very beginning. Finally in 1918, the railroad workers felt themselves strong enough to organize all of the Bolivian railway system into one powerful confederation, the *Federación Ferroviaria de Oruro*, which was the first national union to be organized.[5]

---

[1] Moisés Álvarez, 'La organización, sindical en Bolivia', *Boletín del Ministerio del Trabajo, Previsión Social y Salubridad*, No. 1 (September, 1937), pp. 35–6.

[2] Barcelli, *Medio siglo de luchas sindicales*, pp. 65–8.   [3] *Ibid.* p. 72.

[4] Moisés Poblete Troncoso, *El movimiento obrero latino-americano* (Mexico: Fondo de Cultura Económica, 1946), p. 95; Guillermo Lora, 'Historia del movimiento sindical boliviano', capítulo 'El partido socialista', pp. 2–3.

[5] Barcelli, *Medio siglo de luchas sindicales*, pp. 72–3; W. Álvarez, 'Fundación de la Federación Gráfica', pp. 95–6; M. Álvarez, 'La organización sindical en Bolivia', p. 36.

The new labour strength which was created in the period 1914–20 found expression early in 1920 in a wave of important strikes. In February 1920 the government was forced to use troops to put down a threatened national railroad strike originating with the Federación Ferroviaria de Oruro,[1] and in late June 1920 there was a nationwide strike of telegraphy workers against the state owned and operated lines. This strike greatly agitated the government, which denied the right of government employees to organize, and it destroyed the union by using troops and strikebreakers throughout the various cities of the republic.[2]

During these strikes, Bolivia was experiencing the full impact of the world economic crisis of post-war international trade reorganization which was especially severe in 1920–21. Amidst these two key developments, the Republican plotting reached its culmination. Yet, despite these signs of social and economic discontent and political agitation and plotting, the government was caught completely by surprise when the Republicans rose in a well coordinated revolt in La Paz and the other important cities of the nation on the morning of 12 July 1920. Within a few hours the entire operation was completed and the Gutiérrez Guerra government fell almost without bloodshed.[3] Twenty-one years of Liberal government were thus brought to an end with almost the peace and efficiency of an electoral defeat. New names and new personalities emerged in the succeeding years, but the foundations laid by the Liberals from 1899 to 1920 survived intact for another decade.

[1] *La Razón*, 6 February 1920, p. 5.
[2] *El Diario*, 19 June 1920, p. 1; and *El Diario*, 29 June 1920, p. 1.
[3] Benigno Carrasco, *Siles*, pp. 127–31.

THE REPUBLICAN ERA: SAAVEDRA

Initially the continuity of political institutions and power structures was maintained despite the July revolution of 1920. The
programme of the Republicans was essentially the same as that of
the Liberals, and even the revolutionary slogans which the Republicans proclaimed in 1920 were similar to those proclaimed by
the Liberals in 1899. Representing both young politicians seeking
advancement and old displaced políticos, the new party had its
roots in the same socio-economic classes as its predecessor, and
sought its theoretical inspiration in the same liberal-positivist
philosophy. Even the opposition recognized this essential fact of
homogeneity in the political scene, and the Liberal party newspaper's editorial shortly after the July revolution stated that 'the
political parties which are in conflict at the present time are
mixtures of men of different political schools . . .' Each party had
the same type of liberals, conservatives and progressives, which
meant 'that they are not homogeneous parties, [and] their programmes are more or less the same without real differences.
Because of this, politically minded men believe that it is all the
same to be either in the Liberal, Republican or Radical parties.'[1]

Given this background, it was inevitable that the sudden rise
to power of the Republican party brought in a flood of new men
and greatly strengthened the previously minority party. But the
overthrow of the opposition also created new internal dissensions
for the Republicans, as previously subdued personality divisions
were suddenly accentuated. As the need for unity in the face of
the enemy was no longer paramount, personal factions began to
develop around the three key men of the party: Escalier, Salamanca, and Saavedra.

Of the three leaders, Salamanca, though now in semi-retire-
ment, was the generally best known figure. Escalier, though party

[1] *El Diario*, 18 November 1920, p. 4.

leader and a prime developer of party strategy, was nevertheless kept from continuous active participation by his long absences in Buenos Aires. The third leader of the triumvirate, Saavedra, was the key organizational man of the party from its foundation until the July revolution, a revolution which he alone had led. Unlike the other two men, Saavedra had his base in the commercial and growing middle class interests of his native La Paz, which he had represented in congress for so many years, and not in the provincial landed classes. Although Saavedra had previously subordinated his interests to those of Salamanca and Escalier, with the initiation of the revolutionary movement and the subsequent overthrow of the Liberals he assumed direct leadership of the party and emerged as the head of the revolutionary junta.

In the first days of the newly established junta government, these three men quickly became the foci for the conflicting party loyalties and ideologies, and a three-way power struggle ensued for control of the party and the government. In this conflict, the able Saavedra quickly dominated the situation, organizing a powerful *Guardia Republicana* military organization loyal to his authority, and establishing his own party newspaper *La República* to counter the pro-Escalier *La Razón*.[1] Finally, in a move to gain a wider base of support than his two hacendado opponents, he issued an historic decree in late September recognizing the right to strike and establishing a formal government labour arbitration system.[2]

But neither Salamanca nor Escalier proved capable of responding to Saavedra's acts in any concrete fashion. Salamanca was especially disoriented and went so far in his reaction to Saavedra as to propose the return of the Liberals to power to form a 'neutral' government.[3] All these complicated manœuvrings came to nothing, however, and when a special convention-congress finally met in La Paz in December 1920, it was apparent to all that

[1] For a detailed discussion of the intricate political manœuvrings during this tense period, see Herbert S. Klein, *Origenes de la Revolución Nacional Boliviana, la crisis del generación del Chaco* (La Paz: Editorial 'Juventud', 1968), pp. 75ff.
[2] *El Diario*, 1 October 1920, p. 5. The government also set up an Institute Social Reforms, with university student and labour representation, to study proposals for social legislation. The government appointees to the institute, however, were all men of extremely conservative background, and they held the majority of the votes. *El Diario*, 9 October 1920, p. 5.
[3] Alvéstegui, *Salamanca*, II, 272–9.

Saavedra's quietly efficient work had produced the desired results, and that his supporters represented the majority block in the convention. With the opening up of congress, the power struggle within the party shifted to the floor of the convention, and all thoughts of writing a new constitution were abandoned in the concentration on the presidential issue. The final result of these conflicts was, however, never in doubt. Under the leadership of Abel Iturralde, José R. Estenssoro, and Hernando Siles, the *saavredristas* easily triumphed over the disunited forces of their opponents and on 24 January 1921, they elected Saavedra to the presidency.[1]

The election of Saavedra, however, did not resolve the intra-party struggles, but exacerbated them, for Salamanca and Escalier were so fully committed to their hatred of Saavedra, that once his victory within the party was assured, they resolved to destroy the party. Immediately upon his election, Saavedra attempted to heal the growing split and prevent the two opposition leaders from breaking away from the party. Three days after his election he offered the vice-presidency and four of the six cabinet ministries to the minority groups. But Salamanca rejected this offer and went to the extreme of recommending the establishment of a permanent political opposition in the form of an independent party. At first, the minority deputies were unwilling to go as far as Salamanca in splintering the party, and from February until May lengthy negotiations were held between the government and the minority leaders in an attempt to effect a reconciliation, especially necessary in the face of rising Liberal power. Yet each move toward compromise was bitterly opposed by Salamanca, and by mid-winter he finally succeeded in winning Escalier over to his position. This position of intransigent opposition was finally accepted by the majority of their followers at a special Oruro convention, and in October 1921, they founded the *Partido Republicano Genuino*.[2]

With the establishment of the Genuino Republican party, the traditional political forces of the nation found themselves divided into three major parties, each with its dominant personalities and each with its committed followings. In the next decade and a half,

[1] Alvéstegui, *Salamanca*, II, pp. 285ff.; Benigno Carrasco, *Siles*, pp. 137ff.
[2] Alvéstegui, *Salamanca*, II, 327ff.

the struggle for power between these three parties dominated the Bolivian political scene. And overshadowing these constant struggles were the two key personalities of the original Republican schism, Daniel Salamanca and Bautista Saavedra.

Saavedra shared many of the qualities and attitudes of his predecessor Montes, and was a strong individual who projected an appealing public and private image. He was fifty years old when he was sworn into the presidency on 28 January 1921,[1] and was already established in several professions and still in the prime of life. Born and educated in La Paz, Saavedra had trained for the law and had lived most of his life in his native city, to which he was strongly attached. He had fought for his city in the federal revolution of the 1890s and after the war had begun a distinguished career as a teacher and scholar. Widely-read, he worked primarily in the fields of history and sociology and soon developed an international reputation as one of Bolivia's leading scholars. In the first decades of the century he published several studies on national institutional history and boundary disputes, as well as his famous study of pre-Columbian Indian organization, the *ayllu*.[2]

It was in his capacity as a scholar that Saavedra first entered politics. In 1903 he was selected by the Montes government to do historical research on the Peruvian-Bolivian boundary dispute in the Spanish archives. Returning from Europe at the time of the Villazón government, he served as minister of education for two years, and then took up the diplomatic post at Lima. With the end of the Villazón régime in 1913, he returned to La Paz, and for the first time ran for elective office.

Saavedra was an extremely adept politician and committed himself passionately to this new life. He won the 1913 election as an independent and soon gathered around himself many of the fragmented parts of the old and new groups hostile to the régime. He was thus a key instigator of the organization of the Republican party in 1914. From 1914 to 1920, as head of the important La

---

[1] *El Diario*, 28 January 1921, p. 4.
[2] A 1913 edition of this work had an extremely laudatory prologue by the great Spanish social historian Rafael Altamira. See Bautista Saavedra, *El Ayllu* (3rd ed.; La Paz: Gisbert y Cía., 1955), pp. 7-12.

Paz committee of the party, he was the second most important man in the party, first under Salamanca and then under Escalier, and he suffered several imprisonments and banishments at the hands of the Liberals. He adapted himself naturally to the caudillo role and organized a solid nucleus of supporters who remained committed to his person until his death. A driving force in political affairs, he was to throw his shadow across the political scene for three full decades of the twentieth century, and in success and adversity was never underestimated by his opponents, who always feared his return to power. At first without a political position which was distinct from his predecessors, Saavedra in his long years of political struggle after 1920 became closely identified with the urban middle and artisan classes of largely cholo origin, and came to represent himself as their defender on the national scene.[1]

The years of the Saavedra government were years of tension and strife, in marked contrast to the tranquil Liberal rule which had gone before. The habit of revolutionary violence returned to the political scene, and the previously isolated army and the middle classes became more politically involved and committed. In the economic sphere, a series of short depressions and severe government deficits brought the more dynamic era of government expansion and initiative in public works to a close, and left instead an increasingly constricted and harassed bureaucracy incapable of meeting the problems of the nation. Yet this was also the period, paradoxically, of heavy foreign investment in the Bolivian government, and in the decade of the 1920s private United States capital poured into public utilities and government securities on a scale never previously experienced. But the Great Depression and the increasing government indebtedness and insecurity turned this period into an era of bitterness on the international scene as the impoverished nation began to find its future ever more heavily mortgaged to outside powers.[2]

[1] Alvéstegui, *Salamanca*, II, 305–10; Porfirio Díaz Machicao, *Historia de Bolivia, Saavedra, 1920–1925* (La Paz: Alfonso Tejerina, 1954), pp. 83–4. Hereafter cited as *Saavedra*.

[2] The era of Liberalism, for all its progress, had been achieved at the cost of heavy foreign indebtedness. Since the government refused to tax the tin industry heavily, government revenues never kept up with the expanding public works programmes, and in all but one of the twenty years of Liberal rule, budget

The Republican era was also a period of increasing social tension as the previous social and political cohesion of the Liberal era began to break apart. The lower classes began restively to seek self-expression in all areas, and even the usually isolated rural Indian masses temporarily erupted to strike out at changing conditions. The most dramatic incident of this kind occurred early in the Saavedra period, when in March 1921 Indians in the altiplano cantón of Jesús de Machaca rebelled. The Jesús de Machaca district was an area of free comunidad Indians, in which new latifundistas were beginning to absorb traditional free Indian holdings through the use of government force and bribery. The railroads and roads constructed during the Liberal periods made these reasonably fertile lands, previously isolated from the outside world, available to the expanding urban markets, and white and cholo landowners soon moved into the area, creating landed estates and making the Indians into dependent landless labourers.

The rebellion, when it did come, was short, violent and typical of these almost directionless revolts. Maddened beyond endurance by a local corregidor, whose inhumanity unleashed all the repressed hostility to the changing social milieu, overnight the local communities rose in revolt and the corregidor and a large number of government officials and local hacendados were slaughtered. It was suppressed almost as quickly as it started, and the government troops massacred several hundred villagers, burning, pillaging and raping the primitively armed peasants. When enough blood had been shed, seventy 'leaders' of the uprising were brought to La Paz and incarcerated.[1]

Although Saavedra was sympathetic to the urban cholos and

---

deficits were the result. Even as late as 1920, only 20 per cent of government revenue was coming from the lightly taxed tin industry, which accounted for over 70 per cent of the value of exports and whose gross sales were three and a half times larger than the national budget. Peñaloza, *Historia económica*, ii, 227. To meet their expenses without resort to inflationary monetary policies, the Liberals had resorted to borrowing heavily abroad and left something like $19,000,000 in debts to the following governments. Thus most new loans after 1920 went largely toward refunding this debt and left little for continued government development programmes. Norman T. Ness, 'The Movement of Capital into Bolivia, a backward Country' (unpublished Ph.D. dissertation, Department of Economics, Harvard University, 1938), p. 102; McQueen, *Bolivian Public Finances*, pp. 9–10.

[1] Barcelli, *Medio siglo de luchas sindicales*, pp. 100–3.

the rising working classes, he held the traditional white élitist view toward the Indian. In his defence of the government repression, Saavedra held that the Indians had no cause for grievance and that they were rising not in reaction to injustice, but as fanatical rebels desiring a 'restoration of Incaic communism', and the extermination of all whites. Saavedra charged that a free comunidad type of government was reactionary 'because it maintains an ominous *status quo* which impedes all attempts at reform and progress and maintains, in latent form, the ancient hatred of the Indian against the white race which it accuses of usurpation and oppression'.[1] This was the classic nineteenth-century liberal attitude toward the free Indian community, and this universally held opinion was used to justify the destruction of the comunidad and its collective land ownership patterns.

Although Saavedra was consistent with his predecessors on the so-called 'Indian Problem', he took an entirely new attitude towards the urban working and middle classes of the nation. In contradiction to the prevailing *laissez faire* liberalism, he began to adopt a new attitude toward the social responsibility of the state. He also began to look upon the infant labour movement as an important ally in his increasingly difficult political struggles. For Saavedra soon found himself cut off from the traditional sources of support as Salamanca steadfastly refused all compromise until Saavedra was removed from office. As well as this implacable hostility from the Genuino Republicans, Saavedra faced the natural enmity of the Liberals, and together these two parties largely deprived him of support from the landed classes of the countryside and of the traditional provincial élites. Denied traditional party sources, Saavedra was forced to seek new sources of strength, and turned toward the developing labour movement on the one hand and the burgeoning middle class on the other. He appealed to these elements by initiating, for the first time in Bolivia, a modern programme of social legislation.

Although there had been some pious statements on social legislation in the 1914 party programme and though the junta had been the first government to recognize officially the right to strike in Bolivian law, these were not dominant themes in

[1] *El Diario*, 14 April 1921, p. 5.

Republican policy up to this time. Saavedra, however, now turned to this new field of endeavour in a serious way, and about the same time as the opposition was organizing the Genuino party, he began to develop a major programme of social legislation. In mid-May the convention had turned itself into an ordinary congress and between September and November, Saavedra presented to this congress projected laws on compensation for work accidents, special health and accident compensation benefit laws for miners, an amplified right to strike and arbitration procedure legislation, and finally a minimum hours' code. Ultimately toned down and greatly restricted in their impact by congress, these laws were nevertheless the first ever passed in Bolivia, and undoubtedly represented a major victory for the Bolivian working classes and a primary step in what was to be a long and hard process of social advancement through legislation.

The government, in conformity with these attitudes, also showed a willingness to tolerate strike movements. In 1920–1 a short but drastic depression in tin prices sent the value of tin exports from Bs. 112·2 millions in 1920 to Bs. 42·9 millions a year later.[1] This sudden depression greatly increased political tensions, and it brought on a new wave of strike activity. In July 1921 a miners' strike at Compañía Huanchaca began to take on national importance because of manifestations of support by the railroad unions. Acting quickly, the Saavedra government intervened and with the aid of the United States minister to Bolivia, achieved a peaceful negotiated settlement of the strike.[2]

That all of these developments under Saavedra were more the result of political expediency than advanced social thinking is clearly revealed by the régime's constant retrenchment on basic issues. Faced by serious labour difficulties, the government was often quite inconsistent in its attitude toward organized labour, and on occasion it would revert to harsh suppression of strike movements. Nor did Saavedra ever make a serious attack on the upper élite, for he did not want a real change in the basic socio-economic relations of the nation. In fact he went so far as to enlist the support of the second largest tin family, the Aramayos, in his

[1] CEPAL, *El desarrollo económico de Bolivia*, pp, 10–11, cuadros 4, 5, 6.
[2] *El Diario*, 19 July 1921, p. 5 and 22 July 1921, p. 4.

government, sending Félix Avelino, the head of the family, to the Paris embassy, and his son Carlos Víctor to head the League of Nations delegation. Saavedra also openly encouraged the investment of foreign capital in Bolivia on a vast scale and often with disruptive results.[1] But despite the motivation of political expediency and the mild and sometimes contradictory nature of the actual legislation and attitudes, Saavedra made a profound impact with his new tone in government, and soon received the firm support of the urban masses, a support which enabled him to rule with assurance for the rest of his term.[2]

While Saavedra was finding new and unexpected sources of support in the labour and middle classes, other people were also attempting to organize these groups, though in a far more radical manner. It was from the ranks of the La Paz labour leadership that the first non-traditional political party organization of any consequence developed. On 22 September 1920, the *Partido Obrero Socialista* was founded under the leadership of Julio M. Ordóñez (La Paz FOT chief), Ezequiel Salvatierra, Carlos Mendoza M. and Augusto Varela (all important labour leaders).[3] This La Paz Socialist Workers party (POS) was soon followed by similar parties in Oruro and Uyuni (a major railroad centre). Although these parties were based on working-class support, their aims were largely improvement of the standard of living and the education of the lower and working classes through legislation: the socialism in their title was definitely not Marxist.[4] For as one major radical thinker noted, when recalling his youth in the first two decades of the century, 'The socialist spirit had not yet appeared in Bolivia, [and] even as late as 1920 a socialist current was not clearly expressed.'[5] The actual programme of the POS of La Paz called for the separation of church and state; a prohibitory tax on alcohol and the elimination of taxation on

[1] Basadre, *Chile, Perú y Bolivia*, p. 658.
[2] Barcelli, *Medio siglo de luchas sindicales*, pp. 103–5; Díaz Machicao, *Saavedra*, pp. 114–16.
[3] *El Diario*, 12 November 1920, p. 3.
[4] Lora, 'Historia del movimiento sindical', pp. 3–4; *El Diario*, 14 November 1920, p. 4.
[5] A statement by Tristán Marof contained in his introductory preface to Carlos Aramayo Alzerreca, *Saavedra, el último caudillo* (La Paz: Editorial 'La Paz', [1941], p. iii.

goods of prime necessity; the abolition of the death penalty; civil rights for women, illegitimate children and Indians; worker savings plans; the right to strike; minimum hours and child labour laws. This progressive 'populist' type of programme also called for a government policy of protectionism, a greater stress on education, and, interestingly, a demand for the abolition of Indian *pongueaje* (or personal servitude to patrons) and the legal recognition of Indian comunidades.

By late 1921 the various local POSs felt strong enough to form a national party, the *Partido Socialista*, at a special convention in Oruro in November. To this convention came many labour leaders who were associated with the Republican party, among them Ricardo Soruco, a minority deputy in congress and an important figure in the railroad unions. Others were Augusto Varela, a substitute deputy and head of the La Paz POS, Ricardo Perales, also a substitute deputy to the convention-congress and head of the Oruro POS and Enrique G. Loza, the leader of the Uyuni group. Various unions and confederations also sent delegations along with representatives of the labour press. As a tentative programme, the Partido Socialista adopted the 1920 formulation of the La Paz POS and called for the creation of party committees in the other cities of the republic.[1]

Although the Partido Socialista was the first major experiment in political organization outside the traditional party structure, it lacked the sophisticated labour and radical leadership needed to make any sustained impact. Too many of the labour leaders were still wedded to anarchist concepts of apoliticism, while many others had tied their fortunes to the new Saavedra régime and continued to maintain their traditional party affiliations.[2]

---

[1] *El Diario*, 13 November 1921, p. 5; Lora, 'Historia del movimiento sindical', pp. 4–5.

[2] The party was represented in congress for some time by Soruco and more especially by Ricardo Perales who took his seat as deputy from Oruro in January 1922 (*El Diario*, 17 January 1922, p. 4). Almost immediately upon entering congress, Perales, with the support of Soruco and others, proposed a major piece of social legislation covering the mining industry. His *proyecto* called for the setting up of local unions at all the mines to act as independent bargaining agents. He proposed that these local workers' committees should have control over *pulpería* (company foodstore) prices, and over the metal weighing procedures which determined wages. He called for free commerce in the mining compounds to break company store monopolies and also the elimination of

Thus the new party had little success on the political scene and declined rapidly over the next several years. Nevertheless, this was the crucial first step, and it indicated a fundamental re-orientation on the part of many labour leaders, an orientation which was greatly strengthened by ties which were now developed with the more advanced Chilean labour movement which itself had recently affiliated with the Second International.[1]

But even with the establishment of this first 'socialist' group and the growing politicization of the labour leadership, Bolivia was still one of the least politically radical countries in South America. The first Latin-American Marxist group had formed in Argentina in 1882, and important Marxian socialist movements had been founded in Chile soon thereafter. Bolivia, however, did not produce even a quasi-Marxist grouping until the late 1920s.[2] And although it adopted the socialist label, the first Partido Socialista was essentially a populist labour party which neither propagated any serious alternatives to the dominant socio-economic and political system, nor challenged the foundations of the traditional leadership. Thus the labour movement and the tiny group of moderate reformist intellectuals in Bolivia at this time offered nothing remotely threatening to the established

company police—to be replaced by regular national government authorities. Written contracts were to be mandatory, the workers' councils would participate in dismissal procedures and two weeks compensatory pay would be provided to dismissed employees. Finally the proyecto called for double-time pay for holiday work and the abolition of the fining system (*El Diario*, 28 January 1922, p. 8). In February, he proposed, again with Soruco, major workers' retirement legislation (*El Diario*, 15 February 1922, p. 3), but this was defeated like its predecessor. Shortly thereafter the unity between Soruco and Perales began to disintegrate as Soruco moved closer to the saavedrista group in late 1922 (*La República*, 23 December 1922, p. 8) and by early 1923 the Partido Socialista disowned Soruco altogether (*La Razón*, 3 February 1923, p. 6). With the elimination of Soruco and the defeat of Perales at the polls in the next election, the congressional wing of the party collapsed and it went into a quiescent state, though always maintaining strong hostility to the Saavedra government throughout its career (*El Diario*, 29 April 1925, p. 5).

[1] Lora, 'Historia del movimiento sindical', p. 6.
[2] For a good survey of the socialist movement in Latin America, see Víctor Alba, *Historia del movimiento obrero en América Latina* (Mexico: Libreros Mexicanos Unidos, 1964). The first Marxist group in Latin America was the German immigrant workers' club 'Vorwärts' of Buenos Aires, which was founded in 1882 and was officially represented at the First International. Jacinto Oddone, *Historia del socialismo argentino* (2 vols.; Buenos Aires: 'La Vanguardia', 1934), I, 123, 196.

order and, when compared to the rest of South America, Bolivia still seemed a largely insulated underdeveloped nation, immune to the potentially revolutionary currents emanating from European and more advanced Latin American centres.

Nonetheless, the infant Bolivian labour movement began, in organizational terms at least, to make some headway under the new government. In 1921 a first tentative step was taken in the direction of a national labour federation. Under the leadership of the Federación Ferroviaria de Oruro, a call was issued to all the *gremios* and *sindicatos* of the nation, as well as all the local FOTs, for an organizational meeting in Oruro. All the divergent groups and ideologies representative of the labour movement at that time came to this convention and this very diversity prevented the creation of a national confederation. But the meeting brought these groups together for the first time and, as its title 'Primer Congreso Nacional de Trabajadores' indicated, paved the way for other such meetings in the future.[1]

The undisputed leadership of the railway unions in the national labour movement was again demonstrated early in 1922. In reaction to the constant states of siege and conspiracies, the government in January of that year ordered all nocturnal taxi services to cease and placed La Paz under a curfew. The government's justification for this action was that the noise of the taxis was disturbing public sleep, but in reality it was to prevent the taxis from being used for gun-running at night by anti-government conspirators. The enraged *chóferes* called for aid from the Federación Obrera del Trabajo of La Paz, and the FOT responded by issuing a manifesto calling for its twenty-one associated unions to unite behind the taxi drivers' demand. The Federación Ferroviaria not only supported this dispute but made demands of its own to the Bolivian Railway Company calling for full recognition of its status as sole bargaining agent for the railway workers.[2] On 9 February the FOT, with the support of the *tranviarios* (streetcar operators), railroad workers and printers, issued a call for a General Strike—the first such strike in Bolivian history. By 10 February, the railroad unions were out, national rail traffic came to a complete halt, and the printers succeeded in

[1] Barcelli, *Medio siglo de luchas sindicales*, pp. 97–8.   [2] *Ibid.* pp. 105–6.

closing down all the major newspapers. These two actions and other shutdowns enforced by the unions compelled the government to concede defeat and on 13 February the La Paz municipal council rescinded its nocturnal taxi ordinance, the tranviarios received certain concessions, and the Federación Ferroviaria was granted legal recognition by the government.[1] The government shortly after the settlement attempted to retaliate by temporarily jailing the leaders of the railway unions.[2] The printing trades union newspaper, *Palabra Libre*, was closed down and an anti-strike law was even presented in congress. These measures, however, were soon dropped in the face of strong opposition,[3] and the whole affair proved to be the first large-scale strike victory achieved by the labour movement in Bolivian history.[4]

Although organized labour activity in these first years of the new government was unusually intense, with the return of prosperous times the pace of the labour movement slowed down again. Nevertheless, labour had now shown itself to be of major importance in national life and throughout the decade important local strike activity disturbed the political and economic life of Bolivia as never before. This new importance of labour and of labour relations only added to the sense of change and upheaval which the political climate helped to maintain.

For neither prosperity nor the general popular approval of the social legislation programme brought any tranquillity to the political scene. Rather, the longer Saavedra ruled, the more intense grew the opposition. The decided opposition of a reviving Liberal party was soon added to the constant harassment of the Genuino Republicans. By the end of 1921 the Liberals had formed an astute new leadership which rapidly took advantage of the disunity of the Republicans. Under the direction of José María Camacho, son of its founder, the Liberal party carefully balanced its support to gain the maximum advantage. It allowed

---

[1] *El Diario*, 14 February 1922, p. 5.
[2] *El Diario*, 16 February 1922, p. 5.
[3] A special protest meeting on 2 April drew 3,000 workers to hear FOT leaders attack anti-strike legislation in La Paz, while an equally large crowd heard Enrique G. Loza on this same subject in Potosí. See *El Diario*, 4 April 1922, p. 5, and 5 April 1922, p. 4.
[4] Barcelli, *Medio siglo de luchas sindicales*, pp. 106–8.

several of its leading figures to join the government on a personal basis, and at the same time it formally negotiated with the anti-Saavedra forces.[1]

This growing coalition of all the leading non-saavedrista political forces in a united anti-government front seriously disturbed the government. Though its appeals to labour and the urban classes with social welfare legislation were having an important effect in bringing a needed base of support to the government, the political leaders of the society were still unappeased. In order to vitiate this opposition, as well as to justify the constructive nature of his government in the terms of material progress which all previous governments had used as a crucial determinant of success, Saavedra embarked on an ambitious public works programme. Unfortunately, however, he was faced with a deficit in the treasury, which was heavily committed to financing the previous Liberal development programme. Saavedra therefore decided that his only recourse was to promote foreign investment in the nation's natural resources, and to obtain even more government loans from foreign bankers in order to consolidate the old loans and continue the development programmes.

The first major step in this policy was the opening of Bolivia's oil resources to major foreign control. Although petroleum deposits had been discovered in Bolivia even before the turn of the century, and large numbers of exploitation concessions had been granted to Bolivian entrepreneurs, they had proved incapable of developing this highly capitalized industry. In 1916 the disgusted Bolivian government had finally closed off all new concessions on the grounds that they were only being used for speculation and that no oil had been produced. When the Republican revolt occurred this policy was changed and beginning in 1920 the Bolivian fields were again made available to private concessionaires.[2] This time, however, the world situation was propitious and foreign companies showed a marked interest in

---

[1] Alvéstegui, *Salamanca*, II, 372ff.

[2] Schurz, *Bolivia*, pp. 139–40; Sergio Almaraz, *Petróleo en Bolivia* (La Paz: Editorial 'Juventud', 1958), pp. 74–5. For a complete survey of the history of American involvement in Bolivian oil see Herbert S. Klein, 'American Oil Companies in Latin America: The Bolivian Experience', *Inter-American Economic Affairs*, XVIII, no. 2 (Autumn, 1964), 47–72.

Bolivian holdings. In 1920 and 1921 Richmond Levering of New York obtained a one million hectare grant from Bolivia and William and Spruille Braden obtained a two million hectare concession.[1] But these two concessionaires were acting for a larger concern, and in 1921 Standard Oil of New Jersey bought out these two grants and created a wholly owned subsidiary to develop them, the Standard Oil Company of Bolivia.[2]

Although Standard Oil immediately requested recognition of its purchases, the Saavedra government wanted time to write a new petroleum code. This fairly stringent law was finally enacted in June 1921 and provided for the traditional government claims to sub-soil rights as well as a 100,000 hectare acreage maximum for concessions. The Standard Oil holdings, however, were considered exempt from this acreage limit because of their prior purchase and the fact that Standard was accepting the original Levering contract with its Calvo clause and confiscation proviso.[3] Thus one month later, in July 1921, Saavedra recognized the transfer, and by 1925 Standard Oil of Bolivia was operating the nation's first oil wells.[4]

Although this policy of foreign exploitation was initially successful in economic terms, it was subjected to intense political criticism from the very first days. Such men as Daniel Salamanca had argued as far back as the early 1910s that Bolivia's petroleum potential should be developed by native capitalists rather than foreign interests.[5] This position was supported by a host of conservative leaders, and it was the pro-clerical and leading anti-labour deputy, Abel Iturralde, who led the fight throughout the 1920s against the Standard Oil Company.[6] While these same men

---

[1] Almaraz, *Petróleo en Bolivia*, pp. 80–1; Schurz, *Bolivia*, pp. 141–2.
[2] For a full survey of the motivation behind the move of Standard into Bolivia, see George Sweet Gibb and Evelyn H. Knowlton, *History of the Standard Oil Company (New Jersey): The Resurgent Years, 1911–1927* (New York: Harper and Brothers, 1956), pp. 359–81, 646.
[3] Pedro N. López, *Bolivia y el petróleo* (La Paz: n.p., 1922), pp. 13ff. on the petroleum code, and León M. Loza, *Bolivia, el petróleo y la Standard Oil Company* (Publication No. 3 of Yacimientos Petrolíferos Fiscales Bolivianos; Sucre: Editorial 'Charcas', 1939) for the Levering and Standard contracts.
[4] Almaraz, *Petróleo en Bolivia*, p. 90.
[5] Alvéstegui, *Salamanca*, II, 83–7.
[6] Moisés Alcázar, *Abel Iturralde, el centinela del petróleo* (La Paz: Editorial 'La Paz', 1944).

never questioned the introduction of foreign capital in every other economic activity of the nation, to them petroleum represented a kind of mystique of national sovereignty, and for the next fifteen years Standard Oil remained one of the most bitter issues in national politics.

Nor was Saavedra's action in bringing in new loan capital for government development programmes any more politically successful in allying traditional opposition to his régime. Rather, opposition was if anything intensified by the so-called Nicolaus loan. The largest loan of foreign capital in Bolivian history, the Nicolaus loan was for the sum of $33,000,000, and was primarily used for refunding the major part of Bolivia's internal and external debt load contracted in the previous twenty years for the construction of railways, sanitation works, and the establishment of the Banco de la Nación. Because of its harsh terms and the profits accruing to the loaning companies, it also became the most notorious loan in Bolivian history. So intense was the criticism of the opposition that for a time the Saavedra government hesitated to sign and even set up an independent study commission, which in 1923 issued a report criticizing the loan terms. Despite this, the contract was eventually signed, and by its terms, Bolivia's entire customs receipts were pledged to the loan—that is, 45 per cent of her annual government income—along with other special taxes. Also the government was forced to put up heavy collateral, including its railroad bonds and its Banco de la Nación holdings. And finally a three-man Permanent Fiscal Commission was set up, with two of its three members appointed by the United States banks, to take charge of tax collection in the republic for the quarter-century life of the loan.

Considering the previously good credit rating of Bolivia in the 1910s and early 1920s and the offers of other banking houses, this was an entirely disadvantageous loan that seriously curtailed national sovereignty. So distasteful in fact was the whole operation that the government eventually dismissed the Bolivian agents responsible for the negotiations. The major criticism of the loan by financial experts was that it brought few constructive results in the form of economic development. Only a small percentage of the loan, which was primarily devoted to refunding, was channelled into railroad construction. Bolivia's public works programme throughout the 1920s, as a result, was seriously curtailed, if not altogether halted, because government revenues and new loans were used to pay off the external debt and the constant government budget deficit due to the absorption of huge amounts of its revenue by these foreign loan commitments. As for the fears of internal economic dictation by the Fiscal Commission so loudly expressed by contemporary opponents, the commission, once it was set up, actually functioned quite well and unobtrusively in the economic scene. It played a major part in the systemization of Bolivia's rather archaic tax system and was actually praised for its constructive work both by the government and the opposition. It became, in fact, a rather important and integrated branch of the national government in its very few years of existence, and it never involved itself in the political sphere or brought about United States economic domination of the region as had been feared.[1]

In an effort to alleviate the growing annual budget deficits and also to provide greater revenues for the government now that the traditional sources were pledged to the amortization of the Nicolaus loan, the Saavedra government in 1923 took a bold step forward in the taxation of the mining industry. In November of that year all taxes both on mining company operations and profits and on their exports themselves were considerably raised in a major tax overhaul. As this change came at a time of renewal of mining prosperity following the 1921–2 depression, the new taxes considerably increased government revenue, which actually doubled between 1922 and 1924![2] The 1923 Tax Reform bill for the first time brought equitable returns to the government from the vast tin bonanza, and receipts from all taxes on the mining industry rose from Bs. 3·5 millions in 1922 to Bs. 11·2 millions in 1924.[3] It was primarily to escape this new taxation that Simón I. Patiño in May 1924 removed his mining company headquarters from Bolivia to the United States and incorporated his Patiño Mines and Enter-

---

[1] Marsh, *Bankers in Bolivia*, pp. 96–121, 125–6, with contract reprinted in full in appendix. For the debate in the nation, see Carrasco, *Siles*, pp. 202–5.
[2] CEPAL, *El desarrollo económico de Bolivia*, p. 11, cuadro 6.
[3] *Ibid.* p. 10, cuadro 5; Peñaloza, *Historia económica*, II, 230–3.

prises Consolidated, Inc., company in the state of Delaware.[1] Also in a *quid pro quo*, Patiño lent the Bolivian government £600,000 for railroad construction in return for a guarantee by the Saavedra government not to raise mining imposts for a five-year period.[2]

But this bold and very important development in taxation was not matched by any other radical steps in the social or economic fields. After its initial social legislation proposals and moderate support of elements in the labour movement, the Saavedra régime tended to withdraw from any more advanced position. In fact, the more secure its tenure, the more reactionary it became. This was made clear in the famous Uncía mining massacre of 1923. Early in this year the smaller local mine unions in this key tin mining district succeeded in organizing a major union confederation known as the *Federación Central de Mineros de Uncía*. After large public demonstrations of union strength and sympathy on May Day 1923, the government declared a state of siege and moved troops into the Uncía region. Union leaders were arrested and expelled from the mine areas, and when protest demonstrations occurred on 4 June, troops fired into the crowds, killing several dozen miners and their families. The government's reaction to the massacre was immediately to close down all the opposition newspapers in Bolivia in a drastic move to suppress public knowledge of the massacre.[3] It also sent Hernando Siles on a special mission to the region to work out some kind of settlement between the miners and the Patiño company. The result of these moves was a patched-up compromise and the dissolution of the confederation.[4]

In his defence of the government action in the Uncía mining massacre, Saavedra, during a speech to congress in August 1923, charged that the workers had first attacked the soldiers and that, in all, only four persons were killed and four wounded—a version of the massacre which was immediately labelled as

---

[1] Peñaloza, *Historia económica*, II, 307–8.   [2] *Ibid.* 445–6.
[3] Basadre, *Chile, Perú y Bolivia*, pp. 108–10.
[4] Carrasco, *Siles*, pp. 267–70. The miners in late May had petitioned the government for support for the union against Patiño administrators at La Salvadora and Llallagua mines who were attempting to destroy the confederation. The government rejected this petition and the workers went on strike. Troops were sent to the area and the local commander gave the order to fire on the peaceful demonstrations. *Ibid.* pp. 270–2.

absolutely untrue by the opposition. He also expressed the growing unease of the classical liberal politicians of his age at the faint stirrings of new non-liberal ideology within the previously isolated country. 'There is an agitation in the workers' movements', he declared, 'which does not derive from any fundamental cause. There are a few agitators who, ignorant of the problems affecting the proletariat, are spreading false, fragmentary and illusory ideas among the worker masses, trying to bring to Bolivia the European conflicts of capital and labour.' He stated that strikes produced nothing but harm to everyone involved and that 'it is for this reason that extremist socialism, syndicalism and communism are found to be in discredit in the old world'. Nevertheless, the massacre had obviously shaken his government and he conceded that 'it is lamentable that in Bolivia there is no workers' legislation which supports and regulates labour, salaries, the health and wellbeing of the workers', and called for congress to remedy this situation.[1]

The Nicolaus loan, the Standard Oil contract, and the Uncía massacre all became major political issues with which the Liberal and Genuino opposition could attack the government. The opposition newspapers and the floor of congress became major vehicles for these anti-Saavedra views, and the opposition parties, despite the extreme violence of the elections, continued to make headway against the government. In 1922 especially, the opposition became strong enough after the mid-term elections to paralyse the government and dominate the congressional scene. In sharp political battles and major policy changes, the government began to be seriously hampered by desertions from its ranks, and such older saavedrists as Abel Iturralde and José R. Estenssoro joined the opposition, along with the important parliamentary figure M. Rigoberto Paredes. In the sessions of 1922 Paredes switched to the Genuino ranks and with their support, and the aid of other anti-government groups, succeeded in capturing the presidency of the chamber of deputies after a close and bitter election.[2]

In 1923, so deadlocked and violent had this congress become that the two deputies in the cabinet, Hernando Siles and David Alvéstegui, had to resign their posts in early January and return

[1] Carrasco, *Siles*, pp. 273–4.   [2] *Ibid.* pp. 221–3.

to their congressional seats so as to give the government forces enough votes to break the deadlock. The opposition, however, was not disheartened and on 9 January 1923 it presented a petition calling for the resignation of Saavedra from the presidency. They then boycotted congress through their refusal to form a quorum, which produced from Saavedra an angry decree dissolving congress in late January and a call for elections to reconstitute the entire chamber of deputies in May 1923.[1]

As the election approached, Saavedra indicated that the government would manipulate the elections. The opposition groups which had formed a multiparty unitary slate withdrew from the election in protest.[2] This abstention enabled Saavedra to pack the congress and make it into a docile body, but it greatly embittered the political atmosphere. Saavedra's reaction was a mass exiling of key opposition leaders. In early 1923 such leading Genuinos as Iturralde, Paredes and Domingo L. Ramírez were temporarily exiled. Later, at the height of the Uncía massacre crisis the government closed down the opposition press, and exiled such leading Liberals as Ismael Montes and José Luis Tejada Sorzano, and confined men like the editor of *El Diario*, Fabián Vaca Chávez and Casto Rojas—both important Liberal intellectuals—in distant parts of the republic along with a host of lesser opposition editors from the departmental capitals.[3]

In late 1923, Simón I. Patiño, temporarily returning from Europe, attempted to intervene as a mediator in the local political scene and held a meeting with all the opposition leaders to try to work out a reconciliation with the Saavedra government. But opposition demands for control over cabinet appointments were rejected by Saavedra and this reconciliation gesture, like its predecessors, brought no positive results.[4]

The failure of these moves and the refusal of the government to allow free elections led the opposition not only to abstain

---

[1] Carrasco, *Siles*, pp. 227–34. Saavedra in February also dissolved the Liberal-dominated La Paz municipal council. Díaz Machicao, *Saavedra*, p. 151.
[2] In La Paz the united opposition group known as the Unión Nacional did run its candidates and succeeded in electing both Daniel Sánchez Bustamante and Abel Iturralde to office. Díaz Machicao, *Saavedra*, pp. 155–6.
[3] Benigno Carrasco, *Siles*, pp. 247, 262–3; Díaz Machicao, *Saavedra*, pp. 158–9.
[4] Alvéstegui, *Salamanca*, II, 384–6.

from the May 1923 elections but also to prepare for the violent overthrow of the government. In February 1924, a military uprising occurred in the southern garrison of Yacuiba on the Argentine border, and in July a separatist anti-government revolution erupted in Santa Cruz.[1]

The government easily succeeded in destroying these revolts, but it was obviously shaken by the increasing intransigence of the opposition as well as the cooling ardour of the urban masses as a result of its foreign dealings, and the Uncía massacre. In January 1924, in an attempt to revive this popular support, the government announced a major new programme of social welfare legislation, and that same month a docile saavedrista congress passed much new legislation supplementing the initial programme of 1921. These new laws provided for enforced worker savings plans for several industries, greater accident protection, and an eight-hour day for commercial workers and some industrial labourers.[2] Also, to placate the upper class, the government promoted new railroad ventures, always a hall-mark of concrete 'progress' in Bolivian politics since the days of Arce. In 1924 government lines finally connected with the Argentine railway system and a direct rail link between La Paz and Buenos Aires was established, a truly important achievement.[3]

Because of these various accomplishments and the repeated demonstration of his ability to destroy revolutionary threats to his government, the remaining months of Saavedra's rule proved unusually quiet. All opposition elements now began to prepare for his succession.[4] The rather embittered Saavedra had thoughts of proroguing his government on the grounds that he still had a great deal to accomplish, but even his own party refused to support such a move. He thus resorted to selecting an unknown

---

[1] Díaz Machicao, *Saavedra*, pp. 169–73. These two movements had been preceded by an attack on the La Paz headquarters of Saavedra's Guardia Republicana. *Ibid.* pp. 166–9.
[2] Benigno Carrasco, *Siles*, p. 275.
[3] Díaz Machicao, *Saavedra*, p. 172.
[4] Just how turbulent the Saavedra period had been is indicated by the statistics on government decreed states of siege. According to *El Diario* states of siege had already occupied 890 days of Saavedra's 4 years and 3 months term, as contrasted to a total of 222 days in states of siege in the previous 21 years and 3 months of Liberal rule! *El Diario*, 22 March 1925, p. 4.

but loyal saavedrista, Dr José Gabino Villanueva, to run as his chosen successor. Despite some last attempts by such party leaders as Hernando Siles to prevent this succession, Villanueva was endorsed by the party and Siles was exiled. In the resulting government-controlled election, in May 1925, Villanueva obtained a landslide victory over Salamanca the Genuino Republican candidate.[1]

But after his victory the president-elect suddenly showed signs of independence from Saavedra's control and even began talking of general amnesty and an all-party government. By stating these desires publicly in a newspaper interview in June, he thoroughly outraged Saavedra, who forced through an unprecedented cancellation of the election results on a legal technicality during a bitter September congressional session. Though he succeeded in removing his potentially insubordinate successor, Saavedra was nonetheless incapable of going beyond this gesture to enforce an extension of his own government. Congress elected a temporary president and the party demanded that Siles be recalled from exile and given the party nomination. Against all his political instincts and desires, Saavedra was forced to accept Siles. As a last and futile effort at control, however, he required Siles to sign a formal document promising to accept party discipline on all major decisions. He then tried to insure this pact by requiring Siles to accept Saavedra's own brother as his vice-president. Thereupon Siles was voted president of the republic in an unopposed election on 1 December 1925,[2] and in early January of the new year Saavedra left for Europe.

Born into a leading social family of Sucre in 1881, Hernando Siles had been educated in the law at the local university and had eventually achieved the position of rector. His family were closely tied to the Conservative party but he had by and large remained outside political activity during the twenty years of Liberal rule, and had not become an affiliate of any political party until 1920. In that year he officially joined the Republican ranks

---

[1] Alvéstegui, *Salamanca*, II, 389ff. The official returns were 50,000 for Villanueva to 10,000 for Salamanca. Benigno Carrasco, *Siles*, p. 365.

[2] Benigno Carrasco, *Siles*, pp. 359ff. For complete texts of these documents and Siles' letter of acceptance, see Alcides Argüedas, 'La danza de las sombras', in *Obras completas* (2 vols.; Mexico: Aguilar, 1959), I, 989–90.

and became a leader in the Oruro committee, and a firm supporter of Saavedra in a salamanquista stronghold. Elected to the convention of 1920, he played an important role in the saavedrista ranks and in the election of his mentor. His reward was a special diplomatic assignment; he represented Bolivia in Mexico in the centenary celebration of its independence in 1921, and in late 1921 returned to his parliamentary seat.

In January 1922 Siles was given the ministry of public instruction and in June he was transferred to the important post of minister of war and colonization. In this post, which he held until his return to congress to break the 1923 deadlock, Siles made important friendships with the younger officers in the national army, friendships which were to prove of surprising durability. Returning to the chamber of deputies in early 1923, he again took a leading part in parliamentary activity and was soon thereafter elected president of the national committee of the Republican party. Here again, as in his post in the ministry of war, Siles impressed his dynamic personality on the younger party regulars who began to give him decided support and form a *silista* movement within the party. Following the Uncía massacre in June, he was appointed a special representative of Saavedra, and, after negotiations with all sides, brought the strike to an end and somewhat saved government face after the initial fiasco. In August 1923 he entered the new congress as a senator from his home district, the position his father had held in the previous century.[1]

Meanwhile, as early as the beginning of 1923, Siles' supporters within the party had pressed his name on Saavedra for the presidential succession. But he and several other candidates were too independent for Saavedra, who even went so far as to exile Siles temporarily to keep him out of the running.[2] In the chaos after the nullification of the presidential election, however, Siles' powerful supporters within the party made a strong bid for his selection and forced the party to accept him as its candidate. Thus Siles began his régime in early 1926 with a tight control over the

---

[1] Benigno Carrasco, *Siles*, chs. I–IV.
[2] *Ibid.* pp. 320ff. For a time Saavedra had considered the possibility of making the poet and intellectual Ricardo Jaimes Freyre his hand-picked successor, but the latter refused the offer and left the country.

government Republican party and also a calm political situation as all the opposition forces waited to see how this essentially anti-saavedrista régime would develop.[1]

[1] Even *El Diario*, 19 February 1926, p. 4, took special note of the surprising political calm which the nation was now experiencing, after the riotous Saavedra years; also, see Porfirio Díaz Machicao, *Historia de Bolivia, Guzmán, Siles, Blanco Galindo, 1925–1931* (La Paz: Gisbert y Cía., 1955), pp. 19–29. Hereafter cited as *Siles*.

THE REPUBLICAN ERA: SILES

Helped by a propitious political calm and general support from the opposition parties when he came to office in January 1926 Siles had little difficulty in rapidly establishing his own absolute authority over the new régime. Though he inherited several powerful saavedristas, such as Eduardo Díez de Medina and Pedro Gutiérrez, in his first cabinet, he quickly rid himself of the stifling presence of Saavedra's brother. In late March he sent the vice-president on a special good-will tour of Latin America in a deliberate move toward 'diplomatic exile'. Siles also began to reorganize the army and bring into key staff positions such loyal personal followers as Colonel David Toro. But despite this drift away from his control, Saavedra continued to give his support to the government, both personally and through his newspaper *La República*.

Meanwhile the opposition parties rapidly responded to Siles' gestures of conciliation and soon many influential opposition leaders accepted positions in the new government. As a first step, three leading theoreticians of the opposition parties took diplomatic posts. The anti-saavedrista Franz Tamayo joined the foreign ministry early in the year; in May, Fabián Vaca Chávez of *El Diario* accepted a diplomatic post; and in October the salamanquista editor of the influential *La Patria* of Oruro, Demetrio Canelas, accepted a position in the embassy in Peru.

By July conciliation moves had reached such a stage that Siles was able to bring several leading opposition politicians into his cabinet as independent figures, and by September he had signed an agreement with Escalier for the formal Genuino endorsement of the government. This agreement was put into operation in October when the government appointed two Genuinos, as official representatives of their party, to cabinet positions. He also reinstated in the army the leading salamanquista officer, Colonel

Carlos Blanco Galindo, who had been a special target of Saavedra in the previous period.

Finally in September and October the last vestiges of allegiance to Saavedra were relinquished by Siles when he encouraged mass demonstrations to prevent Abdón S. Saavedra from returning from his diplomatic tour. The vice-president ignored these manifestations and entered the country in late October, but the popular demonstrations were so violent that to save his life he was soon forced to flee. This was obviously the ultimate insult. Bautista reacted violently to this treatment of his brother and in impotent rage he formally disassociated himself from the government by renouncing his ambassadorship on 1 December 1926.[1]

Although Siles broke with the party that had put him into power, he did not intend to embrace his previous opponents. Instead, he proposed to form his own party of loyal followers into a group independent of the traditional political organizations. Endowed with leadership qualities which primarily appealed to the young intellectuals, Siles decided to establish his new party on a previously unexploited source of power, *la juventud*, that is the previously uncommitted university youth and younger professionals.

As early as May 1926 there had been talk in university circles of the need for a party to represent the new aspirations of the university youth.[2] Saavedra, in a letter to his partisans, ridiculed the whole idea. 'The new party which is attempting to organize itself in order to support the government,' he declared, 'is a political impossibility, since political parties do not form themselves by will; the concurrence of great ideals being necessary.' 'At the present time,' he declared, 'such a triumphant ideology does not exist', and in his tradition-bound view Saavedra could not see such a grouping finding 'a programme distinct from that which the existing parties profess'.[3]

But Saavedra was partly wrong. For the first stirring of the university youth was beginning to make itself felt in Bolivia. More and more the restless young people of advanced ideas

[1] Díaz Machicao, *Siles*, pp. 38ff.
[2] *Ibid.*, pp. 49–50.   [3] Quoted Díaz Machicao, *Siles*, p. 50.

began to read Marx, while the continental movement of *Reforma Universitaria*, which had begun in 1917 in Córdoba, Argentina, and provided for university autonomy and student participation in government, was beginning to manifest itself in Bolivia.[1]

Probably the first major public manifestation of this new university spirit occurred in the early days of the new régime. In March 1926 the church, with the full support of the Siles government, launched the Gran Cruzada Nacional Pro-Indio.[2] The whole idea of the campaign, which was primarily a benevolent and constructive one, was to raise funds for Indian vocational schools, scholarships, etc., under the assumption that the major problem of the Indian was lack of education. At first the university students, along with everyone else, gave full support. But on 17 April the Federación Universitaria de La Paz, under its president Enrique Baldivieso, announced that it was in absolute disagreement with the whole crusade. In an official announcement they stated that:

We believe that the incorporation of the Indian into civilization should not be the patrimony of any religious creed. All approaches to the redemption of the Indian should rest upon an eminently economic phenomenon: the ownership ... of the land, and literacy and technical education will follow as a consequence of this postulate ... The experience of four hundred years shows us that the clergy, together with the latifundista and the representatives of authority—today allied—have been slowly and calculatingly exhausting the vitality of

---

[1] Céspedes, *El dictador suicida*, p. 82; Valencia Vega, *Desarrollo del pensamiento político*, p. 96. A leading Peruvian student radical leader, Manuel Seoane, who came to Bolivia for the centenary celebrations of 1925, noted that the Federación Universitaria de La Paz had seemed to him, not only to have expressed its 'divorce from the methods of the old politics, but primarily, its sensibility before the social question'. Quoted in M. Baptista Gumucio, *Revolución y universidad en Bolivia* (La Paz: 'Juventud', 1956), pp. 55–6. Also the soon to be widely read Gustavo A. Navarro—Tristán Marof—published in Brussels at this time an important collection of radical essays under the title of *La justicia del Inca* espousing a strong *indigenismo* ideology and a programme of nationalization of the tin mines and land reform for the Indians. Valencia Vega, *Desarrollo del pensamiento político*, pp. 92–3.

The Federación Universitaria de La Paz, after a three-year hiatus, had reformed and begun a new and radical active political career in mid-1925 under the leadership of its active president Enrique Baldivieso. *El Diario*, 21 May 1925, p. 4, and 16 June 1925, p. 4.   [2] *El Diario*, 24 March 1926, p. 5.

the race and placing the Indian in the wretched situation in which he is found today.

In short it is perfectly evident that the Great National Pro-Indian Crusade has no other end than that of placing the solution of this problem in the hands of the clergy... This task, however, belongs to the state, which should accomplish it without the intervention of any religious profession.[1]

The next day the students held a mass protest meeting in Plaza Murillo—the central plaza in La Paz—and when troops and police attempted to break up the demonstration, Siles ordered them to stop and permitted the meeting to proceed. Siles then heard F.U. president Baldivieso attack the clergy for exploiting the Indian, and state his demand that the Indian should recover his lost estates from the latifundistas.[2] This opposition from university students had immediate repercussions. For not only did the government withdraw its patronage of the whole affair, but by 22 April the bishop of La Paz himself announced the end of the crusade and the return of all funds raised in the few days of collection, thereby admitting defeat by the radical student opposition.[3]

Thus Siles responded to the new sophistication and unity of the university student movement, and attempted to weld it into a major source of support for his government, a support distinct from the traditional elements of authority yet closely allied to the élite. Appealing to this awakening generation, he also united in his political movement leading young and previously uncommitted intellectuals, as well as the more radical young figures of the Liberal party.[4] By the middle of the year Siles felt that the movement was strong enough to begin formal plans for organization, and invited a group of these intellectuals, among them Enrique Baldivieso, José Tamayo, Humberto Plaza, and Augusto Céspedes, to the palace to discuss both the formation of the party

El Diario, 18 April 1926, p. 8; also see Díaz Machicao, *Siles*, p. 44.
El Diario, 20 April 1926, p. 12.
El Diario, 22 April 1926, pp. 4, 8. Interestingly this sudden show of strength and radical ideology by the student movement, while it succeeded in bringing down the moral cruzada, put nothing in its place, for the government continued to do next to nothing in the sphere of Indian education. Nobody was about to carry through land reform, least of all the Siles government, and the defeat of this motion and the truly vast sums which had been pledged to it was in one sense a major loss to the nation, given the lack of any other activity in this area. Finot, *Nueva historia*, p. 368.

and its principles.[1] Members of this group comprised the leadership for the anti-Abdón Saavedra demonstrations.[2] He therefore called on these men to establish cells of the new party throughout the republic. In discussing this organizing trip, Céspedes noted that he and his associates gained the support in Cochabamba of two leading young radicals, Carlos Montenegro and Augusto Guzmán. However these intellectuals were not in the majority and the new party became dominated by men thoroughly steeped in classical liberal ideology and principles, including Rafael Taborga, Enrique Finot, F. Vaca Chávez, and L. Fernando Guachalla, and it was they who gave the tone to the party image and ideology.

At first, Céspedes, Baldivieso, and Humberto Plaza wrote their own 'revolutionary' party programme on their return to La Paz. According to one of its authors, this programme 'contained an essential novelty: a criticism of liberal individualism, [and its] application by the Bolivian parties. In the tactical area it pointed out the intellectual need of the youth to guide the country toward a discrete form of socialism.' But the dominant leaders of the new conglomeration, according to this same author, 'were horrified with its content and edited in substitution a succulent liberal programme, inflating it with a gigantic catalogue of public works ... Our initiative,' charged this young intellectual, 'remained rejected for being "too intellectual" and thus the revolutionary theory of the new party was unmade in its origin'.[3]

Despite this traditional programme, or more likely because of it, by January 1927 the organization of the movement had reached such a point that its leader Rafael Taborga felt strong enough to announce the official creation of the *Partido de Unión Nacional*,[4] which quickly became known as the *Partido Nacionalista*. On 11 January the newspapers of La Paz published the official programme of the party, which, as Céspedes had rightly noted, contained nothing especially revolutionary, while one member of the new party later labelled the whole thing *nacionalismo romántico*.[5]

---

[1] Céspedes, *El dictador suicida*, p. 83.
[2] *Ibid.* p. 84. Céspedes claims that Abdón charged that he and Gustavo Adolfo Otero were the key ringleaders in the mob action against himself.
[3] *Ibid.* p. 84.   [4] *El Diario*, 6 January 1927, p. 6.
[5] Francovich, *El pensamiento boliviano en el siglo xx*, p. 83.

The programme called for the reorganization and modernization of the public administration; a major programme of economic development, including public works; development of national industry and agriculture; and a government policy of protectionism. The usual pious demand for economic and administrative decentralization was made, and a call to modernize the administration with the creation of a professional foreign service corps, and the establishment of a new ministry of health. Following the Saavedra experience, there was now also a strong policy of national social legislation and legal protection proposals for workers, women and children. For the university movement, a formal endorsement of university autonomy was a key proposal. In the field of social legislation, the new party called for a national savings plan and a complete labour code. In the sphere of fiscal policy the nationalists wanted a more rational taxation structure with the elimination of indirect taxes and development-style industrial banks, one for mining and another for agriculture, as well as the establishment of a totally government-owned Banco Central.[1]

Thus the programme rather faithfully represented a middle-class reformist type of ideology in which the younger men in politics, still within the traditional ideological framework, conceived of reforming Bolivia through 'scientific' modernization and progress. They completely ignored the fact that for a 'New Bolivia' to be created one had to do more than modernize the instruments of government and inculcate everyone with a forward-looking philosophy—the nation needed basic institutional reworking, and as yet the younger middle class intellectuals of the late 1920s were not prepared to think in these terms. They were still unwilling to challenge the foundations of a society and government which seemed to them to be fairly well ordered, constructive, and above all fruitful. Only a complete breakdown of that society could alter their basic assumptions.

Despite the fact that there was no really new ideological content to the programme, and that the government was using crude tactics to bring it into existence, the new party nevertheless did seem to be well received among certain independent elements.

[1] The entire *programa* is reprinted in *El Diario*, 11 January 1927, p. 5.

The usual cluster of job-seeking politicians migrated to its ranks, but there was also a serious response from the students and intellectuals of the nation, both from moderates and from those with more advanced ideas. In one way or another, almost every major intellectual of leftist leaning, directly or indirectly, through the Partido Nacionalista or the government itself, participated in the Siles administration in the years 1926–30. Thus in addition to men of the new party, already mentioned, others to join the ranks of the Partido Nacionalista included: Guillermo Francovich, Vicente Leitón, Alberto Ostria Gutiérrez, Carlos Salinas Aramayo, Félix Capriles, Saturnino Rodrigo, Alberto Mendoza López, Max Atristaín, Carlos Medinacelli, Javier Paz Campero, and Benigno Carrasco;[1] while at one time or another Víctor Paz Estenssoro, Ricardo Anaya, and José Antonio Arze were associated with the Siles government. As can be seen from this list, practically every major young Bolivian intellectual of any note participated in some way in this movement, and the future leaders of every post-Chaco War radical party received their early political training in this period.

Thus at least in terms of personnel and tone, if not in terms of ideology or formal organization, the Siles régime and the Partido Nacionalista were to be the precursors of the new political world which would emerge in the post-Chaco War period. After years of control of the political process by ageing veterans of the Liberal era, the youthful Siles evoked a deep response from the national intellectual and youth movement of the 1920s.

The response of the traditional parties to the new movement, however, was hostile. The Genuinos especially reacted to the creation of this new political movement since it threatened the recently achieved unification of the two branches of the Republican party. In their February 1927 convention in Oruro, the Genuinos under the leadership of Escalier decided on a formal break with the Siles government. Their official party organ *La Razón* justified this action by charging that Siles himself had broken the unification compact by supporting the foundation of the new party, and warned that he was forsaking a government of the majority for a minority rule.[2]

---

[1] Benigno Carrasco, *Siles*, pp. 382–3.   [2] Díaz Machicao, *Siles*, pp. 61–2.

In the May 1927 congressional elections, the first in which the Partido Nacionalista participated, the government used the usual strong interventionist methods to obtain results and the new party achieved a major electoral victory, especially as the Genuinos had abstained because of the government's refusal to grant guarantees.[1] But this electoral victory was immediately challenged on 4 May by very serious student rioting and a teachers' strike. After much bloodshed and an attack on the Partido Nacionalista's newspaper plant, the government declared a state of siege, exiled leading Genuinos and Liberals, and closed down *La Razón.* The opposition charged that the whole affair indicated that the Siles régime was governing with a minority party.[2] Nevertheless Siles was still able late in May to organize a new cabinet with one Liberal, one Independent, and two members each from the Partido Republicano de Gobierno and the Partido Nacionalista. In June the two latter parties finally came to an understanding, and both agreed to support the Siles government in coalition, although maintaining their separate identities.[3]

The May 1927 congressional elections had not only been a major event in the formation of the new National party, but they also marked the resurgence of a newly revived worker-supported political radicalism. The old Partido Socialista organization was temporarily revived for this election and put up an impressive slate of labour leaders and radical intellectuals including Enrique G. Loza, the young extremists Tristán Marof (Gustavo A. Navarro) and Roberto Hinojosa, and the only publicly avowed Bolivian communist, M. L. Dick Ampuero.[4] The striking quality of this slate indicates how far the old Socialist party had come along the road towards radicalism after its early moderate years. Both Marof and Hinojosa were at least partly Marxian socialists with

[1] Of a total of seven senate seats up for election, four were won by the Nationalists, two by Liberals, and one by a Republicano de Gobierno (i.e. saavedrista), and of the thirty-four congressional seats, the new party took twenty-one, the saavedristas four and the Geninos four. One each went to the Liberal, Socialist and Regionalist parties, and one to an independent. *El Diario,* 3 May 1927, p. 4.

[2] Díaz Machicao, *Siles,* pp. 64–5.

[3] *El Diario,* 2 June 1927, p. 4.

[4] *El Diario,* 3 May 1927, p. 4. The year before, M. L. Dick Ampuero, in his book *Organización sindicalista* (La Paz: Biblioteca Revolucionaria, 1926), had advocated the organization of a communist labour movement in Bolivia, affiliated with the 'Red International' (pp. 11, 54).

strong *indigenista* programmes and both had already been severely attacked by established authorities for their radical opinions. In the elections all were defeated, save for Enrique G. Loza, whose seat a hostile congress refused to validate.[1]

The election seems to have been the last major effort of the old party, but later in the year the Partido Socialista gave birth to a new minority labour party with the distinct title of *Partido Laborista*, though it, too, soon became popularly known as the Socialist party. Under the leadership of the important labour leaders Moisés Álvarez and Ezequiel Salvatierra, and with the remnants of the old party and some new radical blood, the new party was founded in July 1927.[2] Although it proclaimed itself the direct descendant of all previous Socialist parties in Bolivia, it was far more radical than its predecessors and can be considered the first Marxian Socialist party in Bolivian history. As the programme of the party stated:

The character of our party is eminently class oriented, made up of those who live honourably by their labour against the exploiting and non-labouring classes, of the poor against the rich, of the manual and intellectual workers against the racial and creole aristocracy, in short, of those who are working for the socio-economic transformation of the present state in which we live, into a more rational and human society . . . The Partido Laborista is of the workers and for the workers, it embodies the supreme aspiration of the betterment of the people and for the people.[3]

In its second circular, which the party issued in 1928, it stated that, although it had adopted the label of Labour party, 'our doctrinary position remains fully Marxist'. In a later circular the party declared that its doctrines, 'were aimed towards the socialization of all the sources of production. Our points of view', it went on to say, 'are directly intended for the transformation of the present society, because we are convinced that this is the only way to save the people from the social injustice of which they are the victims.'[4]

The Labour party was not the only manifestation of growing

[1] *La Razón*, 4 September 1927, p. 8.
[2] Lora, 'Historia del movimiento sindical', p. 6.
[3] Quoted *ibid.* p. 7. [4] Quoted *ibid.* pp. 7–8.

radicalism within the labour movement. For in 1927 the various confederations were able successfully to organize the third national convention of the Bolivian working classes. In 1925 a Segundo Congreso Nacional de Trabajadores had finally succeeded in establishing a rough type of national confederation,[1] and this new congress gave to the confederation its ideological content. The third congress met in July 1927 in Oruro. Over 200 delegates attended, making it the most important national labour meeting to date. At this convention the class struggle for the first time was openly espoused by the worker movement, and a major programme of political and labour action against the capitalist classes was adopted. Although the majority of the delegates expressed marked sympathy toward the Third International, there was enough anarcho-syndicalist sentiment to prevent open affiliation, and the new national confederation continued to maintain itself independent of any of the major Internationals.[2]

In this same month, the government announced that it had uncovered a 'communist' plot to take over the nation. According to the government, this revolutionary plot was led by Tristán Marof and a 'Council of Ten'. Also implicated in the plot were the Labour party and sindicato leaders Ezequiel Salvatierra and Moisés Álvarez and the radical intellectual Oscar Cerruto.[3] Not only did Marof himself deny the validity of these accusations,[4] but the leading Genuino newspaper, *La Razón*, charged that the whole communist issue was a government fabrication.[5] When the militant leftist labour newspaper, *Bandera Roja*, also added its voice of dissent, it was closed down by the government.[6] The fact that the government used the excuse of this 'plot' to exile several leading traditional leaders would seem to confirm the fact that the whole affair was a manufactured one. This was, however, the first mention of a specifically communist revolutionary attempt in Bolivian history, and indicated a growing concern amongst the upper classes with a potential rising tide of extreme radicalism on the far left. But with communism, just as earlier

---

[1] Barcelli, *Medio siglo de luchas sindicales*, pp. 111–12.
[2] Álvarez, 'La organización sindical en Bolivia', p. 36; Barcelli, *Medio siglo de luchas sindicales*, p. 115.
[3] *El Diario*, 15 July 1927, p. 5.   [4] *La Razón*, 10 September 1927, p. 4.
[5] *La Razón*, 24 July 1927, p. 12, and 26 July 1927, p. 4.   [6] *La Razón*, 22 July 1927.

with socialism, Bolivia was still several generations behind most of the other nations of Latin America. Except for a mild reaction among half a dozen intellectuals in the late 1920s and early 1930s, the Russian revolution, in fact, produced no echo within Bolivia until almost three decades after its occurrence.

In one crucial area, however, Bolivia was not immune to the radical currents disrupting traditional Latin American thought throughout the rest of the hemisphere, and this was in the university student movement. Originating in the famous university reform movement in Argentina in 1917, this new movement conceived of the university as the vital instrument for the basic reorganization of the essentially oligarchic structure of Latin American society. But as the universities were then constructed, they could not play this vital role of reformation. Therefore the University Reform movement proposed that the student's primary concern was to revolutionize the essentially oligarchic university so that it could begin to play a greater role. This meant modernization of the still largely humanistic and scholastic curriculum, opening up the universities to students from all social classes and, most important, permitting the student generation to participate in the autonomous university government. Practically no country in Latin America was immune to this ferment, and Bolivia in this particular case was no exception.

With these ideas of reform of the university came a new philosophy which was profoundly influenced by nineteenth-century European socialism, as refined and expressed for the Latin American world by such synthesizers as José Ingenieros. As one intellectual of this period later recalled:

The speculative interest in historical materialism surged forth in Bolivia with the publication of the *Sociología argentina* of José Ingenieros. Ingenieros was one of the Argentine writers most read in Bolivia between the two world wars. His books of criminology and of sociology had almost the rank of texts in the universities.[1]

Thus, at least within one small part of the university world, a new and potentially revolutionary ideology was taking hold. While still completely marginal to the dominant political and

[1] Francovich, *El pensamiento boliviano en el siglo xx*, pp. 103–4.

social ideology of the day, this new development among the university youth was extremely important, since it finally established on a firm and lasting basis a non-liberal and non-traditional pattern of thought, in this case Marxian socialism.

To give these new ideas and new university movements more concrete form, some of the more radical student leaders decided to organize a national student federation. With the firm support of the Siles government these leaders succeeded in organizing a first national student congress at Cochabamba in August 1928, and among its members were such figures as the poet Carlos Medinacelli, and the radicals José Antonio Arze and Ricardo Anaya.[1]

The key leader of the convention was the young Marxist intellectual Arze, who was a recent graduate of the law faculty of the Universidad de San Simón at Cochabamba. It was Arze who both chaired the convention and was the principal writer of the programme of the *Federación Universitaria Boliviana*, the national student federation created at this convention.[2]

The Statutes of the FUB proclaimed that one of its aims should be to 'create an effective cooperation between the manual and intellectual proletariats, to organize a pro-Indian league, committees of worker-student solidarity and to aid the unionization of secondary and primary school teachers and intellectual workers in general'.[3] Along with its support for 'university autonomy' and 'university reform' on the Argentine model, the FUB programme also demanded full commitment to what is called 'the social question'.[4] Thus the FUB took a revolutionary stand on the Indian problem, and called for 'the incorporation of the Indian into the civilized life [of the nation]. This incorporation being achieved only when the Indian is emancipated from the present agrarian feudalism.' The emancipation required in specific terms 'the forceful breaking-up of the latifundio, as has occurred in Mexico'.[5] The programme approved by the convention also called for cooperation with the Bolivian proletariat in its drive toward syndicalization, and declared itself united with

[1] Primera Convención Nacional de Estudiantes Bolivianos, *Programa de principios, estatuto orgánico y reglamento de debates de la Federación Universitaria Boliviana* (Cochabamba: Federación de Estudiantes de Cochabamba, 1928), p. 3.
[2] *Ibid.* pp. 4, 12, 24.   [3] *Ibid.* p. 13.   [4] *Ibid.* p. 25.   [5] *Ibid.* p. 35.

the workers in their legitimate defence against capitalist exploitation. The principles of the 1917 Mexican constitution were also upheld in the FUB demand for the nationalization of natural resources.[1]

Conceding the right of students to join any traditional political party they wished, the FUB, nevertheless, stated as a general aim the need for a new party based on new economic principles.[2] It stressed the need for democratic government and even proposed a federalist structure for Bolivia. But it charged that 'true democracy is incompatible with the present capitalist régime, because it is founded on the absolute right of private property, which creates a conception of wealth in a few hands, and an ever increasing poverty of the salaried and proletarian workers. Wealth, an essentially collective product, should be collective in its ends.' Therefore, the present competitive capitalist system should be replaced by a cooperative one. 'The only salvation of Bolivia is, therefore, the progressive SOCIALIZATION OF PRIVATE WEALTH.' This meant in concrete terms the nationalization of the mines and of petroleum. It also meant land reform and the possession of the land by the Indians, and finally a major social and labour code (on the model of the 1917 Mexican constitution and the 1919 German one) to protect the proletariat.[3]

Although the FUB 'repeats its conviction that it prefers democratic institutions for the realization of its ideas to their brutal imposition by reactionary tyrannies', if it was forced to choose between 'the clerical type of fascist dictatorship or the socialist type of Russian dictatorship, it would not hesitate in preferring the latter, because it at least represents violence put to the service of a generous future'.[4] Predictably, the student congress also expressed marked anti-clericalism, and called for entirely lay education, the suppression of the monastic orders, and the separation of church and state.[5]

The international programme called for the 'substitution for the Monroist and Panamericanist principles which serve Yankee imperialism, of the principle of Latinamerican solidarity'. It called for 'defense against the action of Yankee imperialism, impeding its

[1] Primera Convención Nacional de Estudiantes Bolivianos, 1928, p. 36.
[2] *Ibid.* pp. 36–7.   [3] *Ibid.* pp. 37–9, 41.   [4] *Ibid.* p. 40.   [5] *Ibid.* pp. 40–2.

interference in international litigations over territories, its interference in internal politics, and its monopolization of the national
wealth'.[1] Finally the congress, despite its disapproval of wars of
conquest, took a nationalistic stand for complete reintegration of
the littoral and defence of the south-east against Paraguay by the
government.[2]

In short, the 'First National Bolivian Students Convention'
propounded some of the most fundamental ideas of the radical
left in Bolivia at a national level for the first time. These classic
Marxian, indigenista and nationalist ideas were the basic themes
of Bolivian radicalism from that day until the great social revolution almost thirty years later. More than anything else, this
congress indicated the advanced state of thought which had developed among the more radical elements in the student movement. The clarity of the thought as well as the numerous specific
proposals indicated total familiarity with the great movements
of contemporary European and Latin American ideas on the part
of its authors and the currency of this thought in at least one part
of the university world. But the immediate influence of these new
radical programmes and ideals was limited, and in fact implied
more for future developments than for the contemporary scene.[3]

For national political life, divided among four traditional parties, continued to revolve around the same issues which had
dominated the political scene since the days of the Conservative
oligarchy. These questions concerned the battle of personalities
and the issues of government interference in the electoral process
on the internal side, and the problems of growing national
indebtedness and territorial disputes in the international arena.
At first, Siles like his predecessors had concentrated on the
littoral question, which especially in 1926 had reached new levels

---

[1] Primera Convención Nacional de Estudiantes Bolivianos, 1928, p. 43.
[2] *Ibid.* pp. 34. The new FUB elected as its president for a two-year term the Cochabamba law student, Ricardo Anaya. *El Diario*, 23 August 1928, p. 6. For a discussion of the importance of this congress within the movement for university
autonomy, see Manuel Durán P., *La reforma universitaria en Bolivia* (Oruro:
Universidad Técnica de Oruro, 1961), pp. 56ff.
[3] It is interesting to note that the work of José Carlos Mariátegui, *Siete ensayos de
interpretación de la realidad peruana*, which appeared in the middle 1920s had a
very early impact and diffusion in Bolivia, and in 1927 a chapter of the Peruvian
APRA party was even temporarily established in Bolivia. *La Razón*, 7 September 1927, p. 2.

of intensity with the intervention of the United States in the dispute. In March and November of that year, Secretary of State Kellogg proposed to Chile and Peru that the Tacna-Arica area be turned over either to a tripartite administration including Bolivia or given to Bolivia as an outright possession. This proposal, known as the *formula Kellogg*, aroused fantastic hopes in Bolivia, whose government had long since retreated from the *reivindicacionalista* stand taken by Saavedra at the League of Nations. Its only result, however, was to push Chile and Peru into direct negotiation, excluding both US mediation and Bolivian observation.[1] After intense discussions the two countries arrived at the inevitable solution in 1929 of dividing the two departments between them and agreeing not to give any territory to a third party without the consent of both nations.[2]

Meanwhile, in late December 1926, the littoral issue began to be submerged for the first time in Bolivian newspapers by news stories on the Chaco Boreal and Bolivia's historic dispute with Paraguay over this territory. By 1927 Tacna and Arica were already relegated to the back pages, as the Chaco dispute took the headlines. In response to the growing tension on her southeastern frontier, Bolivia in December 1926 secured from the British armaments company, Vickers-Armstrong, a short term loan of $9 million to be used for the purchase of war material to modernize her army.[3] Despite this seemingly bellicose act, the Siles government also tried seriously to alleviate the tension over this issue, and in 1927 sent a boundary commission to Buenos Aires, composed of such leading opposition figures as Escalier, Daniel Sánchez Bustamante, and Colonel Carlos Blanco Galindo. All negotiations with the Paraguayans broke down, however, and both sides resumed their intensive activities to construct fortresses in the unpopulated and unexplored no-man's-land in the Gran Chaco.[4]

Along with growing foreign problems, the Siles government also began to experience a serious economic crisis. Faced by a

---

[1] Alvéstegui, *Salamanca*, II, 441–2.   [2] Basadre, *Chile, Perú y Bolivia*, p. 660.
[3] Ernest Galarza, 'Debts, Dictatorship and Revolution in Bolivia and Peru', *Foreign Policy Reports*, VII, No. 5 (13 May 1931), 105–6.
[4] Carlos Alberto Salinas Baldivieso, *Historia diplomática de Bolivia* (Sucre: n.p., 1938), pp. 164–6.

growing shortage of funds for normal government operations as
well as lack of money to complete several major public works and
railroad construction projects, the Siles government soon found
itself in a rather tight financial situation. It therefore resorted to
further increases in indirect taxation, with imposts on stamped
paper and beer, and a particularly unpopular and burdensome
tax on personal identification cards which were issued to all
Bolivians.[1] The increasingly desperate government also carried
through a forced loan of some Bs. 3 million in the middle of the
year from the local banks, and when Patiño's Banco Mercantil
refused to contribute, Siles impounded its books.[2]

But these actions only temporarily relieved the situation, for
Bolivia's annual budget deficits between 1926 and 1929 left her
with little or no ability to liquidate her total debt obligations
which in 1926 represented 33 per cent of the value of national
income for that year. These budget deficits fluctuated from a low
of 3 per cent of government income in 1926 to an incredible
high of 31 per cent in 1928.[3] Bolivia once again turned to the
international money market for new funds, despite its already
heavy indebtedness due to the Nicolaus loan. In early 1927 it
succeeded in securing a $14,000,000 loan from the New York
house of Dillon, Reed and Co., for work on three uncompleted
railroad projects. To finance this loan the government had to
pledge a whole new series of tax revenues uncommitted to the
Nicolaus loan.[4]

In an attempt to reorganize the archaic and mortgaged government revenue and tax structure, the Siles government contracted
for assistance from the United States Kemmerer mission which
arrived in La Paz in March 1927.[5] Walter Kemmerer was an
internationally known government finance and currency adviser
and professor of economics at Princeton, who in the late 1920s
undertook missions to advise several major Latin American
governments on the reorganization of their finances. In 1927,
after completing such a mission to a neighbouring country, he
was invited to Bolivia for a three months' study tour, in which

[1] Galarza, 'Debts, Dictatorship and Revolution', p. 106.
[2] Céspedes, *El dictador suicida*, p. 86
[3] López Rivas, *Esquema de la historia económica*, pp. 76–7.
[4] Peñaloza, *Historia económica*, II, 446–9.   [5] *El Diario*, 30 March 1927, p. 5.

he was given the full assistance of the Siles administration. Kemmerer's primary recommendations concerned the reworking of the Banco de la Nación Boliviana into a Banco Central modelled on the Federal Reserve System of the United States. This would give the bank control over both internal currency and rates of exchange, as well as the handling of foreign currency and its conversion for local importers and exporters. Kemmerer also recommended an overhaul of the inefficient budget system, and the replacement of the chaotic and burdensome indirect tax structure, with heavy direct taxation on property and personal income. By and large, in the following months and years, most of the Kemmerer reforms (with the major exception of those on taxation) were made law by the Siles government, thus bringing about important changes in the financial structure of the nation.[1]

But future reforms could not relieve an increasingly tense economic situation. Another approach was tried when, in a rather unexpected fashion, the panicky Siles régime announced that it intended to nationalize the property of the Bolivian Railway Company, then in rather difficult financial straits. But six months after this announcement had been made, and not acted upon, the government quietly dropped the whole affair. Only a half-hearted gesture in the first place, the nationalization programme evoked little public response, as it was presented with no clear-cut ideological justification. It seemed that the government was more interested in saving the company as well as safeguarding its own heavy financial investment in the railroad than in trying to solve Bolivia's problems through a radical programme of nationalization.[2] But in any case these and numerous actions of the Siles régime were only temporary gestures to deal with the severe problem of impoverished sources of government revenue, and this pragmatic programme could not resolve the basic structural deficiencies which were the essence of its problem.

Throughout 1927 the Siles government concentrated its attention both on the serious economic problems and on its efforts to

---

[1] Benavides M., *Historia bancaria*, pp. 105–14; Galarza, 'Debts, Dictatorship and Revolution', p. 106; Francisco Mendoza (ed.), *La Misión Kemmerer en Bolivia, proyectos e informes* (La Paz: Arnó Hermanos, 1927).
[2] Díaz Machicao, *Siles*, pp. 66, 75.

broaden its support among more traditionally minded groups. Although giving continued endorsement to his two loyal party supporters, the government Republicans and the Nationalists, Siles also made overtures to the Liberal party, and for a time the Liberal party leader Tomás Manuel Elío served in the cabinet.[1] This temporary alliance, however, ended in early 1928 and throughout most of the year the government maintained press censorship and the state of siege, justifying its actions on the grounds of international tension. As for the financial situation, the Siles government finally brought temporary relief by negotiating a new loan from Dillon, Reed and Company for the sum of $23,000,000. It promised to enact the Kemmerer reforms, in return for the loan, proceeding to do this in a series of congressional bills at mid-year, and by pledging still more government revenues. This loan was used almost entirely for refunding a major portion of Bolivia's previous international debt, and especially to pay off the Vickers loan. It therefore produced little in the way of either public works or new sources of funds for government revenue.[2]

By the middle of 1928 the internal political and economic situation was arousing the tense feelings familiar to the Saavedra period. A major test of strength began to develop in late 1928 when the Liberals and Genuino Republicans announced their intention of abstaining from the coming municipal elections.[3] But before an attempt at revolt could develop over these new inter-party tensions, the entire game of political manœuvre was temporarily upset by the sudden flaring up of the Chaco border. As early as September 1928 sharp border clashes occurred with Paraguayan troops attacking Bolivian soldiers. These minor incidents suddenly got out of hand on 8 December, when a full-scale unannounced Paraguayan assault was launched on the Bolivian fort of Vanguardia.[4]

The impact of the Vanguardia incident on the nation was overwhelming. Immediately the government received support from all political parties, and mass popular demonstrations occurred for three days running.[5] The Siles government cancelled

---

[1] Díaz Machicao, *Siles*, p. 67. [2] Peñaloza, *Historia económica*, II, 449–51.
[3] Díaz Machicao, *Siles*, pp. 78–81. [4] *El Diario*, 8 December 1928, p. 1.
[5] *El Diario*, 9 December 1928, pp. 1–2; 10 December 1928, p. 1 and 11 December 1928, pp. 1–2.

the municipal elections that were to have been held on the
9th, and also broke off diplomatic relations with Paraguay. All
civilian leaders immediately gave the government their cooperation and endorsed this action, and many opposition stalwarts joined hastily-established patriotic committees. In response
to the firm support of all political elements, Siles issued a complete amnesty on 9 December. On 11 December the cabinet
resigned, and a full-fledged coalition cabinet of all the parties was
invested on the 17th. The government also secured major elder
statesmen to take up important diplomatic posts, and appointed
Montes to Brazil, Saavedra to Geneva, and Escalier to
Argentina.[1]

Although Siles shrewdly took advantage of this outpouring of
patriotic fervour to shore up his somewhat shaky régime, he
would not be panicked into war. Under strong pressure, he
called up the classes of 1926 and 1927 and accepted volunteers
for the army. He refused, however, to issue a call for general
mobilization. Although he ordered the retaking of Vanguardia
and the capture of the Paraguayan fort Boquerón by Bolivian
troops, as a reprisal, he accepted at the same time the mediation
offer of Kellogg, the United States secretary of state. Paraguay,
caught in this open act of aggression, backed down, especially
after the successful retaliation of the Bolivians, and, after long
negotiations, an apology was offered and an Act of Conciliation
was signed between the two nations in September 1929.[2]

Internal opposition to the government was renewed with the
relaxation of the war tension, and soon the coalition cabinet
broke down and most of the old party leaders resigned their
diplomatic posts. Meanwhile, the Partido Nacionalista decided to
make a major bid for power. Although they had agreed in
February to put up a joint ticket with the Government Republicans for the coming May congressional elections,[3] they
ignored this agreement, and, with strong backing from Siles,
obtained a landslide electoral victory. In both Oruro and Potosí
there was much bloodshed during these elections. The government even sent troops into Potosí.[4] The count gave the

[1] Díaz Machicao, *Siles*, pp. 82–7.   [2] Finot, *Nueva historia*, p. 369.
[3] *El Diario*, 3 February 1929, p. 12.   [4] Díaz Machicao, *Siles*, pp. 89–91.

composition of the 1929 Congress as 29 Nationalists, 16 Government Republicans, 11 Genuinos, and 4 Liberals.[1]

When the newly elected congress met in August, the enraged Government Republicans showed their hostility to the recent Nationalist actions and to the new aggressive tone of the victorious party, and formally annulled the traditional pact of the two parties, which had been in existence since June 1927.[2] Immediately the Government Republicans in the administration resigned their cabinet posts and Siles was seemingly left to govern with his Nationalist party alone. Siles, however, had strong ties with the old saavedrista faction and when Saavedra attempted to return from Europe in September, he not only prevented Saavedra from entering the country, but used the whole affair as a test of strength to break the control of the ex-president over his own followers. Under strong pressure from Siles the Government Republicans reorganized their ranks and placed silistas in control, thus bringing the party once again into the government. The entire opposition, in sharp contrast to their pre-1926 position, protested against the anti-Saavedra action of the government, and Siles reacted by exiling Ismael Montes and a host of lesser figures among the Genuinos and Liberals. By the end of the year the opposition was so embittered that it refused to participate in the December municipal elections, and Siles was forced to continue to rule under the state of siege that had been in continuous existence since 1927.[3]

With the end of the war scare, and the intensification of political conflict, the government also began to feel the first shock waves of the Great Depression. Since the temporary depression of 1921-2 the economy had experienced a steady growth until a peak was reached in 1928 and 1929. In this last year the total value of tin exports reached the figure of Bs. 102,500,000. But an indication of the gravity of the situation was the fact that this figure, which was considerably below the peak exportation years of 1918 and 1920, was based on almost double the amount of tonnage than had been needed to secure those higher returns ten years before.[4] However, world demand for tin was not inelastic,

[1] *El Diario*, 9 May 1929, p. 6. [2] *El Diario*, 25 August 1929, p. 6.
[3] Díaz Machicao, *Siles*, pp. 92–101; Céspedes, *El dictador suicida*, p. 90.
[4] Peñaloza, *Historia económica*, II, 234.

and the 1929 figure of 47,000 tons exported was never again attained in the history of Bolivian tin mining.[1]

Already in 1927 the excess of world production of tin had begun to provoke a slow but steady decline in world prices. The Great Depression aggravated the situation and greatly accelerated this decline. In terms of United States currency, tin dropped from $917 a ton in 1927 to $794 a ton in 1929, and eventually reached $385 per ton in the bottom year of 1932.[2] As early as December 1929 the government officially began to express alarm at the increasingly severe fall in tin prices.[3] For as tin declined, so did government income, and the Siles régime was in an especially acute financial situation at this time, due to its huge obligations for debt service and the maintenance of a strong military force in the Chaco. It was estimated that 37 per cent of the 1929 budget was marked for foreign debt service, with the military taking another 20 per cent, leaving a bare 43 per cent for the maintenance of all other government services and practically nothing for public works or for any possible emergency, such as the world depression.[4]

Increasingly the economic situation began to occupy the public mind, and added new cause for unrest to the rather tense political situation. Siles, feeling as Saavedra before him the frustration of having ruled for four years and having accomplished no major changes, began to think of extending his rule. In this he had the firm support of the National party leaders who talked of organizing a constituent convention which would write a new constitution and usher in a new political and economic age. Thus the government tried to take advantage of the rather serious economic situation by talking of the need for extraordinary action. In January 1930 Escalier proposed a unification convention of all the parties to select the next president. Siles rejected this idea and in the same month a Nationalist newspaper, *El Norte* of La Paz, began publishing rumours of a presidential extension. By

---

[1] Peñaloza, *Historia económica*, II, pp. 233–4; CEPAL, *El desarrollo económico de Bolivia*, p. 12, cuadro 7. The 47,000 ton figure had been surpassed once previously.
[2] CEPAL, *El desarrollo económico de Bolivia*, p. 12. By using dollar conversions the fluctuations in Bolivian exchange rates at this time are cancelled out.
[3] *El Diario*, 14 December 1929, p. 6.
[4] Galarza, 'Debts, Dictatorship and Revolution', pp. 106–7.

February the news was more fully in the press and on 9 February
Salamanca, from his retirement in Cochabamba, issued a manifesto
denying the validity of any such move.[1] Siles, however, refused
to heed this warning and in April the government officially
announced its intentions to prorogue.[2] In May a new ministry
was organized with two key military officers brought into the
cabinet to indicate the army's support for Siles' action.[3]

The next move in the scheme to prorogue came on 28 May
when Siles formally resigned and handed the government over
to a council of ministers, with the full support of General Kundt
and Colonel Toro, and the new council called for elections for
a constituent assembly on 29 June. But the Siles' resignation
broke the political calm, and rioting and revolutionary plotting
quickly broke out. On 12 June students rioted against the government and on 17 June Toro reorganized the vacillating and ineffectual council and took direct charge of a tense situation.[4]

The first armed attempt to break this stalemate came on the
same day, when a left-wing group of forty followers of the
youthful revolutionary radical Roberto Hinojosa invaded Bolivia
from Argentina.[5] Attacking the frontier community of Villazón,
the small band took over the city and engaged in one successful
encounter with the army. But the arrival of reinforcements
forced them back across the border. There was some sympathetic
worker agitation in Oruro and Potosí, and the labour leader
Enrique G. Loza even arrived on the scene in the last hours, only
to be taken when most of the others made their escape.[6] Altogether
this was a minor affair, and was not in the mainstream of the active
traditional political party plotting which was having ever more
serious consequences on the altiplano. But minor as the affair

---

[1] Díaz Machicao, *Siles*, pp. 102–7.
[2] *El Diario*, 8 April 1930, p. 6. The official text justified the prorogation on the
grounds that the nation was experiencing intense economic difficulties 'because
of the crisis which presses on the mining industry, a situation which is producing
serious social, industrial and commercial problems. Thus the government,
deeply preoccupied in seeking the best solution possible in this complex aggregate
of difficulties, considers it patriotic foresight not to aggravate this general state
with the political agitations which an immediate calling of elections would bring'.
[3] One of these officers was Siles' old-time friend, David Toro; also a new cabinet
post, that of minister of agriculture, was set up at this time.
[4] Díaz Machicao, *Siles*, pp. 109–17.   [5] *La Razón*, 20 June 1930, p. 4.
[6] *La Razón*, 21 June 1930, p. 5; *El Diario*, 21 June 1930, p. 7.

might be in its immediate political consequences, it was the first revolutionary attempt in Bolivian history which had as its avowed aim a concrete and radical social revolution for the nation.

The manifesto which the rebels issued on the first day of their revolt not only attacked Siles and his prorogation plan as undemocratic, but more importantly proclaimed: 'Our revolution is a *Social Revolution*, which comes to save Bolivia, demanding economic transformation of the nation and the liberation of the force and brains of the producing classes, which is the only basis on which to build true republican and democratic institutions.'[1] Its specific programme of principles called for 'nationalization of the mines, petroleum deposits, major industries and potential riches of the soil and subsoil; nationalization of the telephone and telegraph lines, of the railroads and other means of transport; forceful abolition of the latifundios'.[2] TIERRA Y LIBERTAD, and LAS MINAS PARA LOS TRABAJADORES BOLIVIANOS! were the slogans of the revolution.[3] The rebels called for obligatory unionization and a profit sharing plan for the workers;[4] abolition of *pongueaje*;[5] universal suffrage—i.e. the vote for the Indian; and the indirect election of the president through congress.[6] Hinojosa and his followers denied any connection with Russia and in fact with communism *per se*,[7] and the entire movement later received the warm endorsement of Haya de la Torre himself.[8] A subsequent manifesto of the rebels, issued to support the fighting, offered advancement in rank for all those who joined the rebellion and threatened imprisonment and confiscation to all those who opposed it; it also cancelled all internal and external debts and specifically singled out all debts owed by Bolivians to Aramayo and Patiño.[9]

---

[1] Reprinted in Roberto Hinojosa, *La revolución de Villazón* (La Paz: Editorial La Universal, 1944), pp. 7–8.   [2] *Ibid.* p. 25.   [3] *Ibid.* pp. 12, 13.
[4] *Ibid.* pp. 26–7.   [5] *Ibid.* p. 27.   [6] *Ibid.* p. 30.   [7] *Ibid.* p. 22.
[8] V. R. Haya de la Torre, *¿A dónde va Indoamérica?* (3rd ed.; Santiago: Editorial Ercilla, 1936), pp. 126–30. There exists some discrepancy between what Haya de la Torre thinks the rebels proclaimed and what Hinojosa in his book claims that his group proposed. But as the Bolivian newspapers—and Haya de la Torre bases his analysis on these and other Latin American newspapers—provided only a sketchy outline of the revolt and never reprinted the manifestos, I have relied completely on Hinojosa. However, it is possible that Hinojosa may have later reworked these documents and put into them a far more specific leftist programme than contemporary sources indicated.
[9] Hinojosa, *La revolución de Villazón*, pp. 33–6.

But for all the talk of revolution and the considerable amount of bloodshed that occurred, the main movement against Siles was taking place on the altiplano. This movement was led by the traditional political parties in league with important military officers and with the aid of a crucial shock force of university students. On 22 June, the day after Hinojosa recrossed the border into Argentina, student rioting in La Paz reached its height. On this 'tragic Sunday' troops were called out and fired on the students causing much bloodshed. The next day the council of ministers ordered the confiscation of *El Diario* and the imprisonment of its owner, José Carrasco. However, the days of the régime were numbered and on 25 June a well coordinated revolt broke out in several cities of the republic.[1] The Camacho regiment seized Oruro in a bloody twenty minutes of fighting, and the cadets of the Colegio Militar rose in support of La Paz. Kundt and Toro tried to hold down the army and suppress the movement. Armed students, however, joined the cadets and began three days of severe fighting in La Paz. Meanwhile, Cochabamba had fallen on the first day and Sucre and Potosí on the next.[2] From Oruro the rebels issued a manifesto setting up a provisional military junta under the direction of the old salamanquista General Carlos Blanco Galindo and five colonels, and placed military officers in all the prefectures which they had captured. By 27 June the revolt had completely succeeded and Kundt, Toro and Siles all took refuge in foreign legations while angry crowds destroyed their homes and personal effects.[3]

The popular hostility expressed against Siles in the 1930 revolution influenced public opinion about him long after the revolt. This hostility is clearly reflected in the writings of Alcides Argüedas,[4] and in the 1930 congressional investigations into malfeasance in office.[5] But the subsequent Chaco War disaster and the rise of new political movements in Bolivia greatly altered both the popular and the historiographic interpretations of the Siles administration. Whereas even Hinojosa in 1930

[1] Díaz Machicao, *Siles*, pp. 119–25.
[2] *El Diario*, 28 June 1930, pp. 2–3 and 29 June 1930, p. 5.
[3] Díaz Machicao, *Siles*, p. 139.
[4] See especially Argüedas, 'La danza de las sombras', in *Obras completas*, I, 988ff., which was written in the mid-1930s.   [5] Díaz Machicao, *Siles*, pp. 126ff.

attacked Siles for cowardliness in the Chaco and selling out national sovereignty to the Paraguayans,[1] the post-war generation came to appreciate to a marked degree the tact and ability used by Siles to avoid war in the extremely serious Vanguardia situation of 1928, and they compared it favourably with the lack of such tact shown by his successors. In the new developments in political life in the post-Chaco War period, all those who had worked with Siles and the Nationalist party once again emerged in the forefront of the national political scene, and all the new parties one way or another felt a strong tie to this first government that attempted to break the previously traditional mould of politics.

What Siles was actually trying to undertake, however, is difficult to assess. He certainly did not represent a social revolution that challenged the economic relations of national society. He turned over the state network of radio and telegraphic communications to the Marconi Company between 1926 and 1929,[2] and he farmed out government taxes to a private Compañía Recuadadora in the last years of his administration.[3] These actions clearly indicate his conservative views on the role of the government in the economy. His troops crushed Indian rebellions[4] and were used against strikers and radical elements, which at that time made him a bitter enemy of the radical left. Although he did continue the policies begun by his predecessor in the field of labour and social legislation, he was not an innovator in these matters.

His most revolutionary stand was his refusal to be the pawn of any of the traditional parties and the political support he sought from the uncommitted younger elements in the army, the

[1] Hinojosa, *La revolución de Villazón*, p. 37.
[2] Galarza, 'Debts, Dictatorship and Revolution', pp. 103–4.
[3] Céspedes, *El dictador suicida*, p. 87.
[4] In 1927 troops had put down with considerable bloodshed a major Indian uprising in the Potosí cantón of Chayanta. Supposedly one of the greatest such uprisings in the twentieth century, it involved *comunidad* and *colono* Indians who attacked and killed several local latifundistas and demanded land. The government reported 100 Indians officially killed; however, unofficial figures were much higher. The army had also carried out a thorough campaign of burning and rapine throughout the region. Barcelli, *Medio siglo de luchas sindicales*, pp. 115–19. Interestingly, one of Hinojosa's major attacks against the Siles régime was based on the Chayanta massacre. See Hinojosa, *La revolución de Villazón*, pp. 38, 40.

universities and political life. With this shift to new sources of political authority he was evolving a new conception of the political struggle in Bolivia. Yet he never seemed to be aware of the basic aims that he was trying to achieve with this newly politicized force. Even his warmest supporter and intellectual aid, Augusto Céspedes—a representative by his own account of the radical wing of the Partido Nacionalista—could state that Siles had only a vague intention of breaking down the traditional party structure, without an idea of what he hoped to put in its place. It was, declared Céspedes, 'the intention of Siles to create a party constituted as a counterpoise to the traditional *caudillaje*; his plan of destroying only the political apparatus of the Oligarchy, without touching its economic motor, was doomed to failure from the first moment'.[1] It may even be seriously debated whether Siles was not so much consciously rejecting traditional political systems as replacing those who controlled the system with new men committed to his own remarkable personality. But by bringing these new elements into play, he inadvertently initiated the rudiments of a new political consciousness in the younger generation of the nation.

[1] Céspedes, *El dictador suicida*, p. 97.

5

SALAMANCA AND THE COMING OF
THE WAR

The strikes and clashes of students and teachers initiated the revolutionary process against the *ad hoc* Toro caretaker régime, but it was the military that carried out the actual overthrow of the government under the direct leadership of the traditional political parties. The military's involvement in this coup was unquestionably its most dramatic intervention in national politics since the 1890s, but the army was still carefully subordinated to civilian interests and quickly relinquished its power to these forces.

The chief military figure in the revolutionary junta was General Carlos Blanco Galindo, a long-time follower of Salamanca and a man persecuted by the Saavedra government for these sympathies. For Blanco Galindo the all-military junta was a temporary affair, and since the junta members themselves were untrained for civilian rule he turned over effective administration to a carefully selected civilian secondary junta which oversaw actual government operations. Each military cabinet official was seconded by a prominent civilian, and the whole civilian sub-cabinet was ruled by the dynamic Daniel Sánchez Bustamante, an ex-radical and a leading salamanquista. Upon his appointment as chief civilian adviser, Sánchez Bustamante became president in all but name, and his ideas and personality came to dominate the shadow military figures of the junta government.

Although the military officers were by and large content with this arrangement, some of the more radical elements attempted to gain control for a military caudillo on the old style. This movement was led by Lieutenant-Colonel José Ayoroa, who succeeded in persuading a majority of the officers to sign a petition requesting that Ayoroa be admitted to the ruling junta.[1] But rapid

[1] José Ayoroa had been one of the few officers to join the 1920 Republican revolution and as a reward had been given the post of prefect of Oruro by

junta action led to the arrest and exiling of Ayoroa before he could act, and by this action the junta killed the only potential threat of serious military intervention to the traditional *políticos*.[1]

Organizing a powerful government with traditional party support, Sánchez Bustamante brought into the government such leading civilian political figures as Tomás Manuel Elío, David Alvéstegui, Carlos Calvo and Rafael de Ugarte. The return of full-scale political activity on the part of the traditional parties was also encouraged, and almost immediately after the revolution, Saavedra, Montes, and Escalier returned to the country and began talks for a three-party unification electoral slate.[2] The idea of such an all-party candidate, or *candidatura única*, as it came to be called, had been first suggested by Escalier in January. When Siles had rejected it, it had been taken up by Saavedra, who had suggested to the Genuino Oruro convention in February that such a unity slate be organized with just the three opposition parties—his own, the Genuinos, and the Liberals.[3] With the prorogation problem, the whole idea had been dropped, but given the unity of opposition in the overthrow of Siles, it was immediately taken up again under the new government.

Thus, after long negotiations between the three parties and the government,[4] a slate was finally agreed upon, which to a marked degree reflected the current power position of the three parties with the new government. Salamanca received the presidential nomination, Montes the first vice-presidency, and the rather unwanted Bautista Saavedra was given the second vice-presidency position.[5] Though supporting a common presidential slate, all three parties agreed to run their own separate lists of candidates for congress.[6]

Saavedra. However in 1923 the Uncía mining massacre occurred under his orders. A strong saavedrista, he had been exiled by Siles and with the July revolution of 1930 he returned to the country, strongly supported by the junior officers. Ricardo M. Sétaro, *Secretos de Estado Mayor* (Buenos Aires: Editorial Claridad, 1936), pp. 29–33.

[1] Díaz Machicao, *Siles*, pp. 139–42.

[2] *El Diario*, 9 August 1930, p. 7. On 10 August the government formally decreed presidential and congressional elections for January 1931. *El Diario*, 10 August 1930, p. 5.

[3] *El Diario*, 3 August 1930, p. 4.

[4] See, e.g., *El Diario*, 17 August 1930, p. 4, and 19 August 1930, p. 6.

[5] *El Diario*, 22 August 1930, p. 1.   [6] *El Diario*, 14 October 1930, p. 6.

The presidential formula seemed to indicate that all three parties recognized the supremacy of the Genuinos, but the freedom of action in the congressional elections gave each of them the opportunity to test their actual political strength, and this the Liberals exploited to the full. Meanwhile, both Liberals and Genuinos spared no love for the saavedristas, and in December the two parties proceeded to dump their unwelcome companions. On the first of the month, Ismael Montes renounced his vice-presidency and Saavedra was forced to follow suit since the formula pact was thus broken. On the next day the Genuinos and Liberals announced a new formula of Salamanca with José Luis Tejada Sorzano—dropping the second vice-presidency post altogether.[1]

The junta, under Sánchez Bustamante's direction, benevolently supervised the development of a unitary presidential slate for the traditional parties, and attempted to carry out a general liberal reform of the constitution. Responding to some of the more basic political proposals of the past fifty years, Sánchez Bustamante offered amendments to the 1880 charter limiting the state of siege, adopting the right of habeas corpus, and prohibiting the immediate re-election of a president. The government publicly proposed these constitutional amendments in September 1930 and declared that in the January presidential elections these amendments would be voted on in a popular referendum—a procedure never before attempted in Bolivia. Sánchez Bustamante also rewarded the university students for their role in the 1930 revolution by proposing a plan for university autonomy, which would give economic and political independence to the universities, and the right of the faculty and students to elect their own rectors.

That these progressive reforms were the work of Sánchez Bustamante alone is clear from the indifference or outright hostility with which Salamanca, the Genuinos, and some Liberals greeted them. Salamanca in November proposed a counter-set of constitutional amendments, while Montes denied the very validity of the whole procedure. Nevertheless Blanco Galindo,

[1] *El Diario*, 2 December 1930, p. 6; 3 December 1930, p. 7, and 4 December 1930, p. 7.

despite this opposition, stood behind his chief adviser and placed the constitutional amendments on the ballot.[1]

In addition to these political and educational reforms, the junta also attempted to come to grips with the ever-worsening economic situation. To begin with it set up a National Economic Council in June to oversee the Bolivian economy and offer some means of control and planning.[2] It then proposed in September to make this *Consejo de Economía Nacional* a permanent government body through the formal device of a constitutional amendment, providing that the council would supervise government loans and contracts, and advise on all social and economic legislation.[3]

More immediately, the government established a major public works programme in the mining centre of Oruro in August to handle the increasing number of unemployed miners.[4] But these half-hearted measures had little effect as the price of tin declined by 44 per cent from June 1929 to June 1930. In July, Edmundo Vásquez announced that 'the present intense malfunctioning of the national economy has no parallel in any other crises ever suffered by the nation'.[5]

The complete dependence of the Bolivian economy on the tin industry was now recognized by all. As prices continued to decline, in the worst depression the industry had ever experienced, the Bolivian government began to express official and serious concern over the effect of the breakdown of the industry on the internal economy. In October 1930 the comptroller-general

---

[1] Díaz Machicao, *Siles*, pp. 154–9; Trigo, *Las constituciones de Bolivia*, pp. 124–8.
[2] *El Diario*, 9 July 1930, p. 7.
[3] Trigo, *Las constituciones de Bolivia*, p. 125.
[4] *El Diario*, 9 August 1930, p. 7. But this programme had little impact, as the prefect of Oruro noted in September, since workers were only being paid in food for themselves. The prefect also noted growing worker agitation demanding a moratorium on rents, provisions for food plantings for workers, a major public works programme and the end to identity cards and registration fees. *El Diario*, 12 September 1930, p. 9.
[5] *El Diario*, 22 July 1930, p. 4; also Edmundo Vásquez, *La economía y las finanzas de Bolivia (Documentos y opiniones emitidas sobre problemas emergentes de la crisis 1929–1930)* (La Paz: Imprenta 'Atenea', 1931), p. 4. Vásquez noted in this memorandum presented to the new *Consejo de Economía Nacional* that his Permanent Fiscal Commission as early as May indicated to the government the need for wholesale firing of government employees because of the continued decline in government revenues. *Ibid.* p. 5.

announced that Bolivia's total debt (external, internal, and float-
ing) had reached the extraordinary figure of Bs. 207,752,064, and
warned that the economy as well as government finances would
suffer irreparable losses if the tin industry should be forced to
close down, estimating that the tin-mining companies invested
close to Bs. 62 million annually in the nation in the form of
salaries, taxes, purchases, etc.[1]

But although the junta government attempted to control the
economic situation, its measures proved of little use in the crisis.
This was the major issue of the late twenties and early thirties,
but the resolution of Bolivia's economic problem lay more with
international powers than within her own means of control, and
on the international scene, the world's producers still lacked any
effective policy to deal with the crisis.

Four states produced over 80 per cent of the world's tin:
British Malaya, Bolivia, the Netherlands East Indies, and Nigeria.
Of these four states, Bolivia was by far the highest-cost producer,
and was therefore the first to feel the effects of declining prices.
The Far Eastern producers, despite the low prices, were still able
to produce tin profitably because of their low production costs
and exceedingly rich ores. It was at the insistence of Patiño and the
other Bolivian tin interests that the first efforts were made in the
direction of international control over production and prices by
the producing companies.

While tin prices started their disastrous decline only in 1929,
as early as 1927 producers began to worry about the surplus of
production over consumption and the slowly but dangerously
rising stocks. By 1929, both indices—declining prices and rising
stocks—began to assume menacing proportions and in June–
July 1929 a group of 300 tin company representatives (accounting
for 60 per cent of the industry) meeting in London, organized
on a private basis the voluntary Tin Producers Association. The
unquestioned leader of this whole movement was Simón I.
Patiño, and the objective of the association was voluntarily to
restrict production. The low-cost producers, however, refused

---

[1] *El Diario*, 28 October 1930, p. 6. It was estimated at mid-year that *c.* 57 per cent
of the estimated government income for 1930 would go towards servicing this
huge public debt. Vásquez, *La economía y las finanzas*, p. 17.

to cooperate, and by mid-1930 this voluntary scheme was considered to be a failure.[1] The Bolivian producers had more than willingly cooperated with the scheme. Aramayo began to cut production in late 1929 and the Patiño group followed suit in early 1930. But the TPA retrenchment quotas had been less than half met, and these measures had had no effect in pegging the declining prices.[2]

With free market conditions intolerable, and with voluntary restrictions impossible to achieve, the producers decided, in late 1930, on the drastic measure of outright government control over the whole scheme; since only three governments were really involved—Bolivia, the United Kingdom, and the Netherlands—it appeared as if this solution might be successful. In their desperation, the companies thus decided to turn over police powers to these governments to enforce production restrictions and determine quotas. This arrangement suddenly gave the Bolivian government a control over its chief industry which it had never before exercised, and it also brought about a more intimate and open involvement of the tin barons in the government.

Although there was no real difference of position or ideology between Hochschild, Aramayo, or Patiño, there was always a sharp but quiet struggle over the division of the production quota assigned to Bolivia under the new arrangements. As each producer could potentially double his production at any time,[3]

[1] *El Diario*, 6 July 1930, p. 4, discusses these international developments, while the failure of these early schemes was announced in *El Diario*, 15 October 1930, p. 4.
[2] For these early attempts at international control, see: K. E. Knorr, *Tin Under Control* (Stanford: Food Research Institute, Stanford University, 1945), pp. 92–8.
[3] Such is the estimate made by one of the leaders; see Mauricio Hochschild, 'El concepto de la crisis actual', *El Diario*, 6 April, 1930, p. 5.

Mauricio Hochschild was born in Europe in 1881 and studied mining and economics at Freiburg. In the early 1920s he set up in Bolivia as a metal trader in competition with W. R. Grace and Co., and several English and German firms. However, Hochschild had an extraordinary creative ability for the reorganization of old companies and unworked mines. With backing from European capital, he became a major factor in the actual mining of tin and a host of other metals. His greatest success was the Compañía Minera Unificada del Cerro de Potosí, which took over the extensive holdings of the Soux Company and numerous smaller mining outfits and organized them in the late 1920s into a major modern aggregate. Compañía Unificada was his most important creation; however, he also branched out into the mining of silver and a host of other metals and into tin operations in several other areas. By the each was willing to involve himself in the government—which determined the individual company quotas—to gain an added percentage for himself. This was not really a crucial struggle, since the two smaller producers usually recognized the dominant position of Patiño both in the industry and in the government, but there were times in the future when, for an important few extra percentiles, this dominance was successfully if temporarily challenged in both areas.

Throughout the latter part of 1930 secret negotations were taking place among the producers and between them and their respective governments. At the end of the year the TPA announced that the important private companies 'had reached the conclusion that it had become essential in the interest of the industry to enforce the present system of voluntary regulation by arrangements more comprehensive, and more binding and durable in scope'. In January 1931 the TPA stated that the production restriction plan had been approved by the three governments. In February the quota system was worked out for the International Tin Control Scheme, and on 1 March 1931, four days before Salamanca's inauguration, it went into effect.[1]

While these arrangements were able in later years to produce a marked change for the better in the world tin market, they had no immediate positive effect, and in fact the initial impact of the scheme was to worsen Bolivia's economic crisis by greatly restricting her national production.[2] Thus the economic situation was further aggravated by these international developments, and the pre-Chaco War governments were left to solve or at least ameliorate Bolivia's economic problems exclusively through their own resources.

1930s production from his tin mines was slightly ahead of Compagnie Aramayo de Mines en Bolivie, the two taking up *c*. 35 per cent of national production and Patiño averaging around 45 per cent. D. Ibañez C., *Historia mineral de Bolivia* (Antofagasta: Imprenta MacFarlane, 1943), pp. 230–4; Peñaloza, *Historia económica*, II, 319ff; *¿Quién es quién en Bolivia?* (Buenos Aires: Editorial Quién es quién en Bolivia, 1942), p. 120.

[1] The history of international tin negotiations is taken from Knorr, *Tin Under Control*, Chs. VI–IX.

[2] Thus, taking 1929—the best year in tin history—as a base, production was cut at first to 77·7 per cent, dropping to 56·2 per cent in January 1932, and in the ensuing months to 43·8 per cent in June 1932, and to 33·3 per cent in July of the same year. *Ibid.* p. 114.

To this deepening economic crisis, Daniel Salamanca, the undisputed president-to-be of Bolivia, offered only the most evasive and conservative answers. In an interview with *El Diario* in August 1930 he was asked if he would adopt strong measures to combat the economic difficulties and he answered: 'I think that the policy of the coming government should be to limit itself to the strictest economy, without deviating even a point from the reasonable and prudent standard which the situation of the public treasury indicates'. As for public works projects, he indicated he would only carry out such programmes as were within the fiscal resources of the state to handle.[1] Meanwhile, Escalier, the official party chief, stated that the Genuino programme 'is simple: honesty, economy, good administration, tranquil homes, respect for all the rights and duties of citizens, and frankness and loyalty with our friends in international relations'.[2]

The failure of this vapid programme to appeal to the nation in a time of crisis was certainly reflected in the elections of January 1931, for the Genuino party was badly defeated at the polls. The quieter but more efficient Liberals won a fantastic landslide victory which gave them absolute control over congress, even if all the other parties were to unite against them![3]

Thus while Salamanca was now given the presidency because of his unopposed candidacy, his party and apparently the ideas he and they represented were thoroughly defeated by the limited national electorate. This signal defeat was a reflection of the growing discontent with the more conservative policies of the old leader, and showed a restlessness on the part of both older and newer political elements in the face of the severe economic depression on the one hand and the rise of a new political consciousness on the other. This latter development was the result of an increasing awareness among the youth, and the intellectual and moderate reform elements which had developed in the Siles and Sánchez Bustamante periods and within the important university reform movement.

[1] *El Diario*, 23 August 1930, p. 7.   [2] *El Diario*, 27 August 1930, p. 7.
[3] *El Diario*, 25 February 1931, p. 6. In the lower house the Liberals finally obtained 38 seats; the Genuinos, 19; the saavedrista Republicans, 5; 5 Independents and 1 Radical (Franz Tamayo) were also returned. In the senate the Liberals obtained 8 seats, the Genuinos 7, and the saavedristas 1.

These newer elements also began more consciously to oppose the traditional parties and to add to the Bolivian political spectrum their own distinct radical views. The far left in these pre-war years, however, was still a very small and highly fragmented movement, and was far behind the major radical movements in the more advanced states of Latin America in terms of organization. In terms of ideology, though, the Bolivian radical moment in the late 1920s and early 1930s finally began to assume a decided revolutionary and advanced reformist tone more in harmony with leading radical elements elsewhere in the hemisphere. It also began for the first time to bring together the fringe of middle-class radical intellectuals and university students with some elements of the labour movement.

The new political awareness of the labour movement was expressed in January 1929, just before the crisis, when the national labour federation had decided at a general labour conference to commit the Bolivian workers' movement to an international organization. The dominance of the extreme leftist worker elements in the local labour federations in all the key cities is indicated by the conferences' expression of preference for joining the *Confederación Sindical Latino Américana* (CSL), a militant leftist Latin American confederation which was then being organized in Montevideo. This decision of the conference was soon approved by all the local FOTs not present at the convention.[1]

As could be expected, the anarchists, who drew their strength largely from the La Paz *Federación Obrera Local* and similar FOLs in some of the other cities, vigorously denounced this meeting and denied the right of their opponents to bring the Bolivian worker movement into the CSL.[2] The battle between these two major divisions within the labour movement became an open conflict at the Fourth National Workers' Congress, which met in Oruro in the tense days just before the fall of Siles in early 1930. The general political situation was also reflected in this congress and the battles of the anarchists, communists and socialists brought only sterile debates and no basic agreement.[3]

---

[1] Barcelli, *Medio siglo de luchas sindicales*, pp. 119–20.
[2] *El Diario*, 10 February 1929, p. 7.
[3] Barcelli, *Medio siglo de luchas sindicales*, pp. 120–1.

But the anarchists did succeed in bringing enough power to bear to prevent the national confederation from formally taking membership in the CSL, despite previous commitments and the delegates' attendance at their international meetings.[1]

The great debate over international affiliation, however, finally clarified the labels of several of the major union leaders, most of whom had been of a rather mixed ideological background. Starting with Dick Ampuero in the early 1920s an increasing number of labour leaders had begun to choose sides in the controversy over international affiliations, and those who supported the so-called Red (or Third) International began to consider themselves communists. Although many of these 'communists' gained important influence in the labour movement, an official Communist party was never successfully established by these men before the Chaco War. In 1928 the Montevideo meeting of the Communist parties of Latin America supposedly requested the Bolivian communists to set up a party. Although an organization was apparently established that year, it functioned only on the smallest scale, and should more accurately be considered as a political cell rather than as an organized party. Working clandestinely, it had little effect, and was practically unknown outside a small group of intellectuals; the group collapsed in the repressive political atmosphere of the Salamanca era.[2] This does not mean that there was not a strong pro-Russian communist sympathy within the intellectual and labour elements, but rather that this was expressed more in vague personal terms of preference with little reference to national problems or formal party organization.[3]

[1] Robert J. Alexander, *Communism in Latin America* (New Brunswick: Rutgers University Press, 1957), p. 214.
[2] Guillermo Lora, *José Aguirre Gainsborg, fundador del POR* (La Paz: Ediciones 'Masas'), 1960, pp. 14, 19–20. Alexander, *Communism in Latin America*, p. 213, states that by 1926 there were small groups of communists active in La Paz, Cochabamba, and a few other cities, but seems to feel that they never formed such an official Communist party as Lora implies.
[3] The problem of defining who is or is not a communist in the period before the official organization of the Bolivian Partido Communista (PCB) in 1949–50 is an extremely difficult one, especially as many persons proved to be extremely sympathetic to the communist position, but defined their sympathy in their own national ways and when forced to be counted often refused to join the communist organization *per se*. Also there was a whole range of leftists from fellow-traveller-type socialists, through to anarchists and Trotskyites, with each calling

The almost moribund radical political movement of the left was revived in 1930, when a new political party grew out of the short-lived Partido Laborista. Known as the Partido Socialista, this new party was founded in December 1930 at the local head-quarters of the Federación de Artes Gráficos. It was made up almost entirely of old laboristas but also included several new leftist intellectuals. Thus Enrique G. Loza, Moisés Álvarez, and Ezequiel Salvatierra, the leaders of the La Paz FOT, and the most politically conscious labour leaders in the movement, who one way or another had been associated with those left political parties since their beginnings in 1920, were members of the new organization, along with such youthful leftist intellectuals as Alberto Mendoza López and Felix Eguino Zaballa. At its first meetings, the delegates agreed to make a new call 'to all the elements representative of the left sector in order to form a united front' and to invite both the communists affiliated with the Third International and the anarchists to join the new party. But this attempt at a united front was a failure, for, as Salvatierra charged,

the elements of the extreme communist left adopted a tactic of dis-association following the plans which were sent to them from Monte-video, [thus his group] resolved to organize on their own the Partido Socialista with the groups and elements of socialist tendency. They also agreed to postpone meetings whose purpose was to organize a united front until the Partido Socialista was reorganized on the base of its own dispersed elements among the [old] Partido Socialista, Partido Laborista, the Socialist intellectual sector and other groups of revolu-tionary or independent Socialists.[1]

The reference to revolutionary socialists was to the small but intellectually advanced group which in 1929 had organized the

the other Stalinists, etc. Many individuals were themselves rather confused about their own ideology, mixing up tenets from all the different points of view to form their own. Therefore I have been forced to fall back on such general terms as 'radical' or 'extreme' leftists to define much of this movement. I use these terms also to distinguish the groups who called for basic socio-economic change of a far-reaching revolutionary nature, from later socialists and leftist groups who were more vague in their ideological orientation and less committed to violent change—these I have generally denominated as 'moderate' leftists.

[1] Lora, 'Historia del movimiento obrero', pp. 9–10; Alberto Mendoza López, *La soberanía de Bolivia estrangulada* (La Paz: Editorial Trabajo, 1942), pp. 44–5.

Partido Socialista Revolucionario. It was a party of clandestinely organized intellectuals with very little power, as was the case with all the leftist political parties at this time, but it uniquely advocated violent overthrow of the bourgeois government. The party in its manifesto attacked Siles for mortgaging the nation to foreign bankers and for opposing the workers and students. It charged that 'at the service of a dozen millionaires he has converted Bolivia into a fief, where only a privileged class enjoys the natural wealth of the country and the rest obey, subject to the most irritating and abject slavery'. It called for a rebellion of workers, soldiers, and peasants, and in much the same harsh terms used by Roberto Hinojosa the next year, proclaimed that the soldiers should wipe out their officers, the workers destroy the mine operators, and the Indians drench the soil with the blood of their *patrones*. The PSR called for abolishment of the latifundios and nationalization of the mines and attacked all the traditional political parties, including the Nationalists, claiming that they were tools of the imperialist powers which controlled Bolivia. Probably the most original part of its programme was the plan to organize a post-revolutionary peasant-worker government to take over the nation, and its immediate call for the initiation of guerrilla warfare. Unlike most of the far left, including the Partido Laborista, which had attacked Paraguay for military aggression in 1928, the PSR had the courage to maintain a strong pacifist anti-war position. Its 1929 manifesto declared that:

the classic procedure of tottering dictatorships is to provoke armed conflicts in order to obtain sympathy in the hour of danger. . . The Bolivians who speak of patriotism, should know that their country is conquered by foreign capital and in its own land the bourgeois government condemns them to die of hunger.[1]

The only other pre-Chaco War leftist group of any consequence was the important Grupo Tupac Amaru, which had been formed by left-wing intellectuals exiled by Siles in 1927. More than any other pre-war group, Tupac Amaru had an intimate relationship with all the leftist intellectual currents of its day, and it eventually emerged as the most important link between the pre-war

[1] Lora, 'Historia del movimiento obrero', appendix to Partido Socialista chapter consisting of four pages.

radical left in Bolivia and the post-war groups. It also served in the harsh years of the early 1930s as a major rallying group, then located in Argentina, for all the Bolivian radical left, maintaining an active revolutionary propaganda role against Salamanca and later against the Chaco War.[1]

Apart from the propaganda effect of these revolutionary leftists and worker parties, which by and large had little immediate impact on the pre-war student and intellectual classes, there was a major importation beginning in 1930 of cheap Spanish translations, produced in Latin America, of the classic Marxist authors, which did have a major impact on these classes. While Ingenieros, Mariátegui, and Haya de la Torre were much read and appreciated,

the diffusion of theoretical Marxism was produced in its most widespread and decisive form with the reading of the works of European authors, principally Russian, which inundated the Bolivian bookstores like all those of the continent after 1930, thus resulting in the same phenomenon which had occurred with positivism at the beginning of the century. The works of Lenin, Bukarin, Plejanov, etc., circulated everywhere in popular editions made in Argentina and Chile, receiving the same response as those of Comte, Renan, Spencer, etc. forty years before.[2]

Bolivia's major intellectual historian, Guillermo Francovich, also sees a marked difference between this first pre-war generation of intellectuals influenced by Marxism and the post-war use of this same philosophy:

In the history of Bolivian Marxism we encounter two clearly defined stages, the speculative stage, and the political stage. During the first, Marxism is a sociological and historical doctrine, the 'historic materialism', which is studied in the universities, is discussed in the academies and is used to explain the present and past phenomena of the country. In the second stage, Marxism is converted into an active social force which influences the organization of political groups, and acquires the outlines of an unquestioned ideology, taking dogmatic possession of the thought of the new [post-war] generations.[3]

[1] Grupo Tupac Amaru, *Manifiesto, La victoria o la muerte (al pueblo boliviano: soldados, estudiantes, obreros)* (n.p., [1934?]), pp. 2, 7; Alexander, *Communism in Latin America*, p. 214.

[2] Francovich, *El pensamiento boliviano en el siglo xx*, pp. 104–5.   [3] *Ibid.* p. 103.

In short the intellectual climate of the 1930s was pervaded by the basic critical assumptions of classic Marxist thought, which was being applied to the Bolivian situation in much the same way as in the 1900s the new Comtian and Spencerian positivist thinking had led to a new re-evaluation of Bolivian institutions and history. This is not to say that the pre-war generation was either revolutionary or against the traditional government or party, but merely to note that their frame of reference was new. Under the impact of a major disaster this frame of reference proved an important source of new conceptualizations about Bolivia, and these new views found common ground with the pre-war programme and ideologies of the tiny fringe of communists, socialists, Indianists, and anarchists, programmes which before 1932 had little impact on the general intellectual and political climate of their day.

It was thus a newly educated and awakened national political consciousness which set the tone of political thought on the eve of the new constitutional government. Aided by the liberalizing junta government, and deeply concerned over the apparent failure of classic *laissez faire* capitalism to come to terms with the world-wide collapse of national economies, the country waited for the accession to the presidency of Daniel Salamanca with great expectation and hope.

For the great 'hombre símbolo', or symbolic man as he was called, the assumption of the presidency in February 1931 represented the culmination of over thirty years of active political life and two previous attempts at election to the office. The last of the traditional caudillo politicians of the beginning of the century, and the final product of fifty years of Bolivian political development, Daniel Salamanca was an imposing and dominant figure who left a deep imprint on Bolivian history.

Salamanca was born in Cochabamba in 1868 and came of a long line of landholding families of that rich agricultural valley. He had inherited considerable estates on the death of his father. A favoured, though extremely sickly youth, he had dedicated his childhood and early manhood to study, and had been educated at the public schools and the local university. Since there was at the time only one faculty at the Universidad de San Simón

(Cochabamba), he studied law, which suited his intellect. But since he had independent means he had never had to practise his profession. Afflicted throughout his life by extremely severe stomach disorders, he was constantly in pain and forced to eat the most rudimentary of foods. As a result he became an introvert, and he never made intimate friends, an unusual trait for a Bolivian. Because of his wealth and social position, however, it was inevitable that he should be drawn into political life, at least at the local level. While Salamanca's father had maintained a strictly apolitical attitude all his life, his son had been thoroughly imbued with the liberalism and positivism of his day at the university. Drawn reluctantly at first into politics, he soon became obsessed with it, although continuing to deny the fact all his life. But he was always something of an idealist and maverick, and party discipline, even of the party of his own making, weighed heavily upon him. He preferred to follow his own dictates.

Though neutral in the federal revolution and also an admirer of Mariano Baptista, he was asked by Pando to run for the first Liberal congress of 1899. Here Salamanca found his true role in life. Well educated, with a disciplined, logical mind, he proved to be the greatest orator of his day. To his contemporaries, in the twenty years he actively participated in congressional life (1900–20) he could only be compared in Bolivian parliamentary history to his fellow Cochabambino and friend Mariano Baptista. It was this skill, rather than his own personality, which gave Salamanca his political importance. Because of his extreme reserve and introversion, he was incapable of emotionally binding people to him. His oratory, however, marked him as unique among his fellow congressmen and on issue after issue his word came to be accepted and followed.

Of completely opposite personality to the active and charismatic Montes, it was inevitable that the two men would clash, especially as Montes had little respect for congressional authority. Thus throughout the first Montes administration, when there was no organized political opposition, Salamanca became the chief spokesman of those hostile to the régime, and he led the congressional attacks on the Speyer contract, and the treaty of peace with Chile. It was thus natural that when a formal opposition party was being created specifically to fight Montes, its organizers turned to Salamanca to lead it.

Salamanca made an ideal figurehead whose fiery oratory and debating skill proved a major asset to the fledgling party, but he was incapable of effective organizational leadership. In fact it was men like Saavedra who carried out the daily tasks which welded a political organization together, while Salamanca himself became ever more of a symbolic figure. Even party discipline was too difficult for him, and after 1914 his rather harsh moral code made him consistently oppose his fellow party members, and within party circles he could count on only a very limited following of loyal supporters. But Salamanca was the best known opposition figure on the political scene, and the new party found it virtually impossible to gain strength without his support in the early years. Nevertheless by the late 1910s his consistent rigidity and aloofness, coupled with the growing fame of other Republican leaders, caused Salamanca to lose power very rapidly and even to retire from the political scene altogether in the last months before the 1920 revolution. The result was that he had little control over the revolution and eventually refused to accept its legitimacy.

In the splintering of the party in 1920–1, Salamanca's personal antipathy toward Saavedra played a crucial role, and his own action became heavily influenced not by his classic moral code, for which he was so famous, but by personal jealousy and anger. Again forced into retirement by the Saavedra and Siles governments, he also allowed his Genuino party to be led in practical affairs by others, and it was these men who plotted and revolted and carried out the grimy practical everyday affairs, which Salamanca refused to do. Benefiting from their activity, unlike the other leading politicians of his day, he was never imprisoned, exiled or in any way molested by an opposition government at any time during his political career. Because he was never called upon personally to sacrifice himself for his parties, Salamanca never felt great loyalty to any of them.

In the decade of the 1920s Salamanca had continued to live on his estates at Cochabamba, issuing pronouncements from time to time against the government, and continually breaking up compromise negotiations with his opponents. Also, he began to develop a more rabid form of nationalism than ever before in his political career, and came out as the leading *guerrista* in the Paraguyan Chaco dispute. 'We must stand firm in the Chaco' was his famous phrase, with which he castigated the Siles government for cowardice and inaction, thus rallying to his banner the extreme nationalists who were calling for full-scale war to preserve national honour.[1]

To find a consistent ideology and programme which Salamanca believed in all his political career is difficult. Like every major political figure of his day, his frame of reference was classic nineteenth-century liberalism, with a strong sense of limited government, though this was primarily an expression used by all the 'out' politicians of the day. His more positive positions included support for parliamentary supremacy, strong local government and decentralized executive power, and finally the sovereignty of the ballot. He professed, in his long congressional career, belief in liberty of the press, speech and assembly, and the fact that he was out of office for thirty years seemed to add weight and consistency to his firm moral stance on these issues. However when in office he violated all of these principles, and often with a ruthlessness that not even his predecessors could match. To seek his ideological principles in these florid pronouncements for liberal-democratic government is to lose oneself in a maze of fine oratory and little reality.

Yet to call him a dogmatic tool of the mining superstate, or the defender of the landholding classes, as later Bolivian politicians have done, is to go too far to the other extreme. Certainly he was a product of his age and class, and his landholdings did not endear him to radicals of any description. But he was surprisingly nationalistic and opposed the mining industry and especially Patiño. Throughout the 1920s and 1930s he advocated the encouragement by the government of a national capitalist class and defended national rights against the foreign concessionaires. He was also, until the late 1920s, rather unemotional and rational in his approach to foreign affairs, and to most domestic issues. In reality, despite popular conceptions of him as a cold puritanical

---

[1] This analysis of Daniel Salamanca is taken from the excellent three-volume biography of him by David Alvéstegui.

dogmatist, he was surprisingly flexible and pragmatic on some issues and strongly dominated by his emotions on others. It is in his emotional makeup, more than in defined ideology or defence of class interests that the true stimuli for his actions in the years of his presidential rule can be discerned.

Salamanca began his presidential term in an atmosphere of political calm and a general feeling of accomplishment despite the tense economic situation. This was due to the surprisingly productive programme of action carried through by Daniel Sánchez Bustamante in his eight months of government, a fact which the national press and public praised when the junta militar quietly relinquished office in early 1931: but the political calm and party peace quickly dissipated in the first days of the new régime. For Salamanca adopted from the very beginning a partisan and emotional tone which splintered the political harmony and created a tense political situation to match the economic crises.

Salamanca made his first major decision on 3 March, when he announced that his new cabinet would be exclusively dominated by Genuino party stalwarts.[1] On the 6th he addressed the newly elected Liberal-dominated congress and offered a programme of action for the new administration. By and large the pre-election conservative tone was adopted, with Salamanca promising strict constitutionality and legality in government, and moderation in economic affairs, though he did propose to concentrate on the serious economic problems of the day.[2] But he sounded a new and very discordant note when he referred to what he called the 'social' crisis which was facing the nation. This crisis, he charged, was being caused by:

foreign communist propaganda, which has considerably increased its activity in Bolivia. The danger of this propaganda is proportional to the poverty and ignorance of a country. For a government, the difficulty of meeting this threat is a legal problem of a new order, a problem which not long ago could be considered as non-existent. This propaganda takes advantage of all the liberties and all the rights established by the

---

[1] Porfirio Díaz Machicao, *Historia de Bolivia, Salamanca, La Guerra del Chaco, Tejada Sorzano, 1931–1936* (La Paz: Gisbert y Cía., 1955), pp. 18–19. Hereafter cited as *La Guerra del Chaco*. [2] *La Razón*, 7 March 1931, p. 4.

constitution, not only to overthrow that same constitution with all its liberties and rights but to destroy the existent social order. The insufficiency of the usual constitutions to control this danger seems obvious to me, and the necessity of a new law of social defence is absolutely clear ... I believe that the government lacks legal measures sufficient to defend society against this danger, and I will make a vigorous effort to fill this gap.[1]

Compared to the rest of his programme this was extremely forceful and dramatic language that clearly indicated the strong anti-labour and anti-radical nature of the new government. This attitude marked it off sharply from its two predecessors. Along with the anti-labour stand, the new government in the first months in office carried out severe retrenchments in government spending and operations as it reacted to the economic crises with a classic *laissez faire* approach.

The concentration on the 'communist menace' was new in Bolivia, but quite an old obsession with Salamanca. As early as 1924 in a letter written to Alcides Argüedas in Paris he analysed the essence of the post-war political problem of France and Europe as basically the struggle of civilization against 'barbarian communism', and viewed socialism as but a tool of this black anti-civilization force![2] This sentiment, long a private one of Salamanca's, now received open public expression in his inaugural address, and at first the conservative press reacted to it mildly, but also showed some unease over the specific legislation that Salamanca might call for. But having expressed his fears of the communist danger openly, Salamanca offered at first no concrete legislation to deal with the problem. Rather, in the following months, he carried through decidedly reactionary and anti-organized labour policies without resorting to official legislation.

His first opportunity to strike at organized labour came in early April, when the National Postal, Telegraph and Telegraphic Radio Union went on strike. Founded in 1920, this union of government employees had previously received official recognition both by the Saavedra government and most recently by

---

[1] *El Diario*, 15 March 1931, p. 4.
[2] Letter quoted in Alvéstegui, *Salamanca*, II, 88.

the junta militar. Salamanca, however, refused to recognize the union and union leaders were summarily dismissed from their jobs.[1] Salamanca reacted to the strike by issuing a decree giving the strikers twenty-four hours to return to their work, and had troops occupy all the telegraphic and local post offices of the nation.[2] The union, an affiliate of the Federación Obrera del Trabajo of La Paz, asked the latter organization to intervene in its behalf with the government.[3] But the new government not only declared the entire strike to be illegal in the first place, it even refused to negotiate with the FOT.[4] The FOT thereupon called for a general strike of all its members against the government. But in this showdown, Salamanca applied strong pressure, and in the face of this strong government stand only a few of the affiliated FOT unions responded to the call.[5] After the successful suppression of the general strike, the Telegraphic and Postal Union strike collapsed,[6] and six key union leaders were imprisoned and the union destroyed.[7] This was a signal defeat for Bolivian labour and caused many unions to react by splitting into hostile factions.

Although this forceful anti-labour stand may have temporarily relieved the growing agitation over economic issues, it in no way solved the economic crisis. After many cuts in the salaries of government employees during the early months of the year, the government in desperation at the growing budget deficit and declining revenues finally issued a dramatic but ill-conceived decree on 23 July 1931, providing open-ended discounts of salaries with promissory notes being given in place of cash. The government decreed that employees would be paid only from funds that had actually come in in the previous month, and this was in addition to the flat 15 per cent reduction which had previously been enacted by congress.[8] Even the allied Liberal party bitterly attacked this reduction as ridiculous and a threat to the very economic survival of government employees, let alone of government services.[9] A few days later the government took a

---

[1] *El Diario*, 11 April 1931, p. 7.   [2] *La Razón*, 11 April 1931, p. 13.
[3] *El Diario*, 15 April 1931, p. 6.   [4] *El Diario*, 17 April 1931, p. 7.
[5] *El Diario*, 18 April 1931, p. 7.   [6] *La Razón*, 21 April 1931.
[7] *El Diario*, 14 August 1931, p. 7.   [8] *El Diario*, 24 July 1931, p. 7.
[9] *El Diario*, 25 July 1931, pp. 6, 7.

far more critical step by announcing the defaulting on Bolivia's external debt.[1]

Another result of this economic crisis was a sharp increase in political tension caused by the growing conflict between Liberals and Genuino Republicans over government economic policies. The two parties initially had divided over the issue of the constitutional referendum. In May the Genuinos even went so far in their hostility to these reformist proposals as to petition congress, with presidential backing, to abolish them. The Liberal party, however, stood firmly behind the junta militar's reforms and by a landslide vote defeated this Salamanca-Genuino move.[2] The Liberals rather crudely laid down their position to Salamanca at the end of that month, when rumours developed of a possible saavedrista-Genuino compromise and unification plan. The Party officially reminded Salamanca that 'if the Liberals had supported their own candidate, the president [i.e. Salamanca] would not have obtained the absolute majority required, to judge by the composition of the parliament which contains a Liberal majority'.[3] The Liberals in congress also heavily stressed the anti-clerical issue and much to the discomfort of the Salamanca government advocated the nationalization of the clergy, the separation of church and state, and freedom of religion.[4] But they were much more conservative on economic issues, especially as the crisis deepened in the latter half of the year and the government in its desperation began to turn toward radical inflationary solutions.

Despite his extreme retrenchment in normal government services, Salamanca proposed the most ambitious and expensive scheme for military penetration of the Chaco ever envisioned by a Bolivian president. On 2 May 1931, on the initiative of Salamanca and based on his own ideas, the *Estado Mayor General* (general staff) presented a major plan for the penetration, exploration and military occupation of the Chaco.[5] This was a bold plan requiring

---

[1] *El Diario*, 25 July, 1931, p. 6.　　　[2] *El Diario*, 21 May 1931, p. 6.
[3] *El Diario*, 23 May 1931, p. 6.　　　[4] *El Diario*, 27 March 1931, p. 6.
[5] Eduardo Arze Quiroga (ed.), *Documentos para una historia de la guerra del Chaco, seleccionados del archivo de Daniel Salamanca* (3 vols.; La Paz: Editorial Don Bosco, 1951–60), I, 83–96. (The Estado Mayor General hereafter will be cited in its commonly accepted abbreviation, EMG.)

considerable sums of money and major military preparations, at a time when the rest of the government was restricted to the most basic economies and severe limitations of essential civilian services. But Salamanca had been firmly committed to a very rigid position on the Chaco since the late 1920s, and once in office he proposed to counteract what he considered to be the passive policies of his predecessors. Because large areas of the Chaco were still unexplored and unoccupied by either side, this new, more aggressive, stance proposed for the Bolivian forces meant a major shift from a largely defensive to a largely offensive position. Increasingly Salamanca began to turn toward the Chaco problem, which he saw as easily soluble with clear moral implications, while the economic situation became ever more complex and seemingly insoluble.

In line with this more aggressive attitude, Salamanca adopted a more vigorous tone in international relations. On 1 July 1931, following one of the innumerable and inevitable border clashes between Paraguayan and Bolivian patrols, and consequent public attacks by the Paraguyan minister to Washington on these latest incidents, Salamanca officially broke diplomatic relations with Paraguay and recalled Bolivia's minister.[1] According to one of Bolivia's leading diplomats, Luis Fernando Guachalla, Salamanca's action was excessive and was an unnecessarily aggressive diplomatic move.[2]

On 8 August Salamanca went before congress to present a State of the Union message. In this important address, he blamed world economic conditions outside Bolivian control for the present internal economic crisis. He noted that although he had fully supported all efforts of the tin producers to raise prices, there had been as yet no positive results. Meanwhile, public revenue in the first half of the year had been well below estimated income, and the picture for the second half just beginning looked even worse. 'The most painful consequence of this decline,' stated Salamanca (a rather classically-minded economist) 'had been that of suspending the service of our public debt.' While many government agencies curtailed or completely eliminated most of

[1] Arze Quiroga, *Documentos*, I, pp. 57–73.
[2] Díaz Machicao, *La guerra del Chaco*, p. 56.

their services, he proudly noted that no economies had been made in the services of the army or the police! A hasty Bs. $3\frac{1}{2}$ million loan had been secured from the central bank and Patiño's Banco Mercantil, but even Salamanca was forced to admit that the situation would get worse before it got better.

The second semester presents an even darker and more threatening aspect than the first . . . Since there still has not been a favourable reaction in the price of tin, we will have to endure many more difficult and probably more arduous times than the past ones. We can do little or nothing to resolve this situation. Bolivia suffers, in a high degree, the consequences of a world crisis whose causes can never be removed by us.[1]

On the international issue he expressed a desire for negotiation with Paraguay and noted his own pacific intentions. 'Even a hasty glance at our economic situation', he noted, 'is enough to show that it would be madness on our part to provoke international disturbances of a bellicose nature.'[2] Salamanca also stressed his continued anxiety over communist propaganda and stated that under any threat of internal or external crisis he would deal very severely with this opposition. He also warned the workers not to petition and agitate for reforms or new rises in wages as the government did not look kindly on such 'threats'.[3]

In June, the vigorous Demetrio Canelas—editor of *La Patria* of Oruro and a long-time salamanquista—was brought into the cabinet as minister of finance. He broke with the conservative policy of the previous months, and pressed Salamanca on the need for more radical economic measures to combat the crisis. His primary proposal was for an inflationary monetary solution which was then being adopted by many of the countries of the world. From June through September, he advocated the inconvertibility of the national paper currency, increased money issues, and officially going off the gold standard, maintaining that credit had come to a complete standstill because of the hard money policy followed by the central bank—a Liberal party stronghold. Canelas, as was to be expected, immediately became deeply

---

[1] *El Diario*, 9 August 1931, p. 4.
[2] Díaz Machicao, *La guerra del Chaco*, p. 43.   [3] *Ibid.* p. 45.

embroiled with the Liberals over this issue, especially with Ismael Montes, who was at this time head of the central bank.[1]

By the beginning of September, Canelas was ready with his economic reform proposals and the government officially presented them to congress for their ratification.[2] The Liberals at first stood unalterably opposed to any changes in the amount of circulating currency, gold backing or convertibility of national currency.[3] But they were forced to give ground by the sheer havoc which occurred following the September announcement by Great Britain that she was going off the gold standard. Since Bolivia was firmly within the sterling bloc, Britain's move dealt a severe blow to her economy. On 23 September the government decreed the suspension of gold payments and the inconvertibility of paper money on a temporary basis, and authorized the central bank to issue emergency credit.[4] The Liberals and the central bank accepted the absolute necessity of these steps, despite their previous opposition. The bank and the government summoned a special advisory group of leading businessmen and miners to discuss the crisis and arrive at a new exchange rate.[5] Finally on 30 September, congress approved a thirty-day moratorium on the payment of obligations. Almost immediately, however, prices began to rise precipitously throughout the nation, and congressmen began demanding emergency price control measures by the government.[6] A day or two later the government officially asked congress for such powers, and on 2 October it granted the president police powers to control prices.[7] A temporary exchange rate was agreed upon on 3 October,[8] and on 13 October the

---

[1] Díaz Machicao, *La guerra del Chaco*, p. 36; Paz Estenssoro, 'El pensamiento económico en Bolivia', p. 64.

[2] *El Diario*, 17 September 1931, p. 6.

[3] See, for example, *El Diario*, 19 September 1931, p. 7.

[4] *El Diario*, 25 September 1931, p. 7. This emergency decree was continually renewed on a temporary basis until well into 1932. See for example, *El Diario*, 24 January 1932, p. 6.

[5] *El Diario*, 30 September 1931, p. 6. There was a continuous debate from September 1931 into 1932 between the *Cámara de Comercio*, representing the importers and national manufacturers and merchants, and the *Asociación de Industriales Mineros de Bolivia*, representing the miners (i.e. the principal exporters), over the exchange rates set up by the government, with the views of the latter group predominating after intense debates. See, for example, *El Diario*, 9 January 1932, pp. 9, 11. [6] *El Diario*, 30 September 1931, p. 3.

[7] *El Diario*, 3 October 1931, p. 4. [8] *El Diario*, 4 October 1931, p. 8.

government prohibited the exportation of gold and suspended all international obligations for a month.[1]

But the new crisis on the economic scene only temporarily assuaged the growing opposition of the Liberals to the Salamanca-Canelas economic reforms, and soon the Liberals began demanding an end to one-party Genuino government, and calling for a national coalition cabinet. Responding to a *La Razón* editorial defending Salamanca against criticism,[2] the Liberal organ *El Diario* grew irate at the sanctimonious and puritanical attitude adopted by the Genuinos and their leader. They again bluntly stated that if *they* had not agreed to the *fórmula única* of the January elections, Salamanca would never have become president. It was only to prevent social and political disorder, and to stimulate further the institutional reconstruction of the country, that the Liberals had decided to support such a unity candidate. Nevertheless, in his post-election response, Salamanca had not been equally liberal and had refused to form what *El Diario* called a 'national government'. Siles had also tried to rule with just such a small coterie of his followers, warned the editorial, and it implied that the fate which he experienced might befall Salamanca. It denied that Liberals had been hostile to Salamanca himself when they had prevented his abolition of the referendum in congress, but it noted that since July of the previous year Salamanca had known that he would come to the government, and yet even now he still had not presented congress with a major plan of action to confront the serious internal situation, and he still refused to broaden his cabinet.[3] The paper also noted that there were rumours that Salamanca wished to retire from office because of political opposition, 'Porfirian' tendencies in the army, and the communist menace. All such excuses for retirement, *El Diario* noted, were completely unjustified. While the paper admitted that Liberals had fought the Genuinos on many issues, it claimed that the party still supported the government. As for the other charges, it claimed that the army was fully under control and that Salamanca was distorting the communist issue out of all proportion.[4]

[1] *El Diario*, 14 October 1931, p. 7. [2] *La Razón*, 17 September 1931, p. 4.
[3] *El Diario*, 19 September 1931, p. 6. [4] *Ibid.* (separate article).

It is true that the Liberals had not gone into official opposition, but relations had definitely cooled between the two parties, and later in this same month of September, they quietly abstained from giving congressional support to the minister of government, Luis Calvo, when he was attacked by the saavedristas.[1] The Liberals were too powerful for Salamanca to antagonize, and in October he saw himself obliged to sign a special bi-party pact with them, in which the Liberals promised to support his economic and general legislative programme in congress in return for representation on the supreme court. The two parties also agreed to a unity slate in the December municipal elections.[2] Many Genuinos were hostile to this growing loss of their independent position, but had little choice as long as the Liberals so overwhelmingly dominated congress.[3] The saavedristas of course bitterly attacked this formal party pact which left its own members out in the political cold,[4] and both it and the reorganized Partido Nacionalista opposed the unity parties in the municipal elections and did fairly well.[5] Nor did the pact itself greatly change the tense relationship between the two major parties. The Liberals continued to show strong animosity to the minister of finance, and grew extremely wary of their erstwhile colleague's intentions, when in the last days of December 1931 Luis Calvo— Salamanca's minister of government—presented to congress a 'social defence' bill.

From the first day of his administration Salamanca had threatened to enact a *ley de defensa social* which would grant the president extraordinary repressive powers to deal with political opposition and the labour movement. The reaction to this proposal was intense. While congress discussed it behind closed doors, the FOT, Federación de Estudiantes, saavedristas, and all leftist groups in early January held such powerful mass demonstrations against the law that the government was forced to withdraw the whole project for fear of violent bloodshed and revolution.[6]

---

[1] Díaz Machicao, *La guerra del Chaco*, p. 48. [2] *El Diario*, 23 October 1931, p. 6.
[3] *El Diario*, 24 October 1931, p. 6. [4] *El Diario*, 11 November 1931, p. 10.
[5] *El Diario*, 8 December 1931, p. 11, and 15 December 1931, p. 5.
[6] Díaz Machicao, *La guerra del Chaco*, pp. 60–1; Barcelli, *Medio siglo de luchas sindicales*, p. 123.

But the government's withdrawal on one front in no way lessened the growing political tension. In January the tempo of the Liberal attacks on the government's economic policies increased to such an extent that Demetrio Canelas felt compelled to offer his resignation to Salamanca, on the grounds of congressional opposition. Salamanca, however, refused to accept the resignation and gave full assistance to his minister, threatening to resign if he did not get congressional support for his programmes. Toward the end of the month, in a special message to congress, he declared that government income for 1932 would barely reach Bs. 19 million, while estimated expenses were being conservatively calculated at Bs. 35 million. He therefore demanded the right to contract a new loan for Bs. 15 million and also to increase the amount of money in circulation.[1]

The Liberals bitterly fought these moves, attacking the government for incompetence and economic anarchy, and they charged Canelas with endangering the nation with a suicidal policy of soft money and inflation. They also attacked a proposed major programme of government public works as an extravagant affair.[2] In short they fought the entire Canelas economic programme as a direct threat to traditional sound money principles. On 19 February, *El Diario* finally demanded that an all-party cabinet of national concentration be constituted to resolve the economic crisis,[3] and the next day Salamanca accepted the resignation of Canelas and the rest of his cabinet. But Salamanca did not give in with good grace, and, in accepting the resignation of his ministers, he highly praised his friends and lamented that sordid political opposition had brought about their resignation.[4]

These half-hearted surrenders by the president did not satisfy the Liberals. On 23 February their party organ attacked the resignation acceptance decree,[5] and on 27 February the party, meeting under its leader José Luis Tejada Sorzano, officially announced by unanimous agreement that after having studied 'the economic policy adopted by the executive power, and not

---

[1] *El Diario*, 21 January 1932, p. 6, and 7 February 1932, p. 9.
[2] For these attacks see *El Diario*, 14 February 1932, p. 6; 16 February 1932, p. 6; 18 February 1932, and 19 February 1932, p. 6.
[3] *El Diario*, 19 February 1932, p. 6.
[4] *El Diario*, 21 February 1932, p. 6.   [5] *El Diario*, 23 February 1932, p. 6.

being in agreement with it, the Liberal party resolved to put an end to its political collaboration'.[1] *El Diario* explained what this resolution meant in no uncertain terms. It was an ultimatum to Salamanca to bring into his cabinet two or three Liberals, and to give up his attempt to increase the circulation of paper currency and his programme of definitive inconvertibility or else the Liberal party would formally go into opposition. According to *El Diario* the inconvertibility issue was the key to the Liberal party opposition, and they went so far as to remove José Tejada Sorzano from the presidency of the party because of his compromising stand on this issue. Tejada Sorzano was an economist in his own right and in sympathy with the Canelas reforms. He was replaced by Tomás Manuel Elío.[2]

On 1 March 1932, the haughty Salamanca finally admitted utter surrender to the far more powerful Liberal party. He asked Tejada Sorzano to negotiate with the Liberals to end the crisis,[3] and by 7 March agreement was reached to bring three Liberals into the cabinet, to reverse the economic policy of Canelas, and thenceforth to accept Liberal party leadership in all economic legislation.[4]

Along with his trying and ultimately disastrous battle with the Liberals, Salamanca also deliberately provoked increasing radical opposition from the labour and leftists movements by his clumsy and harsh acts of repression and his inability to alleviate the economic crisis. Although he had been able to inflict a severe defeat on the labour movement by his crushing of the Telegraphers and Postal strike, by the end of 1931 organized labour had recovered enough unity to be able to bring heavy popular pressure to bear on the government against the Ley de Defensa Social, and to secure its defeat. Union after union had recovered from the early 1931 disaster only to take a more aggressive stand and acquire more militant strength by the end of the year. A key example of this was the Printers' Union which had been divided over the failure of the general strike in April 1931. Out of the ruins of the old Federación de Artes Gráficos emerged the revolutionary *Sindicato Gráfico* under the leadership of the young

---

[1] *El Diario*, 28 February 1932, p. 7.   [2] *Ibid.*   [3] *El Diario*, 1 March 1932, p. 6.
[4] *El Diario*, 10 March 1932, p. 7; Díaz Machicao, *La guerra del Chaco*, pp. 65–7.

union secretary Waldo Álvarez. The new union issued a mani-festo which proclaimed its desire for radical syndicalism. 'Our syndicalism is revolutionary,' declared the manifesto, 'and springs from the principle of having two factors in production, capital and labour, which divide society into two parts: the exploiters and the exploited.' This generation of class conflict, claimed the union, required that the printers take up a position of active proletarian leadership.[1]

In August and September 1931, the first major anti-govern-ment workers' and intellectuals' demonstrations of a strong radical nature occurred in the two leading mining cities, Oruro and Potosí. In Oruro a crowd of over two thousand protesting miners was addressed by anarchist and communist speakers who called for social revolution and destruction of this anti-worker capitalist government.[2] In Potosí, communist intellectuals led workers in attacks against the installations of Hochschild's Compañía Unificada, and in the subsequent arrests, the police took into custody eleven supposed leaders of this demonstration, among them Víctor Sanjines, Alfredo Arratía, and Albelardo Villalpando.[3] The demonstrators had demanded employment either in the mines or in government public works projects for all unemployed workers, and had attacked the government in harsh terms, calling for a social revolution on communist principles.[4]

In October there was a battle between police and FOL workers in La Paz in which over fifty workers were arrested and about ten people were committed to hospital.[5] This demonstration par-ticularly agitated the paceña middle class, and soon merchants and bankers, under conservative leadership, began organizing a local *liga de la defensa social* whose stated aim was to establish a police force to protect commercial properties in the city against mob violence.[6] In December and January popular radical demon-strations broke out in all the major cities of the republic over the proposed social defence law, and it was these outbreaks which

---

[1] Álvarez, 'Fundación de la Federación Gráfica Boliviana', pp. 97–8.
[2] *El Diario*, 19 August 1931, p. 3.
[3] *El Diario*, 24 September 1931, p. 13.
[4] *El Diario*, 2 October 1931, p. 4.
[5] *El Diario*, 4 October 1931, p. 5; 6 October 1931, p. 12, and 15 October 1931, p. 5.   [6] *El Diario*, 7 October 1931, p. 8, and 8 October 1931, p. 5.

convinced Salamanca of the futility of trying to impose such a law on the nation in time of peace.

Under the impact of the crisis, the year 1932 saw a major conversion of the majority of the labour movement from mutualist apolitical principles of unionism to revolutionary political programmes. More and more middle class white-collar *empleados* began to organize themselves, while local student federations and leftist intellectuals began allying themselves with the labour movement.[1] Finally the public at large became conscious of the foreign companies operating in Bolivia, and voices were heard, more openly, in and outside congress calling for the expropriation of the Standard Oil Company and the Canadian-owned Bolivian Power Company of La Paz.[2]

Nor were radical intellectuals the only ones to take advantage of this growing labour and lower-class unrest. On 8 March 1932 (on the same day as the Liberals achieved their victory over Salamanca), the displaced saavedrista Partido Republicano proclaimed a new 'revolutionary' programme calling for vast new conquests in social legislation and major political renovation. It openly adopted what it considered to be a modified form of European socialism, renaming the party in the process the *Partido Republicano Socialista*.[3] This change accurately reflected the new political thought of the early 1930s, but it essentially represented political self-seeking by Saavedra rather than any fundamental transformation of his traditional party.

More important for the left was the public manifesto proclaimed by the Grupo Tupac Amaru on 1 May 1932. Issued amid the tumultous May Day celebrations of that year, the manifesto declared that:

A minority of latifundistas, of patrons and of exploiters maintain themselves in power behind Salamanca, as they maintained themselves behind Siles. The role of these caudillos is well known: demagoguery in opposition, tyranny in power, and the defence of the interests of a privileged caste, which in partnership with foreign capital is exploiting Bolivia like a private hacienda.

The only possible way to remedy this is by uniting the proletariat

---

[1] Canelas, 'El sindicalismo y los sindicatos', p. 76.
[2] See, for example, *El Diario*, 8 July 1932, p. 9.   [3] *El Diario*, 8 March 1932, p. 6.

and organizing it under the control of a prepared vanguard. This vanguard will indicate the proper policy line, and will carry the masses to the true revolution . . . [which will] benefit all those who find themselves oppressed. This ideological vanguard must come from the bosom of the proletariat itself and cannot be other than the Bolivian communist vanguard . . .

The revolution must first concentrate on the latifundia and eliminate feudalism by every means possible. This can be done by destroying the latifundia and giving the land to the Indians, utilizing the comunidades as cells for the construction of vast agricultural establishments, which will be endowed with the most modern techniques and improvements. It will also be necessary to instruct and educate the Indian, who constitutes 85 per cent of our population and is the basis of our nationality, in socialism. Other reforms will bring nationalization to the mines, exploiting them scientifically for the benefit of the country, the revival of the sentiment of cooperation which was destroyed by the Spanish conquest and finally the making of Bolivia into a country for all those who labour and exert themselves, without distinction of classes or castes. The contracting of fraternal bonds with all the proletariat of America and of the world will be a necessary act, since it is impossible to suppose that an anti-imperialist agrarian revolution would have the sympathy of the great powers.[1]

Despite its open label of 'communism', this manifesto was almost as heavily influenced by twentieth-century *indigenista* agrarian radical ideology of the extreme Indo-American left as by Marxian thought. It also summarized many of the basic revolutionary tenets which throughout the 1920s and early 1930s were developed by Bolivia's own radical thinkers on national problems. Definitely at the fringe of national political thought in 1932 and considered by the overwhelming majority as but the ravings of an extremist and ineffectual minority of embittered and exiled intellectuals, these doctrines and 'solutions' would have a profound impact on the post-war world.

For the moment, they remained only a small minority, and despite the manifestos of this and other revolutionary groups, the labour movement, though consistently increasing in strength, did not unite behind any ideology. Thus, despite the fears of the

---

[1] Printed in the Oruro labour paper, *La Igualdad*, and quoted in Canelas, 'El sindicalismo y los sindicatos', pp. 74–5.

Salamanca government about the influence of revolutionary ideology such as the Grupo Tupac Amaru espoused, the labour movement was not in a state of rebellion, but only of extreme agitation and organizational activity as a result of the economic depression.[1]

Salamanca tasted bitter defeat and dictation from his opponents on the internal political scene; he impotently watched the growth of leftist and labour agitation, which seemed to generate such intense emotional response from him; but his hauteur and grandeur were still untouched on the international scene. He turned all his vast and hitherto frustrated energies to foreign adventures, a sphere where his actions were still uninhibited. Having been defeated, humiliated, and enraged in one area, he more actively expressed his bellicosity and independence in another, especially as the economic situation continued to deteriorate. On 15 January 1932 the EMG worked out its most ambitious Chaco expansion plan to date under the guidance of Salamanca.[2] Its chief, Colonel Osorio, stated at the finish that when we have:

concluded the penetration and consolidated our occupation [through the construction of new forts] . . . we will have realized a truly gigantic national work. Conceived, sustained and realized with all the fervent patriotism which inspires the great visionary spirit of our captain-general [i.e. Salamanca], in his grandiose ideal of leaving the nation better and greater than when he encountered it, this new penetration plan will be the eloquent monument of the materialization of his formidable and overwhelming desire TO STAND FIRM IN THE CHACO, which summarizes all the legendary virility of our people.[3]

Grandiose as this phraseology might be, it captures the psychological state of Salamanca at this important moment of his career, when frustration seemed to mark his every step, the

---

[1] Canelas, 'El sindicalismo y los sindicatos', pp. 75–6.
[2] Arze Quiroga, *Documentos*, I, 135–78.
[3] *Ibid.* p. 173. From his first days in office, according to the Liberal Juan María Zalles, who was his foreign minister, Salamanca showed himself hostile to all ideas of a compromise settlement on the Chaco. Willing to push military occupation to the limit of expansion, he refused to accept the proposal of a Paraguayan port alternative, which was supported by several cabinet members. Juan María Zalles, *Crónicas* (Santiago: Imprenta Universitaria, 1942), pp. 116–17.

phantom of communist revolution seemed to darken his mind, and twenty long years of waiting seemed to have yielded nothing of either grandeur or glory.

The nation soon sensed Salamanca's new aggressive attitude, and public debate grew over probable war with Paraguay. As early as January 1932, the Federación Obrera del Trabajo de Oruro issued a manifesto proclaiming: 'We oppose war, because we have the solemn promise of the workers of Paraguay and of all America, that they will never go to war, that to a declaration of war by their government they will respond with general insurrection.'[1] This was but one of innumerable such manifestos and public meetings organized by the labour and leftist groups against Salamanca's aggressive movements in the Chaco. So effective did this volume of protest become that on 23 March 1932 the ministry of foreign relations sent a circular notice to all the prefects of Bolivia stating that:

This office has heard that there are rumours insistently circulating in all the departments of the republic relating to the imminence of a bellicose conflict with Paraguay, which is creating popular unease. At this time I instruct you to indicate to the citizens of your district that such rumours totally lack foundation, the government not having embarked on any war-like policy. It firmly maintains its proposals of peace and has had until now only a defensive policy in the Chaco, concentrating on repelling the repeated Paraguayan aggressions without attacking the opposite positions.[2]

Yet despite this official denial, rumours continued to circulate with greater intensity, and Bolivian newspapers in early April reprinted international news sources which reported aggressive Bolivian troop movements in the Chaco.[3]

The last link of Salamanca's Chaco penetration plan of January 1932, the uniting of the 3rd and 4th Divisions, was in the process of completion in late April and early May. A Major Moscoso was ordered to build the last linking road and concentrate his

---

[1] Canelas, 'El sindicalismo y los sindicatos', pp. 75–6.
[2] Díaz Machicao, *La guerra del Chaco*, p. 68. Porfirio Díaz Machicao was himself involved in such a leftist pacifist demonstration in Cochabamba at this time. See his autobiography, *La bestia emocional* (La Paz: Editorial 'Juventud', 1955) p. 98. [3] Díaz Machicao, *La guerra del Chaco*, p. 68

forces on the recently discovered Chuquisaca lagoon—the major watering place on the proposed road. On 25 May 1932 Moscoso and twenty-five men under his command began their final march to Laguna Chuquisaca deep in the Chaco.[1] In Washington, at the same time, a specially convoked Neutral Commission proposed a non-aggression pact between the two powers. Bautista Saavedra, the recently re-labelled 'socialist', was the most vociferous in attacking such a 'dishonourable' treaty and publicly proclaimed a militant stand against government 'appeasement'. But the strong and vocal anti-war sentiment persisted despite such ultra-nationalist utterances on the part of some of the traditional parties. So restless did the public become that the chancellery issued a public statement on 5 June claiming that it was bargaining in good faith in Washington and that all recent news reports about aggressive Bolivian troop movements were erroneous.[2]

Moscoso's orders were to occupy the lagoon even though air reconnaissance had indicated the possibility of Paraguayan occupation, and in these orders the EMG seems to have gone beyond Salamanca's specific orders to the contrary, which stated that no aggressive act should be undertaken and only reconnaissance be carried out, not occupation. But the local army commands, backed up by the EMG, seemed to feel that an aggressive act at the lake was worth the risk because of its vital importance—though they certainly had no intention of going to war over this property. Given conflicting orders, Moscoso used his own initiative when he arrived at the lagoon late on 14 June and observed that it had already been occupied by a small Paraguayan fort. Early the next morning his troops attacked and the small Paraguayan garrison fled. Moscoso thereupon dug in, occupying the old Paraguayan fort, which he renamed Fortín Santa Cruz, and called for reinforcements. He quickly received the backing of his commander Colonel Peñaranda who sent troops and supplies, despite EMG orders to the contrary calling for removal of Bolivian forces from the lake. To justify these actions, the various army commands produced a rather complex fabrication to the effect that Moscoso had found the Paraguayan lake fort empty and

[1] Díaz Machicao, *La guerra del Chaco*, p. 71.   [2] *Ibid.* pp. 72–3.

abandoned when he arrived and as a further peaceful gesture he had only occupied the opposite shore of the lake. Although both Salamanca and the EMG knew this version of the events to be untrue, they both eventually accepted it. On 29 June 1932 the expected Paraguayan reprisal occurred and was successfully beaten off by Moscoso, and more troops were sent to the area. Meanwhile there was absolute silence in public about these dangerous developments in the Chaco; no news appeared in the Bolivian press. On 30 June, however, without any official notification, Gustavo Carlos Otero, prefect of La Paz, began to act as if there was a state of siege.[1]

While all this was happening on the Chaco front hundreds of miles from the centres of government, the nation concentrated on the seemingly more serious economic situation which now was approaching chaos. In April 1932 the government established a new exchange rate which completely divided the miners and commercial groups, and caused the latter publicly and bitterly to protest against the government action. On the day following the announcement of the new rates, a protest demonstration of 5,000 people met in La Paz demanding an end to the *Minería* domination of government economic policies. Not only did the various leagues and associations of commercial people join in these manifestations, but students and the FOT as well, and signs were carried calling for *pan, trabajo o muerte*. FOT leader Moisés Álvarez addressed the crowd calling for a 'united front' of workers and *pequeña burguesía* against the miners.[2]

In early May rumours began to penetrate from Europe of the increasingly serious situation and the need to curtail tin production even further under the impact of new falls in prices.[3] So seriously did this new price decline affect the world tin market that in mid-May the International Tin Control organization adopted the radical Byrne scheme which called for a complete shutdown of all tin-producing facilities of all member companies and governments for the months of July and August, and a reduction of world production thereafter to $33\frac{1}{3}$ per cent of the 1929

---

[1] Arze Quiroga, *Documentos*, I, 233ff.; Díaz Machicao, *La guerra del Chaco* pp. 74–80.   [2] *El Diario*, 27 April 1932, p. 7, and 28 April 1932, p. 7 [3] *El Diario*, 7 May 1932, p. 6.

figure—the most drastic cutback proposed by the International Tin Control Scheme and the rock bottom reached in the crisis. By June all the producers had agreed to this drastic programme and it was adopted in London and transmitted to all the governments concerned.[1]

Because of the increasingly unbalanced trade picture and the heavy flight of gold and consequent depletion of national reserves, the government was forced in late May to place all gold dealing directly and exclusively under the control of the central bank. It also tightened its powers over exchange rates and made the dramatic requirement that the miners hand over 65 per cent of their letters of exchange upon foreign and specie currencies to the central bank.[2] Thus at the very moment when Salamanca's aggressive penetration policy was leading to inevitable clashes, and the government was being forced to make decisions of crucial importance on how to react to these border incidents, the Bolivian economic depression was reaching its low point and almost the entire exporting sector of the national economy was literally being shut down for two entire months! There is no question but that this critical economic situation was constantly in the background of all government decisions taken in the following weeks, and was a vital factor in these decisions.

On 5 July in a memorandum to Salamanca, Colonel Osorio of the EMG had finally come round to the position of his field commanders and suggested to Salamanca that Chuquisaca lagoon be held by Bolivian troops and not abandoned. On 7 July a major plan of attack was prepared by the EMG based on the pivotal position of the lagoon. Salamanca's reaction to these two reports was more restrained. He pointed out that international complications were developing on the lagoon issue and asked for moderation— but he did not call for withdrawal—and at the same time said that the war plans of 7 July were not detailed enough.[3]

Throughout these developments Paraguay maintained a discreet silence. Despite its two defeats at the lagoon and its new preparations for a counter-offensive, it still seemed to view the whole affair as just another of the innumerable border clashes,

---

[1] Knorr, *Tin Under Control*, pp. 122–3.
[2] *El Diario*, 21 May 1932, p. 6.   [3] Arze Quiroga, *Documentos*, I, 321–4.

and to believe that once it recaptured the lost post, it would again settle down to protracted negotiations. Thus in early July it organized another assault force, this time heavily armed and consisting of about 400 troops, and at the same time, on 7 July, notified Washington of aggression by Bolivia in the Chaco (area not specified), an action which required that it abstain from further negotiations until the issue was settled.[1] Bolivia's public reaction was to deny the Paraguayan charges of aggression. Bolivia did, however, openly admit that Paraguay must be referring to the Laguna Chuquisaca area, but declared that Bolivian troops had only established themselves in what Bolivia claimed to be previously unoccupied territory. Bolivia also publicly admitted for the first time that one Paraguayan attack had already occurred in this area and had been beaten off.[2]

On 15 July the new Paraguayan attack began and after two days of heavy fighting the fort was retaken from the Bolivians.[3] On 18 July the news of this assault was given to the Bolivian newspapers by the government and caused tremendous popular reactions.[4] The next day at a major public demonstration of support for the government in La Paz, Salamanca made a rabid speech calling for a blood sacrifice from the nation:

If a nation will not react to an action injuring its dignity, it does not deserve to be a nation. And if the government of that nation does not know how to fulfil its duty it also does not deserve to govern . . .

This government is willing to go to the very limit of its resources, but it also demands of the nation and its citizens all the sacrifices, not just of money, which is little, but of life itself in order to prevent the staining of the national honour. Only thus will we really deserve to live as a well organized country. . .

I invite you, fellow citizens, to swear to comply with the obligation that the nation imposes on you and to go to the ultimate sacrifice if it is necessary, in defence of its dignity. Only thus will we demonstrate that we are capable of defending the sovereignty of the *Patria*.

Viva Bolivia! Gloria a Bolivia![5]

---

[1] *El Diario*, 8 July 1932, p. 1.   [2] *El Diario*, 9 July 1932, pp. 6, 7.
[3] Díaz Machicao, *La guerra del Chaco*, pp. 85–6; Arze Quiroga, *Documentos*, I, 283–6; David H. Zook, Jr., *The Conduct of the Chaco War* (New York: Bookman Associates, 1960), p. 74.
[4] *El Diario*, 19 July 1932, pp. 1, 6.   [5] *El Diario*, 20 July 1932, p. 1.

Meanwhile on the night of 18 July in a special emergency cabinet meeting, with the agreement of Colonel Osorio, Salamanca decided to carry through a major reprisal programme in answer to the Paraguayan victory at Fortín Santa Cruz. He ordered the immediate taking of the Paraguayan forts Corrales and Toledo. Osorio opposed this move on the grounds that the Bolivian forces were unprepared for such a major action, and offered his resignation in protest when Salamanca refused to accept his opinion.[1] Salamanca replaced Osorio with General Carlos Quintanilla, and on 20 July decreed an official state of siege. On his arrival in La Paz a few days after his appointment, Quintanilla conferred with Osorio and both agreed that the Bolivian army's 4th Division was in no condition to carry out the reprisal attacks of deep penetration that Salamanca had ordered. He decided to continue opposing him to prevent its execution.

But Salamanca was already bypassing the EMG in his eagerness to see action, and on his own initiative began ordering the local commanders to take the necessary preparatory steps. When the two officers went to Salamanca, he not only dismissed their objections but accused Osorio of seeking a diplomatic solution to the conflict instead of a military one. At this meeting Quintanilla asked that Osorio be continued in his post to ensure army confidence and for a time continued to refuse to replace him. Still refusing to change their position, the two military men met with the minister of war, José Gutiérrez, and begged him to intercede and overcome Salamanca's insane request for a reprisal. They claimed that the situation of the 4th Division was entirely unfavourable for such a move and that it would therefore be unsuccessful. That night they met with the president, but despite all their objections, Salamanca held firm and finally ordered Quintanilla to the front to begin the operations. Osorio claimed that the whole plan was suicidal and would lead to total war for which the army was completely unprepared, and he continued to press Salamanca for a diplomatic solution.[2] Salamanca, enraged at this unwillingness of the general staff to defend what he saw as the

---

[1] Arze Quiroga, *Documentos*, I, 50–1.
[2] Arze Quiroga, *Documentos*, I, 51–2; Díaz Machicao, *La guerra del Chaco*, pp. 87–90.

national honour,[1] finally stated to the officers: 'Execute the order; if there is any merit in it, it will be yours, if there are any reponsibilities, they will be mine.'[2] Osorio, though he opposed the plan to the end, agreed to continue in his post, much to the rage of his chief assistant Colonel Ángel Rodríguez. In summing up this whole sequence of events, Osorio in his memoirs noted that:

The president surely—one has to honour his word—did not want nor think to unleash war; but he could do no less than provoke it with his violent attitude. Perhaps the president also ingenuously believed that with the so-called reprisals that he ordered he was going to frighten the Paraguayan people and that they would not react.[3]

In short, it was Salamanca who deliberately led the Bolivian nation to war, despite the clear opposition of his own high command and despite the lack of Paraguayan initiative. Completely defeated in internal politics, forced to surrender political leadership to the Liberals, frustrated on the communist issue, and unable to stop the economic crisis which was destroying his government's stability day by day, Salamanca turned toward the international scene where he believed that all his personal glory and promise of future greatness could at last find unfettered expression. He was convinced of the righteousness of his cause and the invulnerability of his armies, and he deliberately risked all for greatness. There is no question that the military had long boasted of their prowess and ability easily to destroy Paraguay in the years before 1932.[4] But at the last crucial moment they honestly recognized the fantastic impossibility of the task, given the crudest communications link over the worst terrain in Bolivia in an area long defended and well covered by their enemy, and they

---

[1] Salamanca himself later wrote of this meeting, stating that: 'General Osorio, who showed himself very disheartened, suggested that to resolve the shame of Laguna Chuquisaca, we should resort to diplomatic resources. This conduct of his exasperated me. He had decisively concurred in precipitating the conflict and when the moment to defend the honour of Bolivia arrived, he asked for a diplomatic solution. On that occasion [i.e. this evening meeting] I treated General Osorio with rudeness, reminding him of his responsibilities in these developments, and stated to him the necessity of expiating without delay the shame suffered by Bolivia.' Reprinted in Arze Quiroga, *Documentos*, I, 52. (At this time Osorio was still a colonel, later in the war he was elevated to the rank of general.)   [2] Díaz Machicao, *La guerra del Chaco*, p. 90.   [3] *Ibid.* p. 91.
[4] Ovidio Urioste, *La fragua, comprende la primera faz de la campaña hasta la caída de Boquerón y el abandono de Arce* ([Cochabamba]: n.p. [1933]), pp. 113–14.

tried their utmost to dispel Salamanca's insane illusions. To charges that it would take six months to bring the army into the proper position in the Chaco, Salamanca is supposed to have replied that the war would just have to be started six months earlier. Salamanca would not be frustrated here on this last ground left to him, and he would listen to no counsel but his own.

Almost all Bolivians and Latin Americans believe the war was caused by Standard Oil and Royal Dutch Shell fighting for the disputed Chaco oil fields. The obviously internal nature of the causes—that is the economic tension arising over the depression; the humiliations of the embittered president and the obvious feeling of many leaders that foreign conflict would resolve mounting class tensions—have been ignored in the universal belief that Standard Oil was the chief instigator behind Salamanca. As I have tried to show, Salamanca acted largely on his own in bringing about the war, and was actually hostile to Standard Oil before and during the war years. It is also clear that absolutely no oil lands were at stake in the Chaco territory dispute, and that it was only at the very end of the war when previously undisputed Bolivian territory was captured by the Paraguayans that oil became an issue. Finally the utter hostility of the Standard Oil Company to the Bolivian war effort: e.g. its refusal to refine aviation gasoline locally and its illegal shipments of Bolivian oil to Argentina at the height of the conflict, indicate that the American company had little interest either in the conflict or its outcome and simply exploited the confused war period to make an enormous profit. The mining élite, for its part, had an infinitely more powerful impact on national policy than any combination of foreign banks or companies, and it is clear that many leaders in the mining community were probably enthusiastic supporters of Salamanca's aggressive policies and were disturbed by rising radical agitation in Oruro and Potosí. But even here it should be stressed that the mine workers were totally unorganized during this period and that the companies had little difficulty in dismissing large numbers of miners during the shutdowns induced by the depression.

If public declarations of the urban middle and lower classes are any indication of 'public opinion', then it seems evident that

Saavedra's appeal to nationalism and clear resort to violence—admittedly on a supposedly modest scale—received warm support. The immediate reaction of the political and intellectual forces of the nation, except for the extreme radical fringe, was to give full cooperation to the government in its hour of need. No one questioned the government's version of the chain of events which had led to the 'unprovoked' and 'dastardly' attack by Paraguay on the Bolivian fort of Mariscal Santa Cruz at Laguna Chuquisaca.[1] Support was immediately forthcoming from all the traditional political parties, including the Partido Nacionalista.[2] The nation's leading intellectuals, such as Alcides Argüedas, Ricardo Jaimes Freyre, Fernando Díez de Medina, Gregorio Reynolds, Roberto Prudencio, Gustavo Carlos Otero, Franz Tamayo, Juan Francisco Bedregal, and such moderate leftists as Carlos Montenegro, Víctor Andrade, Enrique Baldivieso, Justo Rodas Eugino, and Vicente Mendoza López, signed an international appeal written in La Paz on 30 July 1932, which stated that 'they found themselves absolutely convinced of the purity of the international policy of Bolivia' and charged that Paraguay had precipitated war in the continent.[3] Finally the urban middle and lower classes came out in mass demonstrations of support for the government in all the principal cities of the republic, seemingly forgetting the economic crisis and the political and social discomforts in their patriotic fervour.[4]

Ten days before this international appeal, the government proclaimed a national state of siege, and immediately rounded up key intellectuals including Ricardo Anaya, José Aguirre Gainsborg, Porfirio Díaz Machicao, as well as a host of labour agitators and

[1] The government's analysis of the causes of the Chaco conflict is contained in a diplomatic circular which was sent to all legations abroad and dated 21 July 1932. For this document see *La Razón*, 22 July 1932, p. 4. The essence of the twelve-point document was that Bolivia had found an abandoned Paraguayan fort when its forces arrived at Laguna Chuquisaca; that although these ruins had been abandoned and were unoccupied, Bolivian troops had even gone so far as to build their own fort on the unoccupied western side, and finally that it was the Paraguayans who initiated armed hostilities and this occurred on 29 June. This attack and the subsequent one of 15 July were, according to the Bolivian government, completely unprovoked.

[2] *El Diario*, 20 July 1932, p. 6; *La República*, 20 July 1932, p. 4 and *La Razón*, 22 July 1932, p. 12.

[3] *El Diario*, 5 August 1932, p. 8, and 10 August 1932, p. 3.

[4] *El Diario*, 22 July 1932, p. 2.

assorted Marxists, anarchists, pacifists, indigenistas, etc. Some of them were fortunate enough to be exiled or confined in distant districts, but many were sent to the front lines. Almost all the leftists conscripted into the army were carefully watched and frequently executed in battle by the local command. Yet this was the greatest opportunity of the Bolivian left, and the power of the extreme leftists grew year after year during the disastrous course of the war, making powerful inroads into the Chaco armies despite government suppression and violence.[1]

When the government ordered national mobilization on 21 July[2] it found that there was great passive resistance to this call among the rural Indians and organized workers, the major sources of front-line troops. At first the government attempted to deal with this resistance by persuasion. Thus in the early months of the war, General Felipe M. Rivera, then chief of the EMG, called a meeting of some eighty labour leaders and asked their co-operation in getting workers to join the army. But this appeal received no response,[3] and rearguard military squads were soon organized to hunt down workers and Indians, even in the most distant and obscure regions of the nation. The bloodshed caused by these roving bands was extreme.[4]

Bolivia's reaction to the retaking of Laguna Chuquisaca took Paraguay by surprise. For once the Paraguayans had retaken this post on 18 July, they notified the Neutral Commission in Washington that they were willing to resume negotiations on the Pact of Non-Aggression, negotiations which they had suspended at the beginning of the month to carry out this operation.[5] That Paraguay still considered the whole issue just another major border dispute allowed the Bolivian forces to surprise Paraguay in the central Chaco by its deep penetration 'reprisal' operation.

---

[1] *La República*, 2 August 1932, p. 4; Díaz Machicao, *La bestia emocional*, pp. 105ff.
[2] *El Diario*, 22 July 1932, p. 1.
[3] Interview with Waldo Álvarez, La Paz, 11 October 1961. Álvarez was one of the participants in this conference, and later in the year was forcibly exiled on trumped-up charges of anti-war propaganda.
[4] A fictionalized account of these impressment gangs is presented in the novel by Oscar Cerruto, *Aluvión de fuego* (Santiago: Ediciones Ercilla, 1935); also see charges against these actions in the 1938 convention debates, Convención Nacional de 1938, *Redactor de la Convención Nacional* (5 vols.; La Paz: Editorial Universo, 1938–9), III, 90–1.
[5] Díaz Machicao, *La guerra del Chaco*, p. 93.

Thus despite the talk of gloom and impossibility by the EMG, it seemed as though Bolivian forces had easily and successfully carried out the mission assigned to them by Salamanca, for they quickly and effortlessly took the key Paraguayan forts of Boquerón, Corrales and Toledo.[1]

However, at this point the unpredictable Salamanca issued a halt to military operations, on 2 August 1932, under the ridiculous assumption that he had achieved a major victory which Paraguay would not contest and that he could get diplomatic recognition for these major conquests. But by his own previous action Salamanca had committed the nation to total war—which the EMG had clearly indicated to him, and as he refused to relinquish these newly taken forts (so vital to Paraguay's defence lines), or even to think of trading them for Fortín Mariscal Santa Cruz, full-scale international war was inevitable. Thus calling a halt to military operations was a grave military error brought on by Salamanca's almost hysterical state of mind.[2]

Another indication of his agitated state was his curiously guilt-ridden note to the EMG written on 1 August 1932, asking for a full scale military investigation of the occupation of the Laguna Chuquisaca position and accusing the EMG of falsifying information.

As the causes of the present situation are of historical interest, and require a complete investigation, I considered it convenient to entrust to you by written instruction the organization of a military investigation concerning the occupation of Laguna Grande [Chuquisaca] or Mariscal Santa Cruz.

As you will recall, señor General, I only changed the imperative and repeated order to abandon that fort on the grounds that the Paraguayan fort had been left unoccupied, while our own was being built on the western side, with the lagoon between them. This order which you assured me had been fulfilled, induced the Government to affirm this change of place in diplomatic documents which compromised the seriousness and honour of Bolivia. As in the course of time . . . I became distrustful of the veracity of the facts which you had affirmed to us, I ended by doubting that the change of the placement of the fort

---

[1] Zook, *Chaco War*, p. 76.
[2] *Ibid.* pp. 76–8. The previous day he sent a harsh note to the Neutral Commission demanding a final settlement to this historical border dispute, with Bolivia retaining the captured forts and demanding a port on the Río Paraguay.

had occurred and I therefore insistently asked that you confirm it to me, you also ending by putting it in doubt. It now appears, when the events cannot be undone, that the new Bolivian fort was not established and that our detachment of occupation remained in the Paraguayan fort.[1]

Surely Salamanca reveals a strange ingenuousness here and an insane belief that the whole war had begun not through his own aggressive actions, but through the machinations of the EMG which had lied to him about Laguna Chuquisaca. He backed up this belief by ordering Ovidio Urioste to the Chaco to begin an official process of inquiry against the officers involved in the Laguna Chuquisaca affair, but the front-line command soon brought an end to the entire proceedings.[2]

This was only the first of many incidents between Salamanca and his high command, both of them attempting to blame the other for causing the war, and it occurred before the Chaco War was a month old! In reply, the EMG on the 30th of this same month sent a memorandum to Salamanca asking him for a detailed war plan, accusing him implicitly of having led the nation into war. Not mincing its words it stated that:

There are many apparent and real causes for an armed conflict and only the supreme government as maker of state policy knows them. Because of its omniscience and central position it is the body called upon to answer to history . . . for the reasons for which it made the war. Its maximum responsibility as a determinate cause is unique and transcendental: to reject or declare war. In whichever of these two decisions, its causal action becomes the reality.

Only the execution of this policy belongs to the military command. But in this execution it alone is responsible for the conduct of operations. Its aim is to obtain the objectives established by the political powers in the best form possible.[3]

The memorandum went on to demand that Salamanca therefore define the political aims which he sought by his policy of war, and that these once defined he should leave the military command free to implement these objectives.

At the present time the supreme government has not concretely expressed in a definitive form in any document, *what it is that the Bolivian*

[1] Arze Quiroga, *Documentos*, I, 239.
[2] Urioste, *La fragua*, pp. 346ff.   [3] Arze Quiroga, *Documentos*, I, 334–5.

state wishes to obtain from Paraguay by resort to arms. The political conduct of the Bolivian-Paraguayan war is neither clear not resolutely
oriented toward positive and practical ends. There has always been
an ideology, but this is not enough for the Estado Mayor General.
We need real objectives and not simple historical aspirations; written
orders and not verbal or voluble instructions.[1]

The memorandum then outlined some fundamental considerations of policy, suggesting that effort should be concentrated on
destroying the capacity of the Paraguayan army, and only after
this was accomplished should the geographic objective of control
over the Río Paraguay be undertaken. But it asked above all that
Salamanca give in essence a defence of his conduct in initiating
the war and a broad and definable plan of what he wanted to
accomplish.[2]

In an answer to this memorandum dated 21 September 1932,
Salamanca charged that:

obviously the object of the referred communication is to avoid the
responsibility of that Estado Mayor General in anticipation, without
doubt, of possible disasters in the course of the war already unleashed
against Paraguay . . . And all this it expresses with absolute falsification
of the truth of the events.[3]

Instead of providing a detailed political plan, he again went over
the orders and counter-orders of the Laguna Chuquisaca affair,
stating—this time in more specific fashion—that he had been
misled through falsified information supplied to him by the
EMG and that the latter had also refused to carry out many of
his orders. To the request that he formulate a specific political aim
for the war, he countered that:

it would have been more logical that the government ask: *What is it
that the chief of the Estado Mayor had wanted when he imprudently unleashed this conflict, in spite of the efforts of the president of the republic
to avoid it?*[4]

Thus at the very beginning of the greatest war in Bolivian
history, before even the first major reverses had been suffered, the
leaders of the nation were already blaming each other for the

---

[1] Arze Quiroga, *Documentos*, I, p. 336.
[2] *Ibid.* pp. 333–41 for the entire memorandum.   [3] *Ibid.* p. 343.   [4] *Ibid.* pp. 346–7.

coming disasters and for responsibility for the whole affair. While it can be admitted to apologists for Salamanca that there were obviously misleading actions carried out by the army command in taking the Paraguayan fort in the first place, this was one of innumerable such incidents in the border history of the two nations. But both Paraguay's limited reaction to the Laguna Chuquisaca aggression and the refusal of the EMG to initiate full-scale war left the responsibility for beginning the war in the hands of Salamanca. It was he who deliberately, against the firm and open opposition of the EMG, decided to make a major *cause célèbre* of the incident and turn it into the opening shot of a three-year holocaust. That both nations were acting belligerently in the Chaco, and that both had armed for possible conflict years in advance, in no way reduces the responsibility of Salamanca. For such tense border affairs have been experienced by practically every state of South America and some of these affairs have continued at a cold war rate for decades. But Salamanca, faced by opposition, frustration, and growing economic chaos at home, felt like many Bolivian presidents before and since that a foreign adventure was just the thing to relieve the frustration of internal affairs and unite the country behind him. His austerity, pride, and introverted sensitivity[1] made him feel his defeat at the hands of the Liberals and their dictation as an insufferable affront, and an easy victory over Paraguay—which his generals had so boasted of prior to 1932—seemed a great opportunity for ultimate vindication for himself. Here at last all the humiliations both he and his nation had suffered from every one of its neighbours could be rectified. But in rectifying its history, in bringing the nation to war, he was destroying the very foundations of the society which had governed Bolivia since the Spanish conquest. The Chaco War sounded the first note of the death throes of the old order, and in the blood and sands of the Chaco the old order in all its horror and weakness was exposed to the view of the world, and more important, to the view of the Bolivians themselves. From this horrible revelation would spring forth a new era.

[1] Particularly revealing of this is the excerpt from Salamanca's personal diary reprinted in Alvéstegui, *Salamanca*, II, 24–65, which reveals Salamanca's fantastic sense of alienation even from his closest political associates, and his truly morbid sensitivity to criticism.

6

THE CHACO WAR

On the eve of the Chaco War Bolivian society was under-developed, highly stratified and in many ways had progressed little since the early nineteenth century. The great socio-economic and political changes in the urban centres of the nation had affected only a minority of the population. Despite the growth of mining and light industry and the increase in urbanization and modern communications, the majority of the population was still engaged in traditional subsistence crop agriculture. The rural population in the census of 1846 was estimated conservatively at 89 per cent, in 1932 it still represented close to two-thirds of the national population.[1]

The few changes that the century of independence had brought to the submerged rural mass tended only to sharpen class and caste lines. The status and condition of the peasantry in fact progressively deteriorated during these one hundred years. As late as 1846 the self-governing, landholding comunidad Indians were greater in number than the landless colonos, being some 478,000 strong,[2] but by 1900 they had declined to an estimated 250,000, and by 1950 to some 140,000.[3]

By 1930 most of the Bolivian people were landless peasants, or colonos, who lived and worked on the great latifundias under

[1] Dalence, Bosquejo estadístico, p. 199; and Oficina Nacional de Inmigración, Censo nacional de 1900, II, 17–18.
[2] This figure does not include the estimated 144,000 forasteros (or agregados sin tierra) who were living in the free communities but did not own land.
[3] Dalence, Bosquejo estadístico, pp. 234–6. George McCutchen McBride, The Agrarian Indian Communities of Highland Bolivia (New York: American Geographical Society, 1921), pp. 20, 24–5. McBride estimated a population of 500,000 comunidad Indians in 1854, which closely supports Dalence's estimates. Dirección General de Estadística y Censos, Censo demográfico, 1950, p. 141. In the agricultural census of the late 1930s it was estimated that there were only 90,000 landowners in the entire nation, and well over half of these were mini-fundistas located in the uniquely sub-divided Cochabamba valley. Rafael A. Reyeros, El pongueaje, la servidumbre personal de los indios bolivianos (La Paz: Empresa Editora 'Universo', 1949), p. 10.

conditions close to serfdom. Even by Latin American standards, the colonos lived a harsh and brutal life. They were required to perform arduous and degrading personal service for the *patrones*; they were subjected to corporal punishment by the *mayordomos*; and they laboured without monetary compensation. The peasant masses were exploited as fully as they could be without being turned into chattel slaves. Since the latifundistas exclusively controlled almost all the arable land of the altiplano, and large parts of the choice lands of the valleys and lowlands, the Indians had no recourse but to supply their labour on the terms demanded.[1]

These terms were harsh. In return for the right to plant his own crops somewhere on his master's land, the general pattern was for the colono to provide free labour, tools, work animals and sometimes seed, for the fields and crops of the patron, for at least three to four days every week. The work included planting, weeding, harvesting, and finally transporting the crops to market. Apart from agricultural labour, the colono had to give the patron a certain additional amount of time for grazing of the patron's animals, and for manufacturing local farm products for him such as cheese and dehydrated vegetable compounds. The colono also had to provide transportation for the finca crops to the nearest markets on his own or borrowed animals, and finally and most onerous of all, he had to submit to demeaning menial personal service (*pongueaje*) to the patron himself, either at his estate, or more often, at his town residence.[2]

---

[1] By 1952, it was estimated that two-thirds of the land on the altiplano was occupied by haciendas or estates and that only 3,787 free communities survived in all of Bolivia. William E. Carter, *Aymara Communities and the Bolivian Agrarian Reform* (University of Florida Monographs, Social Sciences No. 24; Gainesville: University of Florida Press, 1964), p. 9.

[2] For a general discussion of the requirements of the colonos and pongos see: Frank Leuer Keller, 'Geography of the Lake Titicaca Basin of Bolivia, A Comparative Study of Great Landed Estates and Highland Indian Communities' (unpublished Ph.D. dissertation, University of Maryland, Department of Geography, 1949), pp. 44, 75–7; Ben H. Thibodeaux, 'An Economic Study of Agriculture in Bolivia' (unpublished Ph.D. dissertation, Harvard University, Department of Economics, 1946), pp. 194–5; Carter, *Aymara Communities*, Ch. V, and finally Reyeros, *El pongueaje*, pp. 127ff. which discusses the separate category of pongueaje, which was the name usually applied to that part of the free labour which involved personal service to the master and his family. Since a pongo was thus invariably a colono who at the time was working in the house of the master, the terms pongo and colono are often indiscriminately applied to the entire colonato system.

From region to region the number of days, the accounting system, the type of personal service demanded and the amount of materials and seed the colono had to provide for his master's fields and crops varied greatly. For the entire system was one without legal sanction, leaving masters free to charge in terms of labour demands as much as the local market could bear. There was no redress against harsh administrators or masters; there was no protection from corporal punishment which these masters freely used, and strangest of all there were no laws binding the Indians to the soil. But while unbound by law, nevertheless, economically socially and politically the colono Indian had little choice. With no alternative employment available in industry or urban occupations, and unable to prevent white land seizures, he was forced to till his traditional fields to survive.[1]

Because of the marginal nature of the colono plots, or *sayanas* the estate Indians lived on a bare subsistence level and did not participate to any marked degree in the national money economy Their utensils, clothing and household furnishings were home-made, and the few items they produced in excess of consumption went for barter to obtain such indispensable items as salt alcohol and coca.[2] In this subsistence economic pattern the few

[1] The colonato system was based only on a verbal type of lease contract which was supposedly renewed with each generation, or with each change of finca owner-ship, and it gave the Indian colono the use of the usufruct lands only if he continued to meet certain understood conditions. This 'contract', as two govern-ment social investigators noted in 1940, was unique in that it creates 'a unilateral obligation of the Indian colono and his almost absolute submission to the will of the patron. The provisions of the Civil Code do not govern this type of contract; nor does there exist any special law for that object; so that, in fact there is no other norm than that of the patron's will. The patron can deprive the colono of the right to irrigation, prohibit him from selling his own animal and the products which he cultivates for himself, oblige him to yield them at subnormal prices or restrict his transit through the roads of the hacienda; the colono does not have the right of legal action against the landowner, and what-ever complaints he makes expose him to eviction. On the other hand, the patron does not have any obligation or legal limitation with regard to the payment of a minimum salary, the remuneration for assigned personal services [pongueaje] the observance of a working day schedule and of an obligatory rest day, the provision of food, the conditions of lodgings, the protection of maternity, the labour of children and minors, the compensation for work accidents, medical assistance, etc., etc. It treats, in synthesis, of a system typically and character-istically feudal.' Remberto Capriles Rico and Gastón Arduz Eguia, *El problema social en Bolivia, condiciones de vida y de trabajo* (La Paz: Editorial Fénix, 1941), pp. 42–3.
[2] Thibodeaux, 'Economic Study of Agriculture', p. 196.

comunidad Indians were little better off than the colonos, for the lands that were left to the comunidades were usually the poorest and the most inaccessible of the district, and they produced little more than their colono compatriots in the way of food or cash crops.[1] Thus a majority of the nation, what one government report in 1904 estimated at 816,166 persons,[2] and another authority estimated as 64 per cent of the population in 1940,[3] were almost completely outside the money economy.

Not only were the colono and comunidad farmers barely self-sufficient in their own fields, but the production methods on the patron's fields were hardly more advanced, so that the surplus produced by his holdings was a minimum one. In the overwhelming majority of Bolivia's *fincas* or estates, almost no agricultural machinery or artificial fertilizers were used, because they could never compete with unpaid labour.[4] Furthermore, the finca owners were in no way interested in meeting urban consumer demands, for underproduction guaranteed artificially high prices and given the lack of investment in labour, machinery and seeds, the extraordinarily low rate of taxes and the rather low

[1] Keller, 'Geography of Lake Titicaca', pp. 90–2.
[2] The official government report stated: 'It is necessary to eliminate from the productive population [of the nation], the uncivilized element (91,000 inhabitants) which people a large part of the national territory, on the Brazilian Peruvian and Paraguayan frontiers. In addition, the subjugated native class (816,166 inhabitants) is, in relation to the economic process, of little importance.' As far as this rather frank report was concerned, 'National production is associated [only] with the white and mestizo population, numbering together 668,185 people.' Quoted in Ness, 'The Movement of Capital', p. 59.
[3] Reyeros, *El pongueaje*, p. 129.
[4] Thibodeaux, after a year's study of Bolivian agriculture, in the early 1940s, concluded, 'There is no economic incentive for the landlord to acquire labor-saving machinery when all of his labor and power is furnished at no cash cost. True, the use of the land is given for these things. But when it is considered that relatively little of the land is developed [i.e. used or needed by the hacendado], that much of it is low-priced and that real estate taxes are low [less than 3 cents (U.S.) per hectare, p. 82], it is readily seen that labor is cheap.' Thibodeaux, 'Economic Study of Agriculture', pp. 195–6. How wasteful of labour the Bolivian system of agriculture was at this time, can be seen in some of the statistics compiled by Thibodeaux. He noted that 'with the primitive methods used, approximately 352 8-hour days of labor are used to produce and harvest one hectare of potatoes yielding 160 to 190 quintals', in Bolivia, while 'based on production practices in a representative commercial potato area in the United States, the labor used per hectare yielding 312 quintals amounts to an average of only 15 8-hour days if a 4-row tractor, harvester and mechanical grader are used.' *Ibid.* p. 204.

original price of land, they had nothing to lose and everything to gain by maintaining their production levels. To use more modern methods and obtain greater production would not only lower prices in the short run, but would involve investment capital. This way, no money had to be ploughed back into the finca, since production cost nothing, and all profits gained went to personal consumption.[1] Thus despite the fact that over 70 per cent of the national work force was engaged in agriculture,[2] Bolivia was a major importer of agricultural goods, many of which were nationally produced.[3]

A typical finca of the altiplano was the Finca Ingavi, an estate of some 2,000 acres and 100 colonos located between La Paz and Lake Titicaca (Guaqui). On the estate each colono family, of an estimated five persons, was given three acres for its own use in return for three days' labour per week on the lands of the patron. Run by a cholo mayordomo, the estate produced the usual root crops (primarily potatoes), as well as wool from the estate sheep, and various foodstuff manufactures such as cheese and *chuño*. The latter was a dehydrated durable concentrate of potatoes that required a long labour-intensive process of compression and drying and was a major source of income for the patron. In addition to providing labour for manufacturing and agriculture, the colonos were pongos both in the house of the mayordomo and in the La Paz residence of the patron. On Finca Ingavi careful labour obligation records were kept for each family and corporal punishment was freely inflicted.[4]

Less typical of these altiplano fincas, was the more productive and far more modern Finca Taraco. While the moderate-sized Finca Ingavi had its origins in the pre-independence period, the more wealthy and populous Finca Taraco was only of recent creation, organized out of comunidad lands in the first decade of the twentieth century. Taraco consisted of some 3,636 hectares of rich lake-bottom lands on the shores of Lake Titicaca, the

---

[1] Keller, 'Geography of Lake Titicaca', pp. 65–6.
[2] See table 5, p. 394. This was the estimate for 1950.
[3] Thibodeaux, 'Economic Study of Agriculture', p. 5. The figure refers to the period 1936–40.
[4] Frank Leuer Keller, 'Finca Ingavi: a Medieval Survival on the Bolivian Altiplano', *Economic Geography*, XXVI (1950), 37–50.

most fertile region of the entire altiplano. The estate had been established by none other than Ismael Montes, the great Liberal caudillo. The story of the acquisition of this estate was fairly typical of what had happened in the post-independence era to comunidad lands. Montes had visited the Indian comunidad in possession of these lands at the turn of the century, when this previously isolated region was first opened up to La Paz and the rest of the republic through the construction of roads and railroads. Quickly recognizing the value of these lands, Montes bought out a neighbouring property, and then bought actual comunidad fields by purchasing the property of three or four *comunarios*. Although by Indian custom these comunarios had no right to sell what was in theory communal property merely loaned to them, by Bolivian law they were permitted to transfer legal title. Next Montes called in troops from Guaqui on some pretext and the heads of the families of the comunidad were shipped off to La Paz where, under violent threats, they were forced to renounce their land titles. Thereupon Montes prohibited their return to the region and brought in Indians from other areas to work the property as colonos.

The finca, once in operation, was a large affair and after several decades had a population of some 2,500 colonos. Despite the rich quality of the land, the availability of major fisheries in the lake, and even the possibilities of illicit contraband trade with nearby Peru, the colonos lived at a near-starvation level and infant mortality was extremely high. As it was, the colonos were allowed only 33 per cent of the total cultivated acreage of the finca for their own crops, and their plots were insufficient to supply the average six-member family with enough food. Finca Taraco also had a type of piece-work arrangement whereby the number of days worked for the hacendado determined the amount of land a colono was granted. The minimum labour for any land was three ten-hour days a week, which was considered a *cuarta persona* (or quarter family); a half persona amount of land required six days and a full persona required twelve days labour per week, obviously necessitating the labour of several members of the family and possibly even hired labourers, for a good 120 families on the estate had no sayanas of their own. Because labour on the estate was so vital to the survival of a family, since it determined the payment in land the family received, men were more tightly tied to the land than the less productive women, and the latter had a better chance to migrate to the cities than did sons or husbands. All things considered, Taraco was unique on the altiplano for the non-agricultural sources of income available to the colonos (through fishing and contraband), yet even despite this and the unusual fertility of the soil, the situation of the colonos was truly desperate.[1]

Both the hacienda and comunidad Indians were part of an essentially similar sub-culture, bound to local villages and ruled by varieties of the typical native civil-religious government. These elected governments of elders who alternately exercised civil and church functions were common to almost all of Indo-America. The great distinctions between the free communities and hacienda peasant communities were in terms of their freedom to elect people to upper-level governing positions. In the haciendas, the patron appointed all key officers and exploited the internal taxing and tribute arrangements for his own personal consumption.[2]

In both communities, but more especially in the free communities, the pattern of ritual impoverishment predominated, and the exhaustive patronage of religious feasts reduced all wealthy peasants to a common denominator. In the hacienda community all surplus was effectively siphoned off by the hacendado and his administrator since they had complete control over selection for the various work obligations. Thus both comunidad and hacienda peasant communities tended to remain at a given level of economic growth, repeating a constant cycle of savings and consumption. The main differences were in the availability of education and freedom of movement for the free peasants, which enabled them to become part of an urban and mining part-time labour pool.[3]

The physical conditions for comunidad Indians were

---

[1] Edmundo Flores, 'Taraco: monografía de un latifundio boliviano', *El Trimestre Económico* (Mexico), xxii, No. 2 (1955), 208–30.

[2] Carter, *Aymara Communities*, pp. 43ff.

[3] *Ibid.* Chs. IV–VII are the best description available of how this system operated in Bolivia.

unquestionably better than those for colonos since they had greater control over their own labour and produce. But both types of Indian groups were similarly isolated from the minority society of non-Indians which fully exploited the submerged peasant masses either on the land, in the mines or in the towns.

To the Indians, the Spanish-speaking population formed a separate non-Indian whole, but this minority too was divided along harsh class and modified 'racial' lines. The division into urban lower, middle and upper classes was paralleled by the stratification of society into cholos and 'whites', with the former being most closely identified with the lower classes, and the latter with the upper class. The middle class was rather mixed and by the middle decades of the twentieth century the cholo categorization defined only the most recent Indian immigrants to the cities, with actual racial mestizos melting easily into the white grouping through education, dress and language criteria. Thus by the 1930s, the middle class was almost all white by the less rigid twentieth-century definitions. Although racial criteria had been strongly modified, class lines if anything had hardened as society became more complex.

This rigid class structure remained essentially unchallenged up to 1930. Though a few urban unions had organized themselves by then, the majority of Bolivia's non-agricultural labour force remained unorganized, with the single most important industry, mining, lacking any unions whatsoever. The vast majority of urban artisans, whose numbers in 1950 equalled those of all factory workers,[1] and the bulk of the urban proletariate had no conception of class and were largely a docile element in national political affairs. The only self-conscious elements to oppose the class structure of Bolivia before 1930, were in fact a few university students and intellectuals, who by and large formed a very small part of the white middle class.

To ensure their control over the peasants and the lower class, the upper and middle classes carefully excluded everyone but themselves from participation in national political life by an efficient literacy test which denied the vote to all but a tiny minority. Until well into the twentieth century this élite was a

[1] See table 3, p. 392.

stable grouping whose numbers did not greatly expand. Thus the total numbers of voters from the elections of 1884 to 1904 rose from only 30,000 to some 43,000, this latter figure representing only 3 per cent of the population.[1]

Though the number of eligible voters began to expand more rapidly in the twentieth century, reaching over 70,000 in the elections of 1913, 1917 and 1926,[2] the minority nature of this group changed very little. The tiny élite of literate persons in 1930 represented some 450,000 persons, and was itself rather carefully divided between a small middle class and an even more minuscule upper class, both of which were primarily urban.[3] The upper class consisted of hacendados, mine owners, leading merchants, bankers and the new industrialists, and their legal retinue, and made up a self-conscious oligarchy, or *Rosca* (as they were later to be labelled by the radicals), which directed the socio-economic and political life of the nation. United by close ties of marriage, common absentee possession of estates, membership in the same clubs and education in the same few schools, these leading families dominated the leadership of all the major parties and controlled the key administrative positions in the government bureaucracy. Despite the various changes of fortune common to any free market economy, the oligarchy proved surprisingly stable, and unusually able to maintain not only its political power, but its economic leadership as well.

But the oligarchy could not rule the nation alone, and depended for its political power on the constantly expanding numbers of the urban middle classes. Made up of professionals

---

[1] Rodolfo Soria Galvamo, *Últimos días del gobierno Alonso*, pp. 139–40. The 3 per cent figure is reached by dividing the 1900 population into the 1904 electorate.

[2] Andrés de Santa Cruz Schuhkrafft, *Cuadros sinópticos de los gobernantes de la República de Bolivia 1825 a 1956 y de la del Perú 1820 a 1956* (La Paz: Fundación Universitaria 'Simón I. Patiño', 1956), pp. 38, 40. In the Salamanca election of 1931, there were only some 38,000 votes cast (*ibid.* p. 41). In the last election based on a literate electorate, that of 1951, the high figure of 126,000 eligible voters was reached, but these still represented only 7 per cent of the total population. Henry Wells *et al.*, *Bolivia Election Factbook, July 3, 1966* (Washington: Institute for the Comparative Study of Political Systems, Operations and Policy Research Inc., 1966), p. 32.

[3] This is a rough estimate taken by dividing the differences between the 1900 census, which listed some 217,000 literates, and the 1950 census which gives some 708,000. Oficina Nacional de Inmigración, *Censo nacional de 1900*, II, 34; and Dirección General de Estadística y Censos, *Censo demográficio 1950*, p. 114.

and teachers, tradesmen and artisans, white collar workers (*empleados*), public employees, and the officer class, this increasingly self-conscious middle sector of Bolivian society formed the crucial base upon which all the political and economic institutions rested. For it was these groups which supplied the votes and the literate rank and file to keep the system operating. Prior to 1932 this middle class had been subservient to the oligarchy's interests, which it equated with its own, and gave the oligarchy essential political obedience and support. But the Chaco War revealed divergences of interest between the middle class and the historical leadership, and also led it to re-evaluate its relationship to the 300,000 people who made up the Bolivian labour force.[1]

At the start of the great war, however, none of the discord among the governing and politically active classes of the nation was as yet visible or even contemplated. Salamanca's announcement of virtual war in early August 1932 at first brought only paroxysms of patriotism and protestations of sincere unity and support from all the literate classes of the nation. Declaring to the opening sessions of the new congress in August that Bolivia refused to give up her conquests, Salamanca brought about the immediate suspension of mediation efforts, and Paraguay reacted by decreeing general mobilization and by ordering a full-scale military commitment, thus precipitating both sides into the all-out war for the Chaco.[2]

Though war brought seeming unity of thought and commitment to the righteousness of Bolivia's action from the general public, Salamanca's continued political ineptitude renewed the old political wrangling within a very short time. Despite universal demands for a national all-party government and cabinet, Salamanca decided from the beginning that the war situation gave him every right to rule alone and even permitted him to divest himself of the obligations and concessions he had been forced to make to the Liberals.

---

[1] This is an estimate of workers and their families, based on the figures supplied by Capriles and Arduz, *El problema social*, pp. 18, 21.

[2] Díaz Machicao, *La guerra del Chaco*, pp. 102–4. At this 6 August meeting, congress fully endorsed not only all the actions of the president since its last meeting the previous May, but formally presented him with a vote of confidence on his international policy.

In line with his new sense of freedom, Salamanca brought Canelas back into the government in July at the ministry of finance.[1] This was a deliberate challenge to the Liberals, who had forced Canelas' exit only a few months before. Nor had Canelas in his absence endeared himself to the Liberals. From the columns of his newspaper *La Patria* of Oruro, he had viciously attacked them for their opposition to his economic programmes. The response of the Liberals to this deliberate provocation was to go into opposition to the government. On 27 August, at a special party assembly in La Paz, they demanded the immediate organization of a coalition cabinet and declared that all their compromises with the Genuinos were abrogated. The assembly also obtained the resignation of the two Liberals in the cabinet, who were asked to resign so as to force the government to organize a broader-based national unity cabinet.[2]

Meanwhile, Bautista Saavedra and his Partido Republicano Socialista, through their newspaper *La República*, began to attack Salamanca's conduct of the war almost from the opening days. Although on 19 July the PRS agreed to a temporary truce in the party battles,[3] it pressed Salamanca hard for more dramatic action. In sharp contrast to the initially cautious attitude of the Genuino newspaper *La Razón*,[4] and to the Liberal organ *El Diario*, *La República* took a decidedly *guerrista* tone and demanded an immediate and formal declaration of war against the aggressors.[5] The party also demanded a decree of general political amnesty for the traditional *políticos*,[6] a demand which was later seconded by the Liberals.[7]

The government gave its response to these proposals on 2 September when it closed down the Liberal party newspaper in Cochabamba, *El Tiempo*, for calling for a coalition cabinet and a decree of general political amnesty.[8] In response, the Liberal party had its two cabinet representatives, Juan María Zalles and

---

[1] *El Diario*, 20 July 1932, p. 6.

[2] José Quiroga Ch., *La política interna en el primer período de la guerra (Documentos producidos en el proceso para formar el gabinete de concentración nacional)* (Cochabamba: Editorial 'El Imparcial', 1932), pp. 1–2. This party manifesto also called for a decree of political amnesty.

[3] *La República*, 20 July 1932, p. 4. [4] See editorials of 9 July and 14 July.

[5] *La República*, 22 July 1932, p. 4. [6] *La República*, 27 July 1932, p. 4.

[7] *El Diario*, 3 September 1932, p. 6. [8] *La República*, 2 September 1932, p. 4.

Alfredo H. Otero, resign.[1] This precipitated a two-month cabinet crisis of major proportions and proved to be the opening skirmish in a long battle between Salamanca and the other traditional parties. This feud quickly grew more intense as the first major news of disaster began to come in.

By the beginning of September, the Bolivian advance had been almost completely halted, and the Paraguayans were able to begin their counter-offensive. Their prime target was their old Fortín Boquerón, a key to the defence of their Chaco line and now held by some 600 Bolivian troops. The battle for Boquerón began on 9 September and lasted until 30 September.[2] Despite the crucial nature of the post and the initial ineptitude of the Paraguayan assault, the army high command seemed incapable of doing anything to prevent encirclement of the position or of bringing in essential supplies. The Bolivians began the war with only 1,500 troops in the Chaco, and their supply lines from the distant altiplano were in a chaotic and primitive state, incapable of maintaining adequate levels of men and equipment. It therefore took months for these items to go from the altiplano by train to Tarija, the railway terminus, thence by truck to Villamontes at the edge of the Chaco, and from there to the distant forts. The lack of planning, resources and experience of the Bolivian officer corps also quickly manifested itself, and the troops at Boquerón were left to stop the heavy and well-coordinated Paraguayan attack as best they could.[3]

Salamanca's reaction to the encirclement battle of Boquerón was to continue to reject neutral nations' offers of negotiation, still insisting on retention of the Paraguayan forts he had ordered to be taken as reprisal for Laguna Chuquisaca. He also added his own ineptness to the growing breakdown of the Bolivian military command by constantly over-ruling or ignoring his EMG and taking his constitutional role as captain-general as an active one, to the point of ordering and counter-ordering front line troops on his own initiative, much to the chagrin of his bitterly hostile upper officers and commands. Salamanca cared

[1] *La República*, 7 September 1932, p. 4.
[2] For a detailed eyewitness account of this battle see Mayor Alberto Taborga T., *Boquerón, diario de campaña* (La Paz: Editorial Canata, 1956).
[3] Urioste, *La fragua*, pp. 9ff.

little about the feelings or even opinions of his officers, since he had never received much support from the officer class in all his long political career, and in fact many of the leading front-line officers had been closely involved with Siles and the previous régime. Thus in the first battles a sharp conflict developed at the very centre of the Bolivian command between Salamanca and his civilian government and the Bolivian general staff and its subordinate commands. This gulf produced not only a mound of conflicting and incriminating communiqués, but more importantly was to lead to a confused and embittered war leadership on the Bolivian side.[1]

Meanwhile Salamanca, refusing to work out a national coalition cabinet along party lines, tried to obviate criticism by inviting two leading opposition politicians to join his cabinet: the Liberal Casto Rojas and the Republicano Socialista Juan Manuel Sainz. Since he refused to accept party instructions on these choices or allow the party to control the ministers, the respective parties forced both men to reject the proffered posts.[2] With this rebuff, Salamanca decided to try going it alone with a reshuffling of his own followers.[3] But congress showed its hostility to the president by refusing to vote for the continuation of the state of siege, a move which the government simply ignored despite its unconstitutionality.[4]

On 30 September, completely surrounded and under continuous bombardment for twenty-three days, the forces at Boquerón surrendered. In the last days the high command had debated over the alternatives of evacuation or a renewal of an attack on the Paraguayan encirclement, and deciding on the latter sealed the fate of the Boquerón forces who lacked food, water, ammunition and other essential supplies.[5] In the first days of October the public was informed about Boquerón. The effect was extraordinary. Gone were those first naive sentiments of nationalism and

---

[1] For this conflict in commands see Zook, *Chaco War*, pp. 84ff., and for the political alignment of the officer corps, see Urioste, *La fragua*, p. 131. Also see Díaz Machicao, *La guerra del Chaco*, pp. 117ff.

[2] *La República*, 16 September 1932, p. 4; Quiroga Ch., *La política interna*, pp. 6, 7.

[3] *La República*, 21 September 1932, p. 5.

[4] *La República*, 22 September 1932, p. 8.

[5] For battle of Boquerón, see Zook, *Chaco War*, Ch. IV.

patriotism, gone was the dream of Bolivian invincibility and Paraguayan weakness. In the cold reality of the fall of Boquerón the first doubts were sowed, the first horrors of the long and costly war.

On 4 October, according to an anti-government source, some 20,000 persons rioted in La Paz, attacking the official government paper *La Razón*, and then demanding the resignation of Salamanca and the return of General Hans Kundt. Kundt was the famous leader of the pre-World War I German military training mission to Bolivia who later served as chief of the Bolivian general staff during the 1920s. A naturalized Bolivian citizen and a decorated veteran of the Great War in Europe, he was nevertheless distrusted by large numbers of the Bolivian officer corps. Popular demands for his recall indicated the profound national distrust of the officer corps which pervaded the nation.[1] On 6 October several deputies presented a petition to the government demanding the return of Kundt. This petition quickly won full congressional endorsement on 8 October, which indicated congress' support of the growing public clamour against the government and the high command.[2]

Neither Salamanca nor his officers approved of Kundt's return,

[1] *La República*, 5 October 1932, p. 3. In 1911, Bolivia had contracted for the services of a military training mission in Germany, to take charge of the reorganization of the national army. Head of this mission was Major Hans Kundt, who was given a colonelcy in the Bolivian army and also served as chief of the EMG from 1911–14. Another member of this mission was Captain Roehm, later famous in the founding of the National Socialist party in Germany. With the outbreak of World War I, Kundt and the mission returned to Europe and Kundt served with distinction on the Russian front, rising to the rank of general. In 1920 Kundt returned to Bolivia as a private citizen, but Saavedra contracted for his services, making him a Bolivian citizen, giving him a generalship and his old post as chief of the EMG, which he held from 1921–26—an act for which Saavedra was bitterly attacked by the opposition *políticos* and also by the officer corps. In 1926 Kundt took leave of absence to visit Europe and more than 150 officers signed a special petition requesting Siles to prevent the return of Kundt. So Kundt stayed abroad and it was not until the Vanguardia incident and the consequent bungling of the EMG that he was brought back and given his old post, which he held until June 1930. In the revolt of that month Kundt did all in his power to prevent the army from revolting and for this support of the government was forced with Siles and Toro to flee the country and seek safety in exile. Colonel Julio Díaz Argüedas, *Como fué derrocado el hombre símbolo* (*Salamanca*), *un capítulo de la guerra con el Paraguay* (La Paz: Fundación Universitaria 'Simón I. Patiño', 1957), pp. 326–9; Alberto Ostria Gutiérrez, *Una revolución tras los Andes* (Santiago: Editorial Nascimiento, 1944), pp. 59–60, 62.

[2] Díaz Machicao, *La guerra del Chaco*, pp. 139–40.

and Quintanilla angrily wrote to the high command that 'Neither General Kundt nor anybody else will be able to remedy the lack of effective personnel, deficiencies in armament, munitions, means of transporting supplies and in general innumerable organizational failures which characterize the present situation. Asking for the return of General Kundt clearly indicates lack of confidence in the capacity of the general command'.[1] Salamanca, however, took advantage of the public clamour for action by ousting General Osorio as chief of the EMG, and replacing him with José L. Lanza, the hated Osorio being sent to the front.[2]

But the army officers were reaching the point of open hostility towards Salamanca, and under the proddings of the astute and politically-minded Colonel David Toro, his chief aid, General Quintanilla sent his famous telegram of protest to the government. This scathing communiqué was sent from the front on 8 October and declared:

In the name of the commanders and officers of the Fourth and Seventh Divisions and this command, we wish to express to the government the following—First. The field army knows that the only one responsible for the present situation is the government, whose present warlike propaganda contrasts with the slovenliness and lack of foresight it exhibited in endowing and organizing the army. Rather, it neglected the most basic necessities in preparing the army to respond to its *guerrista* policy. Second. *The president of the republic and the cabinet forced the army to initiate operations precipitously and inopportunely, with the exclusive object of obtaining sensational results which were related only to internal political ends.* Third. The president of the republic assumed actual direction of operations, thereby limiting the freedom of the military command, which saw itself obliged to surrender its exclusive role to give way to government orders. Fourth. The army is convinced that the dismissal of the chief of the Estado Mayor General at the present moment constitutes a grave offence against its honour and dignity before itself and others, since it explicitly indicates that the present situation is only due to the ineptitude of the military commands. Fifth. Given the above reasons, the army continues to recognize the authority of General Osorio and the other commands, which it feels cannot be changed, thus finding itself disposed to disavow the orders

---

[1] Arze Quiroga, *Documentos*, II, 247.
[2] Díaz Machicao, *La guerra del Chaco*, p. 140.

of the government on the points indicated. Sixth. The army believes itself capable of continuing to defend the national honour with the present command, with unalterable faith in final success.[1]

This was tantamount to open rebellion against Salamanca. In his answers to Quintanilla, Salamanca categorically denied all charges and demanded compliance with the change of command orders and threatened serious consequences, specifically mentioning treason and rebellion in the face of the enemy. On 10 October, Quintanilla, opposed by a strong pro-Salamanca wing of officer loyalty, backed down and was thereupon ordered to give up his command and return to La Paz.[2] Thus the first open flare-up between Salamanca and the high command was resolved in Salamanca's favour. Colonel Lanza quietly took over the position of temporary chief of the EMG and the change of command was accepted by the officer corps.[3]

But this was only the first skirmish in the long war between the president and his high command. Lanza himself proved no more pliable than his predecessor, and on 19 October he sent a memorandum to Salamanca notifying him that according to regulations a chief of the field army should also be appointed and since no one had been placed in this position he assumed that the president would therefore himself specifically direct military operations in his capacity of captain-general. In short Lanza was challenging Salamanca finally and openly to accept the reality of the position and either fully take upon himself the name and responsibility as supreme military officer—a function which he was already carrying out without title—or give such a post to a military officer and relegate himself to a political and overall general non-military function as President Ayala was doing in Paraguay. Lanza also asked for a specific war policy—that is whether the president wanted an offensive or defensive action and whether he or the EMG should initiate it. In his usual way, Salamanca answered this memorandum on 22 October by claiming that he neither thought to direct military operations nor had any desire of naming a general-in-chief![4]

---

[1] Arze Quiroga, *Documentos*, II, 248, italics mine.   [2] *Ibid.* II, 248–50.
[3] See *ibid.* II, 250–5, for correspondence between Toro and EMG on the issue.
[4] *Ibid.* II, 262–6.

At the same time as Salamanca was experiencing open rebellion and disobedience from his military commanders, his refusal to organize a coalition régime led him into a constant struggle on the internal political scene. Offers of cabinet posts to individual Republican Socialists and Liberals were turned down throughout the early weeks of October.[1] On 14 October Salamanca went so far as to increase his offer to the Liberals to two full-fledged cabinet appointments—to José Luis Tejada Sorzano and Casto Rojas—and after long negotiations a tentative cabinet was organized, only to break down when news came of the fall of the Bolivian fort, Arce, to Paraguayan troops.[2]

Having reorganized its forces and retaken the lost forts, Paraguay now began a major penetration into Bolivian territory and in early October proceeded to outflank Colonel Peñaranda's forces at Fortín Arce, which after some fighting was precipitously evacuated by the Bolivians at the approach of Paraguayan troops on 21 October.[3] It was a full-scale rout and at the news of the disaster the cabinet negotiations immediately broke down. In response to this, Salamanca took the extreme action of organizing his own cabinet of Genuinos, giving the arch-enemy of the Liberals, Demetrio Canelas, the crucial ministry of government portfolio.[4]

The reaction to Salamanca's action was intense and congress, showing a Republicano Socialista-Liberal coalition majority, not only voted a censure of this new cabinet, but demanded the organization of a coalition cabinet within twenty-four hours.[5] *La República* even went so far as to ask for the resignation of Salamanca.[6] The government's response was to resort to mob violence, and crowds began attacking the parliament building, forcing congress to move its meetings to the La Paz municipal building; and the homes of both Montes and Bautista Saavedra were stoned. The government, of course, refused to make arrests

---

[1] Quiroga Ch., *La política interna*, pp. 7–11.   [2] *Ibid.* pp. 12–17.
[3] Zook, *Chaco War*, pp. 102–6. A major mutiny of Bolivian troops occurred at this battle, and five regiments were disbanded after they refused to fight. Ovidio Urioste, *La encrucijada, estudio histórico, político, sociológico y militar de la guerra del Chaco* (Cochabamba: Editorial Canelas [1940]), p. 67.
[4] Díaz Machicao, *La guerra del Chaco*, pp. 144–5.
[5] *La República*, 28 October 1932, p. 4.   [6] *La República*, 27 October 1932, p. 4.

for these actions and blamed the whole affair on regionalist senti-ment.[1] Montes replied to this on 4 November by charging that Salamanca was attempting to organize a dictatorship and in-sisted that he either re-organize his cabinet or resign from office.[2] Throughout November and December the struggle between Salamanca and the two major opposition parties continued, with the government 'discovering' plots involving leading politicians, exiling newspapermen associated with *El Diario* and *La República*, and jailing traditional political party leaders.[3]

The government also increased its attack on the left. From the first day of the conflict, Salamanca had unstintingly attacked the small Bolivian radical and labour movements. Almost immed-iately upon the outbreak of the war the government had begun to intervene in the labour movement. What was left of the local FOTs and FOLs in the major cities of the republic was finally destroyed in November 1933, when the government decreed the non-recognition of all unions which had other than simple mutualist and beneficient ends; only nineteenth-century-style benevolent associations which made no demands for wages or better working conditions and did not strike, were permitted to survive. By his consistent exiling or conscription of labour and leftist leaders from the beginning of the war, Salamanca was finally able to carry through his long-desired 'law of social defence', and under the excuse of war temporarily destroyed the Bolivian labour movement as a structured organization.[4] But despite all the repression, the continued disastrous course of the war was a major source of support to the Bolivian left, and its voice was at last beginning to be heard not only at home, but also on the front lines as Bolivian forces continued to lose ground.

In December 1932 General Hans Kundt, called upon by the people and congress to replace both the badly discredited high command as well as Salamanca, returned from Europe to take over as commander-in-chief of the Bolivian armies. The arrival of Kundt was a key defeat for Salamanca in several ways. Kundt

---

[1] Díaz Machicao, *La guerra del Chaco*, pp. 145–7.
[2] *El Diario*, 4 November 1932, p. 4.
[3] Díaz Machicao, *La guerra del Chaco*, pp. 149, 154.
[4] Canelas, 'El sindicalismo y los sindicatos', p. 77.

had stood out till the end against the Genuinos in 1930, always remained a loyal supporter of Siles, and was thus a political enemy of Salamanca. Secondly his contract with the government gave him—on his own terms—full and unqualified control over the Bolivian military establishment, over the immediate direction of the war effort and even over long-term policy.[1] In short, Salamanca was finally forced to give up his bitterly held control over the army.

But Kundt was unprepared himself for the Chaco conflict and his generalship and long Bolivian experience proved of little use. An expert in organization, Kundt was able by January to create Bolivia's second army of the campaign by rebuilding destroyed or captured units,[2] re-equipping the Bolivian forces, and infusing them with new spirit. But he decided to throw this new army into one major all-or-nothing attempt to take the Paraguayan position of Nanawa, an excellently defended and supplied fortress, though not a strategically key one as Kundt thought. From January through July of 1933 Kundt carried out a murderous continued assault against these fortified positions and while he was thus destroying his own forces piecemeal,[3] the Paraguayan forces at Toledo in March inflicted a severe defeat on the badly led Bolivians. In the battle of Toledo, 2,000 Bolivian troops out of 3,500 were lost and the 3rd Division after this bloody defeat saw the mutiny of two infantry regiments, a mutiny supposedly caused by leftists and pacifist agitators.[4] On 4 July Kundt made his last great effort to take Nanawa and out of 7,000 troops sent against the fortifications that day, 2,000 were killed. Despite this enormous sacrifice no results were achieved.[5]

The 4 July disaster finally brought an end to the mystique of Kundt's invincibility, and the embittered Bolivian officer corps now began openly criticizing the German general. Kundt was even forced to remove his old associate David Toro from command for the latter's open hostility toward the Nanawa strategy.[6]

---

[1] Urioste, *La encrucijada*, p. 72.
[2] It was estimated that after only four months of war, Bolivia had already lost 2,500 troops either killed, wounded or made prisoner! *La República*, 28 October 1932, p. 4.
[3] Zook, *Chaco War*, Ch. V.   [4] *Ibid.* pp. 130, 132.   [5] *Ibid.* p. 146.
[6] Colonel David Toro R., *Mi actuación en la campaña del Chaco (Picuiba)* (La Paz: Editorial Renacimiento, 1941), pp. 33–42; Díaz Machicao, *La guerra del Chaco*, p. 179.

A temporary lull now developed on the front, except in the 4th Division area, and it was not until September that Paraguay again went on to the offensive.

These important military events coincided with major developments on the internal political scene. In anticipation of the coming May 1933 elections, the Liberals and Republican Socialists—classic enemies in the previous thirteen years of political history—finally recognized their common grounds of hostility against Salamanca, and in February 1933 signed a unity electoral agreement.[1] The May elections for congress, however, proceeded along the usual lines of Bolivian government dictation, and despite all his moral stands and defence of the constitution in the preceding thirty years, Salamanca used every crude means possible to ensure the victory of his own supporters. He thus succeeded in packing congress with loyal followers.[2]

But congressional domination did not reduce criticism of the government. In February 1933, Bautista Saavedra reached the high point of his personal attack on Salamanca when he published his famous article 'Sartor Resartor' in which he charged that Salamanca had only been 'a legalist in the opposition because he did not have the opportunity to violate the laws'. Saavedra not only denied that Salamanca was a statesman or even a moral politician, but he claimed that the 'hombre símbolo' had even 'lost his sense of reality. He has lived in a world of his own exclusive subjective making, far from the most urgent problems of his country'. Nor did Saavedra mince words about the causes of the war which was still no more than six months old, declaring that Salamanca in order 'to escape the political torment which threatened to discharge upon his head, carried us to this inhuman war, which is exhausting the nation and carrying the country to its ruin', and to add insult to injury 'he took seriously his title of captain-general, he in whom the sight of the military uniform produces nausea'. Yet despite his actual leadership in the conduct of the war 'he doesn't believe himself responsible', and he throws 'the blame for the disasters onto the military chiefs'.[3]

[1] *El Diario*, 9 February 1933, p. 4.   [2] Díaz Machicao, *La guerra del Chaco*, p. 176.
[3] *La República*, 3 February 1933, pp. 5, 6. This article was expanded, a short time later, into a pamphlet of over a dozen pages in length, and in this form had wide circulation throughout the nation.

While this was the most extreme and widely discussed attack to date against Salamanca, it was not the only one, and in July the Partido Nacionalista added its voice of dissent by condemning Salamanca's foreign policy for not preventing armed warfare in the Chaco.[1] But Salamanca continued his policies, despite these attacks, though he finally reached his limit with Saavedra and his party, and in October 1933 permanently closed down *La República*.[2] But cabinet instability and congressional hostility continued uninterrupted as the war situation deteriorated.

In early September 1933, the Paraguayan General Estigarribia began the Guaraní offensive and soon captured the Bolivian fort Campo Grande along with two entire regiments. Despite opposition from Toro and the officers, the public refused to abandon its one hope of victory, Kundt, and the government in late September categorically refused to replace him. In November the Paraguayans continued their slow advance, and by early December they succeeded in achieving a major breakthrough. In one of the encircling movements for which the Paraguayans were now becoming renowned, Colonel Peñaranda succeeded in extricating himself and some 2,500 of his troops, and the government, now desperate for even a shred of good news, turned the whole retreat into a great moral victory and made Peñaranda into a 'hero', quickly elevating him in rank and position.[3]

By 12 December the government finally decided it could no longer support its high-paid German general and again turned the army over to Bolivian officers. At first it had been decided to return it to the competent Lanza, but it was given instead to the 'hero' of the hour, General Enrique Peñaranda, a slow-witted, though loyal officer. In reality, it was the resourceful Toro, who earlier in the war had instigated the insurrection of Quintanilla, who soon became the dominant figure in the new high command.[4]

Kundt's tenure as chief of the Bolivian army had proved an unparalleled disaster for the nation and in the one year of his

---

[1] Díaz Machicao, *La guerra del Chaco*, p. 178.
[2] *Ibid.* p. 191. Three newspapers altogether were closed by the government at this time: *La República, Acción* of Sucre, and *La Crónica* of Cochabamba.
[3] Zook, *Chaco War*, pp. 158–68.
[4] *Ibid.* pp. 194–5.

leadership some 77,000 men had been mobilized, of whom 14,000 had died in action, 10,000 were made prisoner, 6,000 deserted, and 32,000 were evacuated because of sickness and wounds. This left but 7,000 troops in the field (8,000 were in rearguard services), a pitiful remnant of the great army which Kundt had so laboriously constructed, and a remnant whose morale had been shattered.[1] As for the nation, the going of Kundt brought an embittered disillusionment and a sense of utter futility.

Shortly after Peñaranda took office, a temporary armistice was effected and the Bolivian command was given a crucial breathing space in which to undertake the rapid construction of what came to be called the Third Army. But the respite was only a short one, and in early January 1932 the Paraguayan drive was resumed.[2] Fort after fort fell to the rapidly advancing Guaraní, with the demoralized Bolivian troops either surrendering in large numbers, deserting, or retreating in utter chaos. In February 1934 the tense government exiled its chief opponent Bautista Saavedra, and in March tried a new cabinet reorganization as Bolivia suffered another major defeat at Cañada Tarija.[3]

In April, open hostility toward Salamanca reached such a pitch in the army that the cadets of the Colegio Militar revolted and demanded an end to the government. Only with difficulty was order restored and the cadets returned to barracks. With the dismissal of Kundt, Salamanca had again begun to intervene actively in command decisions and the relationship between the executive and high command quickly deteriorated to its old disharmonious and acrimonious state. In late April 1934 Salamanca precipitated a showdown when he demanded to have his own civilian representative on the EMG and named his loyal supporter, Joaquín Espada, as *Inspector del Ejército*. Colonel Oscar Moscoso, leader of the troops at Laguna Chuquisaca, and now

---

[1] Díaz Machicao, *La guerra del Chaco*, p. 203.

[2] Zook, *Chaco War*, pp. 170–4. For organization of the Third Army see Julio Díaz Argüedas, *La guerra con el Paraguay, resumen histórico-biográfico 1932–1935* (La Paz: Intendencia Central del Ejército, 1942), pp. 66–74.

[3] Díaz Machicao, *La guerra del Chaco*, pp. 205–7. According to the official army historian, Julio Díaz Argüedas, the disaster at Cañada Tarija was due in great part to communist propaganda which succeeded in influencing large numbers of troops to surrender without fighting. Díaz Argüedas, *La guerra con el Paraguay*, p. 92.

head of the EMG, protested at this action and for his insubordination was replaced by Colonel Felipe Rivera, thus causing a deep rupture in the high command. Peñaranda protested at this move from his field headquarters, but Salamanca refused to listen. Nevertheless, there was enough opposition from the officer corps to prevent Espada from actually taking up his position, and Salamanca's move for absolute domination in this struggle was stalemated by the army.[1]

By the end of April, Peñaranda had finally created a new army of 55,000 men, which in May temporarily halted the Paraguayans at the battle of Cañada Strongest—one of the few total victories achieved by Bolivia, in which 1,400 Paraguayan troops were taken prisoner. But the victory was only temporary. From June onward the Guaraníes pressed hard on the Ballivián sector hoping to achieve another breakthrough of the new shortened Bolivian defence line. In August, after several months of holding operations, Toro wrote a memorandum to the government suggesting that peace be signed with Paraguay. He noted that a moral and material equilibrium had been achieved with this recent victory, that Bolivia now had a large number of Paraguayan prisoners and that the strong new Guaraní offensive had been seriously held down for several long months, bringing considerable discomfort to the enemy.[2]

But before the government could act on this suggestion, the equilibrium was shattered and Estigarribia after long months of probing finally found a weak spot and achieved a breakthrough. On 14 August the Paraguayans punctured the Bolivian defences at Picuiba and began a race toward the upper end of the Chaco, an advance force reaching the Bolivian Andean foothills near Carandaití on 27 August.[3] This dramatic movement changed the entire picture of the campaign: the Chaco War now turned into an undisguised battle for the oil fields. With the disputed Chaco territory firmly in their hands, and the Bolivians thrown back to Villa Montes by November, the Paraguayans now had more territory than they had ever claimed even in their wildest

[1] Díaz Machicao, *La guerra del Chaco*, pp. 208–10.
[2] *Ibid.* pp. 211–15; Toro R., *Mi actuación*, pp. 76, 379–404 (the latter is a full reprint of this extraordinarily frank document).
[3] Zook, *Chaco War*, pp. 196–7.

pronouncements. But the Chaco was only potential national wealth, and the hard-pressed tiny nation now saw before it the possibility of taking nothing less than the rich petroleum fields of the Andean foothills in the Bolivian states of Tarija, Chuquisaca and Santa Cruz.[1]

In the midst of this crisis the climax to the long bitter feud between Salamanca and the high command was reached. In the face of continuing retreat Salamanca began demanding a reorganization of the top command and the removal of Rivera and his assistant Rodríguez from the EMG. In late September he met with Peñaranda at Tarija to demand these changes, only to have Peñaranda refuse, and after several days of useless arguing the President returned to La Paz.[2]

Meanwhile, tension increased on the altiplano as the November presidential elections approached. The two major candidates were the Liberal, Juan María Zalles, and the Genuino Franz Tamayo, who was the government-backed candidate. The Republican Socialists demanded the return of their leader and threatened abstention if this was not carried out. The issue of the return of Saavedra became an important one, and despite the Genuino domination of congress the saavedristas carried a vote of censure against the minister of government, Joaquín Espada. Espada, forced by law and precedent to resign, was nevertheless reappointed a few days later to the finance ministry, since he was a staunch salamanquista and had been in practically every cabinet since 1931. Another of Salamanca's stalwart supporters (among whom figured Tamayo, Canelas, Luis Calvo and Salamanca's brother-in-law Rafael de Ugarte—all of whom formed the basis time and again for all the Salamanca cabinets), Ovidio Urioste, replaced Espada in the government portfolio.[3] Urioste, on his own admission, was a strong guerrista and anti-army figure and his presence in this key post exacerbated internal political and army-executive relations.[4] On 11 November the

[1] Zook, *Chaco War*, p. 192.
[2] Díaz Argüedas, *Como fué derrocado el hombre símbolo*, Ch. VII.
[3] Díaz Machicao, *La guerra del Chaco*, pp. 223, 230–1.
[4] Urioste, *La encrucijada*, pp. 167–9. Urioste advocated setting up concentration camps and the formal establishment of a dictatorship. He shows in this work his utter contempt for the political opposition to Salamanca and to the entire officer corps, yet he claims he carried out free presidential elections!

government-backed slate of Tamayo and Rafael de Ugarte was victorious, but the elections resolved nothing and the internal political situation continued tense.[1]

On 11–15 November the last major fortress area between the Paraguayans and the Villa Montes heartland, El Carmen, was surrounded by Paraguayan forces and 4,000 Bolivian troops were taken, some 2,500 being killed in the battle, and the entire line collapsed. The primary cause for this defeat was the independent expedition led by Colonel Toro which threw the defence off balance and exposed the whole line to attack, a movement of which the Paraguayans took full advantage. With the fall of El Carmen the troops retreated along the entire front to the Pilcomayo river and Villa Montes.[2]

To Salamanca, El Carmen was the last insult, and he decided to get rid of Peñaranda altogether as well as the entire EMG. On 25 November 1934, he travelled to Villa Montes with Canelas, Ugarte, and General Lanza to meet Peñaranda. Anticipating the reason for Salamanca's visit, Toro and his aides decided to destroy the entire effort at its core and convinced Peñaranda to rebel openly. On 27 November Salamanca met Peñaranda only to be informed that the army was making him prisoner and demanded his resignation. They threatened him with physical violence and also with signing an immediate armistice with Paraguay if he refused to resign. All potentially loyal military officers were now fully under control of the rebels, and Salamanca himself was securely held in the Chaco fortress of Villa Montes. Under these circumstances he was forced to accept the ultimatum. The government was handed over to Vice-President José Luis Tejada Sorzano. The Liberals now seized their chance to return to power and gave full endorsement to the new state of affairs, while all political opposition joined in supporting the army action. On 2 December the army released Salamanca and the disheartened and embittered man returned to his native city, where he died on 17 June 1935.[3]

The fall of Salamanca and the consequent retreat of the Bolivian

---

[1] Díaz Machicao, *La guerra del Chaco*, p. 234.
[2] Zook, *Chaco War*, pp. 206–10.
[3] Díaz Argüedas, *Como fué derrocado el hombre símbolo*, pp. 157ff.; Díaz Machicao, *La guerra del Chaco*, pp. 235–42.

forces to the Andean foothills had a positive effect on the Bolivian war effort. The establishment of the flexible and astute Tejada Sorzano in office, by the will of the officer corps, created a docile executive willing to allow complete military direction to the high command. Also the great Paraguayan breakthrough in the last quarter of 1934 left Bolivia with an excellent defensive position, close to its own railroads and supply lines, in a settled and familiar foothill region, and in broken country which left little real room for manœuvre. The Paraguayans who were now out of their own element and far from their previously secure and dependable supply lines, were in the opposite position. Also, the Paraguayan government was dangerously close to the end of its resources in its bid for the oil wealth of Bolivia.[1]

Tejada Sorzano was the right person for the role he was now called upon to fulfil. He was an able economist and politician, as well as an excellent administrator, and put all his energies into unleashing the full potential of Bolivian wealth and manpower in the defence of Villa Montes. Tejada Sorzano also brought internal political cohesion as it had never existed before in the Chaco War. He invited Bautista Saavedra to take up the ministry of defence, and while the old caudillo declined this post, the new cabinet was nevertheless a broadly based one. It included such Salamanca figures as David Alvéstegui, but also such men as Carlos Víctor Aramayo, the tin baron who was given the post of minister of finance, and the mildly leftist young nationalist intellectual Enrique Baldivieso who was made minister of public instruction. Zalles and Tomás Manuel Elío were also given cabinet posts in recognition of the importance of the Liberal party in the new government.[2]

The Tejada Sorzano government began the new year with major exploratory peace talks—previously approved by the army—and in January unconditionally accepted the peace terms proposed by the League of Nations. The Paraguayans, however, as the exploratory talks commenced, still refused to commit themselves, for their forces had begun to recover from the Villa Montes defeats and to make new headway. As the result of these

---

[1] Zook, *Chaco War*, pp. 232–3.
[2] Díaz Machicao, *La guerra del Chaco*, pp. 245–6.

new reverses, the discouraged Peñaranda submitted his resignation, but Tejada Sorzano refused to accept it. Meanwhile Peñaranda came to rely more and more on a new military figure, the young Beni officer, Major Germán Busch, who began to emerge as the key strategist and leader in the Villa Montes battle. In January and February the Paraguayans had taken the first of the Bolivian oil fields and half of the state of Tarija fell into their hands as they swirled around Villa Montes and spread to the north. But this northern and western movement aimed at Tarija and Santa Cruz had no hope of ultimate success unless the Villa Montes stronghold could be taken, and throughout February and March the great battle for Villa Montes raged, with the Paraguayans at one point coming close enough to shell the city. By April, the Paraguayan attack on Villa Montes was acknowledged a failure by the Paraguayan high command and though their forces still made advances in Tarija, by the middle of the month a major Bolivian counter-offensive was in full swing. By the end of April all of Tarija and Santa Cruz was cleared of Paraguayan troops and by May the oil fields were again firmly in Bolivian hands and Bolivian forces had once again reached the Chaco lowlands.[1]

With the re-establishment of the lines, the peace efforts of the Tejada Sorzano government began to be warmly received in Asunción and in Argentina, which was Paraguay's chief ally. Paraguay was near economic exhaustion, and, although her veteran army could probably hold the Chaco indefinitely from deep Bolivian penetration, it could never hope to invade the Andean foothills as the Villa Montes failure had just indicated. Thus in March, under League of Nations pressure and with strong Argentine support, a peace conference was set up in Buenos Aires with Bolivia, Paraguay, Argentina, Chile, Peru, Uruguay and the United States in attendance. In April, Tejada Sorzano met leading Bolivians to discuss the peace moves, and in early May appointed Bautista Saavedra and Tomás Manuel Elío to the Bolivian peace commission. The ultranationalist Saavedra was quietly replaced by Elío as chief before the delegation left Bolivia. On its way to Buenos Aires, the peace commission held special conferences with the army and definitive terms were

[1] Zook, *Chaco War*, pp. 228–33.

agreed upon by all parties. By 27 May all the delegates had arrived in Buenos Aires, and under the leadership of the Argentine chancellor and dominant figure in the Argentine-Paraguayan alliance, Saavedra Lamas, the peace conference began. The Bolivian delegation of Saavedra, Elío, Carlos Víctor Aramayo, Eduardo Díez de Medina, and the officers, Colonels Rodríguez and Felipe Rivera, worked out a complete set of compromise proposals, with Saavedra taking the extreme position for continuation of the war effort. After intensive negotiations, reasonable and realistic terms were agreed upon; an armistice protocol was signed on 9 June and the armistice began on 14 June 1935.[1]

Thus after three bloody years of fighting, the Chaco War had come to an end, with Bolivia a defeated nation and the great Chaco Boreal firmly in the hands of the enemy. Bolivia's losses in human life were appalling. Roughly 25 per cent of the combatants, or over 65,000 youths, were either killed, had deserted, or died in captivity, and this figure does not include the wounded and maimed.[2]

Apart from the obvious deficiencies of military leadership and supply, and confusion about ultimate objectives, Bolivia failed because Bolivian society was incapable of sustaining such a foreign war. The mass of the army was made up almost exclusively of Aymara and Quechua Indians, a majority of whom were colonos (or peasant labourers) on large landed estates. Fighting hundreds of miles from their highland and valley homes, in arid useless regions, against a homogeneous people with no caste distinctions, they had little will for fighting and dying for their country, or even understanding why they were in the Chaco in the first place. Nor did their presence in the army even achieve an amelioration of their own socio-economic status. As all veterans have reported, the caste system was rigidly maintained in the Bolivian army from the rearguard positions right up to the front lines and beyond.

---

[1] Zook, *Chaco War*, pp. 233–41; Díaz Machicao, *La guerra del Chaco*, pp. 259ff.; Eduardo Díez de Medina, *De un siglo al otro, memorias de un hombre público* (La Paz: Alfonso Tejerina, 1955), pp. 351–3.

[2] Zook, *Chaco War*, p. 240. The breakdown of these figures is as follows: 52,397 killed in action, 10,000 deserters, and 4,264 died in captivity out of the 21,000 prisoners taken by Paraguay.

From the time of their entrance into the army, the Bolivian Indians were segregated from the whites and mestizos. The intellectual Jesús Lara, for a time a sergeant in the recruiting station in Cochabamba, testified to the fact that whites and mestizos were often rejected completely from military service for the slightest excuses and, when drafted, were more often than not designated incapable of front line duty. The Indians, however, were consistently declared capable for active service.[1] In fact, so universal was conscription of Indians, who formed the major racial group of the nation, and so complete was their exclusion from the officer ranks that whites and mestizos were almost never present as front line common soldiers. Porfirio Díaz Machicao recounts the fact that he was the only white common soldier in his entire unit, and this was because he had been labelled as a political undesirable—a communist—and all such persons were placed in the front lines to be carefully watched by the officers.[2]

Another white civilian, Augusto Céspedes, who served as a non-commissioned officer, noted that 'we whites possessed certain privileges of caste, conserved from civilian life'. This meant white domination of all rearguard positions, the famous *emboscados*, and control over all positions of command. Only whites 'together with the mestizos, assumed functions of command, when professional officers were lacking'. 'In exceptional moments of fighting a kind of camaraderie took hold of certain combatants. In other moments [however] the habits of a lifetime reasserted themselves rudely, with small privileges and evasions of obligations being distributed along caste lines, which no amount of fighting could efface.'[3]

Thus even at the front lines, it was the Indian who did the work and who risked the most. Indians were the shock troops, the front-line common soldiers, and it was they who gave their lives for the nation. Though caste distinctions temporarily broke down in moments of crisis in this mass conscript army, the all-pervasive system always reasserted itself when the heat of the battle had ended. Thus the Aymara and Quechua Indians of

[1] Jesús Lara, *Repete, diario de un hombre que fué a la guerra del Chaco* (2nd ed.; Cochabamba: Editorial Canelas, 1938), pp. 10–12, 21ff.

[2] Díaz Machicao, *La bestia emocional*, pp. 170ff.

[3] Céspedes, *El dictador suicida*, pp. 136–7.

Bolivia never experienced a break with their own socio-economic past and when the war was over they were reintegrated into the old order with relative ease, as the war had brought them nothing but an even more dangerous form of servitude than they had known before. Cut off from the other classes, speaking their own tongues and dying together for a useless and inexplicable cause, they had no chance to enlarge their horizons or challenge their old assumptions. All attempts at rebellion in the front lines were immediately suppressed, and when peace came, the overwhelming majority quietly returned their weapons and resumed their former place in the social and economic system without protest.

But the war did have a profound effect on the civilian white and mestizo intellectuals who were drawn to the front. These civilians were for the first time thrown into a war of relentless slaughter, and as in practically every such war where the sacrifice is without reason and achieves no results, there was born among these men a new sensitivity and a new pattern of expectations. Revealing all the nation's glaring faults, the Chaco War produced the *generación del Chaco*.

As one veteran put it, 'The drama of the Chaco opened a wide furrow in our consciousness. The generations prior to 1932 speak one language; those who come after an entirely different one. For those who live through this unbearable experience there is a transmutation of . . . values.' The political and military errors, the administrative corruption, the absenteeism and libertinism of the plutocrats cause 'even the strongest to stagger, the weak ones to lose faith. The vast territory lost, the harvest of 50,000 lives, the bankruptcy of the institutions and of the trappings of command, . . . incubate a sentiment of frustration.'[1]

The most immediate release for this sense of bitterness and frustration was a great outpouring of social realist novels which began to flood the Bolivian literary scene in the first months of the war and continued to dominate national literature until well into the next decade. Bitter proletarian novels became the Chaco genre which gave rise to a new set of national writers and intellectuals, re-awakened the revolutionary zeal in many pre-war figures and gave Bolivia a major standing in continental

[1] Díez de Medina, *Literatura boliviana*, p. 342.

literature.[1] As the famous critic, Fernando Díez de Medina, noted 'This war literature concentrates itself on the living event, in the lacerating truth of the social process. It is the vehement desire to discover, to fix, to fathom itself: land, races, habits, conflicts of class, regions and souls. The truth, however bitter it may be.'[2] In novel after novel, the cruelty of the war, the wasted blood, the hunger and the thirst, the incompetence, treason and cowardice, the corruption and decadence of the rearguard and the office caste are underlined in bold print. The Chaco War novel brought to the literate élite of the nation a new outlook on life and a most intimate experience of the whole frustrating and disastrous war. As much as any single form of political ideology or revolutionary propaganda, the realism of the Chaco War novel had a profound impact on the men of its day and the future generation of Bolivian intellectuals.

But most Chaco War novels described the bitterness of existence, without providing prescriptions for the revolution or reform of the society which created this harsh reality. The novel, however, was not the only area where the frustration and self-awareness springing from the defeat found expression. For the whites and cholos who would listen, there was a steady voice which throughout the war explained to them the reason for the useless dying and showed them the way to salvage something from the sands of the Chaco. This, of course, was the voice of the old radical left, which maintained a remarkably active front line, anti-war and anti-traditional society propaganda through persecution, martyrdom, and exile. Proclaiming their old *programas* and slogans, they charged that the war was the last resort of the oligarchy and the imperialistic overlords, and only a social revolution could bring a new Bolivia. And as defeat followed defeat, and the lost generation of the war sought to understand why, these voices were heard with a new clarity, and

---

[1] Díez de Medina, *Literatura boliviana*, Ch. XIII; Augusto Guzmán, *La novela en Bolivia* (La Paz: Editorial 'Juventud', 1955), pp. 109ff.; Oswaldo Arana, 'La novela de la guerra del Chaco: Bolivia y Paraguay' (unpublished Ph.D. dissertation, Department of Modern Languages, University of Colorado, 1963), especially Ch. V; and Murdo McLeod, 'Bolivia and its Social Literature before and after the Chaco War: a historical study of Social and Literary Revolution' (unpublished Ph.D dissertation, Department of History, University of Florida, 1962).

[2] Díez de Medina, *Literatura boliviana*, pp. 358–9.

often for the first time, by the majority of literate and non-literate Bolivians.

The pre-war radical philosophy of Bolivia was best represented by Tristán Marof (Gustavo A. Navarro). Without question, Marof was the outstanding figure among the older generation of extreme radicals, who combined a strong current of European Marxism with a deep commitment to American *indigenismo*. Throughout the early 1920s both in Bolivia and in Europe he had published novels, political tracts, and essays to promote his ideas, and in the mid-1920s had also become deeply involved in the internal political scene in Bolivia as an agitator and party organizer. In 1927 the internationally known Marof was imprisoned by Siles but succeeded in escaping to Argentina. Remaining on Argentine soil, despite temporary arrests and exiles, for most of the next ten years, he maintained an active revolutionary life and continued to foment the Marxist movement in Bolivia from abroad. With the outbreak of the war he moved to the Argentine north and from Jujuy and Tucumán carried out active anti-war propaganda.[1] Marof's major activity at this time was to encourage desertions among the soldiers being sent to the front, a policy supported by the anarchists and a group of so-called 'communist nationalists'.[2] Ovidio Urioste, who formed a special commission to study this problem, stated that Marof, Alipio Valencia Vega, and others set up *comités de desertores* to care for the men fleeing the front and also to carry on major propaganda over the border at the southern rail and communications cities of Tarija and Tupiza.[3] The radicals were eminently successful, as the minimum official estimate of 10,000 military desertions indicates. But the group also attempted to formulate a clear revolutionary ideology to answer the problem of the Chaco War generation.

It was in response to this need that Marof wrote his most important work, and the fullest analysis he ever made of Bolivian society. Written in 1934, *La tragedia del altiplano* is an important summary of the pre-war, radical, leftist, interpretation of Bolivia

[1] Tristán Marof, *La tragedia del altiplano* (Buenos Aires: Editorial Claridad, 1934), p. 6, for his war-time work.
[2] Alexander, *Communism in Latin America*, p. 214.
[3] Urioste, *La encrucijada*, pp. 108–10.

and a major analysis of that society on a par with Alcides Argüedas'
classic, *Pueblo enfermo*. Just as Argüedas' work served as a summary of the positivists' interpretation of the reality of the republic
almost thirty years before, Marof's stated the native Marxist-
indigenista interpretation of Bolivia for the new generation.

For Marof, Bolivia was but a feudal colony of the imperialist
powers, which were represented by the mining capitalists, but
more importantly by the Standard Oil Company. To him the old
Incan and Tiahuanacan empires were Bolivia's greatest glories
and he placed great emphasis on his indigenismo and *anti-his-
panicismo*. The *conquistadores* brought nothing but slavery and
misery, which the independence movement did nothing to
change. Minerals were the only source of national wealth, and
this wealth had never benefited the nation, being first controlled by Spain, then by Anglo-Chilean capital and now by
North Americans and such non-Bolivians as Aramayo and
Patiño.[1] As for the Indians, they had lost their freedom and their
lands, and he echoed the words of Mariátegui to the effect that
the problem of the Indian was the problem of land ownership.[2]
But until now the Indian had fought his battles alone and hated
the upper castes. Unless a revolutionary vanguard loyal to the
workers could be organized, he argued, and the Indian convinced
of the ability of this new group to destroy the old oligarchy and
give him back his lands, any revolutionary movement faced the
possibility of being destroyed by the ignorant, down-trodden
Indian masses acting at the instigation of the old oligarchy.[3]

Marof denied the charge that his indigenismo was mere rom-
anticism, or racism.[4] He respected the Indians for their past and
he concentrated on their needs because they were the majority
of the nation and the base on which the feudal structure rested.
To destroy feudalism in Bolivia meant liberating the Indian.[5]
Racism, he charged, was really the class defence mechanism of
the whites. To understand 'the profound hatred which is felt for
the mestizo and the scorn for the Indian, one must search for the
cause in economic motivations. The white, as a ruling class, has
reserved for himself all the benefits of power, and of economic

[1] Marof, *La tragedia del altiplano*, p. 29. [2] *Ibid.* p. 46.
[3] *Ibid.* p. 53.   [4] *Ibid.* pp. 58–61.   [5] *Ibid.* pp. 62ff.

and social advantage. It is natural for this class to see in the cholos and Indians its inevitable competitors.'[1] The whites have therefore deliberately created the myth of the useless Indian and dangerous cholo and tried to encrust them in a caste system in order to prevent them from competing for economic power. Thus, claims Marof, both Enrique Finot and Alcides Argüedas attacked the cholos for causing all the evil in Bolivian history, instead of attacking the oligarchic class, which since the conquest had impoverished the soil and peoples of Bolivia for its own advantage.[2]

In a rather sophisticated argument for nationalization of the mines, Marof noted that foreign capital was sometimes beneficial to a state, if the state was of an advanced economic nature, if the people were of independent initiative, or if the product was agricultural and required intensive development, as occurred in Argentina. But in Bolivia, as in other mining states, 'The natural treasures were taken by foreigners and exploited not for the benefit of the nation, the society or its future, but for the private benefit of the discoverers'. In such a country, 'encumbered by a useless *laissez faire* attitude, an industrial and mercantile bourgeoisie could not be developed which could compete with the initiative of foreigners. The enrichment of the natives was not the rule, but the exception. The sources of production were incessantly exhausted by the foreigner without leaving a trace.'[3] But, 'all of the life of Bolivia, present and future, resides in the mines. Its potential as a country or a region depends on its mineral development. If the mines did not exist, Bolivia would be considered in America like a Liberia, an Ethiopia or a Tibet, mysterious with its legends and flocks.'[4] For this reason the paralytic, impoverished and meaningless Liberal pseudo-democratic state presently controlling Bolivia must be transformed 'into a strong socialist state ... which will administer the mines and exploit them for the benefit of the workers'.[5] In sum, Marof once again was advocating and elaborating his socialist revolutionary code of TIERRAS AL INDIO, MINAS AL ESTADO.

---

[1] Marof, *La tragedia del altiplano*, p. 68.
[2] *Ibid.* pp. 68–9.
[4] *Ibid.* p. 104.

[3] *Ibid.* p. 111.
[5] *Ibid.* p. 111.

Turning to the causes of the Chaco War, Marof reiterated the by now popularly held belief that the machinations of the Standard Oil Company were to blame, a theme first expressed in the Argentine press in the early months of the war to account for the Bolivian attack on Paraguay.[1] He approvingly quoted the dictum of José Aguirre Gainsborg to the effect that ' The Genuino Republican party, bespattered with the blood of thousands of victims, passes into history as the "genuine" representative of petroleum.'[2] Marof, however, did not dwell on this issue, but rather saw the war in the context of the tin barons, the Guggenheim interests, etc., all of whom he charges with directing the policies of the Bolivian government.[3] Nor does he discount as a causal factor the personality of Salamanca, the *hombre símbolo* of the feudal caste, who to save his government and his class 'has not vacillated in precipitating his country into war'. 'Without the war, Salamanca would have been overthrown by a growing popular opposition, or by the military caste as had been the case with Siles.'[4] 'Not being able to solve the terrible economic situation, the unemployment and the hunger, the only thing which occurred to this "brilliant mind" was to repeat his vain and empty phrase: "We need to stand firm in the Chaco".'[5] But what was Bolivia fighting for in the Chaco, asked Marof. For national honour, as the intellectuals' manifesto of 30 July 1932 stated? No! The war was being fought to obtain an oil port for Standard Oil and to defend the four million hectare domain of Standard against the Royal Dutch interests. 'Never was there any war so stupid and absurd as this!'[6]

But Marof saw one great potential of the war: it could be converted into the instrument of destruction of the old régime. 'The Chaco War can be the liquidation of the old feudal and *caciquista* Bolivia, provided that the soldiers, students and workers have courage and determination, and are provided with an energetic and trained proletarian vanguard, which must arise in the middle of this pain and blood.'[7] Such a potential vanguard organization was the Grupo Revolucionario Tupac Amaru, claimed Marof, a

---

[1] Marof, *La tragedia del altiplano*, pp. 160–1n.   [2] *Ibid.* p. 134.
[3] *Ibid.* pp. 157ff.   [4] *Ibid.* p. 148.
[5] *Ibid.* p. 159.   [6] *Ibid.* p. 206.   [7] *Ibid.* p. 119.

group that from its exile in Argentina since 1927 had been fighting to prevent the war and overthrow the feudal society. Now, noted Marof, this group was 'fighting to transform the war, at the service of imperialism, into a social revolution which will cast out of the land four centuries of slavery'.[1]

Grupo Tupac Amaru, the most powerful and important of the revolutionary groups in exile had active agents in the front lines, but was still only one of many such exile groups. In Chile under José Antonio Arze was the *Izquierda Boliviana*, and in Peru there were *Kollasuyo* and *Exilados*.[2] Marof, however, was unquestionably the dominating figure as the greatest revolutionary of the pre-war world and for a short time he became the key transition figure between the pre- and post-war leftist generations. This can readily be seen in the pronouncements and manifestos of the Tupac Amaru group. One such vibrant manifesto written in 1934 echoed the major tenets of the Marof book, defining Bolivia as a feudal colony of foreign imperialism and calling for a social revolution to oust the oligarchy.[3] Only through fraternization of the workers and the soldiers in the front lines would it be possible to achieve the great revolution, noted the manifesto.[4] 'The hour has arrived for creating and forming a new Bolivia. The old is buried in the blood of the Chaco.'[5] This manifesto, which was distributed in the front lines, called for the immediate end to the war, nationalization of the mines, distribution of the latifundios to the soldiers and Indians, recognition of all worker and employee *sindicatos* and all soldiers' councils, and finally demanded a united front to create a 'República Obrera Socialista'.[6]

This call for a united front, primarily under the leadership of Marof, brought a strong response from the Izquierda Boliviana group in Chile and the Exilados in Peru. As a result, in December 1934, a special *Congreso de Córdoba* was held to form a united party.[7] The consequent organization of the *Partido Obrero Revolucionario* (POR) was of major importance in the history of the Bolivian left, for it was the first revolutionary party of the new era, and in later decades formed part of the vanguard of the

[1] Marof, *La tragedia del altiplano*, p. 213.   [2] *Ibid.* p. 222.
[3] Grupo Tupac Amaru, *Manifesto*, pp. 3–4.   [4] *Ibid.* p. 4.   [5] *Ibid.* p. 23.
[6] *Ibid.* pp. 20, 24.   [7] Lora, *José Aguirre Gainsborg*, pp. 29ff.

revolutionary movement. At its founding, however, the POR was more a confederation of the exiled groups willing to work under the united direction of Marof and the young José Aguirre Gainsborg (a recent convert to Trotskyism),[1] than a party with a united cadre and coherent ideology. Each sector preserved much of its own identity and programme, although all now united under Marof to carry out greater pacifist and revolutionary agitation among the troops in the last months of the war. The number of local mutinies, desertions and abject surrenders— some 20,000 Bolivians were captured, many for no military reasons, and some 10,000 deserted from the ranks to seek refuge in Argentina—attests to the effect of this agitation.

But the new party, like its older counterparts, was a small affair of intellectuals in exile, and while their propaganda did reach the front lines and had some effect, the most important cause of the complete defeatism and pacifism of the Bolivian troops was the utter stupidity and corruption of the government and the officer-caste leadership which brought defeat after disastrous defeat. Given this corruption and defeat, any revolutionary doctrine was able to strike a deep chord of response among the soldiers. Revolutionary doctrines came from elements other than these organized leftist groups, for many leftists like Porfirio Díaz Machicao, Jesús Lara, and hundreds of previously activist labour men, were in the front lines as soldiers. In their own individual disorganized ways these intellectuals and labour radicals propagated anti-government agitation, encouraging discontent, and preaching a new order.[2] They created great unrest and a strong pacifist movement developed, with the entire army and nation coming to believe that the war was totally unjustified and indefensible and was caused solely by the Standard Oil Company as an imperialist venture. This mythology of the war for oil became accepted by all, regardless of previous affiliations, and had a marked effect on the internal post-war political developments.

As Marof and his followers correctly perceived, the Chaco War was to be a major cause of the breakdown of the traditional

---

[1] Aguirre Gainsborg, who had been exiled to Chile in July 1932, there joined the Communist party of Chile, was a major participant in the party's split between Trotskyites and Stalinists and had joined the *Oposición de Izquierda*, the Trotskyite wing. *Ibid.* pp. 26–9.   [2] Lara, *Repete*, pp. 20ff.

order. To Bolivians of any intellectual standing, the utter defeat of Bolivian arms, despite greater wealth, manpower and resources, indicated that something was terribly wrong with Bolivian society. Men who had signed the intellectuals' manifesto of July 1932 saw circulating in the newspapers ever more alarming versions of the initiative of Bolivia in causing the war, of the clandestine activities of the Standard Oil Company in total mockery of Bolivian sovereignty, of the desertion, stupidity and drunkenness of a Bolivian officer corps incapable of producing a cadre even half as efficient or intelligent as the Paraguayan one, despite all the pre-war pride in the invincibility and education of the army.

While in any army men grumble about the rearguard troops, about the inefficiency, corruption, and the favouritism displayed towards the privileged, these grumblings can become extremely dangerous in defeat. When an elaborate military machine breaks down time and again, and through sheer stupidity men are left thirsting for water or in hopeless military situations, these grumblings become outright mutinies, and cynicism and defeatism replace the last shreds of faith or patriotism. The number of desertions of officers from their troops was truly extraordinary. Yet each attempt by the government to bring officers to trial was obstructed by their fellow officers, and time and again trials for cowardliness were stopped, delayed or dropped altogether, so that no army officer was ever convicted for such an offence, at least among the regular officers. But this respect was never shown to the civilian reservists or common troops, and numerous common soldiers were shot for desertions and minor irregularities with a fearful vengeance.[1] Embittered by defeat, the

---

[1] Urioste, *La encrucijada*, pp. 201–2. The regular officers were in most cases trained at the Colegio Militar which was notorious for its poor standards and the fact that its students usually represented either the most ignorant or undisciplined sons of middle class and upwardly mobile mestizo families. *Ibid.* p. 189. Urioste tells of many reserve civilian officers who came in contact with RA officers and were truly shocked by their ignorance of even the basic geography of the nation! *Ibid.* p. 203. Graft was rife among the officers and many commands had champagne and women no matter what was occurring at the front. Birthday parties seemed to have been especially orgiastic occasions. Urioste recounts one such party which incapacitated the command in the midst of a key battle at Villa Montes in April 1935, and Toro's famous debacles during the great defeats of 'El Carmen' and 'Picuiba'. *Ibid.* pp. 191–6.

middle class civilian intellectuals had, for the first time in their lives, come into intimate contact with the other classes of the nation, and for the first time had been called upon to sacrifice themselves for the existing order. Those who survived the Chaco experience provided the stimulus which eventually would give rise to a new political order in Bolivia.

7

THE TRANSITIONAL GOVERNMENT
OF TEJADA SORZANO

The overthrow of Salamanca, though the first military coup since 1800, seemed to imply no major change in the political climate, for it brought the traditional Liberal party back into power. Tejada Sorzano and the men who surrounded him were pre-war politicians of the old order; and many of the saavedristas, Liberals and Nationalists appeared to believe that they were ending little else than the rule of Salamanca and his supporting clique. But the real situation in the post-war period was very different. The return to pre-war politics was only a transitional stage before the complete breakdown of the traditional political system. The calm before the veritable storm reflected more the preoccupations and initial disorganization of the new post-war political forces than it did the strength of traditional patterns. So long as the army was engaged in concluding the war and carrying out the initial stages of demobilization and peace, and so long as the returning veterans and intellectuals were still groping for an ideology and consolidating their forces, the pre-war leaders would be left undisturbed with the pretence of their old power. Once the initial period of consolidation was over, however, these same politicians were rapidly shorn of even this pretence.

For the new emerging forces, and for a time for the old political groups, retaining the neutral Tejada Sorzano in the presidency was a necessary stopgap measure until the new realities of the situation could be fully explored. In consequence, on 28 February 1935, congress and all the traditional parties agreed to prorogue the presidential term which Tejada Sorzano was completing for Salamanca until the following August.[1] In the months which followed, the Tejada Sorzano government concentrated

---

[1] Díaz Machicao, *La guerra del Chaco*, pp. 255–6.

on the overtures for peace and later the signing and execution of a peace treaty. The internal political calm, however, was finally broken once peace was restored and the end of the presidential prorogation period neared.

In July, after growing agitation among the political parties to select a presidential candidate, the army high command requested that Tejada Sorzano remain in office until the definitive conclusion of the peace settlement, and asked him to remain beyond August.[1] But the traditional political parties refused to see the naked power of the army and its new role as final arbiter in national politics, and continued their negotiations and bargaining to determine the succession issue. The discredited Genuino parliamentary majority sought the installation of the Tamayo-Ugarte slate which had been elected in 1934. The saavedristas demanded the complete renovation of the salamanquista-dominated congress and called for new congressional and presidential elections, while the Liberals and the small Nationalist party pressed for the continuation of the Tejada Sorzano régime.[2]

Tejada Sorzano accepted the army's request for a continuation of his régime,[3] and the labour and student movements, then in their initial stages of reorganization, fully endorsed the move.[4] But many of the old-style politicians remained opposed. Refusing to recognize the new situation, they attempted to deal with the problem of the presidential succession in the old manner and heeded only their own intra-party interests. All four traditional parties continued to struggle over the issue throughout July, with the two Republican parties in bitter opposition to the continuation formula. In response to these delaying tactics, there was a huge demonstration on 27 July of some 30,000 persons in La Paz in support of the prorogation move.[5] Yet on the same day, ignoring this demonstration and the army endorsement, the PRS announced its hostility and withdrew its two cabinet ministers from the government.[6] These men were replaced a short time later by two military officers.[7]

Ultimately the Liberals were required to use the threat of a

[1] *El Diario*, 5 July 1935, p. 5.   [2] *Ibid.*
[3] *El Diario*, 7 July 1935, p. 5.   [4] *El Diario*, 18 July 1935, p. 5.
[5] *El Diario*, 28 July 1935, p. 5.   [6] *Ibid.* p. 8.   [7] *El Diario*, 6 August 1935, p. 5.

full-scale military takeover to force the parties to come to some compromise agreement. On 3 August the Liberal paper *El Diario* warned that if the political parties did not come to a rapid agreement on the form of the post-war government, the country would soon find itself under a military dictatorship. 'It is not that we are advocating this solution,' declared *El Diario*, 'but simply that we see it coming', and the paper warned that 'if the civilians are incapable of putting their ideas in order, the army will do it for them'.[1] Under this threat, the Republican-dominated congress finally accepted the inevitable the very next day, and continued the government for another year, until 5 August 1936.[2]

Nevertheless, the Republicans refused to be reconciled, for they hoped to take advantage of the collapse of their chief opponents, the Genuinos, to stage a full-scale political come-back. In mid-August Saavedra resigned his post on the Buenos Aires peace commission and returned to Bolivia.[3] Although he held reconciliation talks with Tejada Sorzano, nothing was accomplished,[4] and the government was therefore required to remain in power with the support only of the Liberals, the Nationalists and a few dissident Genuinos.[5] While this solution ended the political tension over the issue of succession, the nation itself was beginning to experience a profound political agitation as never before in its history.

Something of the political temper which was fomenting this agitation was illustrated when the nation learned of the death of Daniel Salamanca at his home in Cochabamba on 17 July 1935. The reaction to the news was probably best summed up by *El Diario* itself, once his strong supporter, when it wrote: 'The most singularly conceited figure of the Bolivian political scene has ceased to exist. The man who agreed to a war which he could very well have averted, has disappeared almost simultaneously with the promissory event of peace. . . History,' continued the editorial, 'will have to pronounce on his acts, and meanwhile, it will be very difficult for anyone who has suffered in the war to cultivate his memory.'[6]

[1] *El Diario*, 3 August 1935, p. 4.   [2] *El Diario*, 6 August 1935, p. 5.
[3] *El Diario*, 16 August 1935, p. 4.
[4] *El Diario*, 27 August 1935, p. 5, and 30 August 1935, p. 4.
[5] *El Diario*, 31 August 1935, p. 5.   [6] *El Diario*, 18 July 1935, p. 5.

The bitter spirit expressed in this editorial reflected the intense hostility of the nation to the whole conduct of the war and its fruitless outcome. But whereas the traditional parties laid all the blame for the useless conflict on Salamanca and his followers, the restless youth began to challenge the very foundations of the society that had led them into war.

For the Chaco had opened up a gulf of generations, and had destroyed the authority of the traditional leadership. Having experienced the 'ferment of the Chaco', as one veteran called it,[1] the younger officers and the civilians, the professionals and the university students, the intellectuals and the middle class elements, all rejected the old forms and old leadership, and engaged in a confused but determined search for new patterns to follow. Disgusted with the pre-war political parties, they gave concrete expression to their hostility and desire for change by organizing new political movements untainted by traditional party ties. By this wholesale desertion of the pre-war parties they launched a period of extreme flux in Bolivian political life, for they destroyed the middle class and young intellectual-professional base upon which the old parties had securely rested.

One of the crucial needs of a government is the basic acceptance of its legitimacy by the mass of active citizens. Without this acceptance, no government or political system can function. This 'legitimization' of the political system is normally an unthinking response. The citizen accepts the general rules of government and the structure of authority as valid and given and adjusts his conduct to these norms. This acknowledgement that the needs of government are proper demands and that the present political system is essentially sound, need not conflict with the existence of corruption or inefficiency. One can be cynical about the bureaucracy or even refuse to accept taxation and other controls which are considered unjust and improperly applied, without in any way challenging the foundation of the government. In fact, a moderately inefficient government has little trouble surviving so long as its legitimacy is accepted. Nor need the government be democratic, or even free from palace coups d'état. For consensus is not what is asked for, only acceptance, and even rapid changes

[1] Céspedes, *El dictador suicida*, p. 143.

among the leadership can be seen merely as surface problems not threatening the general acceptance of the right of certain groups to rule, or the more fundamental pattern of class structure and governmental responsibilities and motivations. But once the legitimacy of a government is challenged, then neither force nor any other factor can preserve either the government, or more especially the system which has made it possible.[1]

This crisis of legitimacy is exactly what occurred as a result of the Chaco War. Suddenly accepted norms and patterns had no validity for a majority of the politically active population. The system had failed in a crucial hour, and that failure compromised it forever.

The first public manifestations of this unique crisis began to appear in the winter of 1935 when the returning veterans injected a new current of energy into the political left. Almost overnight the word *tradicional* came to be accepted as the standard pejorative term for describing the Liberal and Republican parties, and between them and the pre-war fringe of the radical Marxist-indigenist left, there now appeared a whole new moderate leftist movement which had not existed in the political spectrum of pre-Chaco Bolivia. Energies formerly used to buttress the traditional parties were turned toward forming innumerable 'socialist' clubs and political groups, and overnight a host of new names began to dominate the political scene.

As early as July 1935, news began to circulate of the creation of a political organization of young radical intellectuals called *Beta Gama* (the Greek letters signifying *Bolivia Grande* or the new Bolivia ideology). While not particularly radical in its initial reform proposals,[2] the new group nevertheless represented a self-conscious break with the past. It charged the traditional parties with responsibility for the war and disclaimed any connection with them. It also demanded a new voice in government for the youth who had sacrificed themselves in the Chaco.[3] Consisting

---

[1] For an excellent discussion of the problem of legitimacy, see Seymour Martin Lipset, *Political Man, The Social Bases of Politics* (New York: Doubleday and Co., 1963), Ch. III.

[2] Its preliminary operative programme called for constitutional reform, support of the prorogation, a coalition government and the old warhorse of administrative decentralization.   [3] *El Diario*, 25 July 1935, p. 5.

of far left and moderate elements, the majority of its members had formerly been in the ranks of the Republican and Liberal parties. Although still incapable of clearly formulating a revolutionary ideology, this restless youth was convinced that something must change, and something new be created, and this conviction inspired them to a great burst of activity.

Beta Gama was only the first of a host of such post-war groups. For in every major and minor city of the republic, innumerable parties and clubs were being organized. In La Paz there were *Grupo Henri Barbusse, Andes,* and *Bolivia*; in Cochabamba, the *Grupo de Izquierda*; in Sucre the *Grupo Ariel*; in Oruro the *Bloque Intelectual Obrero 'Avance'*; and in Potosí, a hotbed of political radicalism, there were numerous radical student and worker groups. Although most of these organizations were nothing more than ephemeral café gatherings, they nevertheless represented the starting point for a major movement away from the old parties. They gave these youths and intellectuals a sense of their own importance and capacity for leadership, and they helped to instil a more sophisticated philosophical and political attitude in their members. They created in short, an exciting if chaotic era of awakening, which gave a new dimension to Bolivian politics.

One of the few traditional leaders to understand the revolutionary ferment of these first post-war months was the astute old caudillo Bautista Saavedra. So sensitive was he to these currents that he actually succeeded in immersing his old party into the movement and for a time was even accepted as one of the 'new' leaders of the post-war era. Recognizing the chaos as well as the creative ferment, he attempted to fill the leadership gap by appealing to these groups with his pre-war Republican Socialist party, desperately attempting to take full advantage of the heavy withdrawal of the younger men from the traditional parties, to place himself again in power. In mid-1935, he published a pamphlet provocatively entitled, 'Where we are and where we ought to go'. Saavedra, once the most guerrista of the old políticos, now made himself out to be the most pacifist of anti-war advocates.

In this official party manifesto he noted that 'to us who are present during the painful epilogue of the tragedy of the Chaco, belongs the task of erecting a new nation', and speaking of himself and the party he claimed that 'we are the only ones who can speak to the country with purity of heart and with sincerity of thought, because we are beyond all culpability for the disaster'! He sought to respond 'to the deep restlessness which agitates the Bolivian soul' in the tragic, confused hour of its need. Saavedra recognized that to carry out his programme of regeneration 'we need the assistance of youth because we need the aid of awakened and vigorous vanguards'. Saavedra also charged that the so-called 'socialist' movement in Bolivia was without true leadership or organization, and this could only be found in an established party like the PRS.[1] Finally, the pamphlet appealed to the war experience as a source of national rejuvenation, and clearly echoed the crisis of legitimacy which the nation was experiencing, when it declared that the nation had been:

profoundly shaken by the war, which has revealed to us that nothing consistent existed in the country, and that in 100 years of autonomous life we have not accumulated anything which could have supported us in the disastrous defeat which we have experienced in the south-east of the republic. All the moral, institutional and political values upon which we believed we had built the structure of our nationality, have been destroyed. Our primary task is therefore the enormous one of creating a new national structure.[2]

This declaration of the failure of the old order by one of its caudillos demonstrates the profound awareness of the crisis on the part of sensitive political leaders, old and new. That Saavedra was echoing the basic needs of the new post-war generation, was reflected in the vital role he and his party would play in the new left and reform movements, despite their previously intimate association with the traditional order, and despite the essentially conservative and unimaginative nature of their programmes, which were neither new nor revolutionary.

Using much the same language as the old leftists parties, but without anything of real content, the manifesto attacked classical liberalism as having failed and then asserted the need to analyse

---

[1] Bautista Saavedra y Edmundo Vásquez, *Manifesto Programa: donde estamos y a donde debemos ir* (La Paz: Partido Republicano Socialista, 30 September 1935), pp. 1–4.   [2] *Ibid.* p. 11.

things from a viewpoint of historical materialism.[1] Of course, it carefully noted that the PRS was a party of evolutionary socialism which sought to change everything through education of the people, and that it abhorred communism and atheism.[2]

Its specific proposals called for a moderately directed economy, diversification of national production and a gradual programme of nationalization of the mines and petroleum production. In the agricultural area it could think of nothing more revolutionary than a call for crop diversification and protection of the small property holder from the latifundistas and the mortgage banks. The programme also revealed a strong anti-Indian bias in its proposals to encourage the immigration of what it called, 'vigorous and progressive races. Closing the doors of the republic to Chinese, Negroes', etc.[3] It denied the validity of revolutionary syndicalism for Bolivia, but asked rather for the unionization of all workers on the model of the Italian corporate structure. Claiming credit as the initiator of social legislation in Bolivia in 1932, the PRS called for more extensive laws governing hours, wages, pensions, accidents and safety.[4]

In short, the PRS was simply presenting a major programme of social legislation and was attacking the traditional authorities in industry and more especially in mining with vague threats of control and heavier taxation. Although this programme was probably representative of the most conservative elements in the new political movements, the themes developed by Saavedra and his followers were to dominate the moderate leftist movements in Bolivia throughout the rest of the decade of the 1930s. The emphasis was on social legislation and control of the mining oligarchy. It should be stressed that these were essentially urban white and cholo middle class positions, and it was to such elements that the new groups made their greatest appeal. It was no coincidence, therefore, that though these movements, and those espoused by the more radical army officers, constantly mentioned social justice, they were rather fearful of organized labour

---

[1] Bautista Saavedra y Edmundo Vásquez, *Manifesto Programa* (1935), p. 6.
[2] *Ibid.* p. 10.   [3] *Ibid.* pp. 13–18.
[4] *Ibid.* pp. 21–2. It also called for corporate organization of parliament (*ibid.* p. 26) and for major veteran legislation (*ibid.* pp. 35–6).

itself. They constantly flirted with Italian fascist ideas of corporatism as a way to bring reform without challenging the traditional structure of society.

Equally important, all these moderate programmes indicated an attitude of indifference, if not open hostility toward the Indian. When not openly ignoring the whole latifundia system, pongueaje, and the rural masses of society, such programmes as the PRS's called for new immigration, better education or more legislation to protect Indians. This willingness of the new moderate leftist movement to consider eventual nationalization of the mines and advanced social welfare legislation for the urban and mine workers, and their concurrent refusal to discuss the land tenure situation was one of the key distinguishing characteristics of the movement in its early stages. It was, in fact, one of the chief factors, along with its fascination with corporatism, which distinguished this new post-war leftist movement from the extreme radical pre- and post-war Marxian left. Like the more radical elements of these post-war moderate movements, Marof, Gainsborg, Anaya and Arze also talked of the mines and social legislation, but in addition advocated revolutionary worker organization, radical land reform and the abolition of the whole pongeauje and colonato system. The movements of the moderate left which eventually gave rise to some of the majority parties of the early 1940s were at heart anti-indigenista and anti-organized labour, and thus reflected to a marked extent the biases of their major supporters, the urban white and cholo middle classes.

In many ways, Saavedra showed a remarkable grasp of what the Bolivian middle class wanted and needed in this time of emotional crisis, and throughout the rest of his life he was intimately tied to that moderate leftist movement which it fostered. He held this leadership no matter how often more advanced or younger elements tried to oust him, and no matter how many times he revealed his basic insincerity of thought and naked desire for power. For Saavedra spoke for the small but very important middle classes of Bolivian society, which had formed the base for the traditional political party system. Literate and overwhelmingly urban, this minority group was formed of cholo artisans and white collar workers, of the members of the liberal professions and the army officer corps, of the small merchants and innumerable smaller miners, and amounted to at most some 20 per cent of the population. But it accounted for almost 90 per cent of the voting population, and its defection had a crucial impact on the Bolivian political system. In election after election in the years from 1935 to 1951 the middle classes expressed their increased self-consciousness by abandoning the traditional political leadership in ever larger numbers until by 1951 they literally voted the traditional system out of office and supported an openly revolutionary candidate.

The most remarkable sign of this awakening consciousness was the proliferation of political organizations which occurred after the war. Equally important, though at first of no obvious immediate political impact, was the development of an entirely new pressure group hitherto unknown to Bolivian political life. This was the veterans' movement. The returning civilian veterans finding traditional channels of expression to be useless, very rapidly began organizing themselves into a powerful pressure group. But so imperative were their immediate demands that these organizations were at first hostile to direct political association and throughout the 1930s they remained largely aloof from the great political struggles of the post-war era. Wedded to a mutualist position, the leadership of the veterans' movement was successful in sympathizing with the new forces, while remaining essentially uncommitted.

The veterans' movement first got under way seriously in July and August as Bolivia began demobilizing 100,000 troops under the terms of the armistice.[1] By September, local veterans' groups had sprung up across the country and the movement was soon recognized by the government.[2] On 13 September the recently organized *Legión de Ex-Combatientes* (LEC) of La Paz met with the president and the minister of war to work out special arrangements for those reserve officers who wished to stay on in the army, and payment and rehabilitation plans for invalid and mutilated soldiers. The government at this meeting indicated its

[1] *El Diario*, 1 July 1935, p. 5.
[2] See, for example, *El Diario*, 11 September 1935, p. 2; 14 September 1935, p. 5, and 29 September 1935, p. 2.

full acceptance of the mutualist, apolitical aims of LEC and promised to give its full support.[1]

By the end of September and beginning of October, the ex-combatants' organizations had reached such an advanced state of development that they were able to organize departmental and national councils and to write a complete charter which they presented to the government for approval. The government quickly granted juridical recognition to the new entity, which henceforth received preferential treatment in its dealings with the executive.[2]

In its charter the LEC carefully restricted its membership to *combatientes* only, that is to those who saw active front-line service, and excluded rearguard soldiers. At the same time it unequivocably restricted its aims to 'protection and mutual aid' for its members, and a general 'vigilance for the security and well-being of all veterans'. It promised to put pressure on the government for 'the creation of laws and regulations for the benefit of veterans', to facilitate civilian re-employment of its members and to push for government support for the mutilated and widowed families.[3]

Despite its statements to the contrary, many saw the creation of the LEC as a powerful political force which could be used as the nucleus for the creation of a new political system. Thus throughout its period of active existence, the LEC found itself constantly forced to suppress internal attempts to hand it over to an organized political party, and rejected outside appeals from men, groups and parties which called on it for support. Repeatedly it became deeply involved, and at no time in the 1930s was its voice ignored by any politician. But by and large all attempts at converting the LEC into a political party ended in failure due to the stubborn resistance of those leaders who refused to see the mutualist aims of the ex-combatants submerged in the political struggles of the day.

This political and organizational ferment which began in the first months after the armistice soon spread to the traditional parties themselves. Most importantly, it invaded the one traditional party

---

[1] *El Diario*, 14 September 1935, p. 8.
[2] *El Diario*, 3 October 1935, p. 5.   [3] *El Diario*, 4 October 1935, pp. 7–8.

most heavily dependent upon the younger generation, the Partido Nacionalista. In the first days of October, at the same time as the LEC was being organized, a national convention of the Partido Nacionalista was held in La Paz, which most observers predicted would sound the death knell of the old party.[1]

On the first day of the convention, the traditional leadership proudly reviewed the party's history and defended its action since the overthrow of Siles. Honorary President Rafael Taborga, who had handed over active leadership of the party to José Tamayo in 1932, in the opening speech claimed that the work of Salamanca had justified the actions of the party when it had supported the frustrated prorogation attempt by Siles. Vindicating the party's foresight, he demanded, 'Would that prorogued government [of Siles] not have been more convenient than the government of Salamanca, to which the nation owes the most formidable blood-letting and economic débâcle which Bolivia has suffered since its foundation?' Acting President Tamayo also took the floor to discuss the stewardship of the party under his direction, and noted that the party had abstained from the 1933 and 1934 elections under the Salamanca régime, but had wholeheartedly joined the Tejada Sorzano government in November of the previous year, and had been represented in the cabinet by the former student leader Enrique Baldivieso.[2]

On the second day of the meeting, however, a new note was sounded when the younger and more leftists elements of the party made a surprising move toward dissolution and the creation of a new revolutionary party. After several general speeches, including one by Carlos Montenegro, the delegate from Cochabamba, Antonio Rico Toro, took the floor and announced that the leftist wing of the party could no longer adhere to the old organization. 'There are within the party', he noted, 'two clear, definitive [and] fatally distinguished tendencies . . . ; the democratic individualist tendency, the political atomism, that is to say the right' and the left which in direct opposition to the rightist ideals, 'aspires to create a new socio-economic state, proclaims

---

[1] See predictions of Baldivieso and José Tamayo in *El Diario*, 11 September 1935, p. 5.
[2] *La Razón*, 2 October 1935, pp. 4, 5; *El Diario*, 2 October 1935, p. 5.

the necessity of entirely transforming the nation from its most important institutions of government, to its simplest contributory elements, that is to say, from the public power to the individual'. Given these basic and irreconcilable antagonisms of the right and left within the party, the latter group, he announced, had decided to withdraw from the party and leave the convention to the conservatives.[1]

Thereupon in a tumultuous uproar the motion of dissolution was seconded by the labour leader Felipe Tovar, and the left proceeded to walk out, thus in fact dissolving the old Partido Nacionalista. Later that same day, the leftists returned en masse to the empty convention hall and began to organize themselves into a new political grouping which they denominated temporarily as the *Célula Socialista Revolucionaria* with an *ad hoc* executive board consisting of José Tamayo, Carlos Montenegro, Felipe Tovar and several others.[2]

Immediately the Célula began making overtures to the other nascent political groups which were being organized at the same time. The most important group to which it appealed, of course, was the Legión de Ex-Combatientes. After several meetings the LEC took this invitation for political cooperation to an open meeting of its general assembly, and there it was decisively rejected as being contrary to the announced apoliticism of the new organization.[3] The Célula Socialista Revolucionaria, however, found a better response in the burgeoning leftist youth groups which were then being organized in several cities of the country. By the end of the month, it was discussing a united front and a leftist convention with such newly formed groups as Beta Gama, Andes and Bolivia.

On its own initiative, Beta Gama began holding conversations with the Cochabamba Grupo de Izquierda, which was led by Anaya and Arze and seems to have been the old exiled Izquierda Boliviana of Chile. Although this group had been one of the founding organizations of the Partido Obrero Revolucionario, the latter party seems not to have been brought back from exile by the returning pre-war radicals. For one of its key leaders, José

[1] *El Diario*, 3 October 1935, p. 5.
[2] *Ibid.*
[3] *El Diario*, 19 October 1935, p. 8.

Aguirre Gainsborg, upon his return to Bolivia in late 1934 joined the Beta Gama group, and made no mention of the POR, while Marof, its actual head, remained in exile, despite the ending of the war. Apparently, while the nucleus of Marxists kept the organization going in a skeleton form abroad, no move was made to bring it into Bolivia, and it was thought by many to have been only a temporary war-time coalition grouping.[1]

On 14 October, Beta Gama and the Grupo de Izquierda signed an agreement to work together to organize a leftist youth congress and to try to create a united ideological programme.[2] Later in the month Beta Gama met with the CSR and the groups Andes and Bolivia (which had just organized themselves into a Partido Socialista Boliviano) to work out a plan of action for the congress and for a united front of the left.[3] At the end of the month there was a reorganization of the leadership of Beta Gama. Luis Iturralde Chinel became secretary-general, and an executive committee was formed, consisting of Hernán Siles Zuazo, José Aguirre Gainsborg, Víctor Andrade and Julio Zuazo Cuenca, among others.[4] The new leadership proved hostile to the CSR's organizational activities and especially to the programme being worked out for the so-called *Confederación Socialista* as the new united party grouping was being called, and in early November announced its withdrawal from this movement.[5]

In late November, Beta Gama added a new title to its name, calling itself *Acción Socialista Beta Gama* and openly declared its desire to participate actively in politics. It began to produce a bi-weekly newspaper under the editorship of Aguirre Gainsborg to publicize the ideas of the party, which was now beginning to take a far more leftist and radical slant than when it had first appeared on the political scene in July.[6] In the first number of the newspaper, the Acción Socialista Beta Gama declared itself to be, above all, 'an anti-imperialist organization'. It called for Bolivia's 'economic and political liberation from the great empire of international finance capital' and proposed a union of all Latin American anti-imperialist parties in a great 'Confederation of Latin

[1] Lora, *José Aguirre Gainsborg*, p. 41.
[2] *El Diario*, 18 October 1935, p. 5.   [3] *El Diario*, 26 October 1935, p. 4.
[4] *El Diario*, 31 October 1935, p. 5.   [5] *El Diario*, 8 November 1935, p. 7.
[6] *El Diario*, 28 November 1935, p. 7; see also *El Diario*, 24 November 1935, p. 7.

American Socialist Republics'. The ASBG held that such a confederation would have as its aim 'the internationalization of canals, rivers and seas in benefit of all the countries of the continent'.

This latter concept was obviously borrowed from the Aprista movement in Peru and implied that Bolivia could obtain her outlet to the sea through the socialization of America. The ASBG also stated that it was anti-feudal, and proposed to foster the comunidades, agricultural education among the Indians and their incorporation into national life. While it attacked servitude, it did not come out openly for land reform. It proposed the syndicalization of the workers, and as its members were socialists, they promised to work for the betterment of the proletarian classes. Point Four of their new programme stated that the socialist state which they proposed to organize would be based on the proletariat, peasants, and petty bourgeoisie and would be established by them, as the vanguard of the socialist movement. It upheld the small proprietor and the cooperative movement and also proposed the unification of the isolated portions of the nation through colonization and development of communications.[1] In all, it was a moderate programme which was to the left of the CSB, although far less radical than the pre-1935 programmes of the old Tupac Amaru and POR groupings.

At the same time as it was taking its anti-Confederación Socialista Boliviana stand and announcing its own programme, the ASBG began making overtures to several other groups including the Grupo Izquierda of Cochabamba—its old ally—the Grupo Henri Barbusse of La Paz, the Grupo Ariel of Sucre and finally the Bloque Intelectual Obrera 'Avance' of Oruro.[2] These alliances allowed major freedom for local groups and were specifically directed against the moderate Confederación Socialista Boliviana which was continuing to gain ground.[3]

Under the active leadership of Enrique Baldivieso, the CSB was able to overcome the opposition of the more radical or politically aware of the younger intellectuals, and to draw most of the new political movements into its organization by the end of the year. The concentration on the issues of change and social

[1] *El Diario*, 28 November 1935, p. 7.   [2] *El Diario*, 3 December 1935, p. 2.
[3] *Ibid.*; also *El Diario*, 26 November 1935, p. 4.

justice in the vaguest terms seemed to be an ideal one, and the carryover of a large number of the cadre from the old Nationalist party provided a degree of experience and continuity which the other groups lacked.

That its programme was far from radical, even by traditional political standards, was clearly revealed in the initial plan of action which the CSB issued in late November. While stressing the hostility of the traditional parties to the collective welfare of the popular classes, its own proposals for reform were mild indeed. It called for public housing and rent control laws, re-adjustments of salaries and wages to take account of inflation, and elimination of injustices in the price control apparatus with popular representation on price control boards. In the political sphere it asked for the end of the state of siege and the improve-ment of public services. In short, it appealed to the most immediate demands of the upper level of urban workers and the middle classes, with proposals for better and cheaper housing and con-trol over the post-war inflationary developments which were beginning to disturb a good number of the urban middle classes.

Interestingly, though, there was one part of the programme which was a radical departure and very clearly reflected the post-war bitterness over the conduct of the Chaco War. This was a declaration (No. 2) calling for 'the establishment and judgement of individual and collective responsibilities for the war'. The CSB demanded an official inquiry into the cause of the war and especially and bitterly singled out the responsibilities of the mining industry in the conflict. It denied the validity of the thesis that the mine owners had paid for the war, and noted that through their huge loans they had escaped paying taxes. The statement also spoke of political misjudgements, mismanage-ments and treasons, and of all the crimes committed during the war on the home front. There was no specific mention, however, of the same things in reference to the army officer corps, for this would have been a deliberately provocative proposal that would have destroyed the growing alliance between the CSB and the younger officer cadre. But even confining the attack to the trad-itional political parties and the tin barons, the issue was still too explosive to pursue. Despite its pledge to follow through on this issue with all its force, now and in the future, the party soon found it more convenient to forget the issue. It was therefore left to the most embittered and extremist groups to attempt to raise this subject once again in national politics in the following year.[1]

In early December, the CSB issued an official programme which outlined its aims in greater detail. Although no new revolutionary pronouncements were added to its early programme, the new platform more clearly stated its basic principles, which were distinctly anti-traditionalist in tone. The Unified Programme, as it was called, stressed the collective over the individual good, and the social responsibility of private property. It also came out as completely pacifist, requesting international arbitration machinery to settle border disputes in Latin America.

More importantly it proposed positive government intervention in the economy. It called for the creation of state industries, nationalization of the means of communication, new economic and banking legislation, obligatory unionization, encouragement of consumer and producer cooperatives, government participation in the profits of the tin industry and finally the nationalization of the gold and more especially the petroleum fields. The latter obviously reflected the by now universal hostility toward Standard Oil. Although calling for nationalization in these areas, it also proposed the encouragement of foreign capital investment in other natural resources, and suggested a major protectionist programme for national industries and a rationalization of the tax system. It advocated an end to government monopolies in such things as match production, and a complete reworking of the government bureaucracy to eliminate corruption. While it asked for greater government activity in agriculture and heavy taxation of unused land to encourage greater production, no mention was made of land reform.

Strongly supporting a major plan of social welfare legislation, the programme not only demanded full civil rights for women and illegitimate children, but it also demanded the creation of new government ministries in these fields. It proposed the establishment of a ministry of labour and the enactment of a complete

[1] *El Diario*, 23 November 1935, p. 8.

Labour Code (*Código*) along with such other pro-labour legislation as an annual paid two-week vacation; prohibition of child labour; minimum hours and wages; social security and unemployment insurance; establishment of company schools, play areas and infirmaries; equal salaries for women and protection of working mothers; free legal aid; worker scholarships; and creation of technical schools, etc. Creation of a ministry of public health, major public works development, state grocery stores, encouragement of immigration and internal eugenics laws and family maintenance allowances were also among the proposals which were made. The CSB advocated a major revolution in education through the creation of technical schools and night secondary schools, *universidades populares* (adult education), nationalization and 'socialization' of teaching, etc. The Indian, it noted, should be incorporated into national life and protected as a small landholder whenever possible and attempts should be made to abolish discriminatory taxation and pongueaje. Such proposals, however, could only be pious hopes so long as no land reform measures were proposed.

The army was treated very gently in the programme. Proposals were made for its modernization, more enlightened attitudes towards conscripts and the development of a national armaments industry—this latter being in sharp contrast to its pacifist proclamations at the beginning of the programme. The only semi-hostile statement in this chapter was the prohibition of all secret societies within the armed forces. For the veterans, widows, etc., it demanded a host of special enactments for those who had suffered on account of the Chaco War. And finally the CSB platform proposed the active organization of the entire socialist movement, which would find ultimate expression in a national convention and the creation of a united socialist party.[1]

With this progressive, but by no means radical programme, the CSB were able to appeal successfully to all the new elements, including the most radical. By early 1936 such groups as Beta

[1] Confederación Socialista Boliviana, *Programa Unificado* (La Paz: n.p., 7 December 1935), pp. 1–22. This programme also asked for the 'establishment of a Tribunal of Responsibilities of War, principally with reference to the economic and political conduct of the conflict'. *Ibid.* p. 20.

Gama and Avance found themselves absorbed into the organizational activities of the CSB.[1] Though a dissident group of the most radical members of Beta Gama, led by José Aguirre Gainsborg, Hernán Zuazo and others, seceded from Beta Gama and formed an independent *Bloque Socialista de Izquierda*,[2] even they found themselves irresistibly drawn into the new movement.[3]

Meanwhile the CSB in the early months of the new year was feverishly organizing regional congresses, and in March the local CSB congress in La Paz founded an official Partido Socialista under the leadership of both Baldivieso and Carlos Montenegro.[4] Other leaders of this initially La Paz-based party were José Tamayo, Luis Iturralde Chinel (old head of Beta Gama), Alberto Mendoza López (a leader of the pre-war Partido Laborista) and the pre-war labour leaders Felipe Tovar and Moisés Álvarez.[5] Meanwhile other regional socialist parties were being organized around the CSB nuclei, and by March it was decided that the belated national convention would finally take place in the following month, and that the new party would at that time announce its own presidential candidate for the coming elections.[6]

The Liberal government was not unaware of this feverish new political activity and from mid-1935 actively attempted to confront the new political situation by adopting ever more radical measures. As has been seen, it gave full support to the organizations of the Legión de Ex-Combatientes throughout the nation and tried to resolve some of their major grievances with liberal pension plans and other welfare measures. On 25 October 1935, in an obvious bid for popular support, it initiated court actions against the Standard Oil Company of Bolivia for having constructed an illegal pipeline from its Bolivian fields to its Argentine holdings across the Bermejo River.[7] A clandestine pipeline had first been publicly disclosed in the Argentine congress by a group

---

[1] *El Diario,* 4 January 1936, p. 2; 15 January 1936, p. 2; 21 January 1936, p. 7 and 24 January 1936, p. 3.
[2] *El Diario,* 25 January 1936, p. 4; 29 January 1936, p. 4 and 30 January 1936, p. 5.
[3] *El Diario,* 31 January 1936, p. 6.
[4] *El Diario,* 30 January 1936, p. 5; 13 February 1936, p. 5.
[5] *El Diario,* 5 March 1936, p. 5.
[6] *El Diario,* 6 March 1936, p. 7. At the last minute the Bloque Socialista withdrew along with the labour leader Waldo Álvarez; *El Diario,* 13 March 1936, p. 6.   [7] *El Diario,* 26 October 1935, p. 4.

of dissident congressmen who charged that the oil was being shipped illegally to Argentina and then transshipped to Paraguay and sold to Bolivia's enemy.[1] The existence of this pipeline was revealed at a time when the company was publicly claiming that it could not produce enough oil commercially and therefore had to sell Bolivia extremely high-priced oil for the war effort from its Peruvian fields.[2] The government charged that this illegal pipeline had been in existence since 1925, unknown to Bolivian authorities, and some nine million barrels of untaxed oil had been shipped out to Argentina in the ten-year period since its construction.[3] The Standard Oil Company denied the charges, and said such a pipeline had only operated for a few months in 1925–6 with the full knowledge of the Bolivian government, and the few hundred barrels shipped out had been used strictly for drilling on the Argentine side of the river, only a small excess being sent by tank car for refining in southern Argentina.[4] It therefore began a long legal fight to prevent court action on the issue and for the moment prevented the government from taking any outright action.

Though temporarily halted from action on the Standard Oil issue, the government made concrete moves to deal with the more immediate problem of inflation. In December 1935 it gave government employees a major wage increase and called for private industry to follow this example.[5] At the same time it attempted to meet the demands of the CSB programme of December by proposing in the same month a constitutional convention for May of the new year and calling for the writing of a new constitution.[6] Finally in early January it proposed the creation of a ministry of public health, labour and welfare to replace the special wartime ministry of defence.[7]

But these Liberal gestures seemed to have little impact. As early as October 1935 rumours of an impending military *golpe* were so widespread that chief of staff Colonel David Toro had to deny

---

[1] *El Diario*, 28 January 1935, p. 4.
[2] Carlos Montenegro, *Frente al derecho del estado el oro de la Standard Oil (el petroleo, sangre de Bolivia)* (La Paz: Editorial 'Trabajo', 1938), pp. 54ff.
[3] *El Diario*, 31 October 1935, p. 4.   [4] *El Diario*, 8 November 1935, p. 7.
[5] *El Diario*, 10 December 1935, p. 5; and 11 December 1935, p. 5.
[6] *El Diario*, 10 January 1936, p. 7.   [7] *El Diario*, 13 January 1936, p. 7.

publicly that the army had any political ambitions.[1] By the end of the year the government, fearing major political unrest, prevented congress from meeting and suspended municipal elections called for that month.[2] Its justification for the latter move was that the new elections had to await the return of all demobilized troops and prisoners. It also acted under threats from the CSB that such elections would be premature for its own organizational plans and would threaten political stability.[3]

Thus the Tejada Sorzano government appealed to the newer elements by adopting some of the proposed 'socialist' reforms and at the same time suspended political activity till these new movements were fully organized.[4] Though bitterly resenting these delays, the other traditional parties accepted the new developments of 1936 and began to prepare for the coming conventional and presidential elections. Deliberately excluding the Genuinos, the Liberals and Republican Socialists under the respective leadership of Juan María Zalles and Bautista Saavedra, signed a poltical non-aggression pact as a preliminary move toward a common candidature slate in late January.[5] In February, Zalles handed over party leadership to Tomás Manuel Elío and there began to be talk of an Elío-Carlos Calvo platform under the assumption that as both men represented different geographical regions and had both been leaders in the peace convention, they would make a popular slate.[6] Calvo, however, soon let it be known that he refused to run.[7] On 12 February the government officially decreed election day as 31 May for the convention delegates and the presidency.[8]

An interesting indication of the transformation that was

El Diario, 13 October 1935, p. 12. [2] *El Diario*, 18 October 1935, p. 5.
El Diario, 1 December 1935, pp. 5, 6.
In January and February of the new year this anti-traditional political activity received new impetus under the impact of the first public accusations between leading Genuinos and high army officers in the Bolivian newspapers over who was responsible for causing the Chaco War. See Díaz Machicao, *La guerra del Chaco*, p. 275; Demetrio Canelas (ed.), *Documentos Políticos* (my copy of this work lacks the title page and final pages, but I believe the work was published in La Paz under Partido Republicano Genuino auspices in 1938), pp. 21–38, for the Genuino manifesto against the Toro accusation of responsibility for the defeat and the initiation of the war.
El Diario, 27 January 1936, p. 6. [6] *El Diario*, 11 February 1936, p. 4.
El Diario, 18 February 1936, p. 4. [8] *El Diario*, 13 February 1936, p. 5.

occurring on the political scene at this time was an interview *El Diario* published with the new head of the Liberal party, Tomás Manuel Elío. Asked about the ideological position of the party, he stated:

Our policy has its roots in the universally known liberal principles. But it is also progressive since it supports the innovations which the social and other sciences indicate are useful and necessary to the moral and material order. No party can reasonably attribute to itself the privilege of the truth and pretend to condemn the other group by marking them with the seal of traditionalists. In the life of the people as in the life of the individuals, we cannot renounce the past, since it dominates all human endeavour. Our aspirations for progress have to be coordinated at all times with our history, psychology and own temperament.[1]

Clearly, the Liberal party was beginning to feel sensitive about the attacks which were being levelled against it by all the new political groups and parties, and was beginning to fight shy of what was becoming a damaging political label, that of tradicionalistas. Liberal isolation from the new movements was further accentuated at the end of the month by the news of electoral unification talks between Saavedra's Partido Republicano Socialista and the Confederación Socialista Boliviana, with the Liberals appearing to be left only with the unwanted aid of the Genuinos who were a secret asset but an open liability.[2]

In the beginning of March, Elío left the government both to work on his own presidential candidacy and to prepare the party for the coming elections. In response to the rumours of PRS-CSB cooperation, Elío proposed that instead of a direct election, the constituent assembly name the president and vice-president.[3] He then presented his proposal to the government and asked all parties to express their opinions.[4] Saavedra and Baldivieso both indicated hostility, while the Genuinos stated that they would abstain altogether from the elections.[5]

Despite this rejection, Elío refused to give up, and the Liberal party, probably fearing that an open election would destroy it,

[1] *El Diario*, 16 February 1936, p. 7.
[2] *El Diario*, 20 February 1936, p. 4, and 21 February 1936, p. 6.
[3] *El Diario*, 1 March 1936, p. 7. [4] *El Diario*, 12 March 1936, p. 4.
[5] *El Diario*, 15 March 1936, p. 6, and 16 March 1936, page numbers in disorder.

continued to negotiate with the two other active groupings. Toward the end of March, Elío proposed an outright three-way division in the coming election, with each party getting thirty seats in the assembly.[1] The party reached the point of despair when on his return from abroad, the titular head, Juan María Zalles, proposed not only that the new government should be composed of the best men and not based on party (i.e. should be a national unity government), but that the army should intercede in the party deliberations to reach such an agreement.[2] Zalles' plan, given the delicate political relations with the army, was suicidal and obviously represented a last desperate effort by the Liberals to prevent themselves from being completely destroyed. Zalles suggested that a cabinet crisis should be engineered, that the government should then be handed over to a full-fledged military cabinet and that these 'neutral' elements should then preside over free May congressional elections, with army officers taking over all prefectures and sub-prefectures in the nation. The plan concluded by proposing again that the president and vice-president be indirectly elected by the constituent assembly and that the parties divide up the assembly seats beforehand on an equal basis; and in a defence of this move he cited, of all things, the threat of communism.[3]

What the Liberals obviously feared was a compact between the military officers and the new political parties, and also an open election where the majority of voters would be Chaco War veterans who were hostile to the old parties. Toro answered for the army, stating that if all political parties agreed, it would take over the government.[4] By April, however, Zalles admitted great opposition to his plan not only from other parties but from many Liberals themselves, and decided to drop it.[5]

With the failure of Zalles' moves, President Tejada Sorzano himself began talks with Saavedra and Baldivieso to organize a government of national conciliation. On 3 April, the government announced the discovery of a Genuino revolutionary plot and arrested Canelas, Ovidio Urioste, Enrique Hertzog, José

[1] *El Diario*, 24 March 1936, p. 7.
[2] *El Diario*, 26 March 1936, p. 4.   [3] *El Diario*, 28 March 1936, p. 5.
[4] *El Diario*, 31 March 1936, p. 6.   [5] *El Diario*, 1 April 1936, p. 6.

Gabino Villanueva, Rafael de Ugarte and other stalwarts of the old party.[1] But despite the definitive removal of this bitterly hated group from the political scene, negotiations between the Liberals, the Socialists and the Republican Socialists still brought no results, since neither Saavedra nor Baldivieso would commit themselves. There was talk of postponing the elections even further until the complete return of the Bolivian prisoners of war, who were scheduled to arrive in May.[2]

But delay was no longer a reasonable alternative for the government. Baldivieso began to establish intimate relations with key members of the Estado Mayor General, believing that the party could gain more through collaboration with the powerful military than through the normal political processes, In early May, Baldivieso announced that he believed the army should take over the government and that the new military régime would be the best way to realize a major socialist programme for Bolivia. The Liberals reacted to this move, which they believed meant the signing of a secret pact between Baldivieso's socialists and the army (a pact which had been in the negotiating stage for several weeks), by declaring that they would abstain from the coming election since the army would not respect the results of such an election.[3] In desperation, President Tejada Sorzano announced on 6 May that he would make one more attempt to overcome what he called the 'political strike' of the parties and their refusal to run candidates for the elections.[4] In the midst of these talks, news began to circulate of the creation of a new party from among the traditional elements. Carlos Víctor Aramayo, the tin magnate and owner of the newspaper *La Razón*, had attempted to take over the leadership of the Genuino Republican party at the beginning of the year and had been rebuffed.[5] Now in the first days of May, just before the elections, he announced the organization, with the assistance of the financier Federico Gutiérrez Granier, of the *Partido Centralista*, which was to be the last political organization to be created under the Tejada Sorzano government.[6]

[1] *El Diario*, 3 April 1936, p. 12.   [2] *El Diario*, 28 April 1936, p. 4.
[3] *El Diario*, 3 May 1936, p. 7.
[4] *El Diario*, 6 May 1936, p. 4; *La Razón*, 8 May 1935, p. 4.
[5] *El Diario*, 20 February 1936, p. 4.   [6] *La Razón*, 8 May 1936, pp. 4–5.

While the political parties were manœuvring, organizing, and reforming, the economic situation of the nation began to deteriorate rapidly and the resultant crisis soon forced all groups to precipitate action. Although money in circulation was ten times greater in 1935 than in 1931,[1] Bolivia still had not experienced serious inflation during the war years.[2] This was largely due to heavy internal financing through the central bank[3] and to government supported exchange rates favourable to the consumer.[4] Also, after 1933, the tin market began a powerful comeback and prices were continually increasing together with production.[5] In fact, the moderate price rises which did occur during the war were considered by Bolivians as a necessary concomitant of the conflict, and did not shake confidence in any way, as indicated by the surprisingly rapid growth of bank savings in these years.[6]

But immediately following the end of hostilities, Bolivia began to experience a severe inflationary spiral, despite the laudatory articles by national economists to the effect that sound economic financing of the war and lack of immediate post-war depression indicated rosy years ahead for Bolivia and immunity from the post-war crises traditionally to be expected.[7] Whereas the annual average increase in the cost of living in the years 1932–5 had been 16·6 per cent, it suddenly rose in the period 1936–9 to an annual average rate of increase of 50·7 per cent.[8] This inflation was actually due to the better economic situation, the sudden demand for goods and services, and the expansion of imports after the end of war controls. Between 1936 and 1939, imports rose to double what they had been in the war years. Also, internal industrial production began to increase steadily in the period after 1936.[9]

---

[1] CEPAL, *Desarrollo económico de Bolivia*, p. 60.   [2] *Ibid.*
[3] Vicente Mendoza López, *Las finanzas en Bolivia y la estrategia capitalista* (La Paz: Tip. Salesiana, 1940), Ch. IV; also see Banco Central de Bolivia, *El Banco Central de Bolivia durante la guerra del Chaco* (La Paz: Editorial 'America', 1936). The central bank lent the government £3·1 million; Bancos Mercantil and Nacional another £58,000; the Big Three Patiño, Hochschild, and Aramayo £1·7 million and £200,000 came from other firms. Finally, the three banks guaranteed a £1 million loan contracted by the government.
[4] CEPAL, *Desarrollo económico de Bolivia*, pp. 60–1.
[5] Knorr, *Tin Under Control*, pp. 124ff.
[6] CEPAL, *Desarrollo económico de Bolivia*, p. 61.
[7] See, for example, such a forecast in *El Diario*, 19 December 1935, p. 4.
[8] CEPAL, *Desarrollo económico de Bolivia*, p. 62.   [9] *Ibid.* pp. 62–3.

But government income proved incapable of meeting war obligations and the demand for internal development and increasing government deficits led to major deficit financing in peace time and a lack of confidence in the public money market.[1] Allied to the increased internal demand for goods and services, greater imports and deficit government financing, a final contributary cause of the inflation was the greater exportation of capital during the post-war years.[2]

It was therefore an expanding economy which was experiencing this inflation, and in such a situation, the revived labour movement could operate perfectly. By all accounts the economic boom after the war caused a great demand for skilled workers, and a major absorption of many Indian veterans who refused to return to the soil. Thus, a tight labour market in an expanding economy accompanied by a sudden runaway inflation created the ideal background for a major burst of activity and major growth of the Bolivian labour movement.

Even before the end of the war, Moisés Álvarez, Ezequiel Salvatierra and Enrique G. Loza, the old warhorses of the labour movement, had succeeded in temporarily organizing a *Confederación de Trabajadores de Bolivia* (CTB) and reorganizing on paper the old La Paz FOT;[3] both, however, were premature. The real reorganization and rebirth of the movement came after July 1935, as militant labour leaders returned from the front and from exile in Chile and Peru. The most important union to organize itself, and one of the first to do so successfully, was the old *Sindicato Gráfico*, founded by the militant young leftist Waldo Álvarez in 1932.[4] From his base in the reorganized union, Álvarez, who was secretary for inter-union relations, and many of his fellow printers actively intervened in many of the other

---

[1] While bank credit expanded tremendously, bank deposits increased only slowly. Also bank deposits, which had increased by greater percentages than the money in circulation in the war years, were in an opposite relationship in the post-war period. While the official exchange rate had remained steady at Bs. 20 to the pound throughout the war, it declined in the two-year period from 1937 to 1939 from Bs. 20 to Bs. 141. As for the cost of living, it rose from 214 per cent in 1936 to 578 per cent in 1939 (base is 1931 and figures are for La Paz). *Ibid.* pp. 58, 61–3.

[2] *Ibid.*   [3] *El Diario*, 27 January 1935, p. 5.

[4] Interview with Waldo Álvarez, La Paz, 11 October 1961; and *El Diario*, 24 October 1935, p. 5.

trades to help revive their old organization. So successful was this movement that by the beginning of the new year the old La Paz FOT had been fully re-established along with the FOT in Oruro, Tarija and other cities.[1] As early as November, these unions began calling for protection against the rising prices and the continued inflation, demanding a 100 per cent salary increase, reduction of rents and prices of consumer goods, etc.[2] In December a one-day strike at the major mining centre of Corocoro produced a rise in salaries in answer to workers' demands.[3] Workers began intense agitation in all industries and all areas of the nation in the face of labour shortages and price rises. But the movement by and large kept itself distinct from the feverish political activity. Although various labour leaders became involved in the new post-war movements, they initially represented only themselves and not their local unions. Apoliticism was still a strong force in the labour movement.[4]

In early 1936, the strike movement began to increase in tempo and in scope. In March the tobacco manufacture workers (mostly women) went out on strike in demand for higher pay.[5] In April under its secretary-general, Waldo Álvarez, the FOT presented a nineteen-point petition to the Tejada Sorzano government calling for a 50 per cent reduction of prices of consumer goods of primary necessity and their free importation; 100 per cent increase in public and private employees' and workers' salaries; suppression of the consumer goods monopolies; prohibition of night work for women and minors; suspension of states of siege and freedom of association and the press, and the syndical organizations of workers; new social legislation and jobs for veterans and a host of petitions for the mutilated and orphans of the war.[6] According to FOT disclosures to the press, the organization stressed the salary increases above all else in this petition.[7]

Despite the refusal of the labour movement to join the leftist

---

[1] See, for example, *El Diario*, 1 December 1935, p. 2; 27 December 1935, p. 4, and 11 January 1936, p. 5.

[2] *El Diario*, 29 November 1935, p. 7.   [3] *El Diario*, 6 December 1935, p. 6.

[4] Thus, for example, the Sindicato de Mineros de Oruro rejected an invitation to join one of the regional leftists councils being organized by the local CSB and Avance groups. *El Diario*, 4 March 1936, p. 2.

[5] *El Diario*, 19 March 1936, p. 3.

[6] *El Diario*, 12 April 1936, p. 7.   [7] *El Diario*, 25 April 1936, p. 5.

political parties, it was willing to cooperate with them on major issues, and these political groups in their turn saw great possibilities in the agitation of the labour movement. Thus the FOT received the sponsorship not only of the apolitical LEC, but also of the PRS, Partido Socialista, Bloque Socialista de Izquierda and the anarchists, when it decided to hold a mass meeting to present its nineteen-point demand to the government.[1] The government, of course, refused permission for the meeting to be held, but it did formally accept the FOT petition.[2] When the government refused to act quickly, it was the Sindicato Gráfico which decided to force its hand.

On 6 May 1936, the Sindicato Gráfico presented a petition to all the La Paz newspapers and publishers demanding a 100 per cent increase in salaries to be effective immediately.[3] The publishers asked for time and government arbitration, but the Sindicato Gráfico refused to accept the delay and issued a strike call.[4] Thereupon began the greatest strike movement that Bolivia had experienced. On 10 May the strike began and all the newspapers were shut down. Then the FOT, under the Gráficos leader Waldo Álvarez, and with the support of the anarchist FOL, began a major general strike movement in support of the printers' union. This general strike, demanding the 100 per cent pay increases for all workers, was called for an indefinite duration. Tejeda Sorzano, fearing violence of a revolutionary nature, ordered the *carabineros* (or national police force) into their barracks, while Colonel Busch promised the workers that the army would not intervene so long as there was no rioting. Thus La Paz was left to the control of the strikers, and workers themselves patrolled the streets to keep public order. But the workers were seeking nothing more than wage increases, and did not take advantage of this unique situation to overthrow the government or impose revolutionary political solutions.[5]

For the political and military opponents of the Liberal government, however, the general strike and the complete collapse of the government in the face of labour agitation provided a perfect

---

[1] *El Diario*, 16 April 1936, p. 8.   [2] *El Diario*, 18 April 1936, p. 5.
[3] *El Diario*, 7 May 1936, p. 5.   [4] *La Razón*, 9 May 1936, p. 5.
[5] Barcelli, *Medio siglo de luchas sindicales*, pp. 138–41; M. Álvarez, 'La organización sindical en Bolivia', pp. 37–8; W. Álvarez, *Federación Gráfica*, pp. 98–9.

opportunity.[1] On 16 May the army began to take over the government, under the leadership of Toro and more especially of Busch, who was now chief of the EMG. For a time the affair remained undecided and Busch even had to seek temporary asylum in the Peruvian embassy.[2] But by 17 May, Tejada Sorzano had been successfully ousted and Busch had taken over the government, and with the arrival of Toro on 20 May, a formal junta militar was established under his presidency.

Thus after fifty years of struggle, the civilian political party system was overturned by a reawakened military establishment. Infected with the same disillusionment as the civilian veterans, the younger officer class decided that only they had the moral purity to lead the nation to new vitality and spiritual rebirth. Taking advantage of the post-war political anarchy, the military were able to initiate the first experiments to establish a new order. Still essentially conservative, despite their revolutionary leadership, they attempted to lead the nation through their own conception of social reform which they proudly called 'socialismo militar'.

[1] According to Álvarez the workers were not in contact with the revolutionaries and were caught by surprise at its occurrence, and were in fact at first hostile to the change. Interview with Waldo Álvarez, La Paz, 11 October 1961; also see Barcelli, *Medio siglo de luchas sindicales*, pp 138–41.
[2] Díaz Machicao, *La guerra del Chaco*, p. 276.

8

DAVID TORO AND THE ESTABLISHMENT OF MILITARY SOCIALISM

The revolution of 17 May 1936 was carried out by a tripartite coalition of junior officers close to Toro and Busch, the Baldivieso Socialists, and the Republican Socialists under Saavedra. Planned and prophesied long in advance, the revolution was achieved without bloodshed and was willingly accepted by the majority of Bolivians. For most now felt that the army was the only viable instrument for creating the new political atmosphere and 'social justice' that all were demanding. The incapacity of the traditional parties, numbed by their involvement in the war and overwhelmed by the military preponderance, prevented them from meeting these demands, while the majority of the new political groups were still too disorganized to take the initiative on their own.

Men like Baldivieso had encountered a kindred spirit in the younger front-line officers who now ruled the military establishment, and found them eager to lead the nation. For the army too had experienced the revolt of the younger generation against the old leadership. The war had proved the incapacity of the senior officers and had also sparked off the meteoric rise of able pre-war lieutenants to positions of power and rank. These new men were bitter over the failure of the war leaders and were highly sympathetic to the aspirations of the civilian veterans for a new order. Much more politically self-conscious than their elders, and extremely sensitive to charges against the army's conduct of the war, they were eager to efface their military disaster with political radicalism.

Apart from political idealism, many officers were driven by an undercurrent of fear of threats of civilian investigations into the conduct of the war and responsibility, which would have implicated the entire military establishment. To many officers the only way to meet this threat was by controlling the government and carrying out a popular reform programme. Finally, according to one civilian veteran, 'The taking of the government signified [for these officers] the illusion of responsibilities as it satisfied the thirst for power which the habit of commanding civilians in the Chaco had developed in them.'[1] Faced with these new men and needs, the old army leadership was forced to give ground completely and allow these younger officers for the next three years to lead the military establishment where they would.

The key figure and leader of this younger group was Lieutenant-Colonel Germán Busch, one of the few real 'heroes' of the Chaco War. As a young lieutenant of twenty-eight at the beginning of the conflict, Busch had been one of the few competent officers on the Bolivian side, and through his brilliance had risen in the last days of the war to leadership of the field troops in the great defence of the Camiri oil fields. For this action he was finally rewarded with the second highest post in the army, chief of the general staff, shortly after the end of the conflict.[2] But for all his military insight and leadership, Busch was politically unsophisticated and, although he firmly believed in the need for some type of social change, he was at this point incapable of clearly formulating his own ideology or leading a government. Recognizing these deficiencies in himself, Busch, like the younger officers who surrounded him, came to accept the leadership of Colonel David Toro.

Of all the officer corps, both the younger and older generations, between which he formed a vital link, David Toro was unquestionably the most politically adept and sophisticated figure. Elevated to the rank of major at the age of twenty-seven in 1925, he was an intimate associate of General Hans Kundt and President Hernando Siles. Under Siles' policy of committing the army politically, Toro was a leading activist, and in the last months of the government he held the cabinet posts first of development

---

[1] Céspedes, *El dictador suicida*, p. 146.
[2] The general-in-chief of the army was pliable Enrique Peñaranda, who replaced the German mercenary Hans Kundt in this position in December 1933, and retained the office until his retirement in January 1938. Zook, *The Chaco War*, p. 168; *El Diario*, 12 January 1938.

and communications and then of government, the chief position of political control in the régime. Because of his political involvements, Toro was forced into exile with the 1930 rebellion, but the Chaco emergency brought him back into the ranks even more powerful than when he left.

During the war, Toro's intellectual calibre and political astuteness won him the respect and devotion of the higher officers who soon came to depend heavily on his judgement. His opposition to Salamanca prompted several attempts at insubordination by the men he worked under, such as Carlos Quintanilla and Enrique Peñaranda, who were led by Toro himself. When Kundt fell after the battle of Nanawa and was replaced by Enrique Peñaranda, Toro, who had been opposed to Kundt's leadership, was given almost unlimited authority and became the most powerful officer in the army.

But for all his intellectual brilliance and military skill, Toro was too politically minded and too dissolute to carry through to successful completion many of his complicated military manoeuvres, and more than once was the chief cause of a bitter Bolivian defeat. Yet, no matter how disastrous his field operations, Toro never lost his control over the upper officer corps on the one hand, and his fellow young officer veterans on the other. Thus when Busch and his followers began their plotting, it was Toro who they decided should lead them.[1]

On 20 May, Toro returned from the Chaco and took over the leadership of the government. On the same day he issued a statement to the press in which he declared that:

The army does not have any interest in implanting caudillismo or in encouraging the predominance of any particular groups or parties. The *golpe de estado* had a long gestation and occurs with the unanimous consensus of the army, whose ideology is in harmony with the new ideology of the country. Its firm intention is to implant state socialism with the aid of the parties of the left.

He then promised that neither 'I, nor any other officer of the army, have any illegitimate ambitions, neither do we pursue power.

[1] For the biographies of these two men, see Díaz Argüedas, *Como fué derrocado el hombre símbolo*, pp. 330–1, and Zook, *The Chaco War*, pp. 194–218.

After constitutionalizing the country, the army will return to its technical functions. The country will then elect the government, in which government no military officer will accept a position.'

In this statement of aims and policies of the new government, he also announced that although his administration was collaborating with the parties of the left, it nevertheless asked the co-operation of all men of good will. He also announced that the army had ratified the designation of Enrique Baldivieso, Fernando Campero Álvarez (both of the Partido Socialista), Gabriel Gosálvez and Pedro Zilveti Arce (both of the Partido Republicano Socialista) as members of the new government.[1] Toro also offered Busch the key post of minister of government, but the latter refused the position and indicated his preference for remaining as head of the EMG.[2] Toro was thus seemingly left with full discretionary power to act in his own right by this rejection of office, but in reality it left Busch with full control over the army, the most potent force in the new régime, and thus with ultimate veto power over the government.

The response of the traditional parties to these developments was surprisingly moderate. For its part, the Liberal organ *El Diario* declared that it accepted the army move and its promises of major reform and early return to civilian government in good faith, and ended by wishing the army success in this venture and promised its support.[3] *La Razón*, now representing Aramayo's Partido Centralista as well as the Genuinos, also announced its support of the revolt and was full of high praise for the new government.[4] These responses seem to indicate that the traditional parties viewed the whole affair as a temporary expedient that was needed to calm the feelings aroused by the Chaco disaster, and thus pave the way to a return to normal traditional party government which they felt Toro was prepared to give them.

This faith seemed to be maintained, despite the growing radicalism of Toro's public statements. In an exclusive interview with the Associated Press correspondent in La Paz, for example, Toro more explicitly elaborated on the main themes of the new

[1] *La Razón*, 21 May 1936, p. 4. [2] *El Diario*, 21 May 1936, p. 5.
[3] *Ibid.* p. 4. [4] *La Razón*, 31 May 1936, p. 5.

government. This time he declared quite specifically that the origins of his political movement had been in 'the political, social and economic problems arising after the Chaco War, whose solution was impossible within the traditional political structure, and that this made the intervention of the army in defence of the interests and rights of the working classes and the ex-combatientes a necessary act'. He also announced his desire to work for a socialist solution and gave only a vague non-committal response as to when the new government would hold elections. Finally he reiterated the already public position of the new government that the army had no desire to disturb the Buenos Aires peace talks or in any way to upset the present international *status quo* in the Chaco.[1]

In the area of working class 'interests' the Toro government acted quickly to meet outstanding claims by the workers. Although Busch had temporarily granted an increase in salaries for all workers and employees of private concerns and thus had ended the strike, the strike leaders demanded that the new régime ratify the Busch agreements.[2] The FOT also demanded that Toro should ensure that the government immediately create a ministry of labour and allow the FOT to name the first incumbent. Toro met Waldo Álvarez, the strike leader, and after consultation with the FOT acceded to all the workers demands and even agreed to appoint Álvarez as the nation's first minister of labour.[3] Thus on 21 May the government publicly announced the historic creation of Bolivia's first labour ministry, and the appointment of Álvarez made him the first worker ever to hold a cabinet post in Bolivia.[4]

Labour reacted to the news of the Álvarez appointment by holding a public demonstration in support of the government, and at the government palace cheering crowds listened to speeches

---

[1] *El Diario*, 21 May 1936, p. 8.
[2] *Ibid.* p. 4.
[3] Interview with Waldo Álvarez, La Paz, 11 October 1961.
[4] *El Diario* noted that Waldo Álvarez at this time was a thirty-three-year-old linotypist who was employed in the *El Diario* plant and represented not only the FOT and his sindicato in office, but also the *Bloque de Izquierda Socialista*. *El Diario*, 22 May 1936, p. 6. However, this was the last mention of the Bloque of José Aguirre Gainsborg in the Bolivian press, and the group seems to have quietly disappeared with Aguirre returning to his own POR group.

by Álvarez and Toro. In his speech, Toro said to the 'camaradas', as he fraternally called them, that:

Our social doctrine has been born in the sands of the Chaco, in the trenches where civilians and military men have shed their blood for the nation, giving it the maximum sum of their energies and sacrifices.

It was there in the Chaco that the ideology of our present revolutionary movement was crystallized. And this ideology has as its aim, not the enthroning of civilian or military caudillos, but rather the demand for rightful social justice.

He called for the vindication of the rights of labour and the veterans of the war, and declared that his régime aspired to guarantee 'that the blood shed by our fellow citizens in the sands of the Chaco' would not be shed in vain. This, he declared, could only be achieved through social justice for all, and respect for authority and order on the part of the workers themselves.[1]

What this Chaco-originated ideology was, and what the new leaders meant by that all-encompassing term of socialism, remained for the leading civilian of the new government to elaborate. Upon being appointed minister of foreign affairs, Enrique Baldivieso, head of the Partido Socialista, declared in his investiture speech that:

Both the structure of the state and political developments are nothing more than the external manifestations of a more essential reality: the economic organization of the people. The Liberal democracy was the expression of capitalism at the service of a minority.

Each day the terrible economic inequality of the Liberal régime was accentuated. On the one hand there were those who possessed nothing but their labour, and on the other, there was the accumulation of privilege in a few hands, the monopoly of wealth and the dictatorship of uncontrolled egoistic capitalism.

On the one hand, there existed the false democracy which made the citizen the subject of rights, political abstractions and the nominal depository of sovereignty, and on the other was the evident reality in which all political power was concentrated in the hands of the privileged.

For Baldivieso, the movement which he headed aimed at

---

[1] *El Diario*, 26 May 1936, p. 12.

destroying not a person or a party, but an entire system—the 'egoistic capitalism' which was maintained by 'the old machinery of the democratic liberal state'. But political independence, both for the nation and the manual and intellectual workers, means nothing without economic independence, which is the prime requisite for true liberty. Thus the aim of the movement which the army and the parties of the left had carried out is the restoration of the economic sovereignty of Bolivia. 'Against the political rights so many times proclaimed, we want to affirm the economic rights of the citizen: the right to live, the right to work, and the right to receive the full benefit of that work.'

Baldivieso declared that his socialism and that of his government was not a doctrine taken from aliens, but was defined by the economic, racial and geographical reality of Bolivia. He recognized that Bolivia was 'not prepared for the advent of complete socialism'. This was because it lacked any real industry or technology and was but 'a semi-colonial producer of raw materials'. In nations 'where the stages have followed according to the laws of economic development, the formula of capitalism against socialism is a true one'. In Bolivia, however, he believed that the lack of capital and industry necessitated a continued dependence on capitalism. But this capitalism was not to be the old 'egoistic and absorbent capital which flees from Bolivia without leaving any benefit', but rather the 'fecund and productive' variety which would invest in the country, and 'which remunerates labour with justice, and which is a progressive and beneficial factor' whose aim is the creation of a viable and diversified industrial base in Bolivia.[1]

This was the essence of the ideological programme of the new middle class moderate leftist movement in Bolivia, a movement which in the next decade gave birth to the *Movimiento Nacionalista Revolucionario*, and in the decade of the 1930s was the majority and dominant ideology among the veterans and leading younger political figures of the day, whom Baldivieso so well represented. It sought evolutionary social reform at home, with prime concentration on the responsibility of the state both for the welfare of its citizens, and for the reduction of the exclusive power and

[1] *La Razón*, 24 May 1936, p. 4.

economic monopoly of the mining oligarchy. Allied to this was the desire for economic development and the encouragement of good' foreign capital. Conspicuously absent from all of these early post-war moderate programmes was the question of latifundismo and of the Indian masses. While the extreme left called for the nationalization of the mines, land reform for the Indians and revolutionary governments led by workers, the moderate socialists at this early stage stressed evolutionary reform within the system, primarily to benefit the middle-class urban sector.

The moderates soon discovered, however, that such a mild programme could never really succeed. For these moderate measures were continually defeated by the old oligarchy, through both pacific and violent means, and more and more the moderates were forced to listen to the radical proposals of the extreme left, which never for a moment expected to achieve any truly major reforms without violence and revolutionary programmes of nationalization and decisive land reform. In the decade of the 1930s, however, the extreme left, though far more powerful than in the pre-war period and growing stronger every year, was still a small minority, and it was the moderates like Baldivieso who were left with the power to attempt to achieve significant change through evolutionary reform.

To elaborate more completely what the new government proposed, the cabinet of the junta militar issued on 25 May a fifty-two-point programme of immediate action. The heavy influence of Italian fascism among the officers of the new government was evident from the key proposals for the establishment of obligatory syndicalization and a corporate type of functional régime in parliament to replace the existing direct election system. It also proposed that the state should assume responsibility for seeing that all people were provided with work or unemployment compensation, that obligatory worker savings plans be established, that social security coverage be provided for all, and that laws be enacted to give social equality to women and children. State-subsidized food stores were to be established to overcome the impact of inflation on the middle and lower classes, and finally a host of proposals were promised which were designed to guarantee the rights of veterans and see to their preferential treatment. Despite all these expensive proposals, the government also promised a balanced budget and frugal administration, claiming that new taxes would provide the funds required. Although strong on general social welfare programme, aid to veterans and the promise of a new non-liberal corporate type of government, this programme was strikingly silent on the Indian problem, promising merely to set up a *Patronato Nacional* to study questions of relevance to the indigenous population. And finally, there was embedded within this long list a promise to judge those responsible for the disaster of the Chaco War, a proposal obviously designed for propaganda purposes only.[1]

As an immediate concrete step toward implementing the new programme of social reforms, the government set about establishing a host of new ministries, the most important ones being labour, and mines and petroleum.[2] The setting up of the labour ministry was probably the most radical act of the new government at this time, especially as it was led by the outstanding labour leader Waldo Álvarez. Surrounding himself with a small coterie of radical intellectuals, the new minister of labour quickly created a radical leftist niche in the otherwise conservative to moderate government and took seriously the proposals to vindicate labour's rights. The two top positions in the new ministry were given to the Marxist intellectual from Cochabamba, Ricardo Anaya, and to the secretary-general of the printers' union, Hugo Sevillano A. To these were soon added leading members of the Grupo Izquierda of Cochabamba, and within a very short time Álvarez and his very active followers began to arouse the traditional forces

[1] *La Razón*, 26 May 1936, p. 9.
[2] This was truly a major change in cabinet structure and one of the most important modernizing moves of the new régime. Whereas before the Toro government there had been only six ministries at the most (N. Andrew N. Cleven, *The Political Organization of Bolivia* [Washington: Carnegie Institute of Washington 1940], p. 128) there were now ten altogether. A department of Indian affairs was organized in conjunction with the public education ministry. Agriculture was separated from a previous coalition ministry and raised from departmental status to that of a self-contained ministry and the same occurred with industry and commerce which had formerly been subordinated to the finance ministry. Also, there was the outright creation of two new ministries of what previously had been subordinated departments, that of mines and petroleum—indicating the new government's concern over the prime wealth of the nation—and labour and social security.
[3] *El Diario*, 26 May 1936, p. 6, and 20 May 1936, p. 5.

against the government and create the first serious unease on the right about the aims of the new régime. Almost from the beginning of its tenure, the traditional newspapers, especially *La Razón*, constantly attacked the 'creeping radicalism' of the labour ministry.

But the labour ministry radicals were not the only divisive factor embarrassing the new régime. For all was not well among the victors. Many key Socialist party members were beginning to rebel against the leadership of Baldivieso and Montenegro over the issue of their negotiations with the Partido Republicano Socialista, which many still regarded as a traditional party despite all Saavedra's 'socialist' protestations to the contrary. Throughout the last days of May the Partido Socialista was racked by internal dissension, and Baldivieso even temporarily resigned.[1] But this gesture did not resolve the issue. The growing hostility of the rank and file to the PS-PRS pact began to drive more and more regional committees into rebellion against the leadership in La Paz. In early June the Oruro branch of the PS decreed that it would not accept such a pact with the enemy, as it defined Saavedra. Later in the same month, it in fact broke with the La Paz leaders, declaring them traitors to the revolutionary movement.[2] The La Paz committee, meanwhile, also expressed hostility, and in a special party assembly on 2 June it declared invalid the pacts written between the two parties. To many observers it looked as if this move was made not only for ideological reasons but as a deliberate move to oust the saavedristas from the government. With the political pacts annulled, it was predicted that Saavedra would be forced into a trial of strength to show who had the support of the majority of the public and, more crucially, of the army.[3]

It seemed at first that the army wished to prevent such a confrontation and asked all civilian cabinet ministers to continue in their positions.[4] But the military were beginning to feel uncomfortable in the presence of the dynamic Saavedra and tried to force him into diplomatic exile by offering him the presidency of

[1] *El Diario*, 23 May 1936, p. 4.
[2] *El Diario*, 1 June 1936, p. 2, and 19 June 1936, p. 3.
[3] *La Razón*, 3 June 1936, p. 4.
[4] *El Diario*, 14 June 1936, p. 4.

the Buenos Aires peace treaty delegation. But the wily old político refused to bow out so quietly and rejected the post.[1] Then Saavedra began to put counter-pressure on the government. His PRS held mass meetings which produced some rioting, and in the party paper *La República*, Saavedra charged that the 'communists' in the government were bent on destroying him.[2]

This action of Saavedra and the political machinations which had begun under the junta greatly angered the rather straight-forward Busch, and without informing Toro, Busch carried out a golpe de estado on 21 June. The prime objective of the golpe was the deportation of Saavedra and the abolishment of the tripartite system of civilian party and military pacts, leaving the army free to govern on its own, with only the aid of individual civilians who represented no political parties.[3] The whole movement took place without bloodshed and indicated beyond question the pre-dominance of Busch, quietly working in the shadows of Toro's government.

It was Busch himself who issued the manifesto to the nation on Sunday, 21 June, justifying the move of the army. He stated that in the *17 de Mayo* movement the army sought national regenera-tion, and not desiring power itself, had decided to rule with the parties of the left.

Unhappily, the political reality which we encountered did not corres-pond to the noble aspirations of the army. The parties of the left, united by pacts which seemed solidly defined, did not hesitate in breaking them, giving us the spectacle of totally opposed interests. In this inconceivable fight ... the maximum responsibility for what now has come about belongs to the Partido Saavedrista.

The army, stated Busch, had had enough of these sterile pol-itical battles, and had decided to go it alone, without the aid of the political parties, basing itself rather on 'the veterans and the organized labour movement'.[4] Here for the first time was Busch's own avowed programme, which he later attempted to carry through. Impatient with political machinations, he believed that

---

[1] *El Diario*, 11 June 1936, p. 4.
[2] Porfirio Díaz Machicao, *Historia de Bolivia, Toro, Busch, Quintanilla, 1936–1940* (La Paz: Editorial 'Juventud', 1957), pp. 25–6. Hereafter cited as *Toro, Busch*.
[3] *Ibid.* pp. 26–7. [4] *El Diario*, 21 June 1936, p. 12.

the army could truly regenerate the nation with the veterans and labour movements, forces which he was to discover were as difficult to direct and depend upon as was the political party system. The manifesto went on to ratify the army's support for Toro's régime, to ask for the future cooperation of the workers and the veterans, and in a significant move, to imply the complete dissolution of the party system by proposing that the government rule alone without asking the support or advice of *any* political party.[1] Toro tardily joined the golpe, and following Busch's lead issued his own manifesto to the nation the next day, which stated that he fully accepted the decision of the army on this matter and asked the nation to cooperate in this new partyless government.[2]

Although Toro specifically exonerated the Partido Socialista from subversive tendencies in an official communiqué,[3] the ousting of the party from the government by Busch brought about its rapid decline and quick demise. On 23 June Baldivieso resigned as party leader, charging both that the recent golpe invalidated his position, and also that the party newspaper *La Calle*, under the direction of Montenegro and Augusto Céspedes,[4] had maligned him and his policies.[5] *La Calle*, which began publication in this month, was to continue long after the fall of the party and after the political decline of Baldivieso as well, and was to be a crucial link between the short-lived Partido Socialista of Baldivieso and the parties of Bolivian socialism of the late 1930s and early 1940s. Also most of the personnel of the PS became involved in these later movements. Without government support and clear leadership, the Partido Socialista quietly disappeared from the political scene before the year was out.[6]

From its first days in office, the Toro government exhibited in all its diverse actions a rather bizarre mixture of ideologies, personalities and interest groups. In swift moves designed to gain popular support and to indicate to the nation that it was a government of action, the Toro administration issued a series of important

---

[1] *El Diario*, 21 June 1936, p. 12.   [2] *El Diario*, 22 June 1936, p. 5.
[3] *El Diario*, 26 June 1936, p. 6.   [4] Céspedes, *El dictador suicida*, pp. 149–50.
[5] *La Razón*, 25 June 1936, p. 5.
[6] One of the party's last public acts was to announce its full support of the Spanish Republic in August 1936. *El Diario*, 4 August 1936, p. 4.

liberal decrees. The five-year old Chaco War state of siege was finally ended,[1] and the ministry of labour began to set up several important study commissions to work on legislation for social security, a labour savings plan and a complete labour code.[2] On 1 June the government issued a new pay rise decree for government and private employees, augmenting considerably the previously decreed salary rises under the Tejada Sorzano régime.[3] The new ministry of mines and petroleum also announced that taking into consideration recommendations of the Tin Investigating Commission of 1935, it was planning the creation of a Banco Minero, which would become the prime mineral-purchasing agent for the small miners and a major government instrument of control in the industry.[4]

The régime, however, also exhibited a strong authoritarianism and an anti-labour attitude. Under the leadership of Pedro Zilveti Arce, minister of communications, for example, it prohibited the right of government employees to form unions or to strike.[5] At the end of June the government announced that it was actually considering an extremely stringent anti-communist and anti-anarchist decree.[6] It also began informal conversations with the Aramayo Partido Centralista over the entrance of the latter into the government.[7] But the government was too heavily dependent on labour support to carry out these threatened laws or to formally identify with a frankly conservative party. Rather it proceeded by quieter measures to enlist leading conservative civilians as government advisers, and made changes of personnel which would weaken leftists influence. Finally, in the first cabinet organized after the Busch golpe, Baldivieso was removed and replaced by the professional diplomat Enrique Finot.[8]

This drift toward government that was, though reformist,

---

[1] *La Razón*, 24 May 1936, p. 6.
[2] *La Razón*, 31 May 1936, p. 7; *El Diario*, 6 June 1936, p. 12.
[3] *El Diario*, 7 June 1936, p. 7.
[4] *Ibid.* p. 6, and *El Diario*, 10 June 1936, p. 4. Curiously the government also completed the work begun by Daniel Sánchez Bustamante in 1930 in the field of university reform by decreeing economic autonomy to the universities and also re-establishing his old *Consejo Nacional de Educación*. *El Diario*, 2 July 1936, pp. 4, 5.
[5] *El Diario*, 14 June 1936, p. 7, and 15 June 1936, p. 5.
[6] *El Diario*, 26 June 1936, p. 6.   [7] *El Diario*, 30 June 1936, p. 4
[8] Díaz Machicao, *Toro, Busch*, p. 33.

partyless and increasingly authoritarian, proved to be the junta's response to ever more complex problems which it seemed unable to resolve. The most pressing of these problems was unquestionably the severe post-war inflation. This was an extremely sensitive issue which affected not only labour and veterans who were continually petitioning and agitating over it, but the vital middle class as well. To resolve this issue the army attempted a series of drastic measures to control market prices, measures which were often conflicting and usually of little effect. Building on the work of the Tejada Sorzano régime, which established a *Dirección General de Consumos Nacionales* in early 1935, the Toro government reorganized the Dirección into a Special Subsistence Department under the ministry of industry and commerce and in June, August, September, and October several anti-speculation and price control laws were decreed.[1] Finally in early July the government established state food stores to sell items of prime necessity at prices subsidized by the government.[2]

In the labour field, meanwhile, Álvarez on his own initiative was carrying out radical measures. In July he began regular meetings with all the sindicato leaders, organizing them into an *Asociación Nacional Permanente de Organizaciones Sindicales* (ANPOS). This was a kind of overall committee, which included representatives from all the FOLs and FOTs in the nation, organized to supervise the development of a much debated obligatory syndicalization decree and other measures important to the labour movement.[3] It also served as a key institution for uniting the growing labour support and preparing the ground for the creation of Bolivia's first national labour federation.

The Álvarez ministry also represented the interest of labour in its hostility to the rural migrants who were flooding the labour market with unskilled workers. In a move designed to force vagrant peasants and Indian veterans back to the fields or into industry, the government issued an obligatory work decree for all men between the ages of eighteen and sixty who were of sound mind and body. This decree was designed to deal with the great increases in the city populations as a result of returning Indian

[1] *El Diario*, 17 October 1936, p. 7.
[2] *El Diario*, 6 July 1936, p. 4.
[3] *El Diario*, 5 July 1936, p. 6.

Chaco War veterans who, because of their war experience, were unwilling simply to return to the caste system and feudal arrangements of the countryside.[1]

A few of these restless veterans stayed on their holdings and agitated for a change in the organization of the agricultural system through self-organization and militant leftism, but this movement was confined solely to Quechuan colonos of the Cochabamba valleys. A few hundred of these colonos by 1936 succeeded in organizing peasant syndicates through which they rented the lands they worked from the absentee landlords. The most important of these few unions was created on the Santa Clara monastery estate in the Cliza valley, near Cochabamba. With strong support from the FOT and leftist groups of Cochabamba, in which they were represented, and with the benevolent support of the Toro government, these ex-combatant Quechua colonos obtained a five-year lease on these estates for them to work cooperatively with a possibility of renewal if they were successful. The ministry of agriculture provided them with free technical aid in the form of a resident agronomist, and the Cochabamba FOT provided a liaison official. The government also guaranteed to the monastery full respect for private property and intervened directly in the contract negotiations.[2] In short, it was something of a hot-house experiment, even if it contained radical overtones, and with the fall of the leftist governments at the end of the decade, the experiment was easily suppressed. Nor did the movement of *sindicatos campesinos* spread outside the small Cliza region to the rest of the great valley, let alone to the altiplano Aymara. Thus the only real expression of discontent that manifested itself in the post-war years was a heavy migration of the more advanced and restless Indians into the larger cities. In fact, the post-war years for a while were surprisingly free of the chronic Bolivian Indian uprisings, despite the vast number of returning

---

[1] Waldo Álvarez interview, La Paz, 11 October 1961; Sección de Prensa de Palacio de Gobierno, *Bajo el régimen militar socialista. ¿Hay labor gobernativa?* (La Paz: Imprenta Intendencia General de Guerra, 6 August 1936), p. 95.

[2] *El Diario*, 7 November 1936, p. 4; also see the detailed study by Jorge Dandler-Hanhart, 'Local Group, Community and Nation: Study of Changing Structure in Ucureña, Bolivia (1935–1952)' (unpublished MA thesis, Department of Anthropology, University of Wisconsin, 1967).

Indians who had been carefully trained in the use of modern arms during three years of warfare.[1]

Meanwhile, the most publicly discussed issue under consideration by the government was the proposal for an obligatory syndicalization decree. Later in the month of July the minister of government, Lieutenant-Colonel Julio Viera, presented his own version of this decree, with the backing of Javier Paz Campero and Carlos Romero, while Álvarez presented his own counter-plan defended by two ministry of labour advisers: Ricardo Anaya and José Antonio Arze.[2] The initiative for the decree came primarily from the younger officers who had in mind Mussolini's corporate state organization. Although Álvarez and his aides did not initiate such a proposal, nor support the corporate idea, they fully supported the proposal, hoping to take full advantage of it to unionize the workers.[3] Shortly after the full cabinet debate on the issue, *El Diario* bitterly attacked the whole scheme as ridiculous and dangerous, charging that Bolivia was a backward country in which the workers did not understand the meaning of syndicalism and it would thus be placing a powerful tool in labour's ignorant hands.[4]

In a special interview, Álvarez denied that the 'obligatory syndicalization' decree was specifically designed to destroy the political party system. Nor, he claimed, was it designed to replace that system with a corporate syndical structure, as many of the papers and public were charging. Nevertheless, the law would state, he went on to note, that 'the syndical organization will be the base for the functional constitution of the public powers', which he interpreted to mean that all future political parties would have to be based on the sindicatos and on economic and social class interests.[5]

[1] Government statistics indicated that all the major departmental capitals—particularly La Paz and Cochabamba—had seen a post-war population expansion of at least 30 per cent, almost exclusively due to veterans' migrations to these cities. 'The ex-combatants who previously were agriculturalists and herdsmen prefer to establish themselves in the cities and work as carpenters and in other manual activities where the salaries give them a fair economic situation.' It was estimated that the population of La Paz had risen to 214,000 and that of Cochabamba to 60,000. *El Diario*, 28 August 1936, p. 7.
[2] *El Diario*, 21 July 1936, p. 4.
[3] Waldo Álvarez interview, La Paz, 11 October 1961.
[4] *El Diario*, 22 July 1936, p. 4.   [5] *El Diario*, 25 July 1936, p. 4.

So intense did the discussion on this proposed decree become that Toro decided to issue public declarations on the subject. Speaking in late July, he discussed the basic philosophy of the government behind this move, and behind the overall structure of what was being called 'functional democracy',—an obvious euphemism for the corporate state, though in much of the discussion Mussolini or the Italian fascist model were rarely mentioned. He observed that:

The country is passing through a state of disorganization of its political and social institutions. This is due not only to the world crisis . . . but also to the decomposition of our parties and our old oligarchies and to the problems derived from the Chaco War. The atmosphere is characterized by the absence of large healthy groups, by the inertia of the masses, by the predominance of special interests and by the existence of small egoistic groups which seek to dominate the state . . . The old politics has not educated the masses nor has it created in them the consciousness of their obligations and their civil rights . . . For this reason there is no true public opinion and the latter is guided by aberrant sentiments such as *caudillismo, burocratismo* and regionalism, and is blind to the great permanent interests of the nation and to the resolution of the social, economic and cultural problems of Bolivia. The disorganization of the public powers, of the juridical and educational institutions, the administrative corruption and the organizing of groups which have no other end than that of seizing power and the public treasury, indicate that under these conditions the nation cannot continue any longer without running the danger of being destroyed in the most frightful disorganization and anarchy.[1]

He proposed as a solution to this pending institutional and moral catastrophe, and to 'the new economic and social problems which the development of modern industrialism have planted', that a major reorganization of parliament be put into effect. In such a reorganization, half the representation would come from the new syndicates and the other half from the traditional electoral processes. Citizens thus would have a dual vote, a general public vote and a vote as a member of one of the interest groups. This whole process, Toro declared, would educate the popular classes in social responsibility and make parliament more of a reflection of the socio-economic realities of the nation.

[1] *El Diario*, 28 July 1936, p. 10.

Toro modified his definition of syndicates in an attempt to placate growing middle-class opposition, and noted that there were all kinds of syndicalism, from revolutionary to cooperative and mutualistic, and that the government did not propose to impose any particular brand as its own. Nor, he declared, 'does it pretend to implant a form of syndicalism which sharpens the class struggle and creates an artificial atmosphere for the economic and social problems' of the nation. The government, stated Toro:

wants simply to take advantage of this force, to channel it within certain limits, subject it to the control of the state, make it an element of discipline and education of the masses, to root out caudillismo, anarchy and extremist action and convert them [i.e. the masses] into useful factors for the resolution of the problems of the republic. I do not believe that the organization of a few sindicatos of lawyers, doctors, engineers, agriculturalists, shoemakers, industrialists, merchants [and] workers, can intensify the class struggle, since these groupings are functional and will not group the men as capitalists or as proletarians, but rather in their technical and professional aspects. One cannot in the least doubt that the participation of these groups in the solution of certain problems, whose definitive resolution will still be in the hands of the state, will be of great utility and will contribute to educating public opinion in a better knowledge of national problems.

Finally, Toro promised that the whole movement would initially be of modest proportions, and would be carefully limited by state control.

This in essence and in its most articulated form is the philosophy which the small group of politically conscious and advanced younger officers proposed for the rejuvenation of national life and the creation of what they called a 'new Bolivia'. How far Toro himself formulated this doctrine, and how much he was influenced by the small coterie of officers who followed his banner, is difficult to say. There is no question, however, that Toro was certainly the most articulate spokesman for these men and that in the syndicalization debate he outlined the essential ideas of the group on the reasons for the failures of the old régime, and their remedies for the structural and organizational defects in Bolivian society. Certainly, the sophistication of this ideology stands in sharp contrast to the muddled pragmatic approach of the 'socialists' around Baldivieso and his party, and to the even less philosophically articulate traditionalists who surrounded Saavedra. Here in essence was the ideology of the advanced military thinkers, some of whom had received some type of training in Italy in the late 1920s and early 1930s, and their clear conception of what has been loosely defined as 'state socialism'. That Toro was more the articulator than a firm believer in such an ideology is indicated by his continual retreats from his promises and constant compromises with those 'egotistical groupings' and 'oligarchies' which he so lambasted. Yet there is no doubt that this ideology played an important role in the Toro government and did much to set its tone.

In proposing obligatory syndicalization, the government exposed itself to a violently anti-government campaign from the right. But it also faced a new political attack from the radical left on entirely different grounds. This attack came principally from a small group within the veterans' movement. The most important of the post-war veterans' organizations was, of course, the LEC, which despite several upheavals in its leadership in late 1936 and early 1937 continued to be the voice for the mass of veterans who were primarily apolitical and interested in obtaining as many benefits as possible from the state. The LEC, however, was not the only veterans' organization to arise. There were also such politically oriented groups as ANDES (*Asociación Nacional de Ex-Combatientes Socialistas*), which had played an important part in the formation of the Confederación Socialista Boliviana, the *Legión de Ex-Combatientes Nacional Socialistas* and several other smaller and more radical organizations.[1] But the veterans' group which most threatened the army rule and the political scene in the early months of the Toro government was the bitter, and temporarily important extremist group known as the *Asociación de Ex-Prisioneros*, the AEP. Formed from among the 15,000 Bolivian POWs who had spent long years in Paraguayan prisons, this association had a far more deepseated hostility towards the officer castes who ran the war than the veterans who had remained at the front. Both the civilians and officer POWs had felt betrayed by the nation, not only in their original capture, which had most often

[1] *El Diario*, 22 March 1936, p. 6.

been the result of extreme incompetence of the high command, but also in the protracted negotiations for their return which had not been completed until a full year after the end of hostilities. In the prisons, these men had formed organizations which reflected this bitterness—the professional officers in secret military cells like the RADEPA (*Razón de Patria*) and the civilians in organizations like AEP—and upon their return to Bolivia in May 1936 they had begun to agitate politically.

In early August, the AEP circulated a manifesto which touched off a political storm of major proportions. The manifesto in a bitter and sarcastic tone declared that:

Not all who were in the front lines are meritorious Bolivians, nor are all those who worked in the rearguard contemptible. Only an analysis of their behaviour in the course of duty and in the efficacy of the task performed, can determine a just verdict. In the same way, only with the most thorough exposition of the motives which occasioned the surrender of so many prisoners, can one establish if we are all culpable and if all who returned from the front are authentic heroes.

The manifesto, in an obvious reference to Toro, attacked 'theoretical men who were extremely articulate, but useless in action'. It singled out influence-peddling and deceiving officers who won decorations without going to the front, who obtained reservists' commissions and 'converted the war into tourism', and who then had the audacity to call men who were captured 'traitors' and 'cowards'. Who really were the traitors and cowards, demanded the ex-prisoners? We, or the 'choir of angels in certain rearguard posts' or 'the *jefes fracasados*, the strategists and tacticians of simulation, the false breakers of encirclement?' These are the men:

who have called us traitors, cowards, surrenderers, each time they needed to disguise the shame of a defeat. Nevertheless we ask: Who defended Boquerón, stamping a page of legitimate glory in our history?

Who raised the wall of their palpitating breasts in Kilometre 8 and retook Alihuata?

Who struggled at Nanawa and carried the offensive upon Gondra, Rojas Silva, Pirijayo, Pancho 8 and a hundred forts more?

Who held up the enemy advance in Conchitas and achieved such results in Strongest?

The answer of course is 'we prisoners' who represented the vigorous youth of the nation and who were taken by the better armed and better commanded enemy. Shifting from the defence of the POWs to a forceful attack on those whom they believed to be the true cowards, enemies, and traitors of the war, the manifesto declared that:

Now, placed face to face, cowards and heroes, traitors and patriots, those who surrendered and those who supposedly broke through enemy encirclements, we can reconstruct the past, and on the scales of justice impose the weight of historic truth.

Astonished Bolivia is still not convinced of its defeat. A threatening enemy at the foot of the craggy hills of the *cordillera* and daring to climb its slopes, is something that was always beyond the bounds of possibility and even of mere supposition.

We prisoners who have suffered absence from our native soil are not satisfied with the patria that we encounter; it does not seem to us the same; its pain, its silence, its passivity, its indifference, discourage our patriotism. If we ex-prisoners remain silent in this historic moment, we would indict ourselves as guilty.

They therefore urgently demanded a popular tribunal to judge 'the officers who commanded the thousands of Bolivians who fell into enemy hands . . . ' 'We have begun', declared the ex-prisoners, 'with the principle that not all who returned from the line of fire are authentic heroes nor worthy Bolivians, and for that reason we ask for a tribunal which will be the expression of the citizenry's conscience.'

The manifesto ended on the bitter and discouraged note that the ex-prisoners had returned to Bolivia hoping to find a leader to crystallize their aspirations and orient the ideas which had emerged from the chaqueña tragedy, but had found none.[1]

The call for a tribunal to judge military officers and specifically the high command struck deeply at such men as Toro and Peñaranda, both of whom were directly indicated as culpable in the above declaration. It also threatened the very precarious unity of the army, raising before its view the fear of a civilian and public attack on its honour and leadership, one of the very things it had hoped to obviate by taking power and leading the 'rejuvenation' movement itself.

[1] *El Diario*, 12 August 1936, p. 4.

El Diario noted that the request for a war responsibility tribunal by the AEP had caused quite a stir in national political circles, but commented that this was not the first such request that had been made. Almost from the end of the war an investigation had been called for by the press, public assemblies and ex-combatant organizations; however, for one reason or another it was always put off. The old congress refused to carry out such an undertaking, claiming that it would threaten the peace negotiations, and with one excuse or another since then, the proposed investigation had always been dropped. Now, declared *El Diario*, there was no more excuse for delay.[1]

But others were not so anxious to begin this potentially explosive trial, least of all the high command. When asked his opinion about such an investigation, General Peñaranda, commander-in-chief of the army, stated:

I believe that . . . while all the necessary documentation, which permits one to establish a definitive judgement, is being accumulated and classified, it is premature to discuss the complex subject of the responsibilities for the war. Such a discussion at the moment could well generate an inflamed and unprofitable battle of passions. On the other hand, one should not forget that responsibility for the conduct of the war embraces the entire nation and goes well beyond just the initiation of the conflict itself. The war has made evident, in no uncertain manner, the failure of all our institutions as well as the improvidence and irresponsibility of our men.[2]

There is no question that this was a candid threat by Peñaranda to the traditional parties, to the effect that if they supported such a dangerous and damaging investigation, then they, as well as the high command, would suffer the consequences. The government also counter-attacked, and announced that a commission would be set up to study the actions of prisoners during their imprisonment in Paraguay to determine and judge their conduct. This obviously was a direct counter-challenge to the AEP manifesto, and the so-called Tribunal of Honour was held over the heads of the ex-prisoners as a vindictive retaliatory measure should they succeed in carrying through their own call for a popular war

[1] *El Diario*, 13 August 1936, p. 4.   [2] *El Diario*, 3 September 1936, p. 4.

investigatory commission.[1] So long as the high command main-tained its control over the government, however, the possibility of such an investigation being carried out, especially given the equal fear felt by the traditional parties, made the organization of such an investigation highly unlikely, and with the passage of time the matter was eventually allowed to be forgotten.

Having quelled this threat to stability from the radical ex-prisoners, and having postponed the conservative opposition as well by delaying initiation of the syndicalization decrees, the Toro régime concentrated its attention on governmental organiza-tion and social legislation. In July and August, special advisory commissions were set up to study civil rights for women, and the establishment of salaried *alcaldes* (or mayors) to replace the elec-tive system, and the actual decrees for these were carried through in later months.[2] The government also announced proposals for a more equitable tax system, the creation of a national department of health, and the confiscation of all petroleum concessions not being worked according to the terms of the concession contracts.[3] The continual flow of decrees on these and other subjects was designed to give the government the aura of a major revolutionary and dynamic force; the specially established state printing office helped to propagate this impression by issuing a flood of pro-motional literature on the great work being carried forward by the Military Socialist régime. Toro even went so far as to set up a weekly press conference to discuss the major problems of the day with the press corps, a system rather new to Bolivia and one which he used frequently to advantage.[4] Despite this feverish activity, however, little serious impression was made on the public, for a good deal of the major legislation and activity brought few immed-iate concrete changes and seemingly the public remained largely apathetic to the régime.[5]

[1] *El Diario*, 26 August 1936, p. 6.
[2] *El Diario*, 9 July 1936, pp. 4, 5, and 23 October 1936, p. 7.
[3] This latter decree effectively reduced the number of petroleum concessions from 225 containing 12,704,875 hectares to just 6 containing only 379,558. *El Diario*, 10 July 1936, pp. 6, 7. For a full catalogue of the enactments of the government in these first months see: Departamento Nacional de Propaganda Socialista, *Informe presentado por el señor coronel Presidente de la Junta Militar Socialista de Gobierno al Ejército Nacional, de 17 de mayo a 31 de diciembre de 1936* (La Paz: Imprenta de la Intendencia General de Guerra, 1937).
[4] *El Diario*, 20 October 1936, p. 7.   [5] Díaz Machicao, *Toro, Busch*, pp. 39ff.

But the oligarchy was not so apathetic and felt sufficiently threatened by the new situation to give marked support to Aramayo's personalist Partido Centralista, which had been founded in May. This support was clearly indicated by the appointment as head of the party of F. Gutiérrez Granier, who concurrently was also head of the very important big miners' *Asociación de Industriales Mineros*.[1] In reality the Partido Centralista was more of an open oligarchic pressure group created for the times than a coherent political party in the old style. But its very creation and prominence indicated that the upper classes and holders of economic power doubted the capacity of the traditional parties to protect by themselves the established socio-economic structure of the old order in this unique political situation of military rule. And there is no question that in reality, while some power remained in the traditional parties, the war had so discredited them that they had reached a stage of decadence from which they would never fully recover, at least in the style of the pre-war days.

The formation of the Centralista group and other later conglomerations and confederations of the older parties in direct and open concert with the older upper-rank military officers, the industrialists and miners, clearly indicated that the oligarchy in the post-war world could no longer rely on the traditional political structure. In fact, from 1935 to 1952 the oligarchy was constantly searching for new political organs capable of defending its rights and providing the security of the pre-war system. Since the key tin industrialists were nationals, or controlled companies with highly diversified foreign capital, they more heavily relied for protection of their privileged positions on the domestic political system than did foreign capitalists. These latter could always ultimately depend on international pressure when their manipulation of the political system failed. Bolivia's tin miners, however, could not turn with security to such intervention and therefore were less flexible in dealing with the crisis of the political system which had developed. This greater dependence on domestic

---

[1] *El Diario*, 26 May 1937, p. 5, for his mining association and 30 August 1936, p. 6 for his party secretaryship. For a study of this important organization, see William L. Lofstrom, *Attitudes of an Industrial Pressure Group in Latin America, the 'Asociación de Industriales Mineros de Bolivia', 1925–1935* (Cornell University, Latin American Studies Program, Dissertation Series, no. 9, September 1968).

politics may be the key factor in explaining the rigidity of the oligarchy in dealing with the new post-war reformist and radical movements. Instead of co-opting these new groups in the more usual Latin American manner, they constantly fought their entrance into politics. Thus, not only the reformist and radical political movements, but the upper class as well, were experiencing a post-war process of breakdown and reorganization.

In August, the Partido Centralista through the pages of *El Diario* and *La Razón* began an unceasing attack on the economic policies of the Toro government and especially on the ministry of labour and its occupant, Waldo Álvarez, whom they labelled a communist. It charged that the wage increase decrees, the new tax programmes which were planned, and the limitations being placed on the private sector of the economy were all causing a serious loss of economic confidence in the country. They charged that the only remedy to this situation was the establishment of a coalition cabinet which would inspire confidence both at home and abroad.[1]

For a time, Toro was able to hold out against this pressure, especially as several of his ministers were in close social and economic contact with the oligarchy. In early September he even succeeded in raising by 10 per cent the amount of foreign currency drafts (*divisas*) the miners had to turn over to the government.[2] But at the same time, he announced a harsh anti-communist decree, in an attempt to relieve oligarchical pressure on the government.[3] In typical Toro fashion, the decree, which was menacing in its terms, was never put into practice. For Toro still sensed the reformist tone of the nation and while acceding to the traditional forces when he could, tried to maintain the forward momentum of his government. A typical tactic of his was to form working commissions to study radical reforms. Thus he set up a constitutional reform commission, a land reform commission, and even one to investigate war contracts frauds.[4] This was clever manœuvring, but in the increasingly tense atmosphere of nervous oligarchical interests and evangelical military sects, it was becoming more difficult to calm political passions by these methods.

[1] *El Diario*, 30 August 1936, p. 6.   [2] *El Diario*, 8 September 1936, p. 5.
[3] *El Diario*, 22 September 1936, p. 6.
[4] *El Diario*, 23 September 1936, p. 5; 1 October 1936, p. 4, and 25 October 1936, p. 7.

In addition Toro could not seem to meet the inflation crisis. Though this was not a severe crisis by later standards, the annual rate of increase of 51 per cent in the cost of living in the late 1930s was sufficiently different from the rate of 17 per cent experienced in the war years to cause alarm among all sections of the population despite the essentially sound economic position of the nation.[1] Toro himself seemed to recognize the essence of the issue and its political impact in a special press conference in September 1936 when he declared that the whole question was a 'psychological' one since the economy was functioning smoothly. He pointed out that the government had adopted all the traditional anti-inflationary measures and made an unusual appeal to the press to help resolve the problem by informing the nation of its own excellent economic condition.[2]

But inflationary pressures and the drives of traditional and reform forces were taking their toll on the government. In an effort to resolve some of these problems, Toro finally put pressure on his Constitutional Reform Commission to come up with definite proposals and went so far as to declare in the last months of 1936 that he would call for a constitutional convention in May 1937. In his announcements for the coming constitutional assembly Toro declared that the new congress would have only 50 per cent of its members elected by popular vote; the other 50 per cent would be directly designated by the sindicatos whom they would represent. Indicating that these were concrete proposals, the president committed himself to congressional elections by February 1937.[3]

In the midst of these developments new rumours began to circulate that Aramayo, representing his Partido Centralista, was holding discussions with the government on the idea of possible united action.[4] While the government officially denied these rumours,[5] it took advantage of dissension in the labour movement to oust the bitterly-attacked Waldo Álvarez and much of his extreme leftist coterie from the ministry of labour.

[1] CEPAL, *Desarrollo económico de Bolivia*, p. 62.
[2] *El Diario*, 8 September 1936, p. 4.
[3] *El Diario*, 3 November 1936, p. 5.
[4] *El Diario*, 17 November 1936, p. 4.
[5] *La Razón*, 19 November 1936, p. 4.

From the early days of the Toro régime, Álvarez ha
maintained that he was merely representing the FOT in th
government, and would remain in office only so long as the labou
movement continued to give him support. This it did from th
very beginning, with the various individual unions and th
FOTs constantly affirming their confidence in his régime.[1] Late
Álvarez began to state that as soon as a national congress of th
labour movement was convoked to name a successor, he woul
resign. He felt that despite his great activity and accomplish
ments, he was continually facing strong hostility from the rest o
the cabinet and basic indifference from Toro.[2]

Nevertheless, despite this hostility and indifference, Álvarez i
his five-month tenure of office carried out important work. Firs
of all he effectively organized the ministry and temporarily con
verted the old *Departmento General de Trabajo* from a judicial typ
of body into an active ministry with executive operations in th
field of labour legislation as well as major investigatory duties.[3]
He set up study commissions to work out national social securit
legislation and worker savings plans; he gave strong support t
all unionization drives and also established close liaison betwee
the ministry and the labour movement. Throughout his tenure o
office, Álvarez surrounded himself with all the important labou
leaders, both of La Paz and of the other major cities, setting u
under ANPOS special conferences on problems important t
labour to which were invited not only all the labour leaders, bu
many of the leading radical leftist intellectuals of the nation.[4]
Álvarez was also effective in intra-government affairs, and hi

[1] For chauffeurs' and printers' support see *El Diario*, 19 June 1936, p. 7; for textil
union see *El Diario*, 22 June 1936, p. 4; and for local FOTs *La Razón*, 25 Jun
1936, p. 8.

[2] Interview with Waldo Álvarez, La Paz, 11 October 1961.

[3] The *Dirección General de Trabajo* had been established by Saavedra in the early
1920s to try the compensation and worker accident cases, and throughout it
history to 1936, it had operated almost exclusively as an administrative court.
Now it was made the executive arm of the new ministry and endowed
with a host of administrative and labour-organizing functions, and wa
even given the task of carrying out the first industrial census and late
of working out an elaborate labour code. See, e.g. *El Diario*, 7 July 1936,
p. 12.

[4] Both Ricardo Anaya and José Antonio Arze, along with other Cochabamb
radicals, lectured to labour leaders at these conferences. See, e.g. *El Diario*
11 July 1936, p. 4.

determined opposition effectively killed the July anti-communist and anti-anarchist decree.[1]

Meanwhile, Álvarez actively encouraged the meeting of a national congress to give birth to a permanent and united confederation which would embrace all the post-war reconstructed and rejuvenated FOTs. This unification movement gained strong support, and the labour leaders succeeded in organizing a national labour congress. To stress the importance of this congress, they called it the 'First National Congress of Workers', considering the previous four national workers' congresses to be of only minor importance.

This congress, the largest to date in Bolivian history, began its sessions late in November in Oruro, with full representation from the labour movement as well as from all leftist political parties. In attendance were men like Ricardo Anaya and his Izquierda group of Cochabamba and José Aguirre Gainsborg and some of his PORista adherents. There were also numerous moderate socialists, anarchists from the FOL of La Paz, and even Republican-Socialists. For a while the moderate socialists like Fausto Reinaga and Carlos Montenegro joined with such old saavedrista labour leaders as Julio Lara (who represented the La Paz FOT) in attacking José Aguirre Gainsborg and other radical leftists in an attempt to exclude them from the deliberations, but Álvarez and others were able to prevent this struggle from breaking up the convention.[2]

Prevented by Álvarez from deviating into political factional debates, the 100 delegates in five hectic days discussed a host of major issues affecting the Bolivian labour movement, from attitudes toward foreign imperialism and international affiliations, to wage problems, shop stewards, and the establishment of a national confederation.[3] In the early sessions the workers approved

---

[1] *El Diario*, 6 July 1936, p. 4. Among his other actions, in July 1936 Álvarez with Ricardo Anaya, José Antonio Arze and Fernando Sinani among others, had carried out a tour of all the leading labour centres of the republic to discuss problems with the local unions. *El Diario*, 13 July 1936. He had also expressed strong interest in syndicalization of agricultural workers and the abolition of pongueaje. *El Diario*, 23 August 1936, p. 3; 30 August 1936, p. 3, and 31 August 1936, p. 4.   [2] Lora, *José Aguirre Gainsborg*, pp. 51–4. See programme outline, *El Diario*, 24 November 1936, p. 5. The government gave full financial support for the organization of the convention and provided travel expenses for the 100 delegates. *El Diario*, 26 November 1936, p. 7, and 30 November 1936, p. 5.

such acts as requesting the government to end financial support to the Catholic Church, and to nationalize the Standard Oil Company holdings. They demanded a six-hour day for mine workers, and seven and eight for other industries and better enforcement of the wage increase decrees. Finally, they proposed a fifteen-day paid vacation scheme for all workers.[1] In later sessions minimum scales were approved for all industries and tenant protection laws were discussed.

The most important event in all the sessions was the debate over the *Confederación Sindical de Trabajadores de Bolivia* (CSTB), the proposed national confederation. While the outline and organization of the proposed confederación had been accepted beforehand by the labour movement, the crucial questions of political involvement and international affiliations were left to be decided on the convention floor. At first the traditional apolitical positions were proposed by the old-line labour leaders in conformity with pre-war concepts and practices. But the convention defeated these and announced that the policy of the new CSTB and the entire labour movement would be to maintain a close and constant relationship with the parties of the left as had been happening in such cities as Oruro and especially Potosí,[2] that is to form local *Frentes Populares* or Popular Leftist Fronts with these parties. Also it was agreed to seek international affiliation.[3]

On the immediate political issue of electing a successor to Álvarez, however, the convention was in complete discord. Although one Oruro-sponsored candidate eventually did win a majority vote after much balloting, many of the local FOTs later disavowed his candidacy, and the convention unity degenerated into intense internal conflicts among the leadership.[4] At this point, with complete deadlock and disunity in the workers' ranks over the appointment which the government had promised to

[1] *El Diario*, 2 December 1936, p. 4.
[2] In Potosí there existed a 'United Front of the Left' which had been organized by such radical leftists as Abelardo Villalpando—later a member of the PCB and rector of the University of Potosí in the early 1960s—and the local FOT, and this type of relationship existed on a much smaller scale in Oruro. The Potosí *frente* was a remarkably durable one and closely tied to the far left intellectuals and the *Cerro Unificada* miners, both of whom supported each other strongly for many long years.
[3] *El Diario*, 3 December 1936, p. 5; Barcelli, *Medio siglo de luchas sindicales*, p. 146.
[4] *El Diario*, 4 December 1936, p. 5.

hand over to a candidate elected by the labour movement, the astute Toro made a sharp move to the right. Strongly pressed by the oligarchy over the radicals in the ministry of labour and on many other economic issues, he took advantage of labour disunity to support a non-labour man for the post. His selection was Javier Paz Campero, who was a leading lawyer for the Hochschild mining interests and socially and sympathetically a part of the oligarchy.[1]

Immediately after the new minister was appointed, the radicals were removed from the ministry,[2] and the ANPOS organization and conferences and other activist features of the Álvarez régime were allowed to lapse, bringing the ministry into political harmony with the rest of the government, much to the satisfaction of the rightist opposition.[3] Nevertheless, in terms of basic legislation, much of the fundamental social security and worker savings codes initiated by Álvarez were successfully completed by the new minister. Thus, at the end of 1936, Toro seemed to have placated some of the more violent criticism of the right without a rebellion from the left, which still considered him in a highly favourable light. Though his balancing act was successful in giving the régime an aura of reform with a policy of moderation, the general unease due to the continued rule without party and the relentless rate of inflation continued to disturb the middle and upper classes. Also, while Toro concerned himself with popular civilian support, he seems to have been unwilling or unable to establish his independent authority in the army. For Germán Busch, the rather reticent man behind the throne, continued to exert his authority over the army from his position in the general staff without any effective challenge from Toro.

The new year brought with it a major revival in organized political activity as the traditional political parties began, after a

[1] Interview with Waldo Álvarez, La Paz, 11 October 1961: Díaz Machicao, *Toro, Busch*, pp. 40, 44. [2] *El Diario*, 1 February 1936, p. 5.
[3] See editorial in *El Diario*, 19 January 1936, p. 6. Toro's induction speech of the new minister caused true delight in *El Diario* for he seemingly attacked the previous minister for having accentuated the class struggle and expressed his belief that the ministry of labour should serve as a conciliating force between capital and labour rather than the partisan of one or the other. According to the newspaper, this speech was a 'rude blow' to the extremists who wanted radical social-economic change.

long period of inactivity, to prepare for the coming congressional elections. In early January, with the permission of the government, the Partido Republicano Socialista carried out a major reunion of its grand assembly with over 100 persons attending the sessions. In the absence of its exiled titular head, Bautista Saavedra, the national council accepted the resignation of Román Paz as secretary-general, and elected Pedro Zilveti Arce to the post, with Edmundo Vázquez second in command. Others elected to office were FOT president Julio Lara, Roberto Jordán Pando, Waldo Belmonte Pool and a host of other old saavedrista stalwarts.[1]

The Genuinos also began reorganizing their ranks and in early February, their leader, Demetrio Canelas, wrote to the minister of government asking constitutional guarantees for a national convention of the party.[2] Canelas had to wait several weeks for a reply from the minister, Colonel Julio Viera, but when it came it was quite a scathing document. Colonel Viera had held a cabinet position in the Toro government from the very beginning and seems to have been one of the more politically astute and convinced of the officers, and his reply summed up the attitude of the more doctrinaire army men to the traditional political parties and to the aims of the Toro government. The 'Socialist Revolution of May, valiantly purified in June', stated Viera stood for the creation of a true state socialism which sought as a major goal establishment of 'the Bolivian economy on bases of social justice', and the institutionalization of these new forms so as to bring economic well-being to the majority, above the petty egotistical interests of the 'Rosca'.

Hence, the government, whose primary interest is in the reorganization of the nation, . . . seeks the collaboration and support which it needs to realize its reform programme from the political forces of wholly socialist orientation and not in the antagonistic groups which pertain to the demagogic and caudillistic traditionalism of the past . . The Military Government's policy [therefore] is aimed at . . . the liquidation of the old parties which precipitated the moral and economic bankruptcy of the country.

[1] *El Diario*, 12 January 1936, p. 6.
[2] D. Canelas, *Documentos políticos*, pp. 55–6.

Therefore the minister of government considers that they [the traditional political parties] do not exist in Bolivia.

The minister ended by noting that the government would extend full political guarantees to all the leftist parties, but not to the traditional 'non-existent' ones.[1]

Although this was extreme language, it represented a considerable body of anti-liberal and anti-democratic opinion in the military command, especially of the men who were close to Busch. In actual fact, though, this did not in any way mean the end of the influence of the oligarchy on the government—far from it—but rather, it indicated the intense hatred felt for the old politicians and their parties, tainted by the Chaco War. And this hatred would soon lead to a climate that made the continuation of the traditional political parties in their pre-war forms impossible. As for the Viera declaration, while it drew angry replies from the traditional press, it nevertheless put a damper on the temporary effervescence of traditional party activity.

Another factor inhibiting political activity was the Toro government's constant delay in calling for the elections of the constituent assembly. In the first two months of the new year, Toro promoted the activities of the Constitutional Reform Commission, but did nothing concrete about the date of the elections, which had been promised for February. The commission itself, under the leadership of Vicente Mendoza López, was attempting to amalgamate all the different streams of ideology in the new government in a coherent constitution. A mixed syndicalist-corporate state grafted on to the old political party system was contemplated.[2]

But despite the constant flood of words from the government palace, seemingly nothing concrete was happening and many crucial leaders were becoming impatient with the lack of true vitality in the government or of substantial change in the economic situation. They were enraged over Toro's procrastination over the calling of a constituent assembly, and this impatience made itself felt early in March when Busch handed in his resignation

---

[1] D. Canelas, *Documentos políticos*, pp. 57–9.
[2] *El Diario*, 28 January 1937, p. 4, and 2 February 1937, p. 6.

as chief of the EMG.[1] The army officers in the Chaco quickly cabled Busch their support and asked that he should not be removed, while the government's immediate response was to refuse to accept his request.[2] The resignation of Busch was tantamount to a vote of no confidence in the government and the Toro régime was considerably shaken by it. Although Busch was persuaded to stay, the government realized that it had to produce some dramatic action or otherwise it faced the certain future of a golpe de estado. Busch had withdrawn his resignation this time; the next time he would not make his opposition public, but merely act on it.

The first act of the newly rejuvenated administration was truly a startling one, for on 13 March, just ten days after Busch's resignation threat, the Toro government announced the confiscation of the property of the Standard Oil Company of Bolivia. Shaken to its roots, the Toro régime, under the leadership of its minister of labour, Javier Paz Campero, finally brought to an abrupt conclusion the long-drawn-out process of litigation against the Standard Oil Company which had been initiated in 1935 by the Tejada Sorzano government, and had quietly languished in the courts ever since. This truly historic decree, antedating the similar, though far greater, action of the Mexican government by an entire year, stated:

BE IT RESOLVED:
The government declares the forfeiture of all the property of the Standard Oil Company of Bolivia, within the republic, for proved defraudation of the fiscal interests [of the state].

All the goods of the mentioned company which are found in Bolivian territory at the time of dictating the present resolution, pass to the property of the state.

Until the government believes it convenient, the official entity *Yacimientos Petrolíferos Fiscales Bolivianos* (YPFB) will remain charged with the administration and management of all the goods of the company, which in virtue of the confiscation decree pass to the power of the state.[3]

The government justification of the confiscation decree was

---

[1] *El Diario*, 3 March 1937, p. 6.
[2] *El Diario*, 8 March 1937, p. 2, and 4 March 1937, p. 7.
[3] *El Diario*, 16 March 1937, p. 7.

based on clause No. 18 of the Richmond Levering contract of 1920 which stated in part, that:

If during the execution of the contract the government complains about something that in its opinion concerns nonfulfilment [of the contract], it will give notice to the capitalist, who from that moment will have a maximum term of six months to correct the offence which motivates the complaint; in case of their not doing it within the said time, the government will be able to declare the lapse, abrogation or modification of the contract, which also will occur administratively for whatever defrauding of the fiscal interests [of the state which occurred]. The caducity of the contract [i.e. its lapsing] signifies for the capitalists the loss of all their rights to the goods of the company, which will remain in the exclusive possession of the government.[1]

The Standard Oil Company was bound to this contract by subsequent agreements since it had taken over the Levering concessions with the consent of the Bolivian government. The Toro government proved by impeccable documents and the company's own inadvertent admissions that Standard had produced oil in 1925, 1926, and 1927, and had shipped it through its private pipelines to Argentina while stating publicly in its reports to the government in those years that no oil was even being produced.

The Siles government in 1927–8 had demanded that the Standard Oil Company of Bolivia pay new and higher concession taxes to the Bolivian government, since it had, according to government sources, begun producing oil on these lands. The company, however, refused to pay these sums, saying that as of 1928 it still had not begun production of oil, a statement which it repeated in several memoranda to the government in that year. On the basis of these company assertions and after long negotiations, the government committed the company to begin payment of the oil production tax in January 1930.

Under the impact of the accusations in the Argentine parliament during the Chaco War and of the consequent questioning of the Tejada Sorzano government concerning a secret Argentine-Bolivian pipeline which had been in existence since 1925, the

---

[1] Jorge Muñoz Reyes, *La caducidad de las concesiones otorgadas a The Standard Oil Company of Bolivia* (Cuartillas Informatives, No. 5; La Paz: Departamento Nacional de Propaganda Socialista, 23 March 1937), pp. 14–15.

company officially responded in October 1935, by denying the charges of gross exportation of oil to Argentina as false. The company claimed that such a pipeline had been in existence, but only for three years (1925–7) and not for ten as charged by the Tejada Sorzano government, and that it had only shipped out a total of 704 barrels of oil, all of which went from its Bolivian fields on one side of the Bermejo to its Argentine works on the other side where it was used in drilling operations. In admitting this, however, the company forgot about its 1928 statements.[1]

Under the leadership of Jorge Muñoz Reyes, the director-general of the ministry of mines and petroleum, and a recent science graduate of the University of California at Berkeley, the ministry, using only the open admissions of the company, proved that it had broken the 1920 and 1922 contracts in several ways: by not giving the government plans of the pipeline installation which it was required to do; by not paying the 11 per cent government tax on the 704 barrels which it secretly shipped to Argentina; by admitting that it had produced oil in 1925, 1926, and 1927, when it had told the government in 1927 and 1928 that it had not done so; and finally by checking carefully all documents that the company itself had presented and proving that even their figure of 704 was inaccurate, and that by their own calculations it should have been 1,360![2]

Thus, without even trying to prove the greater charges of wholesale secret exportations at the height of the Chaco War, the government in a technical and extremely meticulous fashion was proving that the company had violated by its own admission several clauses in the contract. No matter how small the sum involved, the company had thus been guilty of defrauding the state. As a penalty, according to its 1920–2 contracts, it was liable to complete confiscation with its only recourse against this action being an appeal to the Bolivian supreme court. Obviously, all this careful work of investigation by Jorge Muñoz Reyes and his assistants would have been shelved if the Toro ministry had not felt itself in such dire political straits that it sought to use any

---

[1] Muñoz Reyes, *La caducidad*, pp. 2–7; also Montenegro, *Frente al derecho del estado.*
[2] Muñoz Reyes, *La caducidad*, pp. 8–10. Also interview with Jorge Muñoz Reyes (then rector of the Universidad Mayor de San Andrés), La Paz, January 1961.

available measure to save its government. The confiscation of the Standard Oil Company of Bolivia was undoubtedly the most dramatic and popular action of the Toro government and one that nationalists, both right and left, have been proud of ever since. Nor is there any doubt that with this dramatic move, Toro gave a new lease of life to his government.

In line with this new and desperate attempt to bolster his régime by every possible means, Toro now undertook to find an alternative to his dependence on the army by constructing a national civilian political party to give support to his régime. In early April notices of a *Partido Socialista de Estado* began to appear. On 7 April, in the presence of the minister of government, Lieutenant-Colonel Julio Viera, a Cochabamba branch of the Partido was established.[1] On his return to La Paz, Colonel Viera bluntly stated that the government was officially supporting the new organization even to the point of encouraging public employees to join it, and implied that the government, in support of this new party, would hinder other political parties from operating in an open election campaign.[2]

Meanwhile, other cabinet ministers were being sent throughout the republic to set up local committees of the PSE. In early May, the minister of education, Lieutenant-Colonel Alfredo Peñaranda, spoke at a special organization meeting of the Partido Socialista de Estado in Sucre, where the chief attendants were local workers' groups, public employees and members of Baldivieso's old Partido Socialista.[3] So rapid was the progress of this government-generated activity, that the régime was able to witness the construction of a national committee in mid-May. The honorary executive committee included practically the entire cabinet as well as Toro, General Peñaranda, and some of the leading Baldivieso socialists. The actual operating executive committee, however, was largely made up of politically unknown figures.[4]

Concurrently with these moves, Vicente Mendoza López was attempting to set up a *Partido Socialista Revolucionario*, on his own accord, but in harmony with the government party.[5] To this

---

[1] *El Diario*, 8 April 1937, p. 2. [2] *El Diario*, 10 April 1937, p. 7.
[3] *El Diario*, 5 May 1937, p. 2. [4] *El Diario*, 16 May 1937, p. 6. [5] *Ibid.*

new group many of the old Baldivieso socialist elements soon gave their support, after dropping their old leader José Tamayo. Shortly afterwards, these elements joined with Max Atristain and Augusto Guzmán in helping to form an even larger entity called the *Frente Institucional Socialista* under Mendoza López' leadership.[1] Then, with this important political backing behind him, Vicente Mendoza López signed a unification pact with the fledgling Partido Socialista de Estado in an obvious take-over manœuvre.[2] How important this movement might have become, especially as the CSTB was tentatively considering the possibility of bringing in the labour movement,[3] will never be known, for with the fall of the Toro government, the whole embryonic movement collapsed.

Despite the confiscation of the Standard Oil Company and the organization of a Partido Socialista de Estado, and even the seeming improvement in the economy,[4] Toro's prestige declined considerably in the army and among the officers surrounding Busch, and the chief of the EMG finally decided to enter the political arena in his own right. On 10 July in a tumultuous meeting in La Paz, the LEC voted Busch the *Jefe Supremo* of the

---

[1] *El Diario*, 4 June 1937, p. 7, and 8 June 1937, p. 7.
[2] *El Diario*, 10 June 1937, p. 4.   [3] *El Diario*, 13 June 1937, p. 6.
[4] In April, Toro had been interviewed by a correspondent for *La Razón* of Buenos Aires and had stated that he believed the difficult monetary situation could be fully stabilized by August or September, *El Diario*, 29 April 1937, p. 4. And statistics issued by the *Dirección General de Estadística* seemed to support the Toro optimism. Taking the year of 1931 as base, it listed the history of the general index of prices as follows:

Month	Year	Cost of living index
	1931	100
December	1936	396
January	1937	400
February	1937	403
March	1937	438
April	1937	409

Source: El Diario, 22 May 1937, p. 5

Also in late May the government even announced a Bs. 18 million surplus instead of the expected deficit for the fiscal year 1936 because of the increased taxation and administrative reorganization carried out by the Toro government. *El Diario*, 22 May 1937, p. 5.

veterans' organization, and the colonel gratefully accepted this important public post. By bestowing this position on Busch, the LEC consciously indicated that is considered him the ultimate leader of the veterans' movement over the actual president of the republic. It thus indicated its break with the government, the first to occur since its organization, and its recognition of the primary importance of Busch. In his address to the LEC assembly, Busch stressed the need for basic change in ideas and leadership, calling for these new ideas to be created out of 'the experience and sacrifices acquired' in the battlefields of the Chaco. This stress on new ideology and leadership was without question his announcement of impending change.[1]

On the very next evening, Toro, Peñaranda, and Busch met together in secret session, and Busch announced to Toro that he no longer had the confidence of the army behind his government. Busch then offered, as a gesture only, the position of president of the junta de gobierno to Peñaranda, who of course refused, thus leaving Busch's path clear to assume power.[2] On 13 July the embittered Toro quietly announced his renunciation of the presidency for the good of the nation and went into voluntary exile, thus ending fifteen of some of the most fruitful and bewildering months in Bolivian political history.

An astute and able politician who had successfully led the nation through its first truly reformist period, Toro provided much of the tone and even concrete legislation for the period of military radical rule in the 1930s. Although he had antagonized the important miners, he retained support of the rural landed interests and the urban middle classes by tempering his verbal radicalism with minimal changes of a drastic nature. He had also gained positive civilian support by his constant attention to issues of inflation and social welfare and he won the warm enthusiasm of the extreme radicals and labour movement by his support of the Álvarez ministry. Even in his most anti-radical movements after November 1936, Toro never lost his support of the labour movement nor did he ever actively prosecute the radical left.

But he did fail to retain the support of the army and more especially of the junior officers led by Germán Busch. And it was

[1] *El Diario*, 11 July 1937, p. 7.   [2] *El Diario*, 14 July 1937, p. 1.

this interest group which effectively controlled the major elements of power in the new era. For these fascist and reformist-minded junior officers, the political pragmatism and constant manœuvrings of Toro were seen as signs of weakness and lack of revolutionary fervour. Not sufficiently aware even of their own basic desires, they nevertheless felt that a new régime under Busch had more emotional appeal to offer than had the too articulate Toro. Thus with the fall of Toro the army radicals attempted to rule on their own and finally to express their reformist programmes in a totally military 'revolutionary' government.

9

THE RISE OF GERMÁN BUSCH

Despite his compromises with the oligarchy, and his frequent and sharp retreats from stated radical positions, Toro still had the warm support of the labour movement and the extreme left when his government fell in July 1937. To most of the left, moderate and radical, the advent of the politically unknown Busch thus appeared to represent the overthrow of the experiment in Military Socialism and the return of the oligarchy to power, and especially the return of Patiño influence in the national government. The traditional press, for its part, reinforced this assumption by hailing the coming of Busch as a major renunciation by the army of the 'socialist' policy carried out by Toro.[1]

Nor did Busch clarify his position in the early days of the new régime. His first pronouncement, issued on 13 July, seemed to stress corporate ideology by emphasizing the end of the class struggle between capital and labour, its replacement by national cooperation, and rule without party support. While he stated that Toro had strayed from the principles of the 17 May movement, he was unclear as to how this had occurred.[2] His second pronouncement on the 14th reverted to very personal statements of his own modesty and patriotism —a theme which received ever greater stress in his subsequent speeches—and vague remarks about the need for national stabilization and progress.[3]

These unfocused and slightly menacing declarations seemed to confirm the essentially reactionary impression of the revolt in the minds of the people. So persistent was this belief in a rightist putsch that Busch was forced to deny publicly that the revolt was financed by Standard Oil the day after taking office. Later that

[1] E.g. El Diario, 14 July 1937, p. 4, editorial. El Diario was especially hostile to Toro since he had closed them down the month before his fall.
[2] La Calle, 15 July 1937, p. 4. [3] El Diario, 15 July 1937, p. 2.

same week both he and his new minister of mines were forced to promise that the new government had no intention whatsoever of returning the confiscated property to the American oil company.[1]

But these declarations resolved no doubts, for the first government organized under Busch seemed to reflect a marked shift towards the right in national politics. Such politically radical officers as Lieutenant-Colonel Viera were eliminated from the government, and among the civilians appointed was Federico Gutiérrez Granier, president of the Miners Association and head of the Partido Centralista, and a key opponent of the Toro régime.[2] Busch filled out his civilian cabinet members with his two close friends, Enrique Baldivieso and the old-line saavedrista Gabriel Gosálvez. While the moderate leftist Baldivieso was given the politically non-sensitive post of minister of foreign affairs, Gutiérrez Granier was given the important appointment of minister of finance, a position often attacked by the right in the previous government and one which it ardently desired to control. In a special interview with the press, the new minister of finance stated that: 'The political economy of the new government has to be developed within a concept of law and of respect for private property', and also promised that scrupulous management of public funds would be the watchword of the new government.[3]

In the installation speech to his first cabinet, Busch called on the new government 'to restore national institutions' and promised that the army would 'pursue the return of normality to the country'. He then went on to declare that he had received the spontaneous support of the veterans and the workers—the latter a highly unlikely supposition—and that this new government will not be 'a government of class, nor less a government of political sects. It is characterized by its absolute independence.'[4]

Yet despite Busch's protestations, the traditional political parties were quick to revive their regular political activity and to offer their full support to the new government. Within a matter of days many of the leading traditional party exiles were returning, and

---

[1] *El Diario*, 15 July, 1937, p. 5, and *El Diario*, 18 July 1937, p. 7.
[2] *La Calle*, 15 July 1937, p. 5.
[3] *El Diario*, 15 July 1937, p. 4.   [4] *La Calle*, 15 July 1937, p. 5.

Saavedra himself had telegraphed from abroad his congratulations to the new government and its leader—the very man who had ousted him from the country in 1936![1] By the end of July, such leading exiles as Saavedra, the PRS leaders Pedro Zilveti Arce and Edmundo Vázquez, and the Liberals Tomás Manuel Elío and Juan María Zalles had either announced plans for their return or had already arrived back in La Paz.[2]

Almost immediately, the three traditional parties began holding meetings to achieve a united front and to reach an agreement to support the Busch régime, which they claimed had promised the early return of constitutional government.[3] Feeling that they had found a champion of the old order in Busch, the feverishly active políticos rapidly proceeded to resolve historic differences. They successfully closed ranks in a united front for greater strength and announced their full support for the president. Under the leadership of the Liberal party leader, Hugo Montes, and with the support of the minister of finance, F. Gutiérrez Granier, the Liberals, Genuinos, and Republicano-Socialistas carried out the preliminary negotiations, with Gabriel Gosálvez representing the saavedristas, and Joaquín Espada the Genuinos. On 27 July these men, as representatives of their parties, succeeded in signing a pact of political truce and joint support of the government, and agreed to press for the rapid return of elections, congress and constitutional government to Bolivia. Immediately Busch sent his felicitations to the parties concerned, and thanked them for their moral support of the government, and he reiterated his proposition of quickly returning the country to normality.[4] As for the Partido Socialista de Estado, its demise was officially confirmed by what was left of the incipient moderate leftist movement.[5] Certainly to all intents and purposes, these political developments in July unquestionably indicated that Busch had begun his government in a highly reactionary manner. To the right at least, it seemed as if he was merely a caretaker president preparing for the return of the old order, which would abolish

---

[1] *El Diario*, 15 July 1937, p. 2.
[2] *El Diario*, 23 July 1937, p. 7, and 26 July 1937, p. 5.
[3] *El Diario*, 25 July 1937, p. 7.
[4] *El Diario*, 28 July 1937, p. 5.
[5] *El Diario*, 30 July 1937, p. 6.

forever the gestures, initiatives and actions of the Military Socialist régime and State Socialist concepts of Toro.[1]

In line with the new attitude of the government, the Busch
régime announced that the 1880 Constitution, with its 1920 and
1931 modifications, was still fully operating.[2] The minister of
finance, for his part, began making gestures to end the multiple
exchange rate, which subsidized imports of prime necessities for
consumers, as well as the Toro-initiated system of rationing.[3] The
government closed down all the state foodstores which had been
opened under the previous régime,[4] and in general carried out a
full-scale retrenchment in the area of governmental subsidies of
consumer prices and economic protection for the lower urban
classes.

Meanwhile, the minister of government, Colonel Félix Tabera
issued a number of decrees which set the machinery in operation
for the election of a constitutional congress. It was announced
that the Constitutional Reform Commission, which since the
resignation of Vicente Mendoza López some months before had
become a conservative stronghold,[5] had completed its work and
was ready to present its *proyecto* to such a convention.[6] On 2
August the civil voting registers were opened for the purpose of
inscribing voters for the coming elections. But this decree did
preserve a Toro-sponsored innovation. It announced that the
Legión de Ex-Combatientes and the Confederación Sindical de
Trabajadores de Bolivia could both intervene in the registration
and in all later political acts with the same status as political
parties.[7] This latter statement was the first discordant leftist note
in the otherwise seemingly rightist drift of the new government
and seemed to indicate a continuation of some of Toro's corporate State Socialism ideas. Also, apart from giving permission
to the traditional party leaders to return to Bolivia, a return that
was being strangely delayed, Busch indicated that the leading

---

[1] An indication of this intense hatred is reflected in the post-*golpe* act of the PR
which formally expelled from the party as traitors all members who had collab-
orated with Toro, specifically Javier Paz Campero and Minor Gainsborg
El Diario, 30 July 1937, p. 6.

[2] *El Diario*, 1 August 1937, p. 7.   [3] *El Diario*, 2 August 1937, p. 4.
[4] *El Diario*, 20 August 1937, p. 7.   [5] *El Diario*, 22 April 1937, p. 7.
[6] *El Diario*, 15 August 1937, p. 7.   [7] *El Diario*, 28 August 1937, p.

leftist exile, Tristán Marof, would be allowed to return from exile for the first time since 1927.[1]

After their first rush of activity, the traditional political parties began to experience a strange lassitude and apathy in their rank and file. For after just fifteen months of Toro administration, the traditional party base in the middle classes had been eroded and the parties emerged in the post-Toro period as emaciated skeletons of their former selves. Even *El Diario* felt called upon to comment that the unity pact had been more a product of the imagination than of reality, since the traditional party rank and file were in a state of dissolution, with many of the key leaders still abroad for one reason or another. *El Diario* admitted, however, that there was nothing hesitant about Bautista Saavedra, and noted that 'the chief of Republican-Socialism has one obsession : the presidency'. He was also still an unquestionably popular national figure. But, noted *El Diario*, despite his popularity at large and within his own party, and despite the undisputed dynamism which he possessed even in his advanced years, he was still a conservative caudillo under 'socialist' labels, and it wondered aloud if the nation could easily return to the old conservative traditional era.[2]

In a well prepared tumultuous reception, Bautista Saavedra returned to La Paz in early October, after a year and a half in exile. In his speech to the crowds, he noted his support for the Busch government and its drive toward institutionalization and normalization of the nation and promised open non-party-oriented support.[3] But almost immediately Saavedra began playing his old game with all the passion and cunning of the previous years. Shortly after his return, rumours began circulating to the effect that the PRS was not very interested in the unity pact of July and had begun conversations with the leftist groups throughout the nation with the thought of creating a PRS-leftist block.[4] In fact with the return of Saavedra, the general political temper of the nation picked up considerably, especially among the left, whose scattered groups once more began to raise their heads as the traditional parties continued to falter and show obvious signs of weakness. In October 1937, the leftist press began a major

---

[1] *El Diario*, 9 September 1937, p. 7. [2] *El Diario*, 10 September 1937, p. 7.
[3] *El Diario*, 10 October 1937, pp. 6, 7. [4] *El Diario*, 23 October 1937, p. 3.

attack on the minister of finance, Gutiérrez Granier, charging that he was opposing the leftist tendency being manifested by the new government. To counter this attack Gutiérrez Granier demanded support from Busch, which he quickly received,[1] and which seemed to deny the supposedly 'leftist' tendency which the local radical papers tried to detect. But this was only a temporary move and increasingly unmistakable signs of change became apparent.

In October also the government announced that the coming *convención nacional*, as it was to be called, would elect the president and vice-president for the constitutional four-year term,[2] and as early as September local LEC units and others began to announce their support of the candidature of Busch for the presidency. Though the government denied its validity,[3] the movement to draft Busch for the presidency continued to grow as the weeks passed. At the same time as Busch's own power drives began to manifest themselves in contrast with the hopes of the civilian politicos, his government became more firmly committed to the extension of the corporate idea of government. In a special national assembly in late October, the Legión de Ex-Combatientes, an organization now tightly linked to the government and almost a spokesman for the Busch interests, approved a functional (i.e. corporate) plan of organization for the coming national convention. This plan called for the following representation: that the miners choose four deputies to represent them; that the commercial interests select three; professionals, three; universities, four; teachers, three; newspaper reporters, two; the army, three; the LEC, five; the labour movement, five; three each from the agricultural interests (hacendados), from the *indígena* class and the feminist groups. This plan also carefully elaborated which organizations would take part—for instance, the big miners' association would name two of the four allotted to the industry and the small miners' association would name the other two. Provisions were made for valley and altiplano interests, for the CSTB and the local universities. This was a carefully drawn up plan which proposed to include the widest geographical distribution, but

[1] *El Diario*, 19 October 1937, p. 6. [2] *Ibid.*
[3] *El Diario*, 9 September 1937, p. 7.

which also gave disproportional weight, as can be seen, to the left and labour movements.[1]

In November the orientation of the new government finally became unmistakably clear. In the middle of the month, with much publicity and the charge that 'a leftist tendency, with which I personally disagree, has been growing within the composition of the junta', Federico Gutiérrez Granier resigned his cabinet post as minister of finance.[2] As *El Diario* rightly guessed, this resignation clearly defined the orientation of the Busch government.[3] At the same time, the inevitable friction between Busch and Saavedra finally began to manifest itself in an intense struggle for power. On 27 November the government issued a threatening statement to the effect that despite the decree of general amnesty and full civil liberties recently granted, the government did not view threats to law and order kindly. It warned that recent disturbance of the public order by certain parties if not immediately ended would be dealt with harshly.[4] Finally acting on its threat, the government on the evening of 27 November jailed Saavedra and forcibly exiled him, despite the loud protests of his party.[5] Three days later the entire cabinet, except for the two traditional políticos, Gosálvez and Hector Ormachea Zalles, voted support for the executive's action.[6]

Meanwhile, the government began to take definite action of a leftist nature. In mid-November it gave careful study in a public announcement to the recommendations of the local directors of the ministry of labour for a complete and rather radical *Código del Trabajo*. The plan had been written at a national meeting the previous January while Waldo Álvarez was still in office, and reflected all the tendencies of his régime.[7] Finally, rescinding an earlier decision, the government announced that it would again support state subsidized food stores.[8]

On 22 November, the government officially called elections for March 1938 for the national convention which was scheduled to

---

[1] *El Diario*, 23 October 1937, p. 7. [2] *El Diario*, 20 November 1937, p. 5.
[3] *El Diario*, 21 November 1937, p. 6. [4] *El Diario*, 29 November 1937, p. 4.
[5] *El Diario*, 2 December 1937, p. 7. [6] *El Diario*, 1 December 1937, p. 4.
[7] *El Diario*, 6 February 1937, p. 4; also see Waldo Álvarez' anti-proyecto for this meeting in *El Diario*, 3 December 1936, p. 7.
[8] *El Diario*, 27 November 1937, p. 6.

273

meet in La Paz as a single legislative body on 13 May. The convention, stated the decree, would write a new constitution 'conforming to the national temperament of the post-war period' and would also elect the president and vice-president of the nation. After this the convention would, like its 1920 predecessor, turn itself into an ordinary two house congress by 6 August of the coming year.[1]

Considering the decree of convocation of elections a momentous act, the cabinet resigned to permit Busch to create a new one in conformity with his new tendencies.[2] But only minor changes were made. Baldivieso came in again in his usual temporary manner, and Gabriel Gosálvez, no longer representing the saavedristas, but now rather the major adviser to the Busch group, was given the extraordinary post created specially for him, that of minister secretary-general of the cabinet without portfolio.[3] Soon the LECs in the various cities throughout the nation began actively to set up candidate lists for the coming elections, and persistently the name of Busch for the presidency was proposed[4]; shortly thereafter Baldivieso and Ormachea Zalles resigned their cabinet posts to run for convention seats.[5]

In all the political manœuvring for the coming elections, and involvement in civilian politics, Busch never forgot that the army was his chief source of power. That the army was still the dominant political power in the nation was clearly emphasized by the 1938 budget proposed by Busch in early January. Projected as a balanced one of Bs. 274·1 million, the largest single share of the budget, some Bs. 86·7 million (or 32 per cent) was devoted to the army—an army that had been reduced by the peace treaty terms to only 5,000 men! The single next most important item was debt payments which came to Bs. 70·7 million, while education was a poor third with only Bs. 23 million.[6] This imbalance was maintained throughout the years of Military Socialism, for the army, though loyal to Busch, had to be kept continually supplied with funds to guarantee its support. As it was, a new force began to rise as a potential challenge to Busch, when in January the

[1] *El Diario*, 23 November 1937, p. 7.   [2] *El Diario*, 23 November 1937, p. 6.
[3] *El Diario*, 24 November 1937, p. 6.
[4] See *El Diario*, 2 December 1937, p. 7, and 7 December 1937, p. 3.
[5] *El Diario*, 10 December 1937, p. 7.   [6] *El Diario*, 18 January 1938, p. 6.

pliable Peñaranda resigned as general-in-chief of the army and was replaced by the politically more aware General Carlos Quintanilla.[1] One of the few Bolivian officers trained abroad, Quintanilla had spent five years in Germany in the early years of the century.[2] He had a rather indifferent record in the Chaco campaign, having once actually been demoted,[3] but nevertheless emerged as one of the leaders of the old guard of the army in the post-war years. Although seemingly loyal to Busch, he was to prove far more independent of his direction than had Peñaranda.

The theme of the dominance of the army in political life was also heavily emphasized by one of the traditionalist parties in its national convention. In late January, the Partido Republicano Genuino, under the direction of Demetrio Canelas, held a national convention in La Paz with some seventy delegates and demanded 'political normalization and the return of the army to its proper functions . . . We contemplate, with increasing distress, the symptoms of anarchy fermenting in the bosom of the armed forces.'[4] This feeling was shared by all the traditional parties in their increasing unease with the Military Socialist experiment.

There had been no serious attack on the economic power of the native oligarchy, and concessions continued to flow to Aramayo and Patiño, but the Toro and Busch régimes raised serious doubts in the minds of the upper class. Both governments had given great impetus to the labour movement and had fostered the growth of numerous moderate and radical leftist organizations, all of which were sapping the strength of the already weakened traditional political parties. Also there seemed no way to guarantee control over the rather erratic Busch without the traditional opposition party in a reasonably vocal and independent national legislature. But the Bolivian congress had not been called into session for almost three years, which was an extremely dangerous precedent for the traditional parties and the normal patterns of political life.

Despite executive dominance in the structure of Bolivian

---

[1] *El Diario*, 12 January 1938, p. 7.
[2] Díaz Argüedas, *Como fué derrocado el hombre símbolo*, pp. 318–19.
[3] Zook, *Chaco War*, pp. 103, 109, 230; Elter [Luis Toro Ramallo], *Una página de la historia de Bolivia* (Santiago de Chile: Editorial Nascimiento, 1938), pp. 97–8.
[4] *El Diario*, 21 January 1938, p. 7, and 23 January 1938, p. 4.

government, ever since the organization of political parties in the 1880s, congress had almost continually been a vehicle for the tempering of executive power and for the organization and maintenance of opposition parties. But now the traditional political parties were being denied this vital parliamentary forum and were also denied participation in cabinets. The inability to use these institutional supports was extremely detrimental to party cohesion. Party discipline progressively dissolved as leading party members joined the government as individuals and broke their traditional political ties. Without the discipline of a continually operative parliamentary wing, the skeleton national committees seemed incapable of preserving the strength of their parties. And in actual fact, these fears were fully justified. For in almost four years of Military Socialism—a period of hiatus in party activity—the basis of the old parties had definitely rotted away, and when they again came to the fore at the end of the decade, they were but weak remnants of the former giants who had waged the historic battles of the pre-war world.

On the other hand, the period of Military Socialism, while seemingly chaotic as far as the moderate and far left was concerned, was nevertheless extremely creative. In the end, the left emerged as the dominant factor in the political life of the nation, in complete contrast to the experience of the traditional parties. Over and over again the same names appeared in the little café-fostered groupings and more and more they gained vital political experience.

A revival of active organization on the part of these scattered post-war radical and reformist movements began in the early part of 1938 as the Busch government announced its preparations for the constitutional convention. A new note was introduced when the labour movement and the now more politically committed LEC indicated their willingness to join forces with these movements. Thus with the backing of the CSTB, the independent national railroad union, the LEC, and the numerous partidos obreros and partidos socialistas, a *Frente Único Socialista* was organized in February 1938. Pledged to present a united list of candidates, the FUS backed the Busch government[1] and seems to

---

[1] *El Diario*, 18 February 1938, p. 8.

have had reciprocal support from the latter as representing a government party. Also unique to this confederation of workers, veterans and political parties was the adhesion to the Frente of a *Partido Republicano Socialista Antipersonalista*—a small group of leftists who had recently broken off from the saavedrista majority. As the preference of the Busch government was clearly given to the new group, many of the old political parties withdrew from the election race,[1] and the March elections saw the complete triumph of the Frente Único Socialista candidates throughout the nation.[2]

The tempo of political activity following the March election increased greatly as the presidential slate was debated. In the midst of this activity, an attempted frontier revolt led by Toro was suppressed with ease, and only served to reinforce the power and growing popularity of Busch.[3] By late May it had become clear that Busch had chosen as his vice-presidential candidate Enrique Baldivieso, a choice publicly espoused by the LEC.[4] Though none dared challenge the Busch candidacy, a fierce struggle soon developed for the office of vice-president, with the Liberals making a major bid for the nomination.[5] At first the name of the diplomat Luis Fernando Guachalla was mentioned, but soon the head of the Liberal party and nephew of its great caudillo, Hugo Montes, began actively to campaign for the post, receiving strong endorsement from some of the Oriente delegates for the coming convention.[6] Busch, however, soon put an end to this candidacy at a special palacio meeting which both Baldivieso and Montes attended, and Montes upon the request of Busch publicly withdrew his name.[7]

---

[1] *El Diario*, 27 February 1938, p. 4.   [2] *El Diario*, 15 March 1938, p. 6.
[3] At the end of March, Toro invaded the frontier town of El Palmar from Argentina and called upon the army to revolt (*El Diario*, 4 April 1937, p. 4). Carlos Quintanilla, then inspecting the Chaco troops, stood firmly behind the government, and the high command, under Busch's direction, issued orders for the execution of all captured rebels. When the army refused to revolt, Toro and some of his followers escaped across the frontier. A few officers were captured, however, and some of these were later executed by the government. *El Diario*, 5 April 1938, p. 7, and 6 April 1938, p. 6. For the government side of the case see, *La revolución de 'El Palmar', principales documentos jurídicos del proceso* (La Paz: Editorial 'Universo', 1938); and for a pro-Toro view of the event, see Elter, *Una página de la historia de Bolivia*, pp. 55–164.
[4] *El Diario*, 29 April 1938, p. 6.   [5] *El Diario*, 4 May 1938, p. 6.
[6] *El Diario*, 8 May 1938, p. 6.   [7] *El Diario*, 19 May 1938, p. 6.

Thus on the eve of the national convention, the Busch government had firmly revealed its full allegiance to the reformist and
corporate ideologies which had been enunciated by the Toro
régime. It had alienated traditional party support by its rejection
of the vice-presidential nominees of the old parties, and by its
stated intention to continue a military régime in office under the
new presidency. Although the traditional political forces were
still not totally opposed to the Busch régime, they were seriously
disenchanted. In their turn, the electoral victory of the United
Socialist Front group and the successful calling of a constitutional
convention heralded the possibility of a major breakthrough in
post-war political development for the left. And in fact, the constitutional convention of 1938 was to prove a vital turning point
in Bolivian history. The convention finally repealed both the
oldest functioning constitution in Bolivian history, the 1880
charter, and also entirely re-wrote the basic concepts of constitutional government. It adopted what Latin American scholars
have come to label 'social constitutionalism'.

The era of social constitutionalism in Latin America formally
began in 1917 with the revolutionary Mexican constitution of
that year. This charter broke sharply with the nineteenth-century
concepts of limited government and the protection of inalienable
individual rights, of which property was foremost. It stressed the
positive responsibilities of the state for the social and economic
welfare of all citizens at the expense of individual rights if necessary. The social theories behind this movement quickly spread
throughout the Americas at the beginning of the twentieth
century, and soon nation after nation began to change its fundamental charter. In each case, detailed chapters were added to the
old constitutions providing for the social responsibility of capital,
the economic rights of the worker, state responsibility for the
protection and security of the family, and for the physical and
mental welfare of all citizens and classes. One of the most basic
individual rights of nineteenth-century liberal thought, that of
property, was now defined not as an inalienable human right in
the Lockean tradition, but as a derivative right granted by the
state and held only so long as it fulfilled a legitimate social function. While most of these ideas were inherited from European

radicalism and socialism, they also borrowed from the twentieth-century Latin American movement of *indigenismo*, at least in the Indo-American states, and many constitutions attempted to re-evaluate the role of the submerged Indian masses by destroying the feudal bonds which held them apart from national life, and by accepting many of their non-western forms of property and legal customs.[1] In the case of Bolivia, its indigenista ideology had its roots in the late nineteenth- and early twentieth-century Peruvian *pensadores*, above all in José Carlos Mariátegui, and in the same period, the Bolivian Franz Tamayo.[2]

As with the case of the classic constitutions of the nineteenth century, these new social constitutions were usually the work of advanced minorities, who more often than not were actually writing their charters well in advance of the revolutionary changes which were necessary to secure the enactment of the new ideas of social justice. But the radical innovators were not troubled by this problem, for they conceived of their constitutions as programmes of action for the future. With the writing of these detailed programmes of social justice, they

---

[1] A detailed nation-by-nation survey of these new social and economic provisions is given in Academia de Ciencias Económicas, Buenos Aires, *Las cláusulas económico-sociales en las constituciones de América* (2 vols.; Buenos Aires: Editorial Losada, 1947–8). On the revolutionary character and impact of the Mexican constitution of 1917, see Russell H. Fitzgibbon, 'Constitutional Developments in Latin America: A Synthesis', *American Political Science Review*, xxxix, no. 3 (June 1945), 518–20.

George I. Blanksten has defined this expansion of constitutional scope in twentieth-century Latin America as a 'fourth function' of constitutionalism. 'The classic view of written constitutions is that they are designed to perform three functions: to limit the power of government, to set forth the basic outlines of its structure, and to state certain of the broad hopes and aspirations to the constitutions' framers. Today many of the constitutions of Latin America attempt a fourth function: to render mandatory certain operations of government designed to contribute to the social welfare.' George I. Blanksten, 'Constitutions and the Structure of Power', in Harold E. Davis (ed.), *Government and Politics in Latin America* (New York: The Ronald Press, 1958), p. 237. This 'fourth function' has been called 'social constitutionalism' by Latin American legal theorists; see Oscar Frerking Salas, 'Las cláusulas económico-sociales en la constitución política de Bolivia', in Academia de Ciencias Económicas, Buenos Aires, *Las cláusulas económico-sociales*, p. 64.

[2] The classic work cited over and over again by Bolivian intellectuals was José Carlos Mariátegui, *7 ensayos de la interpretacion de la realidad peruviano*, first published in Lima in 1928. Antedating Mariátegui, though stressing primarily cultural *indigenismo*, was Franz Tamayo whose ideas first appeared in periodical form in *El Diario* in 1909 and were later republished under the title of *Creación de la pedagogía nacional*.

consciously hoped to lay the guidelines for all future socio-economic change both within the existing order, which was to be judged by these new standards, and for the coming revolutionary generations.

Such was essentially the experience of Bolivia when in May 1938 she belatedly joined the majority of the other Latin American nations in revising her constitutional charter along these lines. Prior to 1938 there had existed a basic uniformity in the numerous constitutions which had guided the destiny of Bolivia. In this respect the famous constitution of 1880 differed little in essentials from the ten constitutions which had preceded it in the short life of the republic. The pattern provided for a liberal form of constitutional representative government, with limited powers in relation to the individual, for a *laissez faire* attitude toward the economy, a centralized republic and a relatively independent legislature tied to a powerful president.[1] In common with the other constitutions of nineteenth-century Latin America, the emphasis was on the purely legalistic defence of personal property and liberty against the state, with no thought whatsover of defining the social duties of the state towards its citizens.[2] Although the constitutional referenda of 1930 had slightly modified the 1880 charter in the direction of a more self-aware attitude toward the citizen,[3] Salamanca's subsequent abandonment of these amendments made them obsolete. Thus when the conventionaires of 1938 turned to review the basic charter of their republic, they found it essentially the same charter which had been adopted over fifty-eight years before.

But before the convention could even begin to discuss constitutional reform, it found itself in bitter political conflict with the major organs of the national press. With *El Diario* leading, the conservative press attacked the convention for being composed of previously unknown political figures, radicals or

---

[1] For the constitutions of Bolivia, see Trigo, *Las constituciones de Bolivia*. In most of these nineteenth-century constitutions and especially in the 1880 charter, provisions for a type of parliamentary government were made through congressional right of interpellation and censorship of the cabinet. William S. Stokes, 'Parliamentary Government in Latin America', *American Political Science Review*, XXXIX, no. 3 (June, 1945), 527–8.

[2] Fitzgibbon, 'Constitutional Developments in Latin America', pp. 511–18.

[3] Trigo, *Las constituciones de Bolivia*, pp. 124–8.

'unwashed' incompetents.[1] The convention in fact did have a strong radical wing, which included such men as Carlos Medinacelli, Fernando Siñani, Waldo Álvarez, Walter Guevara Arze and Ricardo Anaya. And certainly these, and several other leading radical or fascist-oriented deputies, bitterly attacked the traditional press as well and even went so far as to vote the suppression of *El Diario*.[2] But despite the extreme fears expressed by the conservative press, the convention soon found a large body of moderate opinion which came to dominate its proceedings and to successfully modify the more radical proposals of the so called *sector izquierda* or *sector obrero*.

Nevertheless, even this 'moderate' opinion was far in advance of traditional pre-war ideology and completely accepted the concepts of 'social constitutionalism'. And both moderates and radicals alike seemed constantly obsessed by the need to articulate the inchoate reformist drives emerging from the Chaco disaster. As vice-president Baldivieso declared, the convention had 'the imperative mandate of a people which in the anguish of war . . . has discovered the lies which it lived and now seeks truth and wants justice'. This mandate 'is not common parliamentary power, but a mandate to mould the intentions of the collective soul into deeds'.[3]

[1] See, e.g. *El Diario*, 25 May 1938, p. 6 and 26 May 1938, p. 6; Trigo, *Las constituciones de Bolivia*, p. 130; Céspedes, *El dictador suicida*, p. 167. Also see the bitter remarks of Alcides Argüedas, defeated for a senate seat for La Paz in the convention, who labelled the majority of the 1938 Convention deputies as 'little men without names, without past, without distinction, almost illiterate and in truth obscure, really insignificant persons, anonymities,' etc. Argüedas, *Obras Completas*, I, 1214–15. The newspapers were also particularly incensed by the swearing-in fiasco of the convention (see, e.g. *El Diario*, 26 May 1938, p. 6). Many of the radical intellectuals and labour leaders refused to swear by the traditional formula and like Medinacelli, deputy from Potosí and a member of its Frente Popular, they swore 'by the cause of the proletariat, by Bolivia and by humanity'. One deputy even swore 'by Christ, who is the greatest socialist'. *Convención Nacional de 1938, Redactor de la Convención Nacional* (5 vols.; La Paz: Editorial 'Universo', 1938–9), I, 31. Hereafter cited as *Redactor*.

[2] Under the threat of resignation by three of his civilian cabinet members, Busch had refused to enforce the censorship law passed by the convention. He had also agreed to eliminate his avowedly fascist minister of government, Elías Belmonte, who had supported the censorship drive in the convention, and had replaced him with the moderate Gabriel Gosálvez. *Redactor*, II, 151–3, 253–4; *El Diario*, 15 July 1938, p. 7; 16 July 1938, p. 6 and 22 July 1938, p. 7; and Díaz Machicao, *Toro, Busch*, p. 83.

[3] *Redactor*, I, 83. For a more detailed analysis of these early speeches and activities of the convention, see Herbert S. Klein, 'Social constitutionalism in Latin America: the Bolivian Experience of 1938', *The Americas*, XXII, no. 3 (January 1966), 258–76.

In this general desire for reform, the radicals went one step further, and demanded that the convention take the revolutionary leadership out of the hands of the military. In a powerful speech, to which many of the delegates later referred, one of the leading radicals, Augusto Céspedes, charged that the convention existed not only to turn the military socialist rule into a *de jure* régime;[1] it had to change completely the chaotic pattern which Toro and Busch had developed and to establish a creative legal government which would not be forced to rely upon the whims of the army, but upon a solid foundation of socialist civilian government. The 'socialism' of the military was fraudulent and it had only frustrated the true socialist needs of the people, which the convention must satisfy in the new order.[2] He saw Bolivia as a colonial nation under imperialist domination, made up of two generations:

one which tries to maintain the colonial organization and another which wants to found an effective and economically free nation. Our crisis is complex, it is a crisis of two generations against a world of change. The older generation, which even now is dominant in politics, the economy, finances, society; in everything in short, except in literature where we new writers have gained control. That ancient generation wants to resolve new problems with traditional systems . . . For its part, the new generation has still not been able to create a system of beliefs . . . and it vacillates before a reality which is still directed and ordered by the beliefs, by the laws, by the creeds, and above all, by the economic interests of the old capitalism of the older generation.

Hence we should not be surprised nor discouraged if we find that from the Chaco War, the revolutionary generation did not come forth perfectly equipped with ideas and solutions. That rather, because it participated in the catastrophe, which disturbed its psychic unity, its conviction in old beliefs and its serenity, it came forth with desires, and passions, not with plans, nor methods, nor systems.[3]

In this state of ideological disorganization, the word 'socialism' had become a beacon for a restless generation. But, charged Céspedes, it was a word exploited not only by the legitimate left,

---

[1] This the convention had already accomplished on 27 May when it had overwhelmingly elected Busch and Baldivieso to a four-year presidential and vice-presidential term respectively. *Redactor*, I, 74–6.

[2] *Ibid.* I, 59–61.   [3] *Ibid.* I, 63–4.

but by the defeated military leaders, most of whom were opportunists. Toro sabotaged the true socialist movement, according to
the radical Céspedes. He thought Busch might continue to do the
same if the convention did not bind him by creating a new constitutional and political order which would dominate all military
elements.[1] In this, Céspedes reflected the extreme distrust that
the far left felt for the military, even in its most radical form. As
for his other sentiments, he represented an authentic voice of the
left speaking to his own generation of young revolutionaries.
While Céspedes was far from representing the majority of the
radical left—he himself being somewhere between the moderate
and radical positions—yet he clearly perceived the historic
moment in which the entire generation found itself and called for
the convention to break the anarchy of the post-war years and
give true meaning to the revolutionary spirit of the age.

But the very background which Céspedes so ably described
prevented the left from reaching any major unity at this point,
or any revolutionary control. In the hectic months of the 1938
Convention it found itself able to express only a part of the
leftist platform in the new constitution and its own organization
continued in the chaotic fashion of the post-war years. For the
left was still an essentially fractured and largely local movement
and it needed the crucible of constant defeat and oligarchic reaction to forge it into a revolutionary movement of overwhelming
national power. But while the left never organized itself co-
herently enough in all its radical and moderate wings to dominate
fully the convention proceedings, it nevertheless took full advantage of the debates to propose and propagandize for all the
revolutionary ideas abroad in the land, expressing most of them
for the first time in Bolivian history in the hallowed halls of the
legislative palace.

In their onslaught on the traditional society and its foundations,
the radicals attacked the most fundamental of institutions, private
property. Though the conservatives were opposed to any but the
classic definition of the inviolability of property,[2] the more
moderate and radical left demanded that Bolivia conform to
the more modern European and Latin American constitutions,

[1] *Redactor*, I, 64ff.   [2] See, e.g. *El Diario*, 27 July 1938, p. 7.

particularly the Mexican one of 1917, and limit traditional liberal concepts of property with the proviso that it fulfil a social function.

While the final article was a moderate statement between these two extremes,[1] the radical left took advantage of the debate to propose some rather revolutionary reforms. Under the leadership of Balcazar, Eguino Zaballa, Víctor Paz Estenssoro and especially Walter Guevara Arze, the radicals proposed a formula whose first part read that: 'The state guarantees the right of property so long as it fulfills a social function',[2] and in the second part called for outright land reform. This second part of their projected article proposed the expropriation of unproductive latifundias and their parcelling out among the agricultural peasants who worked them.[3] Walter Guevara Arze even went further and charged that to break up the latifundias into small individually owned plots would be to return to the liberal ideas of the past, and that they should instead be worked on a collective basis by the local Indian comunidades; in short, advocating the collectivization of agriculture.[4] That these ideas were even voiced and seriously debated in a national Bolivian congress was indicative of the major changes in the political atmosphere which had occurred as a result of the Chaco War, and most specifically of the general currency now enjoyed by the radical ideology of the pre-war left.

The radicals also carried out a major attack on the Church. Although anti-clericalism was endemic in the old Liberal party, the moderates and radicals succeeded in giving it a new impetus in the economic realm. Over the objections of the conservatives they successfully proposed that all church property should henceforth be considered as equal to all other forms of private property and subject to the same taxation, indebtedness, restrictions, etc. Even on this issue the more radical deputies had

---

[1] Article 17 states: 'Private property is inviolable, provided it fulfils a social function; expropriation can be imposed for reason of public utility, being authorized consistent with the law and previous just indemnification' (Trigo *Las constituciones de Bolivia*, p. 424). Other articles of the final constitution, however, considerably modified this bald statement in far more radically leftist fashion; see especially article 6b and articles 106–30.

[2] *Redactor*, II, 529, proyecto Espinoza.

[3] *Ibid.* p. 530.

[4] *Ibid.* pp. 533–5.

advocated the wholesale confiscation of all church property and its devolution to state control, a move which was rejected by the majority.[1]

Nor were national property holders the only group considered by the convention. In a strongly anti-imperialist frame of mind after the recent episode of the Standard Oil Company, the convention passed, with surprisingly little debate, articles which declared that no foreign enterprise operating in Bolivia could appeal to foreign powers in its disputes with the state and that such enterprises were to be considered bound by all the laws regulating national companies;[2] that no foreigner could own, lease, or rent, any soil or sub-soil rights to any property within fifty miles of the frontier;[3] and finally that only the state or its representatives could export oil from Bolivia whether publicly or privately produced.[4] In the debate over this latter article, there was even an unsuccessful call by the radicals for the inclusion of the word minerals, thus proposing that all tin would be sold abroad by the state, and not by the private companies.[5]

As deputy Víctor Paz Estenssoro noted, 'the monopoly of exportation of minerals by the state is the only measure capable of achieving a radical and profound revolution in the socio-economic structure of Bolivia'. There is no question that this represented the closest thing to outright nationalization, and probably was the most feasible immediate plan which the left could hope to pass. But even Paz Estenssoro realized that the left did not have the power to implement such a radical procedure and noted that the mining *superestado*, as he called it, would never allow such a law to be put into practice and would 'put into play all its resources to avoid that it be carried into effect. As it has a power greater than that of the state itself, the mining super-state is capable of creating great difficulties and preventing the

---

[1] See debate, *ibid.* pp. 615–35.
[2] Articles 18 and 110 of the constitution of 1938. The full text of the constitution is reprinted in Trigo, *Las constituciones de Bolivia*, pp. 421–55.
[3] Article 19.   [4] Article 109.
[5] *Redactor*, IV, 91. The convencionales also attacked the penchant of private road builders, notably Nicoláus Suárez in the Oriente and Patiño on the altiplano, for preventing the public from using their roads and specifically provided that any road in the nation, whether public or privately built, was open to the free use of all. For this debate see *Redactor*, II, 600ff.

moderately socialist constitution that we are voting from being sanctioned and promulgated.'[1]

This whole debate led to a major attack on the entire mining industry. Sharp criticisms were made of the labour conditions at the mines,[2] of the flight of capital and small returns to the state of the international holdings of Patiño—especially in Far Eastern tin-mining—which it was charged led to his anti-Bolivian action in the recent depression, and on the impersonal nature of the mining superstate whose real powers lay outside the nation.[3] As to the possibilities of overturning the radical legislation proposed Augusto Céspedes noted that if the convention approved such legislation, the executive would be empowered to carry it through and even if this were unsuccessful, at least the prescription for future action had been proposed and would be carried out by others at a later time, just as had occurred with the 1917 Mexican constitution.[4] Though the majority of the deputies eventually defeated this proposition, it was far from buried by the rightist opposition, and within a year it became the most crucial political issue of the day.

Rebuffed on many revolutionary proposals of immediate action, the radical elements in the convention nevertheless succeeded in having written into the constitution, for the first time in Bolivian history, the general socialist principle that the state should assume direct control over the economy of the nation so as to insure the human dignity of its citizens. In the constitution' chapter on the 'Economic and Financial Régime', article 106 opened by declaring that 'the economic régime should essentially respond to principles of social justice, which have as their aim to secure for all the inhabitants a dignified existence as human beings' And to achieve these aims it provided that:

The state will be able to regulate, with overriding power, the exercise of commerce and industry when the security or public necessity require it. It will also be able in these cases to assume the supreme direction over the national economy. This intervention will be exercised in the form of control, inducement or direct management.

In addition to this unequivocal negation of classic liberal

---

[1] *Redactor*, IV, 91–2.   [2] *Ibid.* p. 95.   [3] *Ibid.* pp. 96ff.   [4] *Ibid.* p. 104

conomic principles, the left also succeeded in inserting in the
onstitution the declaration that all persons had the fundamental
ight 'to dedicate themselves to labour, commerce and industry
only on condition that they do not prejudice the collective good'.[1]

The left also concerned itself with the conflict of capital and
abour, and provided in the constitution that the state recognize
i.e. legally guarantee) the free association of a professional and
yndical nature, and the collective contract of labour.[2] The right
o strike as a means of legitimate defence by the workers was
acknowledged,[3] and despite the cries of destroying confidence in
foreign capital markets and forcing all national business to close,[4]
he convention approved the call for legislation to determine the
participation of workers and employees in sharing the profits of
he enterprise.[5] In one lengthy article, the constitution declared
hat the state would provide obligatory security for accidents,
ickness, forced work stoppage, maternity, etc., and that it would
leclare minimum hours, wages, annual vacations, and medical
benefits:[6] in short, that the government would establish complete
ocial legislation to deal with the protection of labour and the
welfare of the people.

In keeping with this social aim, the convention, with only a
ninimum of debate, wrote an entire chapter in the constitution
on 'The Family'. This chapter proclaimed state responsibility
or the health, education and welfare of the child; equality among
all children—of legal or non-legal union—and the placing of
natrimony, the family, and maternity under the protection of
he law.[7] Another chapter dealing with the 'Cultural Régime'
leclared that education was one of the prime functions of the
tate, officially incorporated into the constitution the system of
university autonomy, and proposed a state scholarship programme
and a plan for the protection of national culture.[8]

The essential aim of the convention in all these articles and chapters was to commit the state definitively to full responsibility for
he health, education and welfare of all its people. Whereas previous constitutional conventions had been concerned with de-
imiting the powers of the central government and with defining

---

[1] Article 6. [2] Article 125. [3] Article 126. [4] *Redactor*, IV, 215ff.
[5] Article 127. [6] Article 122. [7] Articles 131–4. [8] Articles 154–64.

the jurisdictions of the national and local administrations—in
volving themselves in classic liberal definitions of limited con
stitutional government—the 1938 convention irrevocably brok
this mould. For the first time in republican history, it was pro
claimed that the function of the state was to provide for th
complete social welfare of all its citizens. The classic libera
laissez faire government with the minimum of control was now
replaced by the socialist concept of an active state intervening in
all areas of a citizen's life, to provide for the collective good of all

While many rightists held that such social policies should no
be written into a constitution, but should be reserved for secondary
legislation, the left refused to give ground. Over and over again
they claimed that such concepts had to be written in as much
detail as possible into the basic national charter, and that even i
this type of legislation was not immediately enacted, the Con
stitution of 1938, unlike the previous constitutions of Bolivia
would provide a blueprint for the future and as complete a state
ment as possible on the goals of the new revolutionary genera
tion. Although the right continually succeeded in modifying the
more revolutionary aspects of such legislation, a fundamenta
beginning was made, a beginning that again and again would bear
rich fruit in the years to come.

As the debate progressed, two rough groups began to be dis
cerned on major issues. These were, first of all, a right, composed
of four major elements: the few Liberals elected; plus the few
clerics in the assembly; and the *grupo oriental*. This latter coalition
was made up of most of the delegates from the eastern lowland
provinces and had a distinctly conservative, regionalist orientation
with a strong anti-Indian bias. Finally, there was the splinter
Republicano Socialista Antipersonalista led by Gabriel Gosálvez.[1]

The left was made up of a coalition of small parties of various
orientations. This left coalition, known variously as the sector
izquierdo or sector obrero, included such labour leaders as
Fernando Siñani and Waldo Álvarez, the local *Frente Popular*
group of Potosí, the *Grupo Izquierda* of Cochabamba, and a rec
ently salvaged left-wing group of former Baldivieso socialists
known as the *Partido Socialista Independiente* (PSI). This latter

[1] *Redactor*, IV, 322.

roup included such figures as Víctor Paz Estenssoro, Augusto Céspedes, and Walter Guevara Arze, and was to be the direct recursor of the *Movimiento Nacionalista Revolucionario*.[1] At the xtreme end of this left sector were such intellectuals as Alfredo rratía of the Popular Front of Potosí, and, surprisingly, con- idering his later career, Walter Guevara Arze of the PSI, both of vhom led the fight for land reform.

A leader in the earlier demand for breakup of the latifundias, Walter Guevara Arze was also a key figure in the convention's xtremely important debate over the proposed chapter on Peasantry'. This chapter called for legalizing the ancient Indian omunidades, which since pre-Columbian times had formed the asic unit of the agricultural population of the nation and which ince the beginning of the republican era had been denied all legal ights by the Bolivian government.[2]

Guevara Arze and Arratía, in their defence of the comunidad nd attacks on the latifundias, constantly stressed the thesis of Mariátegui—that the problem of the Indian is the problem of and, and not a question of education or anything else.[3] To Re- ublican Socialist charges that the country was underpopulated nd therefore there was no problem about land reform, as the fficial party platform read,[4] and to orientalistas' charges that the ntire problem was one of colonization, the left bitterly replied hat the problem of land reform was vital for Bolivia and could ot be denied.[5] Guevara Arze demanded:

How to resolve the problem of the Indian? The Honourable Arratía as already indicated it. The solution is not in educating him; the

---

Céspedes, *El dictador suicida*, p. 168.

At first basing itself on the liberal beliefs of Simón Bolívar who sought to create a small propertied peasantry in his famous decrees of Trujillo and Cuzco in 1824 and 1825 (see Miguel Bonifaz, 'El problema agrario indígena en Bolivia durante la época republicana', *Revista de Estudios Jurídicos, Políticos y Sociales* [Sucre], VIII, no. 18 [December 1947]), the republican legislation established the non- recognition of the juridical existence of the comunidad, which was charged with being a reactionary institution. This legal attitude permitted the whites and cholos in practice to destroy the property rights of these communities and to dramatically expand the latifundia system with the open aid of the state, which refused to protect in law the property rights of the comunidad. See Urquidi Morales, *La comunidad indígena*; José Flores Moncayo, *Legislación boliviana del indio, recopilación, 1825–1953* (La Paz: Ministerio de Asuntos Campesinos, 1953).

See, e.g. *Redactor*, V, 213–15.   [4] *Ibid.* p. 270.   [5] *Ibid.* pp. 271–2.

problem of the Indian is the problem of the land . . . There are million
of men without a piece of earth against people who have enormou
portions of unworked land. The essential thing is that the Indian ha
land.[1]

Guevara Arze went on prophetically to threaten that if the
convention did not make these constitutional provisions fo
peaceful land reform, a revolutionary socialist party would arise
some day which by blood would impose an even more radical
solution on the nation. 'If today we do not make this pacific
revolution, tomorrow will come the violent revolution'.[2] Their
proposal for the *campesino* (or peasant), as the leftists deliberately
called the Indians, was a major piece of radical legislation which
would have recognized not only the legal personality of the comunidad (which was accepted in article 165 in the final constitution) but contemplated outright land reform, providing that fifty
Indians could solicit for the expropriation of a particular latifundia which would be turned over to them by the state.[3] In the
rather heated debate the institution of pongueaje was attacked
harshly by the left, to the point where one deputy of the so-called
sector obrero alluded to the fact that pongos were used for more
things than manual labour by the females of paceña society, an
allusion which caused a complete breakdown of the session and a
suspension of the deputy.[4]

But the left could not prevail. It was attacked both in and outside the halls of the palacio legislativo as being communist-
inspired and hostile toward private property, a view which the
government seemed to share when it threatened closure.[5] The
right wing of the convention succeeded in wiping out the portion
of the campesino chapter which provided for land reform and
special constitutional protection for the Indian. In their place they
inserted watered-down declarations of pious intent to improve
education and legislate on these subjects, taking into account the
local regional differences.[6]

---

[1] *Redactor*, v, p. 277. Almost all of the deputies were constantly referring to the
Mexican constitution of 1917 when dealing with the problem of foreign invest
ment and the Indian, and Guevara Arze even went so far as to quote the work
of Frank Tannenbaum on the Mexican revolution. See *ibid.* p. 281.
[2] *Ibid.* p. 282.   [3] *Ibid.* pp. 283–5.   [4] *Ibid.* pp. 287–9.
[5] *Ibid.* p. 335.   [6] Articles 166 and 167

Now, under intense pressure from Busch, who feared its radical nature and threatened it with forced adjournment, the convention hastily completed the constitution in the last days of October 1938. Thus after five hectic months of tremendously creative activity, the Convención Nacional quietly adjourned and the nation once again returned to the relatively quiet days of non-parliamentary government.

But the end of the convention in no way ended its impact. For as the early speakers had rightly predicted, the convention had set the tone and provided the guidelines for the future generations of the nation. It had finally and definitively destroyed the traditional constitutional charter of economic liberalism and limited constitutional government, and openly proclaimed the positive role the government must take in providing for the welfare of its people. This was unquestionably the basic idea which emerged in the national consciousness in the post-war period, and it was this desire which the convention delegates succeeded in writing into the fundamental charter of the nation.

The constitution of 1938 was in essence a catalogue of human rights and social responsibilities. That this revolutionary new constitution would not endure as long as the 1880 charter it replaced was clearly recognized by the men who wrote it, for they fully realized that new generations would define in far more radical terms the needs and obligations of the state. But even when new constitutions were written in the following decades, they represented more than anything else appendages to the 1938 charter, appendages which reflected the ever growing power of the leftist and labour movements in Bolivian society.

10

THE END OF AN ERA

With the dissolution of the convención nacional in the last days of October, the nation once again returned to a relatively quiet period of non-parliamentary rule. The heat of the great debates had temporarily died down, and as the leadership of the post-war radical movement again dispersed, Busch gave up his passive role and once more began to take initiative and attract the attention of the nation.

But recapturing national headlines was one thing, and developing a consistent and effective government was quite another. For despite his professed leanings toward the left, Busch erratically shifted back and forth on specific policies and often took extremely conservative stands. During the sessions of the convention, for example, Busch had changed from open support for the convention, to indifference, and finally to open hostility. His administration included conservative leaders as well as all shades of radicals. Thus in his first cabinet as constitutional president, Busch gave the radical Captain Elías Belmonte the post of minister of government, but handed over the finance ministry to the conservative Alberto Palacios, a former president of the central bank and a firm member of the oligarchy.[1] All these developments only reflected Busch's own uncertainty as to his aims and methods. His constant shiftings reflected his socio-economic and political naiveté and his inability to find a civilian group to assist him in turning his feelings for social reform into concrete action.

Unable to define his own political personality and desires, Busch often allowed others temporarily to lead the government as they pleased. Thus, Alberto Palacios, who had inherited F. Gutiérrez Granier's role as leader of the anti-radical and anti-convention faction in the cabinet, succeeded in forcing Busch to renounce the press censorship law passed by the convention in

[1] *El Diario*, 29 May 1938, p. 7, and 31 May 1938, p. 6.

mid-July. Also under his direction, the government proposed the elimination of 400 public employees from the 1939 budget to meet the temporary crisis caused by an unexpected short-term decline in tin prices.[1] By the end of July the rightists in the cabinet were strong enough to help oust Elías Belmonte from the cabinet, and in a seemingly parallel rightist move, General Carlos Quintanilla began a public purge of all politically-minded officers from the ranks.[2] At the beginning of August, Palacios noted that all the conservative economic policies that he had been following—economies in government expenses, the establishment of a single exchange rate to replace the multiple exchange system, and the restriction of bank-credit—had had a marked positive effect on the national economy.

But the self-confidence of the minister and his rightist friends was rudely shaken a few days later, when Busch suddenly forced the resignation of his entire cabinet on the excuse of the signing of the definitive peace treaty with Paraguay. Palacios was eliminated and replaced by the moderate reformer Vicente Mendoza López.[3] Busch also appointed a close friend of Tristán Marof, Carlos Salinas Aramayo, to the ministry of agriculture.[4] A short time later the most right-wing of all, Commander-in-Chief Carlos Quintanilla, admitted publicly his disagreements with the Busch government and attempted to resign his post.[5]

This constant attraction and rejection of his rightist supporters, not only began to alienate them, but also seriously disrupted the whole traditional party structure. Denied an important role in the government even as independent individuals, the conservative political leaders of the nation found themselves cut off from all sources of power. In fact, it was more often than not non-political conservatives, such as bankers and mine association leaders who had little sensitivity to the needs or interests of party discipline, who represented the oligarchy in government.

This breakdown of the traditional patterns of representation, along with erosion from below by the mass exodus of younger elements into the reformist ranks, created ever new tensions for

[1] *El Diario*, 7 July 1938, p. 6.   [2] *El Diario*, 31 July 1938, p. 7.
[3] *El Diario*, 2 August 1938, p. 7.
[4] Díaz Machicao, *Toro, Busch*, p. 83.   [5] *El Diario*, 2 October 1938, p. 6.

293

the traditional parties which were clearly visible by mid-1938. In late September the Liberal party met to elect a new leadership and to work out a programme in the light of the new constitution and the continued development of the military socialist régime. With the death of Hugo Montes, the party suddenly found itself without resources among the younger generation, and admitting its total bankruptcy of leadership, it selected Alcides Argüedas to be the head of the party.[1] While Argüedas had an international reputation as Bolivia's most outstanding intellectual, he was completely inept in political affairs, and had once proved such a total failure in parliamentary debate that his party had removed him from congress and never permitted him to hold such an office again. Thus the election of Argüedas was the party's own tacit admission that it was running out of new leadership and had nowhere to turn except to its older but previously untried stalwarts.

An arch-conservative, oblivious to the needs of the post-war community, Argüedas presented to the convention a programme of action which was reactionary in every respect and displayed ignorance of even the simplest reform demands of the Chaco generation. He proposed the need for a Pacific port, the preservation of the sacred Liberal principles which General Eliodoro Camacho had issued fifty-three years before, and a general programme of education and agricultural training to meet the needs of the Indians. To meet the present political situation, he called for the return of the army to its professional duties and the reinstatement of civilian government, a demand which reflected the party's ever growing concern for its very survival under the anti-traditional-party governments.[2] As this programme met with little response in the ensuing months, Argüedas found himself taking ever more reactionary stands which isolated him and his party from national developments.

But while the right saw only the dark unknown with the continuance of the military socialist experiment, the left envisioned great possibilities and continued to experience the important growth that had begun with the ending of hostilities. The radical left began to flourish mightily as a result of Busch's unique tolerance of political radicalism, which contrasted sharply with

[1] *El Diario*, 26 September 1938, p. 4.   [2] *El Diario*, 27 September 1938, p. 7.

Toro's hostility, and also as a result of the new stirrings of radical feelings at the national convention and at the signing of the Constitution.

In the first days of October, José Aguirre Gainsborg and Tristán Marof organized in La Paz the first Partido Obrero Revolucionario (POR) convention on Bolivian soil, the second of its history. The key mover behind this convention was José Aguirre Gainsborg. One of the original founders of the POR, Aguirre Gainsborg had returned to Bolivia in late 1934 and had worked actively in the ranks of the young leftist groups, such as Beta Gama, as well as in the labour councils of the La Paz FOT.[1] In mid-1936, the Toro government had imprisoned him along with the other leading contemporary leftist intellectual of the period, José Antonio Arze, and had exiled both men to Chile.[2] From Chile, Aguirre Gainsborg finally broke with the idea of working within groups like Beta Gama, which had ended up by joining the Baldivieso and Montenegro Socialists and then the Toro government. He decided to return to an independent revolutionary party base, and to resurrect in Bolivia the old POR which he had founded in 1934 in Córdoba with Tristán Marof.

On his return from exile in 1938, Aguirre Gainsborg began working assiduously towards his goal,[3] especially as Marof himself had just returned from exile shortly before. Through their joint efforts the second *Conferencia* of the POR was finally organized in October 1938. A confirmed Trotskyite, Aguirre Gainsborg wanted the POR to be converted into a Bolshevik organization, strongly class-based and for the moment a clandestine operation. Marof, however, proposed that the POR should be launched as a popular party, that it should leave to one side its class characteristics and its doctrinal intransigence and appeal to a united leftist front.

These two programmes came into sharp conflict at the convention and forced a schism in the infant party.[4] To Aguirre Gainsborg's protestations that the opening up of party lists would ruin the POR with extraneous non-Marxist elements, Marof replied, 'We are armed with a theory . . . then why fear

[1] Lora, *José Aguirre Gainsborg*, pp. 41ff.   [2] *Ibid.* pp. 62–3.   [3] *Ibid.* pp. 63–4.
[4] Lora, *De grupo de propaganda, a partido de masas*, pp. 1–2.

mixing ourselves with all peoples . . .' Besides, he went on to note, 'in this moment a socialist spontaneity and desire for a leader exists' therefore, 'Why not take advantage of this spontaneity over the other parties, to create ours on a solid basis?' Thus he proposed to found a socialist party on the basis of a united front of the left, in conjunction with the labour unions, the students and, in fact, anyone who was willing to join the ranks.[1]

With this, Marof and his followers, who represented the overwhelming majority of PORistas, broke with Aguirre Gainsborg and left the party.[2] The latter and a few dozen other Trotskyites thus retained control of the POR. But a few days later José Aguirre Gainsborg died in a tragic accident,[3] and his loss temporarily reduced the POR to a tiny ideological grouping of little consequence in the larger radical movement.[4]

With the death of Aguirre Gainsborg and the weakening of the small POR, the major impetus for leadership of the radical forces now temporarily fell to Marof. Gaining the support of Walter Guevara Arze, Alipio Valencia, Alberto Mendoza López and many others,[5] Marof succeeded in organizing his own workers' socialist party which soon became known as the *Partido Socialista Obrero Boliviano* (PSOB). In a rousing manifesto to the nation in early November, Marof proposed to all leftist Bolivians that they join this party 'born independently and without compromises' and form for the first time in Bolivia a disciplined and doctrinaire radical political movement. In rather harsh terms he stated that all members would have to obey the commands of the party without discussion and put party interest above all other considerations. Implying, and quite properly, that until now the reformist and radical movements of the post-war generation had been unable to form a disciplined and dedicated group, he proposed to overcome this problem. He blamed 'the lack of socialist theory, the low level of the proletarian masses, the demagoguery and

[1] Quoted in Lora, *José Aguirre Gainsborg*, pp. 65–6.
[2] It seems that Luis Peñaloza was one of the few to remain. *Ibid.* p. 66.
[3] *Ibid.* pp. 67–9; also see eulogistic articles in *El Diario*, 24 October 1938, p. 5.
[4] Lora, 'De grupo de propaganda, a partido de masas', p. 2. Lora notes in this unpublished MS that the POR affiliated with the Fourth International in 1939, but denies this in the *José Aguirre Gainsborg* biography (p. 69).
[5] Lora, *José Aguirre Gainsborg*, p. 59.

extremist infantilism', for preventing the creation of a strong united leftist party.

Until this moment Bolivian socialism has been divided into a hundred leftist groups and small parasitic parties without discipline or uniformity. There has not existed the moral and material bonds which united one for all. Many socialists have hesitated to act, withdrawing into theory . . ., forgetting that socialism signifies experience and movement. Others have participated in politics and distorted the doctrine, adopting it for their personal needs. Finally the workers entered into the electoral battles without compass or rudder.

These, Marof noted, were the reasons for the failure, but now he proposed to build anew and bring the left into a more advanced stage of political development.

To attract the largest following possible he somewhat modified his classic attacks on the oligarchy and did not openly proclaim his famous credo 'tierras al indio, minas al estado'. Though leaving the end results vague, he did charge that 'the results of the Chaco War, which have cost the Bolivian people so much blood, money and territory, constitute the judgement of the old feudal and bourgeois oligarchs. Their ineptitude which was made evident in an uninterrupted career of disasters, demands that history sweep them away'. The oligarchy, he maintained, must be replaced by a militant mass party with rigid discipline. Calling for a unified support of sindicatos, groups and other fragmented pieces of the left, he ended with a demand that 'workers, students, professionals, Indians [and] military' must group themselves into a united 'socialist' party, a party which would be 'above individual interest'. And to overcome the infantilism of the old left, the new party would have 'a discipline of iron for all members.'[1] But despite his essentially correct interpretation of the problem of the post-war Bolivian left, Marof and his considerable band of supporters, including several convention deputies, never succeeded in establishing that 'iron disciplined' party. Though far more militantly leftist than such predecessors as Baldivieso's *Partido Socialista*, the PSOB ended by experiencing in a very short time the same historic trajectory as its precursors.

[1] *La Calle*, 6 November 1938, pp. 2, 3.

Marof could not cure the disease he so ably diagnosed, but the time was quickly approaching when others would be able to achieve what he so brilliantly proposed. This start, however, was made not in national political parties, but rather in powerful locally based coalitions, in which both organized labour and the university student movement played a vital role. The revival of the national student movement under the Busch régime was a major breakthrough in the maturation of the radical political movement. After many unsuccessful efforts following the Chaco War, a rejuvenated *Federación Universitaria Boliviana* (FUB) finally succeeded, in late December 1939, in organizing the Fourth National Congress of University Students in the city of Sucre. The so-called third Convention which had met in Santa Cruz in early 1936 had been a total failure.[1] This new convention, however, was not only an organizational success, but it also succeeded in giving concrete expression to the radical ideology of the university students of the nation. At this assembly the FUB rewrote its Organic Statute and Programme of Principles,[2] and tried to give it a far more radical slant, indicating that the student movement was finally emerging from its dormant state into one of the most advanced elements of the Bolivian left.

The 'fundamental declarations' which began its programme of principles was a truly amazing document and one of the most revolutionary declarations of the period. It began by stating that:

The university youth of Bolivia proclaims and recognizes that the Reforma Universitaria 'is an indivisible part of the social question'. No university reform can be obtained without economic and political reform. No university action is possible isolated from the class struggle. The high ends which the university pursues in its fight for the emancipation of the spirit and culture, and the predominance of peace and justice, are also the political ends which the world working class pursues in its fight against capitalism.

In fact, all the postulates which the FUB expounds have the character of class demands: they will only be possible and wholly realizable in a society which arises from a new economic, social and juridical structure.

In order to obtain this new socio-economic and political

---

[1] *El Diario*, 22 February 1936, p. 2.   [2] *El Diario*, 4 January 1939, p. 6.

reality, the FUB in the document proposed to change its character from a purely professional student organization, to an intellectual workers' vanguard in the fight for social justice. It proposed to become 'an integral part of the working class, taking charge of its ideology, of its politics, and of its tactics', in the fields of culture, education and the universities. It declared that only through their own organizational activities could the workers overthrow their oppression. In this process of organization, the working classes needed a revolutionary vanguard, and the students declared themselves now a part of that vanguard. 'The FUB is an organization at the service of the manual and intellectual proletariat, which fights to construct new collective bases for society. From today onward it presents itself, for that reason, as an advanced organization, with a class content and a defined position.'

By way of defining this position, it proclaimed that the liberalism of the *pequeña burguesía* was at an end, and that the new postwar generation had to 'oppose the reactionary post-war oligarchy' by a new 'socialist affirmation'. To overcome the oligarchy it was necessary to join forces with the peasants and workers to destroy feudalism and oppose imperialism. It also clearly stated that not only did student reforms depend on initiating revolutionary social and economic changes in the society as a whole, but that 'in the epoch of imperialism all national social problems have an international character, as international as the cause which produced them'.[1]

Given this fully Marxist interpretation of the national scene and the sharp clarity of their stand, the programme of action which followed this declaration of fundamental principles was a revolutionary one in the full sense of the word.

In its chapter on 'la FUB, el imperialismo, el fascismo y la guerra' the *programa* maintained that imperialism was a method used by the capitalist countries to exploit the underdeveloped nations of the world as sources for primary materials and markets for finished goods. All these colonial or semi-colonial states had lost their economic and political independence under this system, as well as their possibilities for cultural and economic self-expression. Since 1914, the United States had become the chief imperialist power and its

[1] Cornejo S., *Programas políticos de Bolivia*, pp. 297–300.

authority was dominant in the western hemisphere with Bolivia and the other countries of Latin America being 'nothing more than factories of imperialism'.

The instrument of control used by the capitalist powers in countries like Bolivia was to buy out the local governing oligarchies and then keep them in power. Thus the dominant classes in Latin America served their imperialist masters unconditionally, and handed over to them the wealth of their nations. The Monroe Doctrine and the Pan American Union were, it added, but specific instruments of enforcement of this imperialistic system. As for imperialism itself, it was the ultimate stage of decadent capitalism, and the seeds of destruction were now clearly apparent and were rapidly leading to a great world-wide imperialist war. Finally the capitalists—it was claimed—had recently turned towards fascism, or a White Terror, to suppress the restive lower classes and to put down the inevitable social revolution.[1]

To overcome imperialism, fascism and its war, the FUB proposed a dual attack on international capitalism and the native oligarchy, which would have as its goal the economic liberation of Bolivia. In the international sphere it proposed that Bolivians join forces with the oppressed of all Latin America to overthrow the Monroe Doctrine and dissolve the Pan American Union and replace it with a *Confederación de las Repúblicas Socialistas de América Latina*. Such a body would internationalize the canals, rivers and seas of Latin America and also provide seacoast outlets for all landlocked republics—i.e. Bolivia. Further, the revolutionary republic set up in Bolivia would cancel all foreign debts and carry through 'the nationalization of the mines, transportation and petroleum, and the socialization of the soil; as a means of destroying imperialism and obtaining our political and economic independence'. And as an antidote to imperialistic wars it proposed 'proletarian revolution'.[2]

The programme stated that the Indian agrarian problem was the key economic problem of Bolivia and charged that the feudal landholding and labour servitude system in practice in Bolivia not only retarded agricultural production and enslaved a people, but was the base on which the whole national oligarchy

---

[1] Cornejo S., *Programas políticos de Bolivia*, pp. 300–2.   [2] *Ibid.* pp. 303–4.

and ultimately foreign imperialism rested. Thus the latifundia and pongueaje had to be destroyed root and branch. In terms by now traditional for the South American left, it claimed that 'the problem of the Indian is the problem of the land' and stated that: 'it is not possible to resolve the agrarian question while the present régime based on private ownership of the means of production continues. The march of the peasant revolution will take place through the historic course of the socialist revolution which dissolves the democratic-bourgeois stage, conquering it through socialized production and property'.[1]

As for national politics, it stated that 'the line of action of the FUB—as a class organization—is determined by the class line of the revolutionary proletariat. For that reason its tactics and strategy are that of social revolution'. The FUB, it declared, 'will support the formation of *Frentes de explotados* and will take part in all work which tends towards the taking of power by the workers for the real transformation of society'. It held that a workers' government was the 'only means of obtaining the full realization of our aspirations'.[2]

As could be expected, the FUB was strongly anti-clerical, calling for the separation of church and state, nationalization of the goods and rents of the church and the suppression both of Catholic education and the monastic system. It charged that the recent upsurge of ecumenical congresses in Bolivia was merely the method of introducing fascism into the nation and asked for the suppression of these congresses and action against groups which pursued similar ends, the latter being an obvious reference to the newly formed and student dominated *Falange Socialista Boliviana*.[3]

[1] Cornejo S., *Programas politicos de Bolivia*, pp. 304–8.   [2] *Ibid.* pp. 310–11.
[3] *Ibid.* p. 310. The FSB had been founded in Chile in 1937, among Bolivian students working at the Universidad Católica and National University at Santiago, and was modelled along the lines of the Spanish Falange, though much more heavily Catholic in orientation than the Primo de Rivera party. The founder and leader of the party was an agronomy student at Católica by the name of Oscar Unzaga de la Vega. By 1938 the party had established a cell in Bolivia at Cochabamba and rapidly gained support from students in the private Catholic secondary schools. Until the late 1940s, the FSB was almost exclusively a student organization, powerfully supported by the clergy, and its primary aim seems to have been the totally negative one of fighting the spread of Marxism both among the student population and on the larger political

Though its immediate seventeen-point programme presented to Busch at the close of the congress was a rather mild document demanding increased support for education and more social benefits for workers,[1] the basic programme and the declaration of the Fourth National University Students' Congress were of an unequivocal Marxian and revolutionary nature in the classic sense of the term. Thus the vital revival of the FUB in 1938 and its definitive stand on these grounds marked a major break-through for the radical left. For the 1938 congress showed that the radical pre- and post-war revolutionary ideology had finally permeated the hallowed university halls and that without question the formerly isolated radicals now had firm support in the universities, a base that it never lost. In a sense the establishment of the Falange Socialista Boliviana also indicated this revolutionary awakening of the university students and its potential for revolutionary political action whether of the militant falange right or of the far left, a potential which would be fully realized in the years to come.

Even the moderate left began an active revival after the injection of vitality given by the 1938 constitutional convention. Shortly after Marof began to organize his Partido Socialista Obrero Boliviano, the former president of the Convención Nacional de 1938, Renato Riverín, began talks with various groups to form a united moderate socialist party, proposing a convention for early 1939.[2] Travelling throughout the country in January and February of the new year, Riverín gathered together the Partido Socialista Independiente group (Paz Estenssoro, Montenegro, etc.), the Gabriel Gosálvez Antipersonalista PRS faction, and various LEC delegates, into a temporary *Unión Democrática Socialista* with Gosálvez as chief.[3] Riverín, himself a moderate, brought into this new grouping representatives of the

scene, either through counter-organizational methods, or more usually by resort to violence. Jorge Siles Salinas, *La aventura y el orden, reflexiones sobre la revolución boliviana*, prólogo de Roberto Prudencio (Santiago de Chile: n.p., 1956), pp. 154–5. Siles Salinas, a leading falangista and professor at a Catholic University in Chile, is son of Hernando Siles. Also see the hostile pamphlet Movimiento Nacionalista Revolutionario, *El catolicismo frente al falangismo fascista* (La Paz: Publicationes de las S.P.I.C. [1953?]), p. 3.
[1] *El Diario*, 22 January 1939, p. 6.
[2] *El Diario*, 14 December 1938, p. 7.   [3] *El Diario*, 12 February 1939, p. 7

dominant reformist elements in the government, in what seemed like the makings of another Partido Socialista de Estado under government auspices. But despite the signing of a temporary unification pact in mid-December 1938,[1] the apparent disinterest, if not open hostility, of the executive soon brought a complete breakdown of this crucial attempt and left many of the reformist parties disillusioned and embittered. Thus the continued refusal of Busch to organize this potentially powerful political movement deprived his government of essential organized and directed civilian support.

Another temporary political creation which appeared at this time of rapid political flux, was the unique Partido Orientalista, the most important and cohesive regionalist party in Bolivian history since the federal revolution of the late nineteenth century. A product of the 1938 Convention, the *grupo orientalista* and its subsequent party arose from the grievances growing out of the recent creation of a separate department out of oriente territory, and the bitter regionalist sentiment which had grown strong in the closing years of the Chaco War. A right-wing faction to begin with, the orientalistas added a strong dose of white racism to their appeal and within a short time began to attract a powerful local following. The official *Partido Orientalista* was founded at Cobija early in February 1939, and not only announced a frankly regionalist platform, but declared 'as basic principles the integrity of each one of the oriental departments, [and] . . . the integrity of our racial identity . . . [which] in turn entails the basic principle of defence of our race . . .'[2]

The party, apart from proposing a general convention for Santa Cruz in July, appealed for support from Germán Busch, who was born and raised in Beni. Busch, however, not only rejected the invitation to join in support of the new organization,[3] but took positive measures to destroy the movement, and threatened reprisals if the party was not dissolved immediately. In this attitude he had the entire support of the La Paz press which saw the orientalista movement, no matter what its sympathy to the right might be, as a serious threat to national unity.[4] Within

[1] *El Diario*, 28 February 1939, p. 6.
[2] *El Diario*, 5 February 1939, p. 7, and 9 February 1939, p. 6.
[3] *El Diario*, 11 February 1939, p. 7.   [4] *El Diario*, 15 February 1939, p. 7.

a few days the party leaders admitted defeat and in a telegram to Busch on 14 February, agreed to dissolve their organization, though they denied that they were either separatists or racists as had been charged, but were rather promoters of local development and stated that their racial distinction from the altiplano Aymara and Quechua Indians was one of classification only and not an invidious comparison.[1]

But the suppression of the orientalists in no way dampened the increasing tempo of conservative political reorganization, which received new impetus in early 1939. This revived conservative activity was spurred on by the government's announcement that new elections for congressional additions and vacancies would take place in May 1939,[2] but more importantly by the removal of two key political leaders from the scene. On 1 March, news arrived of the death in exile of the old caudillo and dominant figure of Bolivian political life for the past quarter century, Bautista Saavedra.[3] The delicate balance which the astute old man had maintained between the traditional political parties and the new post-war groups was immediately upset by his death and in the weeks and months to follow, his removal from the scene finally brought clarity to the blurred and confused political divisions in the nation. Also, at this time, by his own choice, the nation lost the key new leader of the moderate socialist factions, Gabriel Gosálvez. In early March Gosálvez announced his decision to leave the cabinet and the country and become ambassador to Italy.[4] By his departure Gosálvez left the government socialist movement leaderless, killed the Riverín attempts at forming a political party and sank his own Antipersonalista PRS faction into oblivion. Also, the loss to Busch of Gosálvez meant a major imbalance in the leadership of the government, for Gosálvez seems to have been the dominant policy maker of the Busch government and an important levelling influence on the often mercurial character and mentality of the president.

---

[1] *El Diario*, 18 February 1939, p. 7.   [2] *El Diario*, 6 February 1939, p. 5.
[3] *El Diario*, 2 March 1939, p. 6. Montes had died at the height of the Chaco War, in November 1933. José María Escalier died shortly after, in August 1934, and one of the other great political leaders of the old era, Daniel Sánchez Bustamante also passed away at this time. Díaz Machicao, *La guerra del Chaco*, pp. 184, 198, 217.   [4] *El Diario*, 10 March 1939, p. 6.

As for Saavedra, his removal from the ranks of the traditional political parties brought to an end the old-time leadership, and the great pre-war era of civilian caudillos. His loss was irreplaceable not only for the traditional parties, but for the reformist movement of the immediate post-war period as well. For Saavedra's almost genius-like political sensitivity enabled him to form a link for the new moderate left with the old era. But with his death the last powerful tie with the past was broken and the moderates were left to fend for themselves. The smaller men of the traditional political parties now found it far easier to assimilate their rather similar groups into a united front, without the disruptive influence of dynamic personalities like Bautista Saavedra.

A few days after his death, news began to circulate of a unity move among the traditional parties which were attempting to create a *Concordancia*, as they called it, of the old rival parties of the past, the Partido Liberal, Partido Republicano Genuino, and Partido Republicano Socialista.[1] Under the leadership of the Partido Liberal president, Alcides Argüedas, talks between the three parties and the *Estrella de Hierro* group led by Roberto Bilbao la Vieja were begun. Their aims were to form 'a united civilian front', as Argüedas called it, to prepare for the coming May elections, to promote the return of the army to its professional duties, and to call for the dissolution of the elected convention-congress of 1938–9. The Estrella group soon withdrew, claiming it was a socialist party, though of a national and not international nature, and that it could find no basis of agreement with the traditional political parties. In doing so, the group also denied as being complete fabrication charges that it was too rigidly doctrinaire in its conservatism for the old parties.[2]

Despite this withdrawal, however, the traditional political parties finally reached an historic unification agreement and on 21 March 1939, the Concordancia issued a manifesto to the nation in the name of the three parties. Outlining its ideas of classic liberal government, it called for the return of civilian government to Bolivia, demanding an end to the army's direction of the nation in specific and threatening terms. It also demanded the end of the *divisas* system of government taxation of the mining industry,

[1] *El Diario*, 9 March 1939, p. 7.   [2] *El Diario*, 12 March 1939, p. 7.

alleging that it was an archaic war-time practice, and finally it rejected the peace treaty of 1938 as a slight on national honour and called for heavy spending on armaments. In all, it was the most reactionary document yet produced by the traditional parties in the post-war world and indicated a complete abandonment of the policy of attempted involvement with the moderate left. The manifesto was signed by Argüedas, Hertzog, Demetrio Canelas, Waldo Belmonte Pool, Justo Rodas Eguino, and José María Gutiérrez as representatives of the three political parties.[1]

The signing of the Concordancia pact was truly an historic occasion in the political history of Bolivia, for it marked the end of the political system which had ruled national life since 1880 and of the traditional intra-class party structure with its classic struggles over forms of liberal government, and the real beginning of the class-oriented and socially disruptive political party structure based on the socio-economic realities of the nation. With the signing of the pact, the traditional politicians abandoned their old system and openly represented themselves as a consciously class-oriented party defending the interests of the oligarchy in a bitter inter-class political struggle for survival. Though the signatories to the Concordancia pact seemed to imply that this was a temporary electoral expedient, the Concordancia endured for a long time to come, for it was the inevitable response to the oligarchy's need for a united front to represent its interests. The Partido Centralista had been a warning to the old groups, and they had finally responded to it by forgetting their traditional petty differences and uniting the remnants of their organizations behind a party front which seemed capable of defending class interests.

Among the leftists, however, the unity moves of the period seemed to lead nowhere, and the post-war state of flux reached even greater proportions. The fumbling government socialist party was finally dissolved when the new minister of government, Vicente Leyton, who had just replaced Gosálvez, announced his refusal to join the proposed party. Also a key radical leftist group, the Frente Popular de Potosí, announced its

[1] *El Diario*, 22 March 1939, pp. 6, 7; also Díaz Machicao, *Toro, Busch*, p. 92.

firm opposition[1] and even José Tamayo declared that he was reforming his old Partido Socialista, completely apart from the
government movement, which was now at an end.[2] The collapse
of this movement came at a serious time for the government,
which was cutting off its chief civilian support at a time when
it faced a major election. In rather grandiose terms it implied
that it would support its own lists of candidates for the coming
May elections, while the seemingly rejuvenated traditional políticos announced that they would run their own slates in complete
defiance of the proposed government intervention at the polls.[3]

At the same time as the government was creating new dissension in the ranks of the moderate reform elements, the Busch
régime itself was beginning to experience internal problems of a
major force. In a surprise rejection, which caused much temporary
heat, Vicente Mendoza López was ousted from the cabinet and
replaced in the ministry of finance by the leading banker and
mine operator, Santiago Schulze.[4] Also, news began to circulate
at this time of major frauds perpetrated against Jewish immigrants by Bolivian embassy officials in Europe and by members of
the immigration service generally.

These charges originated in the radical Busch proposal of June
1938, which called for the free and unrestricted immigration of
European Jewish refugees into Bolivia. Reversing previous government policy, the minister of agriculture and immigration, Julio
Salmón, had announced on 9 June that the government would no
longer enforce special restrictions against Jewish immigration, and
that henceforth the official policy would be that: 'the doors of
Bolivia are open for all men of the world healthy in body and
spirit who want to come to work the fertile lands which we will
freely give to them'. Salmón specifically stated that Jews would
be free to enter like all others and that 'in Bolivia we should not
make ourselves co-participants in the hatred or the persecutions,
[of] the Semitic elements in European countries'.[5] This reversal

---

[1] *El Diario*, 9 April 1939, p. 7.
[2] *El Diario*, 12 March 1939, p. 7, and 23 April 1939, p. 7.
[3] *El Diario*, 15 April 1939, p. 7.
[4] Vicente Mendoza López, acting as temporary minister of education, had signed
a decree giving autonomy to the private *colegios*, which aroused the ire of the
leftist student and teacher groups, and was ultimately rejected by the cabinet.
El Diario, 1 April 1939, p. 7.   [5] *El Diario*, 10 June 1938, p. 7.

of policy was rather an unusual one considering the almost world-wide refusal to admit European Jews at this time. It was also surprising in the light of the strong national-socialist and pro-German sympathies of the Bolivian officer corps, and also of the latent anti-Semitic attitude of the left toward Mauricio Hochschild. However, a determining factor in this change of attitude may well have been the offer by Paraguay, a few months earlier, to settle 15,000 Austrian Jewish immigrants in the Chaco at the time of the German takeover of Austria, an offer which Bolivia had protested as a violation of the Buenos Aires peace terms. And it was obviously with an eye to the settling of the Chaco with these immigrants that in the one-year period following the announcement of the new administrative policy, the government permitted the immigration of some 10,000 European Jews to Bolivia. Whatever the specific origins of this basically humanitarian gesture, the whole conduct of the immigration arrangements by foreign ministry officials, and the subsequent breakdown of the agricultural settlement programme, soon became an explosive issue for the Busch government, and greatly increased social tensions in the war-damaged nation.

The issue suddenly exploded in mid-1939 with the charge that the consul-general of Bolivia in Paris, Carlos Virriera Pacieri, had amassed a large fortune through the sale of Bolivian visas. Contrary to all government rules, he had arranged that all visas obtained by Europeans had to be cleared through the Paris embassy, and from Paris he had been issuing for quite some time approximately 3,000 passports weekly, charging the Jewish émigrés between 10,000 and 20,000 francs a visa.[1] The *affaire* as it came to be called, caused quite a stir in the newspapers, with charges of gross moral violations by the government, despite the executive's belated dismissal of many of the persons involved.

Facing mounting criticism of a severe moral nature on the 'affaire de inmigración' and presented with a total breakdown of civilian support for the coming May elections, Busch suddenly resorted to violent action to change the course of events. Reacting as he had in June 1937, under Toro, he decided that drastic measures of 'purification' and rejuvenation were needed to move

[1] *El Diario*, 27 May 1939, p. 7.

the government towards its main objectives. To the utter surprise of the nation, Busch announced the end of constitutional government and the formal establishment of a dictatorship on 24 April 1939.

The manifesto which Busch issued to the nation in defence of his action was a curiously revealing psychological document. In what by now had become a perennial theme for him, he began the document by describing the long years of selfless service he had given to the nation, including the supreme test of war. He too, he declared, had been a witness to the tragedy of the war and the political and economic machinations it had produced. 'And as a living witness of that deep tragedy, which all those who suffered in the fields of battle shared and still share with me, I conceived the same ideals of . . . profoundly renovating and purifying the national soul. An identical suffering engendered in all of us an identical ideal of patriotic rebirth.'

These ideals were behind the 17 May revolution which he led, and which he refused to use for personal power as his rejection of the presidency indicated. It was only Peñaranda's refusal of the post which finally brought him to the presidency in July 1937, he declared, in what was obviously a somewhat facile interpretation of the facts. Thus being forced to accept the leadership of the rejuvenation, he turned to the nation for support, giving complete freedom to all the political factions. But what had happened, he added, was nothing but anarchy. He had fulfilled his duty, he had created a national coalition cabinet dominated by no one group, he had called into session a constitutional convention to write a new charter, and finally he had brought an end to the international problems of the nation. But none of his actions could stem the anarchy and bring conciliation.

My ideal was the reorganization of the parties and political forces through clear and well defined programmes. I recognized the necessity of dramatic free play . . . for the forces of opposition. I sustained the desirability of an ample freedom of the press hoping that it would result in the ascertaining of goals and the appearance of solutions for the great problems of the republic . . . But it has become clear that far from attaining these objectives, beneficial for the nation, the freedom of the press has aroused licentiousness . . . which is a negation of the level of culture at which the republic has arrived. Also the action of the opposition parties, instead of being patriotic and truly civic, has become a subversive and demagogic fermentation which poisons the national atmosphere.

But there is something much more serious. I do not hesitate to affirm that the country is passing through a period of major decomposition and failure in all its values. It seems that, as a consequence of the war, the resources of the nation have been ripped asunder, destroying those factors which make a people great: the faith in its destiny; moral, political and social integrity; [and] the disinterest and spirit of self-sacrifice. Only two passions can be observed at the base of all these acts: the impulsive desire to overthrow the government, by any available means, and an uncontainable and unscrupulous longing for money.

Even the public administration had reflected this, he charged, in an obvious allusion to the immigration affair. The public and private immorality, this self-righteous and ingenuous military officer declared, 'has become a chronic sickness'. When he thought of the past sacrifice of the Bolivian people in the holocaust of war, he stated, he became outraged at the immorality, at the appearance of racist and regionalist (an allusion to the orientalistas), as opposed to national tendencies.

With all this he saw Bolivia still passing through a post-war economic crisis which was daily affecting the basic needs of the middle and popular classes. As for the army, in an obvious allusion to the action of the Concordancia, he attacked those who wanted to divide the armed services from the civilian classes, a tendency which had as its aim 'the putting into action of an immediate fratricidal war'. Before all these problems he could not remain impassive, but must react in an energetic fashion.

With the same faith, and with the same spirit of sacrifice with which I defended Bolivia in heat of battle, offering my life at each and every moment, I want to undertake a new campaign which will save this decaying nation.

Beginning today I am initiating an energetic and disciplined government, convinced that this is the only road which will permit the invigoration of the republic, in the internal as well as the international field. The country needs order, work and morale to fulfil its destiny.

He ended his dictatorship manifesto by appealing to all private citizens to aid this great drive of rejuvenation, to help in saving the nation from the extremists on the left and the creeping oligarchy on the right. The state, he held, must act as a moderator and regulate social justice in the economic sphere; it must conquer all the extremes. 'It is the economic and social pattern of the country which should inspire our programme of action and not the intellectual or sentimental adhesion to fashionable political theories.' This programme should be to create a cohesive nationality; to defend the natural resources for the benefit of all; to rejuvenate the national defence power; to achieve equilibrium in public spending and thus bring back national economic health; to provide guarantees for the investment of capital and positive guarantees for labour until a régime of equality is proclaimed; to build 'schools and roads and finally an iron discipline which will remake moral values'.[1]

This was, in short, the same moderate and unimaginative programme that he had always publicly proclaimed and had been incapable of implementing. Frustrated by the lack of concrete results and actually incapable of coherent and concentrated political direction because of his own lack of training, this moral crusader appealed pitiably to the nation to support his great puritanical morality drive, a drive which he himself seriously believed in. He was enraged and frustrated at the lack of progress, and believed that a dictatorship was the 'solution' to the basic problem, which was essentially that of lack of leadership on his own part.

A flood of decrees followed the announcement of the dictatorship. Congress was suspended and the new elections were called off. While the 1938 constitution was declared to be still in effect, it was decided that the government would now rule directly through executive decree. A series of laws defining immoral action in business and government came forth from the presidential office as Busch tried to legislate against the moral decay he felt was rotting the foundations of the nation. The Concordancia leader, Demetrio Canelas, in a letter to Leyton, the minister of government, denied that the traditional parties were guilty of subversion and charged that by its action the government had actually taken

[1] Speech quoted in full in *El Diario*, 25 April 1939, pp. 6, 9.

a retrograde step, but to no avail.[1] Of more concrete importance
was the resignation of Santiago Schulze from the cabinet and his
replacement by Fernando Pou Mont, a politically unaffiliated
young public administrator.[2] In late May, the government
officially took action on the *affaire* issue and Eduardo Díez de
Medina left office as minister of foreign affairs and was replaced
by another professional diplomat, Alberto Ostria Gutiérrez.[3] A
new educational code was also passed which provided for major
reorganizational changes in the nation's educational system and
an increase of government control.[4] This first burst of intense
governmental activity following the establishment of the dictatorship was completed when the first national labour code became
law on 24 May.

The *Código del Trabajo* was of great importance as an enduring
piece of legislation, and the only one of the many attempted innovations of the Busch dictatorship to firmly establish itself. The
code, which soon became known as the Código Busch, was a
major triumph for the Bolivian labour movement and marked the
culmination of long years of agitation for major social legislation in this field. Embodying many of the proposals first enunciated by Waldo Álvarez and the later elaborations of several
internal assemblies of local directors of the ministry of labour
called under the Toro government, this code of 122 articles provided a wealth of concrete benefits to the labour movement—
excepting only agricultural labourers.

Elevated to a higher *ley general* category, a few years later, this
fundamental code established a maximum of 15 per cent for
foreigners and 45 per cent for women as workers in any enterprise (article 3). It provided full legal protection for labour contracts (articles 5ff.), including separation wages and pension
provisions (article 13). The justifications for firing workers were
carefully enumerated and all other reasons required heavy indemnification by the company (article 16). It provided for the
recognition of the closed shop and a collective contract binding
on all workers (articles 23ff.), and included special provisions for

[1] Díaz Machicao, *Toro, Busch*, pp. 96–8.
[2] *El Diario*, 26 May 1939, p. 4.
[3] Díaz Machicao, *Toro, Busch*, p. 98; Díez de Medina, *De un siglo al otro*, pp. 388–9.
[4] Díaz Machicao, *Toro, Busch*, p. 99.

apprenticeships and *enganche* contracts—that is hiring for work away from the local community—both being special problems of the Bolivian labour scene (articles 28–31). Entire chapters were devoted to cottage industry problems and to domestic labour (articles 32–40). Annual paid vacations were decreed (article 44) and with specified exceptions a 48-hour week was established for the nation (article 46). It stated the desirability of a uniform salary scale which did not distinguish between nationals and foreigners or between sexes, and called for the development of locally established minimum wages (article 52). Child labour prohibitions and special protections for working women were outlined (articles 58–63). It also tried to promote the obligatory pension scheme which had reached only the smallest number of organized workers (article 66). Safety work laws and factory medical facilities were provided, while special enactments covered *campamentos*, or labour compounds, set up by the companies to house workers in the isolated mine fields. Regulations for hospital facilities and the company foodstores—the famous *pulperías*—were also outlined, though in the most limited way (articles 75–7).

A sizeable proportion of the code was devoted to accident compensation for workers—a long established practice in Bolivia in which company responsibilities were carefully defined (articles 79ff.). The right to associate for the organization of labour unions was recognized, and the unions were given a considerable body of rights in the matter of the representation of the workers, contract negotiations and even in the setting up of their own cultural and labour schools and facilities (articles 99ff.). A complete government arbitration procedure was established to settle potential strikes with direct state intervention in the bargaining procedure. These arbitration tribunals, with representation from labour, capital and the government, could issue final and binding decisions (articles 105–13). The right to strike was considerably modified by giving full rights to strike-breakers and outlawing revolutionary strikes or any type of strike violence (articles 114–19).[1]

In all, this was a vital piece of social legislation, and as one

---

[1] The official text of the Código along with later additions, will be found in Germán Busch, *Código del Trabajo* (La Paz: Gran Editorial 'Popular', 1946), pp. 3–34.

labour critic, unfriendly to the régime, noted, 'the merit of having been the first in giving an ample and generous social legislation falls to the Busch government. It is possible to encounter in it [the Código Busch] a series of gaps and even of errors, but it represented a decisive step in regard to the improvement of the conditions of labour, of the working class, and of the employees'.[1]

The Código del Trabajo was of lasting importance, but another, though temporary, action of the government soon dominated the entire thoughts of the nation. On 7 June Busch ended the long and complicated negotiations on the tin issue by decreeing that the companies would henceforth be required to turn over to the government 100 per cent of their foreign gold earnings. This had first been advocated by the radical left in the convention of 1938, but seemingly had been successfully suppressed by the right. But, given the new demand for action by Busch and the need for a major revolutionary slogan, such as Toro's famous nationalization of petroleum decree, this measure was resurrected and proclaimed to the nation.

In late May the big, medium, and small tin miners had all finally joined together in a *Comité Permanente de Mineros* to force the government to abolish the special taxes and divisa requirements which had been imposed on the industry in the Chaco War. The Busch government, however, had refused to give up these greater revenues and under the leadership of the new minister of finance, Fernando Pou Mont, the historic decree was written.[2] It provided that the miners had to turn over to the central bank 100 per cent of the earnings (divisas) resulting from the total gross sale of their exportations, in payment of first class letters of exchange (i.e. gold notes) prior to their receiving a custom house permit allowing them to export their minerals. Article 38 of the decree provided that 'all passive resistance to the fulfilment of the present decree law: sabotage, lock out, restriction of labour and any direct or indirect measure which tries to disturb the normal progress of the mines . . .will be considered as a crime of high treason to the nation [i.e. subject to the death

---

[1] Barcelli, *Medio siglo de luchas sindicales*, p. 149.
[2] Céspedes, *El dictador suicida*, p. 202; Díaz Machicao, *Toro, Busch*, pp. 101–2.

penalty] and its administrators, directors and counsellors, will be judged summarily, without prejudice [i.e. prevention] of an intervention by part of the state in the management of the guilty enterprise or enterprises'. In short, death and confiscation were promised to all those who should attempt to impede the operation of this law by stopping production of minerals.[1]

In a national radio address on 10 June, Busch explained to the public the full implications of the decree. He stated that its basic aim was to ensure henceforth the economic independence of the nation and to promote cooperatives and small and medium-sized producers in the mining industry, as opposed to its present domination by the Big Three giants. Proudly Busch proclaimed that this decree law 'for the first time in Bolivia, established a system of defence of the national wealth'.

A good part of the rest of the speech was concerned with providing as many justifications as possible for such a revolutionary act. First of all, such an action was fully justified by the 1938 constitution which permitted state intervention in the national economic processes. Also such intervention, he stated, was now practised by practically every nation in the world. Government economic control was not unique to the soviet or fascist systems, but was also practised in the majority of South American states, and even in the United States itself under the New Deal of President Roosevelt.

Not only was this common practice among nations, declared Busch, but it was also valid because of the needs of the suffering Bolivian economy which had just passed through a major war and which was also experiencing a crisis as a colonial monoproducer in the world economy. As for the actual decree itself, it in no way signified the end of private property, nor even the confiscation of the mining utilities. For the constitution fully supported the rights of private property, with the proviso, however, that all rights be subordinated to the general interest. And Busch pointed out that even monarchies like Sweden and Romania had such qualifications on private property.

This decree in no way impeded the private exploitation of minerals, but only asserted the rights of the state to intervene in

[1] Banco Minero de Bolivia, *Tasas e impuestos sobre la industria minera*, pp. 121–37.

the process so as 'to avoid the flight of capital and the impoverishment of the nation'. By the terms of the decree, the state promised to pay the miners at the rate of Bs. 141 per pound sterling on 50 per cent of their gold earnings and allowed them the full use of the other half, though the state would exercise control over it. Nor, pointed out Busch, does the state in any way deny the profit margin to the companies, permitting them to export 5 per cent in gold certificates abroad to pay for their interest on stocks to foreign investors. Finally, the central bank was handling the whole affair, and Busch gave an assurance that on its board of directors were representatives from the mining industry itself.

Busch ended by shifting from the defensive to the offensive. For too long, he said, the state had been poor, despite the wealth and bonanza of the mining industry, and now this imbalance would be corrected. National sacrifices in the Chaco, he declared, demanded a new era, and this act was essential to bringing about such a change. By this decree the government hoped to take the fullest advantage of the rich resources of the nation for all citizens. If such an act brings about the downfall of my government, declared Busch, 'I will have fallen with a great banner: the economic emancipation of my country'. He finally appealed to his fellow military men and his fellow veterans to remember the will of the great marshal of Ayacucho 'to defend Bolivia regardless of all the dangers'.[1]

This speech was a moderate and well organized one by Busch's usual standards and it was clearly designed to win popular support for his government against the expected counter-thrust of the mining oligarchy. But Busch was not content with merely obtaining support for this action from the public, nor did he have any really clear idea of how to back up the decree with a host of radical legislation on all socio-economic fronts. Rather, he saw this one piece of legislation alone acting as a great rallying point for the nation in his own peculiarly-conceived drive toward national moral rejuvenation, and really as nothing more. In his speech to a huge public rally on 14 June, sponsored by the left, the students, labour and veterans, he fully revealed his illusions about the true meaning of this act.

[1] Entire speech quoted in *El Diario*, 11 June 1939, p. 4.

Busch began his speech by apologizing to the great crowd spread out before him in Plaza Murillo for having prepared a written speech, stating that he did this so that his thoughts, intentions and propositions would be clearly understood by all. Thanking the masses for their support, he declared in almost deliberately self-deluding terms that:

few times has the national soul been so moved, so fervently and unanimously, as today. The size of this popular demonstration indicates to me that all the nation, conquering its discouragement and its disillusion, has firmly decided to defend its political and economic sovereignty and to make a definitive and valiant act of faith in its future, in its greatness and in its destiny.

On few occasions has a solidarity so absolute and so intimate been seen between government and governed . . .

In times past the masses had been agitated blindly by civilian and military caudillos, but they had never been moved:

like today, as at this moment, by a great and noble patriotic ideal, so noble and great, that before it disappear the . . . fruitless hatreds, the transient interests and the political factions, leaving firm, unbreakable and invincible the will of all of the people, which proclaims its right to live and its decision to conquer.

The tragedy of the war has not been in vain nor the martyrdom of our soldiers useless. From the disaster has arisen this new patriotic conscience, this new profoundly Bolivianist faith, which is expressed in the fervour of the thousands of men who listen to me. In the face of this demonstration I can affirm: Bolivia is on the march and nobody and nothing will detain it in its decision to be, at last, a true patria, for the present generations, for those to come and for all men of the world who want to share our destiny.

Surely this sudden burst of miraculous faith in the masses and their unity was the height of disillusionment for the quixotic Busch. So desperately did he seek for a united country that he was willing to delude himself that this one popular manifestation would mean the end of all the corruption which he had seen in the country a short month before, and that this one mass meeting could be turned into dynamic, positive and united action.

Again in this speech, as in almost all his others, he cried that he had given his all to the patria, that he had sought only its good, and that even in the darkest moments he had never lost faith. With this act, he declared, we bring economic sovereignty to the nation, and as 'the past generations gave us political independence, it is the debt of the present and future generations to attain the economic emancipation'. He appealed to the veterans, the workers the capitalists and all like-minded citizens to join this mystical march to the future and press their support for the disinterested government which would lead the way.[1] But one government-sponsored popular demonstration without political organization or coherent ideology does not make a wave of revolutionary action, and this almost painful longing of Busch to see that wave of regeneration was doomed to utter failure, at least in the moral-istic crusading terms in which he viewed it.

Although the decree was not immediately put into effect, Busch soon learned of Hochschild's supposed proposal to circum-vent the stipulations of the act and in a fit of rage, according to several eye-witnesses, ordered the arrest and execution of the mag-nate. Once Hochschild had been seized, Busch held a stormy cabinet meeting in which he demanded the death penalty for the tin baron who was a naturalized Argentine citizen. By force of will and through prearrangement with some of his more loyal cabinet ministers, Busch cowed the others into signing the execution warrant. Almost immediately, however, they repented their de-cision and not only put pressure on Busch themselves but aroused the foreign legations to make appeals to the government on behalf of Hochschild. In the face of this intense opposition Busch finally relented, dropped the whole affair, and released the imprisoned capitalist.[2] What was important in this whole crisis was Busch's almost insane desire for action and the vindication of his own worth. According to one witness at a banquet a few weeks before, Busch had stated that: 'I, Germán Busch, will demonstrate to those Patiños, Aramayos, Hochschilds ... that here there is a president that will make his country respected.'[3] And his action against Hochschild, which had no legality what-soever, even under the decree which had yet to be put into effect, indicated Busch's impassioned desire to achieve illusory dramatic

---

[1] *El Diario*, 16 June 1939, p. 7.
[2] Céspedes, *El dictador suicida*, pp. 205–6.   [3] *Ibid.* p. 204.

esults. He seemed to have reached a breaking-point at which he ould only conceive of such dramatic and violent actions as neans both of solidifying the nation and cleansing it of its moral agnation.

More and more the president was dealing in phantoms rather nan reality. Without a hard core of doctrinaire leftist intellectuals ommitted to him, organized in a viable political party, and in laces of power, his supposedly 'revolutionary' dictatorship was ncapable of getting anywhere, and in fact the Busch government vas run by the very same men who had helped to run all the revious governments in Bolivia. Thus while Busch nationalized ne new Banco Minero[1] and brought into its management such eftists as Víctor Paz Estenssoro and Walter Guevara Arze, he urned over its direction to his old oligarchic minister of finance, Alberto Palacios.[2] What was true of the Banco Minero was true f the central bank and all the ministries and departments of overnment. Nor could the dictator make any impact without cohesive political party behind him. Though it is true that the eft was rather disorganized, there existed great potential both mong the groups in exile and among the local united front rganizations. But Busch was both unable and unwilling to rganize either these radicals or the numerous moderate leftist roups into a government party.

Thus while the decrees continued to pour out of the presi-lential palace, they met with little positive response or concrete ndorsement, and soon Busch began to feel as if he were legis-ating in a void. Even on his own terms he began to realize that nothing was being accomplished either in alleviating problems r in cleansing the national soul. He had mistaken a single popular nanifestation for a great emotional resurgence and outpouring or himself. But in the grey after-dawn of that tumultuous June lemonstration there seemed to be nothing left, and the support hat he so ardently believed he had created by giving a few

---

The Banco Minero had been created by Toro in 1936. Benavides M., *Historia bancaria*, pp. 123–6. Busch also later nationalized the central bank, on 3 August 1939, by making the government the sole stockholder and owner of the institution through forced purchase of all outstanding private stock. René Gomez García and Rubén Darío Flores, *La banca nacional* (La Paz: Editora 'Universo', 1962), pp. 182–3.

Céspedes, *El dictador suicida*, pp. 203, 204.

speeches and signing some radical decrees had completely evaporated. A lonely figure without organized support in any political movement or military faction, without a defined ideology of his own, and completely dependent on the old oligarchy to govern his administration, Busch soon sensed the utter folly of his own quixotic and romantic dreams, and on the evening of 23 August 1939, committed suicide.[1]

[1] Probably the best discussion on the great debate which has raged over whether Busch committed suicide or was murdered, is that of Augusto Céspedes (*E. dictador suicida*, pp. 207ff.), in which this eye-witness of the event and at the same time loyal Busch follower, after giving every possible reason for assassination, finally concludes that Busch took his own life. However, rather than seeing it as a useless act of an insane individual, he sees the suicide as a great romantic political gesture, much like Vargas' action in Brazil. It came at the culmination of his political career, and according to Céspedes, Busch did more for the revolutionary movement in Bolivia, with this one vital and bloody gesture, than any single idea, or theory. From the plane of practical politics, Céspedes admits, however, that 'given his ideological incipience, his lack of programme and of revolutionary parties, Busch died when the cycle of his possibilities of ruling was closed. The crisis provoked by the decree of 7 June demonstrates that the dictator was incapable of overcoming it, however much passion that he had . . . He was the representative of utopian nationalism, who marched with the counter-revolution at his side, like an ominous shadow, at times misrepresenting the revolution'. *Ibid.* pp. 216–17.

While the Bolivian left has always charged the Rosca with murdering Busch, and all the ideological divisions of the left have appealed to the martyred president as their revolutionary symbol of vindication, one has to conclude with Céspedes that the proof is overwhelmingly with the suicide thesis, and perfectly consistent with Busch's known personality. Certainly a careful examination of even the public record will reveal the psychological destruction of the driving personality of Busch in the last months of his government. His impassioned, rambling and extremely self-defensive public speeches reveal his distorted romanticized version of political reality and his growing awareness of this distortion, which he was eventually unable to cope with.

Also it should be noted, that while Busch was essentially reformist-minded on the socio-economic problems of his day, he seemed incapable of carrying his thoughts and attitudes toward either expression or resolution. In fact the concrete leftist and revolutionary actions that were carried through during his administration were done either by others, or just as often, done in opposition to his will. He set a revolutionary tone and was undoubtedly a far more sincere expression of the new generation than David Toro, but when the actual records of the two men are compared, it is the Toro one which produced more concrete results. As for the three major events in the Busch period, the Código del Trabajo was written by Toro-appointed officials and essentially worked out before Busch came to power; the *divisas* decree was never carried into realization; and the constitution of 1938, the greatest product of the period, was almost entirely written without his active support and towards the end was actually finished in open defiance of him. However, as Céspedes has rightly noted, Busch did achieve more in his dramatic death than he did in his life, and the symbol of the martyred young president would come to haunt the numbered days of the oligarchic governments.

Busch's death marked the end of the post-war era of military socialism. It was an era which had seen the army attempt to lead the nation along the paths of a reformist corporatism mixed with socialism both in response to its own felt needs for vindication from the Chaco disaster for which it blamed the traditional parties, and as a simple matter of self-defence in an increasingly hostile civilian world. The takeover had been facilitated by the vacuum created by the disintegration of the traditional political parties, which in turn was due to the nation's condemnation of their action in leading the country into the terrible Chaco War. From the time of Toro until the formation of the Concordancia in March 1939, the traditional políticos wandered in the wilderness unwilling to believe that the old days were finished. The oligarchy, however, had finally brought home to them, especially after the loss of the historic caudillos, their own individual lack of political power and had forced them to forget their historical differences and band together openly and consciously to defend the interests of the oligarchy as a completely class-oriented group.

The era of military socialism had been one of remarkable growth for the radical left, but especially for the previously non-existent moderate left, and saw the spread of leftist influence in all ranks of Bolivian society. At times encouraged by the government itself and at others neglected or even persecuted, the growth of the left was unchecked throughout the post-war years, especially among the middle class: the urban professionals, white-collar workers, university students, and literate cholo and white merchants and artisans. These were the very groups which previously had formed the hard core of the old political party system, and hence the political base of the nation. It was these numerically small, but politically important groups, who had been most disillusioned by the Chaco War and shocked by the horror and chaos of the disaster. They refused to return to the pre-war days, and it was this rejection of upper-class leadership and refusal to continue to align their interests any longer with the interests of the oligarchy, which led to the destruction of the traditional party system. Seeking a new explanation for the causes of the tragedy of the old order and the outlines for the new, they turned toward radical and Marxist ideologies. And in the first post-war years of military socialist rule, it was these classes who gave their crucial and growing support to the new moderate socialist movements which were defining a middle-ground position which had not existed in the pre-war spectrum of political ideologies.

For the elements of the radical left, which had its roots, its form, and even its leadership in the pre-war days, the Toro-Busch period was a golden age for political development. The vital groups of labour and university students, the heart of any radical leftist movement in Latin America, achieved new political power and at the same time became, in the immediate post-war period, firmly committed to the radical ideological position which was a post-1935 development. Not only did the Marxist intellectuals of the pre-war period establish their hold over the labour and student movements in this period, but they even began to obtain a hearing for their revolutionary ideology from the educated and middle classes, the very groups which had considered them no more than an almost non-existent lunatic fringe in the pre-war period.

More than anything else, the era of military socialism was an era of incubation and development for Bolivian radicalism, in which the middle and popular classes began to organize themselves for independent political action as never before in Bolivian history. It was also an era of transition between the classic intra-class political party system based on historic and formal debates on the terms of liberalism, and an inter-class oriented and ideologically committed political party system based on the socio-economic realities of Bolivian national life.

But while the era of military socialism marked the great turning point in Bolivian political development, which in its way was as crucial as the developments of the generation of 1880, the new political patterns and institutions were still in the process of formation. Because of this, a great testing of power marked the following decade as the reformist and radical movements organized themselves into ever more powerful groupings and the oligarchy itself attempted to work out a new pattern of control which could replace the old traditional political party system.

Initially, the death of Busch enabled the oligarchy to gain the upper hand in its attempt to re-establish its authority. The sudden disappearance of the protective covering of Germán Busch from the leftist officer group within the army, and the chaos of the political support of the left, was an ideal situation for the resurgence of the right in national politics. For the first time since 17 May 1936, the now naked power of the oligarchy made itself profoundly felt. Yet even here, the pre-war leadership and patterns of civilian government could no longer be created, and it was to the army itself that the rightist forces now turned for support and leadership.

Building upon his continued efforts to isolate the leftist officers from positions of power, General Carlos Quintanilla, commander-in-chief of the army, upon receiving the news of Busch's suicide, acted quickly to bring a definitive end to the experiment in military socialism. With the aid of the EMG, which was under the control of the political manipulator Colonel Antenor Ichazo, he rapidly proceeded to gather support for an attempt to establish himself in power. Meeting with the other leading officers, especially General Bilbao Rioja, who was the recognized successor to Busch among the junior officers, Quintanilla by astute bargaining got them to support his takeover move as in the best interests of the army. Thus when the legally elected vice-president, Enrique Baldivieso, attempted to assume the presidency, he was placed under house arrest by the EMG and his succession declared illegal because of the creation of the dictatorship the previous April.[1]

Leading government leftists and close friends of Baldivieso like Hernán Siles Zuazo and Augusto Céspedes, together with local student groups, attempted without success to rally popular support for Baldivieso and oppose the army usurpation. But the regular troops and the urban populace were completely indifferent to the fate of the vice-president and seemed too stunned by the death of Busch to react. Although the pro-Baldivieso forces even succeeded in drawing the docile and retired General Enrique Peñaranda to their side, no garrison in La Paz would revolt, and after several vain attempts, Peñaranda ingloriously retired again to civilian affairs.[2]

[1] *El Diario*, 24 August 1939, pp. 6, 7; Díaz Machicao, *Toro, Busch*, pp. 11–112.
[2] Céspedes, *El dictador suicida*, pp. 218–19.

On 23 August, Quintanilla issued a manifesto promising the nation to continue the government and policies of the fallen dictator,[1] and as a gesture in this direction he temporarily retained the entire Busch cabinet. Meanwhile, Bilbao Rioja moved up to Quintanilla's old position as commander-in-chief of the army, while Quintanilla himself continued to make obsequious gestures of honour to the fallen president.[2] Busch was posthumously raised to the rank of lieutenant-general, and his remains were buried with much ceremony in the Basílica of La Paz on 27 August. Surprisingly the government permitted all the leading supporters of the old régime to speak over the coffin, and even Baldivieso, escaping from his guard, succeeded in making his appearance and in a bitter speech attacked the army usurpation.[3] But despite all these appeals the stunned public could not be aroused against the army putsch. Quintanilla, for his part, shrewdly played on the theme that he was following in the footsteps of his predecessor and would see his great national programme to completion.

But whatever pretensions Quintanilla might have had to assume the mantle of a 'military socialist' ruler or to adopt a military caudillo régime, they were quickly dropped. Faced by the considerable popularity and apparent commitment of the reform forces to Bilbao Rioja, and by the equally strong pressure from the Concordancia for immediate civilian elections for a constitutional president, Quintanilla was forced to give up very reluctantly whatever ideas he might have had about long term rule. So reticent in fact was he about preparing for the return of constitutional government that the sympathetic Concordancia began to grow restive and threatening.[4] For no matter how much they might trust the conservative tendencies of Quintanilla, they desperately wanted an end to the military junta system from which they had suffered such heavy losses.

By late September of 1939, the Concordancia was openly

---

[1] *El Diario*, 24 August 1939, p. 7.
[2] See, e.g. his radio speech reprinted in *El Diario*, 16 August 1939, p. 5.
[3] Díaz Machicao, *Toro, Busch*, pp. 112–13, 121.
[4] See, e.g. letter of Concordancia to Quintanilla of 29 August, in which they demanded elections in the briefest time possible and warned the army not to dictate its political choice to the nation. *El Diario*, 30 August 1939, p. 6.

warning Quintanilla that 'sufficient time has already transpired' for normalizing the country following the Busch suicide, and noted that the civilian political forces were growing increasingly restless over the delay in calling presidential elections. It also warned the junta to stay out of politics, at least as an independent force, and warned that it would not tolerate any imposed government candidate or régime for the coming elections.[1] When this broad warning produced no effect except a promissory letter from Quintanilla,[2] the Concordancia passed an official proclamation demanding the immediate return to a functioning constitution, the calling of formal elections without delay, and finally proposed a national unity slate of one candidate, such as had occurred in 1930.[3]

Faced with tremendous Concordancia pressure on this issue, as well as general hostility from the reformist and radical left to his continuance in office, Quintanilla finally recognized his inability to continue dominating the government. On 6 October he decreed the imposition of constitutional government by declaring the 1938 charter valid, and by issuing a call for congressional and presidential elections for the coming March, 1940. These elections were for a four-year constitutional government, and incidentally abolished the still existent tenure of the dissolved constitutional convention of 1938.[4]

Once defeated on the issue of retaining his hard won post, Quintanilla quickly revealed his conservative tendencies, and began to accept full dictation in basic policy from the Concordancia. Now that all immediate threat from the Busch supporters against the new government had been eliminated, the Quintanilla régime rapidly started to dismantle the military socialist programme. One of his first new cabinet appointments had been Alberto Ostria Gutiérrez, who had publicly broken with the Busch government over the 7 June decree and Busch's nationalization of the central bank. And although Ostria Gutiérrez insisted on his loyalty to Busch's memory, his appointment was the first portent of things to come.[5] While Fernando Pou Mont

---

[1] *El Diario*, 23 September 1939, p. 6.
[2] See *El Diario*, 24 September 1939, p. 6. [3] *El Diario*, 5 October 1939, p. 6.
[4] *El Diario*, 7 October 1939, pp. 6, 7. [5] *El Diario*, 1 September 1939, p. 6.

was still proclaiming as late as 29 August that the new government would put the 7 June decree into effect, this was an empty gesture. In September and October the government issued decrees which in fact wiped out all the requirements of the 100 per cent divisas law.[1] Also, key men of the last Busch cabinet quickly left the government. First to go was Carlos Salinas Aramayo, and then in September came the resignation of the minister of government, Vicente Leyton, over the decision to dismantle the dictatorship machinery.[2] Finally, throughout the month of September, Quintanilla met with leading miners and hacendados and increasingly his government began to authentically reflect the interests and tone of this oligarchic class.

As Quintanilla drifted sharply to the right, his apparent successor, Bilbao Rioja, began to show strong and unmistakable signs of moving to the left. A supporter of the Quintanilla takeover, which was carried out with his help and that of Colonel Ichazo, Bernardino Bilbao Rioja was nevertheless a liberal figure, very much in the Busch tradition. A young pilot officer at the opening of the conflict, he had risen to a generalship by the end, after showing unusual ability in making the Bolivian air force dominant in the Chaco skies, as well as proving his ability as a leading infantry officer. With as distinguished a war record as Busch, Bilbao Rioja also had similar mild leftist leanings and considered himself a full-fledged member of the Chaco generation group demanding reform.[3] Because of this background, it was inevitable that Bilbao Rioja would instinctively reach out for support from the same groups which had allied themselves with the military socialist régime, and that in their turn these groups would render him unqualified allegiance.

After the first weeks of inactivity, this is exactly what Bilbao Rioja set out to do. Quickly and effectively he took up the mantle of the fallen president and began to use the same public language of reform and a new Bolivia. In early September, before an enthusiastic meeting of the Legión de Ex-Combatientes, he

[1] Díaz Machicao, *Toro, Busch*, p. 130; Luis Peñaloza, *Historia del movimiento nacionalista revolucionario, 1941–1952* (La Paz: Editorial 'Juventud', 1963), p. 31.
[2] *El Diario*, 12 September 1939, p. 6.
[3] For an intellectual portrait of Bilbao Rioja by an eyewitness supporter, see Céspedes, *El dictador suicida*, p. 225.

initiated his campaign publicly by assuming the old Busch position of honorary LEC president, and delivered an important
political speech calling for a furtherance of the goals of the old
régime.[1] An effective speaker, Bilbao Rioja evoked a warm response in the audience, which the conservative press justly saw
as a threat to the new position of the traditional parties.[2] Equally
impressive was the general popular support he received on a visit
to Cochabamba a few days later. The populace demonstrated in
unexpected numbers to greet the new leader of the left.[3] Not
only did Bilbao Rioja begin developing his popular support, but
he consolidated his leadership with the younger officers, and
began intensive discussions with men like Céspedes, Paz Estenssoro,
Alberto Mendoza López, and with the old-line Baldivieso Socialists as well as with labour leaders, to gain their support. Around
him there began a definite revival of the moderate and radical
leftist forces, and by early October the LEC, the labour movement, and leftist elements held a mass demonstration in La Paz
demanding a preservation of Busch's economic programme, and a
socialist government responsive to the demands of the veterans'
movement.[4]

The reaction of the Concordancia to the reviving power of
the leftist coalition which had supported Busch and to the definite
popular appeal of Bilbao Rioja was to turn against the Chaco
hero. Fearing a revival of military socialist rule, it went so far as
openly to attack the formerly sacrosanct LEC and began a massive campaign not only against Bilbao Rioja, whom it charged
with desiring to create a leftist dictatorship,[5] but against the idol
himself, Germán Busch. A few days after the LEC demonstration in La Paz, the Concordancia asked all veterans to disassociate
themselves from the organization.[6] And a few days later, when
Quintanilla issued the call for elections, the Concordancia took
the opportunity to issue an official manifesto under the signatures
of Argüedas, Canelas and Belmonte Pool thanking Quintanilla

---

[1] *El Diario*, 5 September 1939, p. 7, and 10 September 1939, p. 8.
[2] See, e.g. *El Diario*, 11 October 1939, pp. 6, 8.
[3] Díaz Machicao, *Toro, Busch*, p. 127; Aquiles Vergara Vicuña, *Bernardino Bilbao Rioja, vida y hechos* (La Paz: Imprenta Unidas, 1948), pp. 502–6.
[4] *El Diario*, 13 October 1939, p. 7.
[5] Vergara Vicuña, *Bilbao Rioja*, pp. 508–9.   [6] *El Diario*, 14 October 1939, p. 7.

'for having liberated Bolivia from the chaos and oppression' of the previous demagogic and radical government.[1]

Nor was Quintanilla slow in replying to this open endorsement of his anti-Busch actions. On 16 October he asked the Concordancia to draw up a united slate for congress and the presidency, implying government endorsement of these candidates.[2] The last masks of impartiality of the government were completely abandoned on the night of 26 October when the president, with the aid of Colonel Ichazo, succeeded in kidnapping the popular Bilbao Rioja and shipping him into exile. In a rather crude but effective move, Bilbao Rioja was called to the presidential palace for a special meeting on that evening, and once inside was beaten senseless and spirited away in the dark to the rail centre of Viacha, and by morning was in exile in Chile.[3] The government meanwhile declared a state of siege and announced that it had discovered a plot led by Bernardino Bilbao Rioja, and had therefore been forced to exile him.[4] But the removal of the unquestioned presidential candidate and most popular political figure since the death of Busch was not that easy to resolve. Upon the news of the abduction a large percentage of the army rose in revolt under the leadership of Bernardino's brother, who was head of the Colegio Militar. While the rebels soon had the full support of the cadets, the air and communications branches, enough of the army remained loyal for their attempt to be soon frustrated. For a time both sides quietly manœuvred and countermanœuvred. But the rebels, though a powerful group, were incapable of overthrowing the government without a full-scale resort to violence, and rather than carry on to that stage, they ended by agreeing to negotiate. Quintanilla supposedly promised the return of Bernardino Bilbao Rioja to La Paz within the month, but once the rebels had laid down their arms, this promise was broken and all the rebel leaders were forced to seek diplomatic asylum.[5]

In this key showdown within the army, a clear division was

[1] Díaz Machicao, *Toro, Busch*, p. 133.
[2] *El Diario*, 17 October 1939, p. 6.
[3] Vergara Vicuña, *Bilbao Rioja*, pp. 516ff.; Céspedes, *El dictador suicida*, pp. 224–6.
[4] *El Diario*, 28 October 1939, p. 6.
[5] Céspedes, *El dictador suicida*, pp. 226–8; *El Diario*, 29 October 1939, p. 6.

revealed between the young reformers and radicals on the one side and the older conservative officers on the other, over the issue of continuing the military reformist régimes or returning the government to the civilian oligarchy. The effective collapse of the pro-Bilbao Rioja revolt therefore represented a return of the army to the leadership of the older upper-rank officers, many of whom held high positions even before the Chaco War and who had temporarily lost control to the new younger officers in the period from 1934–9. This shift of power was shown not only by the defeat of the rebel officers, but also by the shift of some key middle-ground leaders, the most important of whom was Enrique Peñaranda. When the minister of defence resigned in protest against the abduction, General Enrique Peñaranda replaced him in that post as a now staunch Quintanilla supporter.[1]

The Concordancia was quick to congratulate the government on its fine action against the 'radical' Bilbao Rioja, and also announced their warm support for Peñaranda and the decision he had made during the crisis.[2] This warm support soon turned into open endorsement of Peñaranda as the official candidate of the Concordancia for the presidency, an endorsement which was supported by a fair proportion of the moderate left who still felt that Peñaranda might be sympathetic to their position.[3] By December, when the state of siege was lifted, Peñaranda emerged as the only leading contender for the office and had the backing not only of the Concordancia, and the army, but also of the moderate left, and it appeared that he would be the *candidato único*, much like Salamanca ten years before.

But while the moderate leftist movement was lulled into a false sense of security, the radical left quickly recognized the meaning of Quintanilla's acts in support of the resurgence of the oligarchic power élite. Early in the new year, the by now radical university student movement, the FUB, felt strong enough to proclaim its own candidate in opposition to the candidatura única of Peñaranda. They selected the Cochabamba professor of law and sociology, José Antonio Arze.

[1] Díaz Machicao, *Toro, Busch*, p. 138. [2] *El Diario*, 4 November 1939, p. 7.
[3] For Concordancia support see *El Diario*, 2 December 1939, p. 6; and for the support of the moderate Partido Socialista and Partido Republicano Socialista Antipersonalista see *El Diario*, 26 November 1939, p. 6.

Having lived in exile since his forceful expulsion by Toro, Arze had organized a powerful leftist movement from Chile toward the end of the Busch period in early 1939. Called the *Frente de Izquierda Boliviano* (FIB), this organization was composed of the old Grupo Izquierda of Cochabamba, and as such represented the most advanced Marxist group in the Bolivian political spectrum. Essentially isolated from the governments of military socialism, these extreme leftists had supported the more radical acts of these régimes while deploring their pseudo-socialism and lack of true radical organization. Thoroughly distrustful of Toro and Busch, they nevertheless were incapable of generating national support because of the great appeal of these moderate leaders. But the death of Busch had changed all this. As the FIB noted in its programme, 'before the dangerous regrouping of the right in the Concordancia, the most urgent need of the masses in this hour is to unify themselves into a powerful movement and to form a party of their own . . .'[1] It called for a party incorporating the two million Indian peasants, as well as the working and middle classes, to be based on Marxian-socialist ideology and the principles of historical materialism. Although it represented the closest thing to a Communist party since the ephemeral secret communist cell of the early 1930s, the FIB nevertheless proclaimed 'that it has full national sovereignty to formulate its programme, structure its organization and adopt its tactics of struggle' and that 'it is an organization without affiliation to any political International'. It also proclaimed itself a party in defence of legal institutions, and opposed to revolutionary action against democratic governments. 'We want,' said its programme, 'legal government in order to enlighten the people about the social realities of our country, in order to discipline them in a powerful mass movement', so that they may peacefully attain their goals.[2] In short, the radical left now felt powerful enough to seek full expression as a civilian political party engaging in an open electoral struggle for power.

The first action of the FIB after its initial organization in Chile in April 1939, was to set up a functioning party committee in

---

[1] Frente de Izquierda Boliviano (FIB), *¡Hacia la unidad de las izquierdas bolivianas!* (Santiago: Talleres Gráficos 'Gutenberg', 1939), p. 10.   [2] *Ibid.* p. 11.

Cochabamba, which met in June 1939 to form a 'petit comité'. Under instructions from the exiled leadership, this committee called for a national organizing leftist congress to meet in Oruro in the early part of 1940.[1] With the return of constitutional government and preparation for the election, José Antonio Arze came back from Chile in early February to help prepare, at a special meeting at La Paz, for the Oruro congress. In an interview with *El Diario*, he indicated his pleasure with his nomination by the FUB for the presidency, but felt that the time was not propitious since the country still lacked a mass party.[2] In the La Paz conference which was held a few days after his arrival, Arze brought together the FIB, the important Frente Popular of Potosí, the FUB and various regional leftist groups, all of whom eventually signed a pact of unity. For the immediate issue of the coming elections, they agreed to run candidates independently and not to support any official candidate. At this point, they still felt that they could not run a presidential candidate and decided to abstain from the presidential race.[3]

But very shortly after these La Paz conferences, in which labour unions also took a prominent part,[4] José Antonio Arze and his supporters decided that he would run for the presidency even though a full-scale party of the left had yet to be organized. An unknown figure nationally, Arze was standing for elected office for the first time. Campaigning for only a few weeks, and with only the backing of the FIB, the FUB and other scattered radical groups, he presented himself as the sole opposition candidate to the popular war hero General Peñaranda, who had the complete support of both the traditional right and the entire post-war moderate reformist movement. Nevertheless, to the genuine surprise of the traditional politicians, this previously unknown figure, without a national political organization and with virtually no newspaper support, still obtained 10,000 out of the 58,000 votes cast by the literate and propertied upper and middle-class white and cholo electorate.[5] In other words, 10,000 among

---

[1] Frente de Izquierda Boliviano (FIB), p. 3.   [2] *El Diario*, 13 February 1940, p. 6.
[3] *El Diario*, 14 February 1940, p. 4, and 21 February 1940, p. 12.
[4] See, e.g. *La Calle*, 27 February 1940, p. 5.
[5] *El Diario*, 12 March 1940, p. 17, for early returns; Céspedes, *El dictador suicida*, p. 231.

the most important elements of the oligarchy's political base had deserted the old order and had not only rejected the moderate reformist position as an alternative, but had adopted the most radical position possible! This hard core figure of 10,000 literate supporters of the radical left demonstrated the impact of the Chaco War on Bolivian society in concrete terms, and the numbers of these radicalized middle class elements increased with each passing year.

As for the congressional elections, the hopes of the oligarchy which wished to obliterate the 1936–9 period were even more badly frustrated. For while the senate was taken over by the traditional politicians, they lost the chamber of deputies to the left, and a left that included such radical figures as Tristán Marof, Ricardo Anaya and Abelardo Villalpando, the latter being elected the chamber's vice-president.[1] Thus even in an open election, with a restricted electorate, and the tacit support of the government, the Concordancia was still unable to wipe out the effects of the rule of military socialism. The changes of the post-Chaco era had embedded themselves deep into the political conscience of the Bolivian middle classes.

But at first the Concordancia refused to see the full meaning of the 1940 elections, and it joyfully deluded itself into believing that Quintanilla had saved the old order.[2] On 12 April Quintanilla read his farewell address to the newly elected congress, and in honour of his services the Concordancia pushed through congress the elevation of General Quintanilla to the rank of marshal. This was an extraordinary action and clearly indicated that the right firmly believed that Quintanilla had really saved it from a red terror. For in the history of the republic, only two other men had been named marshal, Sucre the founder, and Santa Cruz the great liberal caudillo. Since their time no person had been thought worthy of such a title, and on the face of it Quintanilla had even less claim than others to such a distinction, considering his

---

[1] *El Diario*'s estimates for the senate were: 6 Liberals, 9 Socialist Republicans and 4 Genuino Republicans (Concordancia—19), and 8 Socialists and Independents. In the chamber of deputies the figures were: 20 Socialists, 15 Independents (almost all moderate to radical leftists), 4 PSOB (Marof's party), for a total of 39 on the left as opposed to 34 Concordancia deputies (17 Republican Socialists, 9 Genuino Republicans and 8 Liberals). *El Diario*, 13 March 1940, p. 7.
[2] See, e.g. *El Diario*, 12 March 1940, p. 11.

absolutely miserable and undistinguished war record. But while Quintanilla may have been a poor military general, for the oligarchy he had proved a great political general in time of peace, and for this the Concordancia honoured him with the highest reward possible.

Nevertheless for all its joyful confidence in the future, the Bolivian oligarchy had not killed the hydra-headed movement that had been born in the sands of the Chaco. Their triumph over Busch was only to be short-lived and their temporary reactionary government only encouraged the rapid maturation of the long adolescent modern Bolivian left.

THE RISE OF THE NATIONAL LEFT

With the election of General Enrique Peñaranda, the frenetic age of military socialist and reactionary governments came to an end, and the pattern of civilian parliamentary government again appeared to prevail. But this interlude of representative government was to be only a short period of peace before the total collapse of the traditional system. It was also to be a crucial time in the formation of the great radical parties of the contemporary period.

Following the surprisingly free elections of the Quintanilla government, the Concordancia, though losing the congress, gained the presidency. But General Peñaranda was a very poor instrument of oligarchic control, for he was an essentially passive figure who neither fully supported nor rejected the tremendous developments which were occurring around him. A supporter of all causes, without fixed ideology or conviction, he was ruled by the moment, and when the forces of the left proved more potent than those of the right, he accepted them as readily as the former. Of very limited education, he was nevertheless a neutral and unusually tolerant figure in national politics, and under his régime the work of undermining the traditional parties, which had begun with the Toro régime, was completed.

In early April of 1940, as congress opened its preliminary sessions, Peñaranda began organizing his first cabinet. As was to be expected, he brought the Concordancia fully into his government, giving Alcides Argüedas the ministry of agriculture and immigration, and the Republican Socialist Edmundo Vázquez the finance ministry.[1] The new finance minister proclaimed himself in favour of monetary stabilization as the only cure for inflation, and thereby created a great stir in national

---

[1] *El Diario*, 11 April 1940, p. 6.

political circles.[1] But along with conservative money management, the government also boldly announced a four-year plan for economic development. The plan had twenty-seven points, and called for large increases in roads, power and communications, for the modernization of the railway system and for a great drive in agriculture to achieve self-sufficiency in food staples. The *Plan de Resurgimiento Nacional*, if carried out, would have constituted a serious programme of economic development, but it required a large amount of finance, from both domestic and foreign lenders. The government was counting on the United States government in particular for foreign capital.[2]

The preliminary sessions of congress quickly revealed the ability of the moderate and radical left to work together and overcome the Concordancia minority. This coalition, in the debates over credentials, succeeded in admitting several more radical leftists, among them the notorious Fernando Siñani of Potosí.[3] After the initial trends became clear, congress went into recess until its first full sessions in August.[4]

In this interim period, the Peñaranda government began to define its attitude on both internal and international policy. In this latter area, one of its first acts was definitely to end all further Jewish immigration and cancel colonization contracts with various Jewish agencies, thus bringing to an end the whole Busch immigration programme.[5] Next it showed itself in favour of immediate cooperation with the United States. Taking cognizance of the European war and the beginnings of massive United States aid in the forms of lend-lease, arms sales and long term basic commodity purchases, the Peñaranda government expressed interest in direct alliance. But despite this expressed interest, the United States Department of State initially refused all offers of cooperation, maintaining that no terms on any issue could be reached until the Standard Oil claims were accounted for. While more sympathetic to these claims than the Toro or Busch régimes, the Peñaranda government was severely hampered

---

[1] *El Diario*, 21 April 1940, pp. 6, 7. For Vázquez's own view of the monetary aims of his administration, see Edmundo Vázquez, *Enderecemos nuestra ruta* (Buenos Aires: n.p., 1946), pp. 114–18.
[2] *El Diario*, 14 April, 1940, pp. 6, 12.   [3] *El Diario*, 23 April 1940, p. 6.
[4] *El Diario*, 10 May 1940, p. 6.   [5] *Ibid.*, and *El Diario*, 3 May 1940, p. 6.

in its freedom of action on the issue. For general public opinion, both of the right and the left, refused to permit the return of the American oil company, and even more importantly, protested against any suggestion of indemnification for any sum.[1] Thus the major task of the Peñaranda government in international relations came to be that of forcing the United States to negotiate without first resolving the Standard Oil issue.[2]

But not all Bolivians supported the government's desire for cooperation with the United States, or its pro-Allied position on the European war. From the late 1930s onward, the moderate socialist paper *La Calle* had come out strongly in favour of the Axis powers on the grounds of defence against the great Anglo-Yankee-Judaic imperialist peril. Under the leadership of Augusto Céspedes and Carlos Montenegro, *La Calle* rejected its moderate Baldivieso socialist origins, and began to promote the formation of a 'national' socialist movement, modelled along the lines of the European parties. Forming into ephemeral groups of independent socialist parties in the period after the breakup of the Baldivieso Socialists, these more radical 'national' socialists gained some coherence at the convention of 1938, calling themselves the *Partido Socialista Independiente* and grouped themselves around the powerful *La Calle*, which came to represent their basic position.[3]

Sensing the new possibilities under the tolerant Peñaranda government, and realizing the need to counter both the resurgence of the Concordancia and the rise of the far left under José Antonio Arze, these national socialists now began to organize themselves into a national mass party under the leadership of the

---

[1] For such an attack see, e.g. *La Calle*, 10 July 1940, p. 5.
[2] Foreign Minister Ostria Gutiérrez points out that he and Under-Secretary Sumner Welles at the first Pan American Conference of Foreign Ministers which met in Panama in September 1939 had reached an understanding in principle on trade and aid plans between the two republics, but that when Welles solicited Washington for permission to sign a formal agreement, Hull refused on the grounds that Standard was the *sine qua non* of all negotiations. Alberto Ostria Gutiérrez, *Una obra y un destino. La política internacional de Bolivia después de la guerra del Chaco* (2nd ed.; Buenos Aires: Imprenta López, 1953), pp. 384–5; also see US Department of State, *Foreign Relations of the United States, Diplomatic Papers, 1939* (5 vols.; Washington: Government Printing Office, 1957), v, 316–22.
[3] Peñaloza, *Historia del MNR*, pp. 37–8.

independent congressional deputies. Triggered off by the government's pro-Allied position, by the dismantling of the Busch economic programme, and by the leftist majorities in the new congress, the deputies Rafael Otazo, Víctor Paz Estenssoro, Germán Monroy Block, Fernando Iturralde Chinel and Atilio Malino Pantoja joined with such intellectuals as Céspedes and Carlos Montenegro to form a party nucleus from almost the first sessions of the regular 1940 congress.[1] Starting as a working congressional block, these men soon began to think of themselves as a unified party and by the end of the year the name of *Movimiento Nacionalista Revolucionario* began to become a popular term for describing this group, even though no formal founding congress had been held.[2]

Joining forces with the left wing of the congress on issues attacking the 'Rosca', the MNR group broke sharply with them on foreign policy. While such men as Víctor Paz Estenssoro always remained relatively vague on foreign affairs, referring to them only in terms of his national interests and his independence from foreign movements, others, such as Montenegro and Céspedes, formed a distinct wing of the party which took a strong pro-German stand on all issues. From late 1938 onward *La Calle* began using only German press sources and its headlines were filled with foreboding about the plots of Zion and the 'Jewish Wall Street Imperialists'. So frankly pro-Nazi did its editorials and news stories become, that it was generally believed by contemporaries, with some justification, that the paper was being heavily financed by the German embassy.

But in national affairs, the party, except for its strong hostility toward the new Jewish immigrants,[3] had an unusual leftist position, which sometimes overlapped into the radical leftist

---

[1] Peñaloza, *Historia del MNR*, p. 35, and Céspedes, *El dictador suicida*, p. 284.
[2] According to Augusto Céspedes, whom all authorities cite, the party was organized under Víctor Paz Estenssoro's leadership on 25 January 1941 (*El dictador suicida*, p. 245, and Peñaloza, *Historia del MNR*, p. 38). Its programme of principles however, did not appear until June 1942. See Movimiento Nacionalista Revolucionario, *Sus bases y principios de acción inmediata* (La Paz: n.p., 1942), which was written by José Cuadros Quiroga. On the role of Víctor Paz Estenssoro in founding the party, see José Fellman Velarde, *Víctor Paz Estenssoro: el hombre y la revolución* (La Paz: E. Burillo, 1955), pp. 77ff.
[3] In its programme of principles it 'denounced as anti-national . . . the manœuvres of Judaism'. MNR, *Sus bases y principios*, p. 41.

camp. Appealing strongly to middle-class elements, of which it was essentially composed at this early stage of its career, the MNR group advocated general social reform for the welfare of all citizens, but primarily emphasized a strong programme of economic nationalism. The major features of the party's policy were: 'Bolivianization' of natural resources; nationalization of communications; and, most important of all, control over the Big Three tin miners—though the party as yet had not adopted a policy of full scale nationalization. It declared that the MNR was 'the organization of the Bolivians for constructing their destiny in a Bolivia governed by Bolivians', and its goals were 'Economic liberation and sovereignty of the people of Bolivia'.[1] On the issue of the latifundia and the colonato, however, its early programmes were notably silent, nor was much real interest expressed in support of the organized labour movement. But the MNR did wax eloquent against the 'international' far left, and its position had a strong appeal for those middle-class elements who wanted reform and nationalism, but feared the lower classes and the radical leftists. Because of this, the new party in its early days quickly came to represent a vital if still relatively minor part of the political spectrum in national politics.

Of far greater initial impact and power, however, was the movement which José Antonio Arze was generating. Following the February meetings in La Paz, the FIB, with the Frente Popular of Potosí and many important labour leaders, began preparing in a thoroughly systematic way for the formation of a truly national leftist party. In May and June local regional conferences were held, and by July preparations were completed for the formal founding congress of the new party, to be held in Oruro on the 25th of the month. With more than 150 representatives from labour and all the radical leftist parties in the country, the Oruro congress was an historic event, for it marked the foundation of the first really national and effective labour-radical party in Bolivian history, the *Partido de la Izquierda Revolucionaria* (PIR).[2]

Led by José Antonio Arze and Ricardo Anaya, the two leading

[1] MNR, *Sus bases y principios*, p. 40.
[2] *La Calle*, 9 July 1940, p. 5; *El Diario*, 24 July 1940, pp. 4, 11, and 27 July 1940, p. 8; PIR, *Programa y estatutos del Partido de la Izquierda Revolucionaria* (La Paz: n.p., 1941), pp. 17–19.

Cochabamba radical intellectuals, the party established a national organization and issued its first major programme. Written by Anaya, the PIR programme of principles, and its sociological-historical introduction by Arze, contained a far more sophisticated statement of aims and policies than the excruciatingly vague and bombastic MNR programme, and at the same time represented the culmination of the whole stream of radical leftist and indigenista ideology that went back to the 1920s.

Disputing with those who maintained that Bolivia was too under-developed to have a class struggle, Anaya in the declaration of principles noted in refutation 'on the one hand, that the division of society into classes with antagonistic interests is a universal phenomenon, and on the other, that at the present level of the evolution of the world, no region is isolated from international developments'. Bolivia, he maintained, was especially involved because it is 'a semicolonial country seriously affected by imperialism'.[1] Thus it was ripe for scientific socialism and the creation of an advanced socialist party to resolve its class conflicts. Anaya maintained the by now classic definition of the far left, that Bolivia was ruled by a native capitalist class in the interests of the international imperial capitalists. Thus its local oligarchy, or 'Rosca' as Bolivians of all persuasions called this class, was a particularly unproductive and anti-national force, which had to be replaced in the leadership of the national economy.[2] The programme of principles recognized that in Bolivia there existed not only the classic economic class structure, but a unique social one as well, which often cut across class lines. While this created strong racial tensions, the key struggle was one of economic exploitation, and the PIR programme maintained that racial lines must not be made the barriers of social conflict. Only demagogues could profit by such racist conflicts, and rather than Indians versus whites and cholos, it should be the united front of the middle classes, the workers and peasants against the capitalists, regardless of race.[3]

This in essence was the theme endorsed by the majority of socialist-indigenista thinkers in Indo-America. In this sense, the PIR, despite its close affinities to a formal Communist party, was

[1] PIR, *Programa y estatutos*, p. 40.   [2] *Ibid.* pp. 40–1.   [3] *Ibid.* pp. 41–5.

still uniquely Bolivian enough to be rather isolated from involvement in and unqualified commitment to the issues and doctrines of the Communist International. Blending a very strong indigenista group (which wholeheartedly echoed the agrarian reform plans of Mariátegui), with a pro-communist wing of the party heavily oriented toward the international scene, the PIR was to maintain its identity as a truly national Marxist-Leninist party throughout the decade. It suffered reverses only when it permitted the international wing of the party and its sympathies for Russia to overcome the resistance of its more indigenista and nationally minded members.[1]

As for the international class struggle, it was logical that Bolivia, as a semi-colony of imperialism, according to Anaya, should partake fully in the struggle of other proletarian groups throughout the world. 'The revolution of the international proletariat for their own emancipation opens the road to the semi-colonial peoples to oppose imperialism; at the same time that all struggle for national liberation contributes to the defeat of the masters of the world.'[2] Thus the PIR recognized this as a common worldwide struggle, without prejudice to the interests of the national proletariat, and guaranteed that the party was independent of all international movements.[3]

Attacking the Bolivian fascist and nationalist movements, it maintained that it too wanted Bolivia's riches for Bolivians, but not for her native capitalists to continue exploiting her proletarian groups. The PIR's prime concern was the economic liberation of the lower classes and their full participation in the economic benefits of the nation, and the programme warned that the fascists and 'social-patriots', as it quaintly called the left-wing nationalists, had neither a sophisticated ideology nor a true commitment to the class struggle, but wished only to confuse and deceive the national consciousness.[4]

The constant reference in the PIR platform and in similar pronouncements of the MNR to other groups seeking the support of the lower classes is a remarkable indication of the great

---

[1] On the two groups within the party, interview with Ricardo Anaya, La Paz, 20 August 1963.
[2] PIR, *Programa y estatutos*, p. 45.   [3] *Ibid.* pp. 45–6.   [4] *Ibid.* pp. 46–7.

complexity of movements which had developed on the left wing of Bolivian politics. Prior to the Chaco conflict, there were few competitors for the minds and votes of the lower classes, but since the rise of the Chaco generation and the experiment in military socialism, the multiplicity of groups and ideologies, all issuing propaganda to the Bolivian masses, created a more politically aware and sophisticated working, artisan and urban lower-class consciousness than existed in the majority of nations in Latin America. After 1940, this incessant education, from the corridors of congress to the mineheads of Catavi, began to create one of the most politically committed labour movements on the continent. The newly aroused labour movement became fully committed to the political struggle with the foundation of the PIR, and until the middle of the 1940s the PIR was the chief political arm of organized labour.

In its immediate programme of action, the PIR called for full-scale agrarian reform, complete nationalization of the mining industry, of petroleum, the railroads and other means of transport. It demanded, as a minimum, the state monopoly of foreign commerce and encouragement of agricultural and manufacturing self-sufficiency and the complete processing of all raw materials within the country. It further demanded full economic planning by the state, 'socialization of public credit', and other measures to reorient the national economy in the interests of the economic well-being of the majority of citizens. In the more practical area it wanted free importation of basic consumer necessities and a national wage scale fixed to a cost of living index, a rather sophisticated innovation for Bolivia. In the political sphere it advocated, surprisingly, what it called a syndical-socialist organization for the legislative and executive branches of government. Much like Toro's early constitutional thought, the proposal was for parliamentary representation based on economic units of production, rather than geographical electoral districts. It called for a type of national executive committee based on the numerous technical boards, which would replace the existing system of public administration. It supported extension of the suffrage, but held back from giving the vote to the illiterate, asking instead that some administrative functions concerning peasants' affairs be performed by the illiterate peasants themselves in a form of limited autonomy and self-government. In deference to what it felt was the strong and justifiable regionalism of Bolivia, the PIR called for administrative decentralization, and local regional economic planning, especially for the oriente, with the aim of creating a unified nation. It expressed itself as a strongly anti-clerical party, especially on education, and proposed general extension of social legislation for all underprivileged groups. In international affairs the PIR called for national autonomy, exclusion of fascism, and alliance with all Indianist parties of Indo-America.[1]

Such was the initial programme of the PIR, proposed at the Oruro convention of July 1940. Embodying most of the themes which had dominated the radical left in Bolivia from 1920 onward, it amalgamated them into a coherent and forceful programme shaped by Marxian socialism, and carried forward by a well-disciplined party which had a firm basis in the labour movement and in the united front groups which existed in all the major urban centres of the nation. Given this unusually well-founded base of organization and the concurrent disorganization of all the traditional parties, the PIR suddenly became the single most powerful political organization on the Bolivian scene.

Because of its sudden importance, which was quickly realized by all parties, the founding of the PIR occurred amidst unusual violence. The convention met only long enough to found the party and prepare its programme. Before it could carry through formal convention endorsement, it was brutally dissolved by mob action under the leadership of 150 armed right-wing falangista youths who, with the obvious support of the government, had been transported to Oruro from Cochabamba. The youths stormed the convention and shot at PIR leaders. They attacked the local university as well as killing one worker. This was the perfect excuse the government needed: it declared a state of siege and imprisoned all the leading delegates to the PIR convention.[2]

---

[1] PIR, *Programa y estatutos*, pp. 64–74.

[2] *La Calle*, 28 July 1940, p. 5, and 31 July 1940, p. 4. This was not the first such action of the Falange Socialista Boliviana, for as early as May 1940 they had attacked a meeting held at the university in Cochabamba at which José Antonio Arze was speaking and succeeded in forcing the speaker off the rostrum. *El Diario*, 15 May 1940, p. 6.

But forcefully dissolving the founding convention and destroying the party were two different matters, and by the time congress reconvened in August, the PIR was a firmly entrenched party with a powerful congressional leadership capable of bringing great pressure to bear on the government. The government, however, still refused to accept the inevitable, and while it issued a general amnesty decree and an end to the Quintanilla-imposed state of siege, it specifically asked congress to exclude the extremists, referring to the PIR, from its benefits.[1] By mid-October, however, Peñaranda, under congressional and popular pressure, was forced to allow their release. He was also forced to accept the election of Víctor Paz Estenssoro as first vice-president of the chamber of deputies,[2] which was a major parliamentary coup for the left, and a portent of future parliamentary developments in the Peñaranda period.

While the left was organizing itself into national parties with stable parliamentary leadership, the Concordancia groups began to break up. As early as the preliminary congressional meetings of April, in the debates over temporary offices and credentials, the three parties of the coalition were noticeably fragmenting. The Republican Genuinos had only reluctantly supported the candidacy of Peñaranda, and because of their continued indifference to the new government began to clash sharply with the Liberals. In the growing split between these two parties, the Republican Socialists began to side with their fellow Republicans.[3] By the beginning of the new congressional term there was short-lived talk of a new centralist or independent party distinct from the Concordancia, whose aim was obviously to detach the more liberal wing of the Concordancia and the more conservative elements of the left, and amalgamate them into a balancing coalition against the two extremes.[4] But all such attempts were doomed to failure, as the left was now too aware of its own power and the weakness of the traditional parties to become submerged in such a centre party. With the failure of these attempts, the two wings of the Republican party began full-scale negotiation

[1] *El Diario*, 29 August 1940, p. 4. [2] *El Diario*, 6 August 1940, p. 7.
[3] *La Calle*, 6 April 1940, p. 4.
[4] See, e.g. *El Diario*, 2 August 1940, p. 7, and *La Calle*, 3 August 1940, p. 4.

again, primarily under the leadership of the senator from the Beni, Dr Enrique Hertzog, and by the end of 1940 and the beginning of the new year, the Concordancia had been broken, the Liberals put aside and a new all-Republican right-wing coalition temporarily organized.

With the largest leftist majority of any ordinary congress in Bolivian history to date, it was inevitable that the sessions of the chamber of deputies and the senate after August 1940, would become scenes of increasing attack and debate over basic government positions. Feeling their own new power for the first time, the left began systematic attacks on the government, forcing Peñaranda time and again to move toward the left, despite the Concordancia base of his government. In October a series of lightning mine shutdowns and a major railroad strike caused fierce debate in parliament.[1] Then in November several ministers came under direct questioning on such issues as mine workers' conditions, nationalization of the railroads, the negotiations with Standard Oil, and the financial policies of the government to deal with the inflation. Men such as Víctor Paz Estenssoro became leading speakers in these great parliamentary attacks and effectively forced concessions from increasingly distressed cabinet officials. Although many cabinet ministers wanted to suppress these bitter attacks, and talked of terminating congressional sessions, Peñaranda was strangely ummoved and would tolerate no direct muzzling of congress.[2] The minister of government, Joaquín Espada, did propose to congress a law of security and public wellbeing, reminiscent of Salamanca's old law of social defence, but this was so effectively attacked in congress by the left that the government dropped the whole matter.[3]

So intense did these attacks become that the Concordancia was

---

[1] *El Diario*, 1 October 1940, p. 7, for wildcat mine strikes, and *El Diario*, 24 October 1940, p. 8. The railroad strike was a perfect example of the new political situation. A total success, the strikers quickly gained firm support in congress from both MNR and PIR leaders, who were effective in keeping their case before the public and preventing the government from using force to break the strike. This close working relationship was to increase tremendously the power of labour against the government and initiated a new era of political party-labour cooperation. *El Diario*, 25 October 1940, p. 6, for congressional debate on the strike.

[2] Porfirio Díaz Machicao, *Historia de Bolivia, Peñaranda, 1940–1943* (La Paz: Editorial 'Juventud', 1958), pp. 34–40.   [3] *El Diario*, 3 February 1941, p. 4.

again fully revived in the early part of the new year. Though the two republican wings had temporarily merged in January to form the *Partido Unión Republicana Socialista* (PURS), thus leaving the weakened Liberals on the sidelines, they found that they could not effectively go it alone.[1] By March they signed a new pact with the Liberals, and with a regionalist oriente grouping known as the *Frente Unido de Beni y Pando*, to form an *Alianza Nacional Democrática*.[2]

While parliament was the scene of intense debate and political manœuvring from August 1940 until well into 1941, the government was deeply engaged in important diplomatic activity under the astute direction of the conservative diplomat Alberto Ostria Gutiérrez. At the same time as he finally resolved Paraguayan relations, Ostria Gutiérrez carried out a major offensive to open up the Bolivian oriente. Having previously completed agreements for the construction of a railroad from the Brazilian border town of Corumba to Santa Cruz during his tenure of office under Busch, in February 1941 he concluded an important treaty with Argentina for the joint construction of a railroad from Yacuiba on the Argentine border to Santa Cruz. This proposed railroad passed through all Bolivia's major oil fields, and provided for the preferential sale of Bolivian government-produced oil in the Argentine market to help pay costs.[3] In all of these railroad and oil treaties with her two powerful neighbours, both Brazil and Argentina tacitly recognized the legality of Bolivia's seizure of the Standard Oil fields, and when United States Department of State officials attempted to intervene in these negotiations, both nations rejected the intervention.[4]

As for the negotiations with the United States, Ostria Gutiérrez slowly but surely forced Washington to back down on its settlement of the oil issue as a *sine qua non* for full-scale cooperation. Threatening to sell to the Axis powers, and hinting of German subversion through the national socialist movements, Ostria Gutiérrez soon got results. By the end of 1940 and the beginning of 1941 Bolivia was participating in lend-lease negotiations,

---

[1] *El Diario*, 28 January 1941, p. 6.
[2] Díaz Machicao, *Peñaranda*, p. 46.
[3] *El Diario*, 23 March 1941, p. 6; Ostria Gutiérrez, *Una obra y un destino*, pp. 269ff.
[4] *El Diario*, 23 March 1941, pp. 288–90.

selling tin and wolfram to the Reconstruction Finance Corporation and working out military and economic missions to Bolivia.[1] Even Standard Oil was forced to recognize the strength of the Bolivian position, both diplomatically and economically, and by late 1941 it began to talk of a minimum cash 'arrangement', which in essence represented a complete victory for the Bolivian legal position on the confiscation issue.

But while Standard Oil was willing to make concessions, the Bolivian left became even more implacably hostile to the idea. In March 1941, the cabinet announced its desire to negotiate with Standard and also inadvertently revealed the contents of some rather harsh notes written by Cordell Hull in 1937 to the then minister of foreign affairs, Enrique Finot. The publication of the notes and the request of the government for senate approval of its right to negotiate touched off a major debate in and outside of congress and led to mass anti-government demonstrations. Although the senate finally gave its approval at the end of the month, the issue left a bitter aftertaste.[2]

On the internal scene a great debate was emerging at the same time over the government's desire to end the multiple exchange rate system in an attempt to resolve the inflation issue. The left severely attacked these proposals and created such internal tension on the question, that the cabinet was forced to resign. In a move to end the left-wing attacks on his government, Peñaranda now offered the ministry of economy to Víctor Paz Estenssoro, one of the chief critics of the single exchange system. But Paz Estenssoro was unable to influence the still Concordancia-dominated government, and after just one week, he resigned his position. The result was a further attack on government policy by the

[1] In November came the tin agreement (*El Diario*, 26 October 1940, p. 6, and 8 November 1940, p. 1; Ostria Gutiérrez, *Una obra y un destino*, p. 385), in May 1941 agreement was reached on an arms loan, and in August came a formal state department memorandum expressing willingness to provide economic development funds and an economic mission. *Una obra y un destino*, pp. 385–7; also see Bryce Wood, *The Making of the Good Neighbor Policy* (New York: Columbia University Press, 1961), p. 195.

[2] Díaz Machicao, *Peñaranda*, pp. 44–5; US Department of State, *Foreign Relations of the United States, Diplomatic Papers, 1941* (7 vols.; Washington: Government Printing Office, 1963), VI, 464–77. While the senate formally approved the government's negotiation plans, the chamber of deputies adjourned without voting on the issue.

MNR and the PIR, while the government decided to carry out the single-rate scheme.[1]

In the ensuing debate, the government was presented, in early July, with a much-needed excuse to crack down on Paz Estenssoro and his followers. On 18 July, the United States turned over to the Bolivian government a document uncovered by its secret agents. This was a letter supposedly written by Major Elías Belmonte, Busch's old minister of government, and now Bolivia's military attaché to the Berlin legation, to the German minister to Bolivia, Ernst Wendler. This letter described plans for a Nazi-like putsch in Bolivia to be carried out in mid-July. The letter also bitterly attacked the foreign policy of Minister Ostria Gutiérrez, promising radical changes in the metals purchase arrangements with the United States, return of the nationalized Lloyd Aéreo Boliviano airlines to German interests and an end to the Brazilian treaties.[2] The Peñaranda government acted immediately on this disclosure and closed down the MNR newspapers *La Calle*, *Inti* and *Busch* (all published in La Paz), expelled the German minister and imprisoned several leading MNR and fascist figures, all of these moves being fully supported by the Alianza Nacional Democrática.[3]

When congress resumed its sessions at the end of the month, the MNR deputies challenged the government and a major debate got under way. Led by Monroy Block, Víctor Paz Estenssoro and Fernando Iturralde Chinel, the MNR debated the veracity of the letter and the whole idea of the putsch, claiming that the state of siege and the closure of its papers were illegal acts.[4]

[1] *El Diario*, 21 June 1941, p. 5; Fellman Velarde, *Víctor Paz Estenssoro*, pp. 98–9; Peñaloza, *Historia del MNR*, p. 42. In actual fact, the intense inflationary crisis which Bolivia had been experiencing since 1935 began to level off during the period 1940–3. Because of the tremendous demand for tin, especially after 1941, and the inability to import manufactured goods because of World War II, Bolivia exported more than she imported. Monetary reserves, which were at only $5·8 million in 1939, shot up to $34 million by 1945 and the government was easily able to maintain the boliviano at 42 to the United States dollar throughout the entire period of the Peñaranda government and even after. Thus the cost of living, which had risen by c. 50 per cent annually in the Toro-Busch period, now levelled off to a 23 per cent yearly increase under Peñaranda, and almost stabilized at only c. 7 per cent annual increase from 1943–5. CEPAL, *El desarrollo económico de Bolivia*, pp. 62–3.

[2] This letter is reprinted in *El Diario*, 24 July 1941, p. 7.

[3] Díaz Machicao, *Peñaranda*, pp. 53–5; also Peñaloza, *Historia del MNR*, p. 43.

[4] *El Diario*, 26 August 1941, p. 6.

While the parliamentary coalition of the left, of which the MNR was tenuously a part, opposed the state of siege and the closure of the newspapers as unjustified acts, few members of the left were found to support the ideological position of the new Movimiento Nacionalista.[1] In fact, although the PIR was still willing tacitly to support the MNR petition, Tristán Marof and his PSOB followers used the occasion of the putsch debate to bitterly attack the MNR as a front organization for Nazi penetration into Bolivia.[2] In three days of acrimonious sessions Marof and leading movimientista deputies, such as Paz Estenssoro and Otazo, charged each other with 'selling out' to either German or North American imperialists.[3] By the 29th, the debate had created such a public stir that the chamber of deputies was forced into early recess and the expedient of using troops to clear the public galleries.[4] In the next day's session Otazo physically attacked the conservative Catholic deputy Levy, charging him with being a foreigner and a Jew, and using his fists to prove his point.[5] Although the end of the debate brought a vote of support for the government's action, the ultimate outcome was only a mild suppression of the MNR, which in a few weeks had reopened its newspapers and secured the release of all its supporters.[6]

Nevertheless, the debate over the putsch episode successfully indicated the deep feeling which had been generated within the national political scene over international developments. Never before in Bolivian politics had a non-Bolivian issue of foreign relations created such deep fissures in internal politics. Bolivia had easily sided with the Allies in World War I and been only moderately engaged in the issues of the Spanish Civil War. But the opening of World War II and the rise inside Bolivia of the falange and national socialist type of movements suddenly brought these issues right to her doorstep, and until these conflicts were resolved on the international scene, Bolivian politics

[1] See, e.g. the declarations of the PIR deputy Arratia, *El Diario*, 4 September 1941, p. 6.
[2] *El Diario*, 28 August 1941, p. 6.
[3] For a collection of these debates, see Tristán Marof, *El peligro nazi en Bolivia* (La Paz: Ediciones del Partido Socialista Obrero de Bolivia, 1941).
[4] *El Diario*, 30 August 1941, p. 7.   [5] *El Diario*, 2 September 1941, p. 7.
[6] For a government analysis of the issues in the whole 'putsch' affair, see, Ostria Gutiérrez, *Una revolución tras los Andes*, pp. 133ff.

would be continuously disrupted by developments beyond her borders.

While Marof's attack on the MNR temporarily broke leftist unity against the Alianza Nacional Democrática, this schism was healed a short time later by the increasing tempo of strike activity. In late September and early October strikes broke out in the Siglo XX mines of Patiño, and among the railroad workers. Although the Siglo XX mine strike was quickly resolved,[1] the railroad strike became a major issue. Both strikes were caused by workers' demands for new national pay increase laws. Under charges that the three-month-old single exchange rate system had sent the cost of living up 30 per cent since its initiation, the workers demanded immediate pay rises and threatened strike action if there was no response to their demands.[2] Concurrently the MNR and PIR both supported an immediate 10 per cent pay increase in congress, opposed by the forces of the right, and the government reacted by decreeing a state of siege. But the strike momentum was too great to overcome, and under the leadership of the Federación Ferroviaria de Oruro a short general strike in support of the pay increase law was carried out throughout the nation. Though the government imprisoned strike leaders and accused a communist-fascist alliance of generating the whole affair, the movement was so effective that the government was forced to release the strikers and to grant a 20 per cent pay increase.[3]

Despite their unity on the putsch issue and support of the government anti-strike action, the Alianza Nacional Democrática coalition began to run into serious difficulties by the last months of the year. The so-called 'independent' congressmen, who under the leadership of Gustavo Adolfo Otero had allied themselves with the three traditional parties, decided to pull out of the coalition and regain their independence in parliamentary debate. This move led to a cabinet crisis, since the Alianza was the chief group

[1] *El Diario*, 23 September 1941, p. 7, and 24 September 1941, p. 6.
[2] *El Diario*, 11 October 1941, p. 6.
[3] Barcelli, *Medio siglo de luchas sindicales*, pp. 151–4. The PIR and MNR even attempted to censure the government over its attack on the temporary railroad strike of October, getting together some 25 votes against the government's 52. *El Diario*, 29 October 1941, p. 4.

represented in the government, and ended in the formal dissolution of the group itself by early December.[1] This breakup of the coalition represented both the desire of the parties to go it alone in the coming congressional election of May 1942, and the continued instability of the rightist parties in the face of ever more effective parliamentary action by the left. Working closely together on the issues of defence of natural resources, opposition to a settlement with Standard Oil and full support for worker benefits and salary increases, the PIR, MNR and various independent socialist groups were beginning to wear down cabinet ministers and force resignations of key men. In foreign affairs especially, their combined opposition finally forced Ostria Gutiérrez out of office over his conservative position on metal sales and the oil issue.[2]

National political issues were temporarily submerged at the end of 1941 when the United States was attacked by Japan at Pearl Harbor. Acting in harmony with the majority of American states, the Peñaranda government quickly expressed its support of the United States government and granted it special treatment as a belligerent power. The government also froze Japanese and German capital assets in Bolivia on 10 and 11 December and openly announced its support of the North American cause.[3] *La Calle* and the MNR opposed these moves, of course, but the PIR officially endorsed the government stand and on 26 January called for the breaking of relations with the Axis powers and the elimination of the national fifth column.[4] Two days later the government carried out this action, breaking off relations with Germany, Italy, and Japan, and the next day passed an anti-subversion law which was designed to stop fascist activities in Bolivia.[5] Although *La Calle* and even *El Diario* continued to publish German-originated news stories about the war for several more months, by the middle of the year this source of massive propaganda had been successfully closed off.

Meanwhile, Anze Matienzo, the new foreign minister, continued Ostria Gutiérrez' policies and at the Foreign Ministers'

[1] See *El Diario*, 5 December 1941, pp. 4, 5.
[2] On the parliamentary cooperation of the two parties see, Peñaloza, *Historia del MNR*, p. 40. [3] *El Diario*, 12 December 1941, pp. 6, 7.
[4] *El Diario*, 28 January 1942, p. 7. [5] *El Diario*, 29 January 1942, p. 6.

Conference in Rio in January, finally reached a settlement of the Standard Oil dispute. Working quickly while congress was in temporary recess, the government agreed to pay Standard Oil the sum of $1,500,000 plus interest, for its oil maps and charts, in return for which Standard delivered these studies to Bolivia and agreed to consider that all claims outstanding between itself and the government of Bolivia over its former oil properties and machinery were resolved. This was a total victory for Bolivian diplomacy and represented the culmination of several years of astute diplomatic and economic manœuvring, which finally forced the company to back down from its original positions.[1]

On the internal political scene, however, this settlement was viewed by the various factions of the left, as well as the more nationalist minded right, as a rightist surrender to North American imperialism and quickly became a major object of attack in the heavy anti-government propaganda campaigns. For the internal political scene was now one of constant agitation, with relief coming only in the short periods during congressional recess. With the national parties of the left acting strongly in congress, the labour movement felt emboldened to seek even greater concessions from the government, and to press its demands as fully as possible. All this kept the labour-leftist party coalition in constant agitation against the government.

In January 1942 came PIR demonstrations against the government in Potosí over the issue of government aid to the city, which led to street fighting and to the initiation of a state of siege by the government.[2] Under cover of this emergency legislation, the government also decided, in late February, to crack down on a newly reviving political movement. This was Aguirre Gainsborg's old Partido Obrero Revolucionario. Under the able leadership of the youthful Cochabamba leader Guillermo Lora, the POR converted itself from a sterile clique of doctrinaire Trotskyites, into a powerful pro-labour movement with increasingly strong ties in

---

[1] For the negotiations leading to the settlement, and its full terms see Klein, 'American Oil Companies'; and Wood, *The Good Neighbor Policy*, ch. 7. Jorge Muñoz Reyes claimed that the actual value of the maps and geological surveys alone was several times more than the cash payment. Interview with Jorge Muñoz Reyes, La Paz, January 1961.
[2] *El Diario*, 10 January 1942, p. 7, and 13 January 1942, p. 6.

the mine fields.[1] Declaring that the POR was an affiliate of the Fourth International and was plotting the overthrow of the government, the Peñaranda régime on 22 February arrested its leading figures and confined them in detention camps. Chief plotter of the group, according to the government, was Guillermo Lora, who had just recently established a branch of this Cocha-bamba-based party in La Paz with thirty members, and whose aim was infiltration of the labour movement.[2]

But no matter how the government suppressed these leftist activities and rejected labour demands, the increasing strike activity could not be stopped. In early March the *Sindicato Nacional de Maestros* called out its biggest strike against the public school system, after some two years of short strikes and constant disputes over wages. Reacting harshly to this latest strike movement the government officially decreed the Sindicato to be an illegal organization and demanded that the strikers return to work immediately. But now that they were nationally organized, the secondary school teachers proved one of the most effectively disciplined unions in the Bolivian labour movement, and they continued to defy government oppression and successfully maintain the strike.[3]

Increasingly frustrated at its inability to control labour and to prevent the successful spread of radical ideology and growth of the new national leftist parties, the government began to adopt harsher measures. In April it issued an extremely stringent law of 'state security' which even the conservative parties feared would end all political discussion in the nation. The new decree began by declaring that it was necessary for the state to prevent and suppress 'all developments which tend directly or indirectly to undermine the social system, the political-constitutional régime, the economic régime, . . . private property', etc. It also gave the executive the right to draft workers and bring juridical action against strike agitators.[4]

But the reaction to this harsh dictatorial decree was so strong that the government was eventually forced to repeal it,[5] and the

---

[1] Interview with Guillermo Lora, La Paz, 20 June 1963.
[2] *El Diario*, 22 February 1942, p. 4.
[3] On the strike, see *El Diario*, 12 March 1942, p. 7.
[4] *El Diario*, 14 April 1942, pp. 6, 12.
[5] *Ibid.* p. 4, and *El Diario*, 14 August 1942, p. 4 for its repeal.

backlash from this opposition directly affected the May elections. For, branded an anti-labour and anti-left government, and accused as well of harbouring dictatorial aims, the Peñaranda régime and its supporters suffered heavily at the polls. In Cochabamba, a former Genuino stronghold, the Genuinos met almost total defeat at the hands of the PIR candidates led by Ricardo Anaya. The PIR also succeeded in increasing its control of Potosí, thus bringing its total in the chamber of deputies to six. The MNR also did quite well, especially in La Paz, and emerged with seven deputies, while a new amalgamation of old Baldivieso Socialists, now led by Carlos Salinas Aramayo, picked up a total of thirteen deputies and six senators.[1] This so-called *Partido Socialista Unificado* had been organized in June 1940, by José Tamayo of the old Baldivieso Socialist group, and Alfredo Mollinedo who controlled the remnants of Gabriel Gosálvez' old Partido Republicano Socialista Anti-personalista.[2] The most effective of the state socialist parties which had been attempted under Toro and Busch, the new PSU achieved only ephemeral success. For in the new age of the national left, men like Gabriel Gosálvez and Enrique Baldivieso, both of whom adhered to the new party, were too ideologically uncommitted and lacked a clearly defined programme with which to combat the successful MNR, PIR and increasingly powerful POR. Although the PSU did quite well in the congressional elections under Peñaranda, their middle position proved increasingly untenable, and by the end of the Peñaranda period, most of these men had been either reabsorbed into the traditional parties, or had become committeed to the PIR or the MNR. Of vital importance in the era of military socialism, they were incapable of surviving in the harsh, sophisticated, political world of post-1940.

The May elections also saw a shift in power within the traditional grouping, as the Liberal party succeeded in advancing its position at the expense of the two republican groups. But though the Liberals emerged with a total of twenty-two deputies, as opposed to eleven Genuinos and fourteen Republican Socialists,[3]

[1] For the congressional results see *El Diario*, 21 June 1942, p. 5.
[2] *El Diario*, 5 June 1940, p. 4, and 7 June 1940, p. 6.
[3] *El Diario*, 21 June 1942, p. 5.

the combined vote of all the traditional parties was quite small. It was estimated by *El Diario*, in an unusual post-election analysis, that the total number of votes which the three traditional parties gained in the election was only 14,163, while the parties of the radical and moderate left (PIR, MNR, PSOB, FSB, and PSU) received a total of 23,401—almost double the number.[1] Thus almost two-thirds of a literate white and cholo electorate, the very peak of Bolivia's narrowly pyramided society, cast their votes for anti-traditional parties who were advocating basic change of the socio-economic organization of which they were a part. Thus along with the presidential election of 1940, the uniquely free congressional elections of 1942 indicated the extent of the failure of the old political system, and the inability of the traditional parties, even under the most favourably disposed government and ideal conditions, to re-emerge as the dominant political force in the nation.

The loss of the 1942 congress to a powerful leftist minority also proved fatal for the Peñaranda government and marked another major turning point in the destruction of the old order. For no sooner had congress resumed its sessions in August, than the tempo of attack on cabinet ministers increased tremendously. Taking full advantage of Bolivia's unusual constitutional provisions for parliamentary rights of interpellation for the chamber of deputies, the left began a systematic attack on cabinet after cabinet and created a type of ministerial-parliamentary system under the ineffectual Peñaranda. The chamber refused to grant concessions or bills, unless given full authority to question and challenge every minister. The resulting attacks on ministers, who often lacked effective backing from Peñaranda, brought a steady stream of ministerial resignations in protest or under congressional censure. After months of opposition to his various negotiations over wolfram, rubber and tin purchase arrangements, as well as EXIM bank loans from the United States, congress finally forced Anze Matienzo out of the foreign ministry in late November 1942.[2]

But the removal of another foreign minister was only the

---

[1] See *El Diario*, 3 June 1942, p. 4 for this vote breakdown.
[2] Díaz Machicao, *Peñaranda*, pp. 73–4.

opening battle of a great anti-régime assault mounted by the new congress. This attack centred around the rising labour movement, for the fate of the Peñaranda government was soon made to depend on its reaction to the new organizational activities taking place in the Oruro and Potosí minefields.

As early as 1940, the various mine union locals had held their first national congress, and had unsuccessfully attempted to organize a national confederation.[1] Although this attempt failed, local union activity proceeded at a fevered pace, despite the open hostility of the Peñaranda government. Aided by the increasing alliances with the national political left which argued their cause in congress, these unions engaged in continual small strikes to achieve better working conditions. And despite the harsh government sabotage laws which had been passed after December 1941, to prevent stoppages, these groups were usually powerful enough to achieve some limited successes. In late November and early December 1942, a number of strikes occurred at the mining districts of Potosí, Catavi, Llallagua and Oruro. In response to these new strikes, the government acted with moderation and even sent the minister of labour Juan Manuel Balcázar to the mine district to negotiate with the workers. On 3 December a settlement of the Oruro strike was achieved,[2] and the same occurred at Potosí on 8 December.[3] The 9,300 workers at Patiño's Catavi mines however still continued to agitate, asking for Christmas bonuses and full enforcement of the Labour Code for local conditions.[4] Although the government had proved willing to negotiate with the Potosí and Oruro unions, it refused to deal with the *Sindicato de Oficios Varios de Catavi*, and instead sent troops under Colonel Cuenca to Catavi to keep the peace. Informed that the strike was illegal under the sabotage act, Colonel Cuenca proceeded to carry out harsh action of his own. When a peaceful demonstration was organized on 13 December to protest against the imprisonment of mine leaders, troops and police broke it up. Then after a few days of calm, on the morning of 21 December, miners and troops again clashed, only this time the soldiers

[1] Barcelli, *Medio siglo de luchas sindicales*, pp. 164–5.
[2] *El Diario*, 4 December 1942, p. 6.   [3] *El Diario*, 9 December 1942, p. 4.
[4] *El Diario*, 20 November 1942, p. 5, and 9 December 1942, p. 4.

opened fire and thirty-five miners were killed. Later that same morning, the women and children organized a mass demonstration with the miners. It was estimated that a crowd of 8,000 unarmed persons took part, demanding an immediate end to the shooting and peaceful negotiations on the issue. However, troops again opened fire, apparently keeping the crowd under rifle and machine gun attack for some time, and hundreds were estimated killed in what came to be called the Catavi massacre.[1]

Coming in the midst of increasingly effective labour unrest and the dynamic early years of the national left, the Catavi massacre had a devastating effect on the Peñaranda government. Having improperly handled the negotiation stage and encouraged a violent response to legitimate worker grievances, the government frantically searched for a defence of its acts. In the first hours of the Catavi demonstrations, it had declared a state of siege in the mining districts, and had defended its action on the grounds that illegal unions were agitating the workers and that extremist agitators were promoting violent anti-government action.[2] It upheld the Patiño position that the workers had no legitimate economic grievances and were instead actually plotting the overthrow of the government.[3] The government also began to search frenetically for a scapegoat on which to place the blame for the disturbances. Under the leadership of the minister of government, Pedro Zilveti Arce, the PIR, because of its supposedly close association with the infant mine union organizing drive, was singled out as the agent of international communism, whose immediate goal was the overthrow of the government. Even before the full scale massacre of the 21st, such PIR labour leaders as Waldo Álvarez and Fernando Siñani were jailed and the party newspaper in Cochabamba, *El Día*, was closed.[4] By the end of the month Zilveti Arce was desperately attempting to suppress the alarming rumours about the massacre by opening up a vicious attack on the very legality of the PIR as a national party, though

[1] Barcelli, *Medio siglo de luchas sindicales*, pp. 161–4. For the government version of the Catavi massacre see Juan Manuel Balcázar, *Los problemas sociales en Bolivia, una mistificación demagógica: la 'masacre' de Catavi* (La Paz: n.p., 1947).

[2] *El Diario*, 15 December 1942, p. 4.

[3] For declarations on this subject by the vice-president of Patiño Mines, José M. Rivera, see *El Diario*, 22 December 1942, p. 4.

[4] *El Diario*, 20 December 1942, p. 5.

he never officially outlawed the group as he had a right to do under Bolivian law.[1]

With the strike movement destroyed by violence and the workers forced back to the mines, the government also attempted to suppress all news of the massacre itself[2] But the disaster could not be hidden and the Catavi massacre became the most famous cause célèbre in the pre-revolutionary history of Bolivia. Although worker and peasant massacres were not unusual occurrences in twentieth-century Bolivia, the Catavi massacre occurred at an unusually opportune time for the left and the labour movement, and quickly became their most important unifying issue and revolutionary symbol.

By the end of December the news of the massacre had spread throughout the nation and on 30 December the MNR issued a public protest declaring that the Catavi strike movement had been a legitimate enterprise of the Bolivian workers against economic grievances, and had been illegally thwarted by the government and by Patiño Mines. It ominously warned the government that worker massacres would not deflect the Bolivian masses from their just goals.[3] Nor was the MNR the only party to attack the government, for on the 29th the Partido Socialista Unificada under Carlos Salinas Aramayo had officially resolved that 'The National Executive Committee of the Socialist party, in the face of the massacre produced in the mining centre of Catavi, where numerous workers have lost their lives, expresses its most energetic condemnation and demands that the government explain to the nation the motives and circumstances of such a mournful development'.[4]

For its part, the PIR, which found itself as the accused initiator of the Catavi 'subversive movement' as the government was calling it, denied all involvement. Reeling under the jailings of key leaders, and fighting off the charges of communist association made by the minister of government, PIR leaders did not produce an official reply until the first week in January. Denying international affiliation, subversion and responsibility for the massacre,

---

[1] See e.g., *El Diario*, 30 December 1942, p. 4.
[2] *El Diario*, 23 December 1942, pp. 4, 5, and 24 December 1942, p. 5.
[3] *El Diario*, 31 December 1942, p. 4.　　　　　　　　　　[4] *Ibid.*

the party then went on to declare in its protest to Minister Zilveti Arce, that 'we admit the justice which attended and attends the workers in their demands, we denounce the unrighteousness and unconstitutionality of the siege and the persecution of our party, and we condemn, with the greatest indignation, the massacres of December in Catavi, as the cruellest and most unjustified repressions of a hungry and undefended people'.[1]

Thus despite all the rationalization and pronouncements of the government on the Catavi massacre, the stage was set for a major attack on the government from the leading parties of the left, who in spite of their ideological differences, formed a powerful anti-government front on this issue. Notwithstanding the government's continuing attempt to isolate the PIR and charge it with being solely responsible,[2] this alliance of the left stood firm. In fact, so strong was their position and the general hostility of the Bolivian public on the whole issue, that even the traditional parties were temporarily forced to express their disquiet with the government stand on the massacre. On 19 January, congressional leaders of all the parties, under the direction of the president of the chamber of deputies, Demetrio Canelas, made a formal visit to the president on the Catavi issue, and on 22 January directed an official communication to the government demanding an immediate end to the stage of siege, and a full-scale investigation of Catavi developments. The communication warned the government that it wanted not only a full documentation of the events, but even more importantly, a formal trial of the government's action. Finally the deputies called for a government investigation of working conditions, especially the wages of mine workers, which an ILO mission had just pronounced as among the lowest in the world. This important letter was signed by Demetrio Canelas (Genuino), Angel Mendizábal (Liberal), Remy Rodás Eguino (Republican-Socialist), Francisco Lazcano Soruco (Socialista Unificado), Víctor Paz Estenssoro (MNR), Ricardo Anaya

[1] *El Diario*, 9 January 1942, p. 4.

[2] In an official circular to the prefects on 16 January 1943, the minister of government finally admitted 19 dead and 30 wounded, but defended the killings as self-defence against dynamite-throwing miners who hid behind women and children. The circular also blamed the PIR, which it described as 'a communist group' for the entire incident. *El Diario*, 17 January 1943, p. 4. Also see *El Diario*, 23 January 1943, p. 4, for later attacks on the PIR by Zilveti Arce.

(PIR) and Gustavo Navarro (PSOB), all either heads of their respective parties, or delegated representatives.[1] Although the Liberal and Republican Socialist parties eventually disallowed the authority of their deputies to commit them on this issue,[2] the document nevertheless continued to represent a powerful protest vote. It was in essence a rejection of the government's defence of the massacre, and it openly promised nothing less than a full-scale congressional investigation of the justice of the case in open sessions when congress reconvened in August.

The government reacted to the congressional appeal in a negative way, and seemed to feel that a continued attack on the PIR would deflect the intense opposition which had built up over the issue. Under Zilveti Arce, the PIR was all but outlawed, its non-congressional leaders jailed, its newspapers closed down and its activities harrassed in every possible manner.[3] But while the Catavi issue seemed to subside after the bitter congressional denunciation of January, it had not been resolved as the government appeared to believe. For the next several months the issue smouldered just below the surface of national politics, waiting for the reconvening of regular sessions of congress to erupt again with shattering force against the government.

Peñaranda for his part now felt secure enough to undertake a most unusual venture for a Bolivian president, and in March and April 1943, began preparations for a triumphal tour of Latin America and the United States.[4] Having committed his government firmly to the United States, the latest manifestation being the signing of a long-term economic aid agreement the previous December, Peñaranda was warmly supported by United States officials. In early April, United States Vice-President Henry A. Wallace made a formal state visit to Bolivia, the first of its kind in the nation's history.[5] During this visit the Peñaranda government issued a formal declaration of war on the Axis powers on 7 April 1943, and on 28 April it subscribed to the United Nations pact and ratified the Atlantic Charter.[6] In reciprocation, the United States formally invited Peñaranda for a state visit to the

[1] *El Diario*, 23 January 1943, p. 4.   [2] Díaz Machicao, *Peñaranda*, pp. 82–3.
[3] See, e.g. *El Diario*, 16 January 1943, p. 4; 17 January 1943, p. 8, and especially 30 January 1943, p. 4.   [4] *El Diario*, 24 February 1943, p. 4.
[5] *El Diario*, 5 April 1943, p. 4.   [6] *El Diario*, 8 April 1943, p. 4.

United States, and the latter hastily accepted this crowning achievement of his career. Making Waldo Belmonte Pool, president of the senate, interim president, Peñaranda in early May began a two-month tour of ten Latin American states, the United States and Canada.[1] The entire tour soon submerged local political considerations as the nation watched with pride the triumphal tour of its president. The only disturbance in this otherwise smoothly organized trip was a sharp public protest issued by José Antonio Arze from his exile in the United States. A visiting professor at Williams College in Massachusetts, Arze received good press coverage in Bolivia and the United States for his attack on Peñaranda and his accusations of dictatorial oppression. But apart from this temporary unpleasantness, all went well. In Washington Peñaranda visited President Roosevelt, signed the declaration of the United Nations, and was promised major military aid.[2] He also received honorary degrees from Columbia and Fordham Universities in New York, and was the first Latin American president officially to visit Canada.[3] On 5 July 1943, Peñaranda returned to Bolivia after his successful tour, apparently the respected leader of the nation and firmly in control of the country.[4]

But the surface appearances were deceptive. Among his own traditional supporters there was growing conflict over the choice of a presidential successor, and in August, with the opening of congress, the inflammatory Catavi issue appeared again on the front pages. In the first days of the new congress, no less than three separate interpellation demands were presented on this issue. The PIR, the MNR, and the Liberal deputy Mendizábal each demanded explanations and defence of the government's handling of the Catavi massacre in a formal congressional inquiry. These demands initiated the most intense debate in Bolivian congressional history.[5]

---

[1] *El Diario*, 1 May 1943, p. 4.   [2] *New York Times*, 6 May 1943, p. 8.
[3] *New York Times*, 13 May 1943, p. 5; 14 May 1943, p. 22, and 19 May 1943, p. 28.
[4] *El Diario*, 5 July 1943, p. 1, and Díaz Machicao, *Peñaranda*, pp. 85–9.
[5] For some unknown reason the official congressional digests (the Redactores) for the period 1940–3 are completely worthless, recording only a limited number of sessions, and excluding almost all floor speeches. The only contemporary records available therefore, are the La Paz newspapers. Fortunately these were so concerned with the congressional debates that they gave daily coverage and

The formal government defence before congress began on 18 August with the entire cabinet present, and from the first moments of this month-long debate, hatred and violence were expressed by both sides. The opening remarks were made by the PIR congressional leader Ricardo Anaya, who took this occasion to destroy the government's rather flimsy case against the party as a cause of the massacre. After attacking the wealthy anti-national companies and the poverty of the masses, the rising prices and the falling wages, Anaya bitterly concluded that 'in the present conditions of life, the conflicts between Bolivian capital and labour do not have to be invented by anybody'. He declared that the 'feudal-bourgeois' government 'has imposed order by massacre. It has obtained peace, but it has been the peace of the dead'. Its defence of the social order, a major justification of the government, was in reality the defence of a system 'which maintains the Bolivian people subjugated to its control', and is in fact nothing 'but the oppression by a privileged minority carried out against the great majority of the nation'.

These were rather revolutionary words for the halls of congress, and were a direct challenge to the government. If we are demagogues, cried Aanaya, for demonstrating to the people their misery and subjugation, then we accept the title. But 'there is only one real way to be a demagogue, to serve as a lackey for the companies who are strangling the country', and in the minds of his audience Anaya left no doubt as to who he thought had betrayed the people. 'The massacre of Catavi,' concluded Anaya, 'is one of the most horrendous crimes which is known in the history of the American continent and the chamber of deputies will fail to fulfil its duty if it does not severely punish those who have committed these crimes.'[1]

Minister Zilveti Arce was not slow in replying to the PIR attack. Still rather naively concerned with the PIR, he spent his whole time defending the government on Catavi by a rather obtuse attempt to prove that the PIR was founded by the Communist International and Chilean agents, all of which had nothing

reprinted in full all speeches, documents and votes of all the sessions. Also several parties saw fit from time to time to make up the Redactor deficiencies by publishing in pamphlet form the major speeches of their congressional leaders.
[1] *El Diario*, 19 August 1943, p. 3.

to do with the government's conduct of the Catavi strike. Amid constant interruptions from the public gallery, Anaya and Zilveti Arce brutally called each other traitor and liar, and the session ended with Zilveti Arce making his undocumented statements on the foreign origins of the PIR.[1] In the following session, the minister of the interior admitted his basic hostility to the new Labour Code, and his intolerance of criticism from the PIR, whom he labelled as foreign-controlled 'communists'.[2]

In all his bitterness to the PIR, Zilveti Arce only acknowledged his own basic political ineptitude. For it was from the nationalists and not the far left that his greatest immediate danger came. As even he admitted, the 'communists' were trying constantly to form a united front with the democratic parties, as was occurring throughout the world, so as to support the allied war effort. Anaya himself admitted at one point in his speech that the PIR had counselled worker moderation so as not to impede the flow of tin supplies to the Allies. But to the nationalists, the pro-Allied stand of Peñaranda could only be offensive, and they were unimpeded by such international considerations in their attacks on the national economic structure. Yet Zilveti Arce refused to see the realities of the situation until it was far too late,[3] and in antagonizing the only national party of the left which might have given the government some support, he drove them to the wall and made them willing spectators of the fall of the Peñaranda government.

By the third vituperative Catavi session most of the deputies were beginning to tire of the minister of government's personal attacks. Demetrio Canelas, past president of the chamber and head of the Genuino party, finally got up and stopped Zilveti Arce in the midst of one of his tirades. He demanded that the government specifically defend its massacre of workers and answer several important questions: (1) What were working conditions at the mines; (2) if the government had known that the PIR was so subversive since the early 1930s, why did it permit them to lead the workers at Catavi; (3) why did the government

---

[1] *El Diario*, 19 August 1943, p. 10.   [2] *El Diario*, 20 August 1943, p. 5.
[3] See his bitter post-mortem denunciations of the MNR in Pedro Zilveti Arce, *Bajo el signo de la barbarie* (Santiago: Editorial Orbe, 1946).

not meet with Catavi union officials when they came to La Paz seeking redress in September 1942; (4) and finally what were the findings of the Magruder Commission, which the government refused to reveal, concerning living standards of the workers? These were the vital issues, alleged Canelas, and not the personalities of the deputies.[1] This position was fully supported by the majority of deputies.

The rather shabby government position was meticulously destroyed by the Liberal deputy Ángel Mendizábal, when he began the second major interpellation. Mendizábal pointed out that in his early reports Colonel Cuenca had actually reported worker demonstrations to be of a peaceful kind. He also wondered how troops could fire into a crowd that the government had admitted to be over 7,000 persons for some time, without killing more than the admitted nineteen persons. He also expressed amazement that, when everyone agreed that women and children had been in the front of the crowd, very few were listed as killed or wounded. He concluded his presentation in the fourth session by stating that the workers lived in dire poverty and had a legitimate right to strike, and that only the government minister Zilveti Arce, and the labour minister, Balcázar, were responsible for the disaster. 'To conclude,' he declared, 'I believe that neither the people nor their delegates have any doubts that the only authors of the crime of Catavi are the ministers of government and of labour.'[2]

The interpellation debate then focused on the MNR and its petition. Leading the attack, Víctor Paz Estenssoro declared that it was not just the two ministers who were responsible, but the whole Peñaranda government which 'has shown obvious partiality in favour of the large companies in dealing with social problems and has employed violence in the solution of these problems, a policy which has culminated in the Catavi massacre'.[3] As to the social problems, he pointed to Inter-American and Magruder Commission figures on the low calorie intake of Bolivians, far lower *per capita* than even Paraguay, to the high rate of

---

[1] *El Diario*, 21 August 1943, pp. 4, 5.   [2] *El Diario*, 24 August 1943, p. 4.
[3] This entire speech is reprinted in full in Movimiento Nacionalista Revolucionario, *Víctor Paz Estenssoro y la massacre de Catavi* (La Paz: MNR, Servicio de Publicidad y Orientación Popular, 1943), p. 9.

illiteracy and low rate of school attendance and the total lack of a safe drinking water system in any city of the nation.[1] Paz Estenssoro also charged that Peñaranda was a tool of the Rosca since his election, and admitted that he and his party had not fully appreciated Peñaranda's pliant personality when they supported his candidacy. The Rosca, he claimed, had used the government to put down the workers, and Catavi was a perfect example of this policy. The company refused to negotiate with the workers, from the first petitions in September to the strike call in December, and when the workers appealed to the government to force collective bargaining on the company, the ministry of labour at the highest level refused to give support and finally ended by declaring that any potential strike would be illegal. The result was inevitable, declared Paz Estenssoro, given the government's firm support of Patiño, its claim that the strike was a political one and its dispatch of troops to the mine fields.[2]

But it was the labour leaders whom the government should have supported, he declared, and it was these men who were legitimately defending Bolivian rights by demanding higher wages from the big imperialist companies. 'The workers who are called social agitators [by the government] are the leaders who, because they have a little more native intelligence or know how to read and write, can give an account of what is happening in Bolivia, and of the exploitation of which they and their companions are victims. This work [of social agitation] is much more necessary in Bolivia, where the labouring masses are completely illiterate and ignorant, because the country is backward, because it is exploited . . . These workers do not commit a crime when they prevent their fellow workers from returning to work . . . They are really defending all the workers of Bolivia.'[3] As for the massacre, he strongly doubted the government's charge that the workers were using dynamite to attack the troops. 'How is it', he asked, 'if the workers attacked the army troops, and the troops only made use of their arms at the last moment, that not one soldier was either killed or wounded . . .?'[4]

[1] This entire speech is reprinted in full in Movimiento Nacionalista Revolucionario, *Víctor Paz Estenssoro y la massacre de Catavi* (La Paz: MNR, Servicio de Publicidad y Orientación Popular, 1943), pp. 12–15.
[2] *Ibid.* pp. 19–26.   [3] *Ibid.* pp. 40–1.   [4] *Ibid.* p. 47.

In response to the government attack on PIR, he declared that 'the conflict of Catavi is not a dispute between the PIR and the minister of government'. It is far graver than that, for Catavi represents the tragedy of our national economy and politics. 'What happened yesterday in Catavi, could happen tomorrow in La Paz, in Oruro, in all parts, where the workers driven by hunger want to better their situation.'[1]

> We, the deputies of the Movimiento Nacionalista Revolucionario are not simple commentators on the political situation. That is a task of historians. We are militant politicians, and we prefer to make history. For this reason, I declare, honourable representatives, that if General Peñaranda, and his ministers are not condemned for the massacre of Catavi, the Bolivian people will have riveted the chains of their slavery.[2]

The threat of the MNR was quite clear, that Catavi represented nothing less than an all-out government drive to destroy the labour movement, and that the MNR would if necessary help labour to destroy this tyranny. But the cabinet refused to be shocked out of its position of blaming the whole disaster on the PIR and thus forged the moderate and radical left coalition on labour.[3]

Finally on 10 September, after three of the most dramatic weeks in parliamentary history, the chamber of deputies voted on the censure resolution. Putting tremendous pressure on its deputies, the traditional parties represented in the government mustered barely 48 votes to the opposition 47, with 15 abstentions. This was a signal defeat for the government. From every major traditional party, despite the pressure of the leaders, there were defectors voting for censure or abstaining, while the left voted solidly in opposition. Of the Liberals, 15 voted with the government, 9 for censure and one abstained; of the Genuino Republicans the votes were 9, 1 and 3 abstentions; even Zilveti Arce's own PRS had two censure votes and one abstention. On the left the

---

[1] This entire speech is reprinted in full in Movimiento Nacionalista Revolucionario, *Víctor Paz Estenssoro y la massacre de Catavi* (La Paz: MNR, Servicio de Publicidad y Orientación Popular, 1943), p. 50.

[2] *Ibid*. p. 55; this speech was also reprinted in part in *El Diario*, 24 August 1943, p. 4.

[3] The régime even resorted to mob action against various parliamentary leaders. See, e.g. *El Diario*, 3 September 1943, p. 9.

Socialistas Unificados group had 11 censure votes, 9 abstentions and one support, the MNR, PIR, and PSOB of course all voted for censure.[1]

The reaction of the government to the vote was the immediate dissolution of the cabinet and a reorganization of the basis of government support. Juan Manuel Balcázar was eliminated from the cabinet, and in fact every other minister from the former cabinet was replaced except for Zilveti Arce and one military man. Members of the Socialistas Unificados joined the representatives of the Liberal, Genuino Republican and Republican Socialist parties. Their president, Carlos Salinas Aramayo, was appointed to the foreign ministry and another PSU member to the education post.[2] But, although the government was willing to bring in the moderate socialists because they split the vote, almost half abstaining from censure, their action on Catavi proved fatal for the party. For almost overnight the temporarily important PSU began to disintegrate, as members, from Baldivieso down, deserted the party on the Catavi issue, thus ending the very last of the reformist groups born of the post-war moderate socialist movement.

Having weathered the Catavi censure move, the government appeared to believe that the storm had ended, and the traditional parties began intense activity for the coming presidential elections. Throughout the rest of September and October the four parties which made up the government carried out a series of conferences with the support of Peñaranda which ended in a joint election pact of the Liberals, the two Republican parties and the Socialistas Unificados.[3]

But the other major support of the Peñaranda régime, the army, was strangely silent during this feverish political campaigning. It was suffering an internal power struggle of major proportions, with the re-emergence of a powerful younger radical junior officer movement. The first public manifestation of this conflict occurred in mid-November with the news of an attempted military overthrow of Peñaranda by the Cochabamba garrison. Instead of taking a strong government stand, Colonel

---

[1] *El Diario*, 11 September 1943, p. 4.
[2] *El Diario*, 14 September 1943, p. 4, and 17 September 1943, p. 6.
[3] Díaz Machicao, *Peñaranda*, p. 97.

Ichazo, then head of the general staff, temporized with the rebels. Although he warned Peñaranda of the attempt, he refused to reprimand the local officers involved.[1] For these officers belonged to the powerful secret military society known as RADEPA (or Razón de Patria). Organized among the junior officers who had been prisoners of war in Paraguayan camps in 1934,[2] this secret military lodge had slowly gathered strength during the military socialist period in the advanced graduate schools of war and artillery which Toro had established at Cochabamba, primarily among the young majors and colonels. With the overthrow of the 'socialist' radical officers in the fiasco of the Bilbao Rioja showdown, the lodge became the single most important ideological group within the army, and during the Peñaranda government it emerged as the decisive group in the still fluid army situation. Though some of its members, like Belmonte, had served with Busch, this group remained secret until 1943. During most of the Peñaranda period, the senior officers had held on to their regained positions with some strength. But the rise of the national left, the deterioration of the parties of the Concordancia, and Catavi weakened the hold of the generals over the army, and prepared the way for the emergence of this new group of younger radical officers. In late November seven junior officers representing the more open Logia Mariscal Santa Cruz, the political arm of RADEPA, formally requested Ichazo's removal from head of the EMG. Although Peñaranda refused this request,[3] and leading officers such as the defence minister, Candía, and David Toro warned of an impending military coup, neither the lodge, nor its more secret parent, were suppressed. This was largely because of their strength and because Ichazo and several of the other leading older officers hoped to use the group for their own ends (despite the fact that they were not actual members of the organization).

By early December, however, the signs of impending revolt were clear enough for the government to begin to take more

[1] Díaz Machicao, *Peñaranda*, pp. 100–2.
[2] Elías Belmonte was one of the earliest leaders of RADEPA. Interview with Colonel Julio A. Saavedra G., one of the founders of RADEPA and Belmonte's co-pilot who was captured at the same time, La Paz, 23 September 1961; also interview with the military historian Colonel Julio Díaz Argüedas, La Paz, 28 June 1961. [3] Díaz Machicao, *Peñaranda*, pp. 102–3.

drastic action, especially as congress had just ended its session. On 2 December, the municipal elections called for this month were temporarily postponed on technical grounds.[1] On the 4th, press editors were warned to refrain from making political comments, and on the same day war was formally declared on the Axis powers. Finally on the 13th, because of the declaration of war, a state security decree was passed giving the army virtual control over the nation and suppressing most civil liberties.[2] Under the new decree the government closed down the German Club and also stopped publication of the MNR newspaper *La Calle*.[3] Finally, hurried conferences were held in La Paz between Peñaranda and all the top generals of the army, such as Quintanilla, Toro, Felipe M. Rivera, and a host of others, where the main discussion was the issue of defections by younger officers and the possibilities of a prorogation of the Peñaranda régime. After four hectic meetings the generals apparently agreed on a joint position, and brought temporizers like Ichazo into line. As a result of these meetings, the generals decided that they would exile the plotting younger officers to distant garrisons on Monday, 21 December.[4]

By this precipitous decision, the young rebels were forced to act. Having appealed for and received support from the MNR, the lodge also asked Anaya and the PIR to join the revolution. Although the PIR declined to commit themselves,[5] the MNR wholeheartedly joined them, along with Major Alberto Taborga, head of the traffic police (Tránsito) of La Paz. On the morning of 20 December, Taborga's policemen captured Peñaranda, Hertzog, Zilveti Arce and most of the cabinet, together with Generals Felipe Rivera, Ichazo and others. By early morning troops had taken the National Radio and announced the overthrow of the Peñaranda government and the establishment of a military junta under the direction of the completely unknown officer, Major Gualberto Villarroel, in alliance with Víctor Paz Estenssoro for the MNR.[6] To the stunned surprise of the nation and the American states, the MNR thus came to power.

---

[1] *El Diario*, 3 December 1943, p. 4.   [2] *El Diario*, 14 December 1943, p. 4.
[3] *El Diario*, 18 December 1943, p. 4.   [4] Díaz Machicao, *Peñaranda*, pp. 107–8.
[5] Interview with Ricardo Anaya, La Paz, 20 August 1963.
[6] Díaz Machicao, *Peñaranda*, pp. 108ff.; *El Diario*, 20 December 1943, p. 1; Peñaloza, *Historia del MNR*, pp. 55ff.

THE COMING OF THE REVOLUTION

Though they were both now committed to a supposedly revolutionary programme, neither the MNR nor the totally unknown RADEPA[1] were certain how to achieve basic socio-economic change. The RADEPA was a secret service society without a defined ideology, but with a strong sympathy for a fascist conception of the social and economic organization of society. The MNR, despite its long years of struggle, still lacked a coherent programme. As for Villarroel himself, virtually nothing was known of him by the public at large. As even *La Calle* was forced to admit on 2 December, everyone was asking 'Who is Major Gualberto Villarroel?'[2]

Villarroel was not a war hero, and had not even played a major part in the internal struggles within the army during and after the Chaco War. He was born in 1908 in a small town in the Cochabamba valley, and received his primary and secondary education in the valley; in 1924 he had gone on to the Colegio Militar in La Paz. An able officer, he rose to staff position in the Kundt command during the Chaco War, and apparently resigned his position after the overthrow of Salamanca at Villa Montes. Although he was a loyal salamanquista, a position which did not indicate a radical future, he remained in the army, and after the war played a leading role as a military instructor in the new post-graduate schools of 'war' and 'artillery', where he then apparently became the key figure in the secret internal reformist movement known as RADEPA (or *Razón de Patria*).

Established in Cochabamba during the Toro government,

---

[1] Even the MNR leadership did not know the name or exact composition of RADEPA until after the coup. They initially dealt only with the Logia 'Mariscal Santa Cruz', which also included such civilians as Víctor Andrade and Hugo Salmón, who in their turn had belonged to the old *Estrella de Hierro* group. Augusto Céspedes, *El presidente colgado (historia boliviana)* (Buenos Aires: Editorial Jorge Álvarez, 1966), p. 113. [2] *La Calle*, 22 December 1943, p. 5.

these post-graduate schools had been a major innovation in the improvement of education for officers. It was therefore natural that the returning veteran junior officers would tend to gravitate towards these new schools, and there re-establish the RADEPA on national soil. Founded among the imprisoned officers in Paraguay, RADEPA included such early Busch leaders as Elías Belmonte. Nevertheless the party seems to have been quiescent during the period of military socialism, and revived only with the fall of the reformist military régimes. Virtually nothing is known of the internal history of the society during this long period, or even of when such non ex-prisoners as Villarroel joined the group. What is evident is that RADEPA by the first years of the 1940s was firmly entrenched at the Cochabamba schools among the teaching staff, with its membership almost exclusively made up of middle-rank veteran officers at the major and colonel level.

Under the régimes of Quintanilla and Peñaranda, RADEPA burgeoned and by the last months of 1943 it was powerful enough to reveal its identity within the army, at least to the point of becoming known as the 'Grupo de Cochabamba'. Its power was finally exhibited within the army when it began issuing demands to the general staff for basic changes in the army.[1] RADPEA negotiated with the MNR and the other parties, and finally became known to the public after the golpe of December. It later consolidated its position by absorbing the last of the secret lodges, that of 'Abaroa', which was made up exclusively of junior officers (lieutenants and captains) in 1945.[2]

The ideology of RADEPA was typical of the immediate post-war period. Its programme stated that the disaster of the Chaco was 'due to the decadence of the oligarchic class' and that 'the conservative political parties had no other end than the gaining and maintenance of power'. Proposing action against 'anti-nationalists' RADEPA had warned in its early programme that 'the basic function of RADEPA is to control the acts of the government and its collaborators . . . throwing the balance of justice toward the sacred interests of the patria and energetically intervening when it is necessary'. Vaguely calling for national control over the economy, it specifically threatened 'to control

[1] Céspedes, *El presidente colgado*, pp. 109ff.   [2] *Ibid.* p. 113n.

the political parties, orienting them towards national service, eliminating those of an internationalist tendency or those which spread anarchist doctrines'.[1]

The ideology of the MNR was almost as imprecise as that of RADEPA, even though the party was well known politically for some time. Although the MNR had long since outgrown its moderate reformist origins in the government socialist movement of the 1930s, it was still undecided on the specific form its radicalism would take. Though clearly opposed to the mining élite, and hostile to foreign economic intervention, it had no clear programme for dealing with these issues. In the Catavi debate it had championed organized labour against the mine companies, and though not an active unionizer like the POR or PIR, its warm support and obvious potential power drew many former POR and PIR syndicalists into its ranks. Nevertheless, the party still had a strong fascist wing which was captivated by the ideology of a corporate state and was unwilling to commit itself totally to a revolutionary socialist solution. As the opposition leader Ricardo Anaya clearly indicated at the time, 'in the programme of the MNR there is no clear, concrete and categorical affirmation on the class struggle nor on the form in which this struggle occurs in Bolivia'.[2]

Given the initial indecision of both the party, and more especially of RADEPA, the Villarroel government found it difficult to develop a basically revolutionary programme of change. Instead, it found itself following the lines of limited reform developed by the military socialist régimes of the 1930s and, if anything, with far less popular support than was granted to Toro or Busch. In addition to its strong fascist cast, the military junta as it was initially organized was heavily conservative. There were four RADEPA officers in charge of ministries, and two civilian allies (one was private secretary to the junta) who were officially members of the Logia Mariscal Santa Cruz. To these six

---

[1] Quoted Céspedes, *El presidente colgado*, pp. 111–12.
[2] This charge was made by Anaya on the floor of congress a few months after the coup, see Convención Nacional, *Redactor de la H. Convención Nacional* (4 vols.; La Paz: Editorial La Paz, 1944), ii, 1429. On the early ideological debates of the party, see Charles H. Weston, Jr., 'The Coming to Power of the Bolivian National Revolutionary Movement' (unpublished MA thesis, Department of Political Science, University of Chicago, 1965), pp. 32ff.

profascist and essentially conservative individuals was added one
political independent with close military connections. The MNR
had only three members in the cabinet (Víctor Paz Estenssoro,
Carlos Montenegro and Augusto Céspedes) and though it often
received the support of the old moderate Baldivieso socialist,
José Tamayo, who took the foreign ministry post, it was clearly
the minority partner.[1]

Even then, the MNR itself was not represented by its more
radical elements, since it initially gave predominance to the most
outspokenly fascist members of the party. This fascist wing was
led by the *La Calle* group of which Augusto Céspedes, Carlos
Montenegro and Armando Arce were the leaders. Although Paz
Estenssoro adopted a middle course, and supported such non-
fascist leaders as Hernán Siles Zuazo and Walter Guevara Arze,
to assuage RADEPA feelings he placed all the most rabidly anti-
Semitic and fascist MNR members in the government. Montenegro and Céspedes were both given cabinet appointments and
La Calle became the official newspaper of the government.[2]

But no matter how pro-Axis the Villarroel government may
have wished to be, the realities of international developments by
early 1944 forced it to recognize the supremacy of the United
States and the inevitable victory of the Allied forces. Utterly
dependent for the economic well-being of the nation on the continued export of tin to the United States, the régime proved
extremely vulnerable to outside pressure. Thus when the United
States and eighteen other Latin American countries refused to
grant recognition to the junta, except after an inspection of the
government by a United States mission and the subsequent
elimination of the MNR from the government, the RADEPA
officers were eventually forced to accept these terms unconditionally. They had first tried to placate American opposition by
eliminating the more fascist of the MNR representatives. In early
February, the military, in spite of objections from Paz Estenssoro
and Tamayo, forced the resignation of Céspedes and Montenegro
from the government on the grounds that they were the most

[1] Céspedes, *El presidente colgado*, p. 132.
[2] An excellent analysis of this division in the MNR is given by Charles H. Weston,
Jr., 'An Ideology of Modernization: The Case of the Bolivian MNR', *Journal
of Inter-American Studies*, x, no. 1 (January 1968), 88–95.

outstanding fascist leaders in the party, and even Céspedes later admitted that an important element of the party strongly supported their removal.[1] These two were replaced by Rafael Otazo and Walter Guevara Arze, who represented the non-fascist wing. But even this gesture was insufficient to win foreign recognition. As a further effort in this direction José Tamayo was replaced by Enrique Baldivieso, and finally in late March 1944 the three-month-old junta cabinet was dissolved and the three MNR ministers formally withdrew from the government. This ministerial reorganization brought immediate United States and Latin American recognition as well as long-term agreements for the purchase of minerals by the United States.[2]

The removal of the MNR was only a face-saving gesture, for the military men had now come to depend totally on the party for their ideology and for the organization of civilian support. The MNR continued to play the leading role in the government from March till its formal re-incorporation into the junta in the following year. Thus the initial alliance of RADEPA and MNR became a permanent development which lasted throughout the period of Villarroel's rule. The resulting régime was a strange amalgam in which the essentially unsophisticated officers were committed to senseless violence and the MNR to an initially timid but potentially far-reaching reformist programme. But though many basic proposals were advanced, especially in the area of Indian-white relations, the coalition government proved incapable of carrying them to fruition. Its experience with the military was so frustrating that the MNR eventually turned to the labour movement as a more hopeful ally, and its sudden championing of the rise of a national miners' federation proved to have a profound effect both on the ideology and organization of the MNR and on the future developments of a revolutionary movement. But for the moment the MNR was wedded to its officers and only moderately supported the organization of the mine workers which was being actively undertaken by the rejuvenated

[1] Céspedes, *El presidente colgado*, pp. 148–9.
[2] On the change of attitudes by the MNR see Ostria Gutiérrez, *Una revolución tras los Andes*, pp. 202–5. For the initiation and termination of the United States State Department diplomatic offensive against Bolivia, see the *New York Times*, 25 January 1944, p. 1, and 22 June 1944, p. 1.

POR under the leadership of Guillermo Lora and of the syndicalist leader Juan Lechín.

To give a legal base to its usurpation of power, the junta called into session a convention-congress and held formal elections for this body in June 1944. Despite its open support of the MNR, and the temporary jailing of PIR leaders, the powerful PIR did well in the elections and such party stalwarts as José Antonio Arze, Ricardo Anaya, and Abelardo Villalpando were elected to congress.[1]

But the régime and its MNR supporters were becoming less tolerant of opposition, and, frustrated at the ballot box, they resorted to new methods of control. In April, for example, the junta accused the opposition of attempting a revolt and jailed Enrique Hertzog and other leading Republicans, as well as Mauricio Hochschild. While such 'created' affairs were common practice for Bolivian governments, the subsequent beatings, which Hertzog and another leading upper-class conservative politicians received in jail, were not. Also the jailing of the formally apolitical Hochschild, and his subsequent disappearance for several weeks, were quite unusual. An even more ominous indication of the trend towards government repression was the attack on the PIR leader, José Antonio Arze. When all attempts to prevent his being admitted to congress failed, police officials, on government orders, attempted to assassinate him, fifteen days before congress was to meet. Gravely wounded, Arze was flown to New York in a critical condition. The nation was shocked.[2] Never before in twentieth-century Bolivian history had political assassination been used as a weapon by the government.

Thus when the 1944 convention congress finally met in August, it became a major battle ground for the PIR and the MNR, with the issue of fascism and government violence dominating all debate.[3] At the same time, the congress became a test of strength between the MNR and RADEPA, which the latter succeeded in

[1] Peñaloza, *Historia del M.N.R.*, pp. 67–9.
[2] Céspedes, *El presidente colgado*, pp. 152–3.
[3] See, e.g. the bitter debate led by Guevara Arze for the government and Anaya for the PIR in the September sessions of the 1944 congress, in Convención Nacional, *Redactor de la H. Convención Nacional*, II, 1041 *passim*. Anaya especially attacked the secret military lodges as 'a danger to the tranquillity of the nation', *ibid.* II, 1045. For more open attacks by the PIR on the régime see the two

winning, imposing its will on the party, which in turn became a subservient defender of all government action. Despite a bid by the MNR for representation in the executive branch of the congressionally-elected, constitutional government, Villarroel both imposed his own candidacy for the presidency and allowed Major Celistino Pinto, head of RADEPA and the EMG, to choose the vice-president, thus eliminating all MNR leaders from the race.[1]

But the strength of the party was actually growing outside the normal areas of governmental and congressional administration. Finding the opposition in congress bitterly hostile and effective, and seeing their role in the administration as heavily dependent upon RADEPA, the MNR sought to create a new revolutionary élan by working closely with the rapidly organizing movement for national mine labour. Already in the first days of the junta the MNR had secured the sub-prefect position at the mining town of Uncía for Juan Lechín, the most important mine leader in the movement. Lechín was the son of a Lebanese merchant and a Bolivian mother, and had received a classical middle-class education, attending the Methodist Colegio Americano in La Paz. He had been an above-ground clerical employee in the mines, and had become a well-known figure in the mining area through his football prowess. He had then moved rapidly into a position of leadership in the mines.[2]

Under his leadership, and with the active support of the railroad unions (Confederación de Ferroviarios) which had been helping the miners to organize since the first abortive national mine congress in 1940, the first successful national congress of mine workers gathered at Huanuni in early June 1944. Bitterly attacked by the national labour federation (the CSTB) as pro-fascist, the miners' congress, with its thirty delegates—who claimed a membership of 60,000 persons—nevertheless finally succeeded in organizing a national federation. This *Federación Sindical de Trabajadores Mineros de Bolivia* (FSTMB) immediately became

pamphlets by Ricardo Anaya, *Unidos venceremos, PIR Mensaje al pueblo boliviano* (Santiago de Chile: n.p., July-August 1945); and José Antonio Arze, *Bolivia bajo el terrorismo nazi-fascista* (Lima: Editora Peruana, November 1945).

[1] Fellman Velarde, *Víctor Paz Estenssoro: el hombre y la revolución*, pp. 128–9.

[2] Céspedes, *El presidente colgado*, p. 157.

the single most powerful, militant, and in fact, the largest union in the nation. Electing Lechín as its secretary-general, the FSTMB gave full support to the Villarroel régime and attacked the policy of non-recognition of the United States.[1]

Thus the FSTMB, under the steady hand of Juan Lechín, who remained its unquestioned leader for the next twenty years, introduced an extremely powerful and entirely new element into the ranks of the previously middle-class-oriented MNR. Though not totally controlled by the MNR, since Trotskyite elements always remained an important minority group within the movement, the steady support of the miners proved of crucial political value to the party, and even more importantly, helped to clarify the party's ideological programme and position. Especially under the proddings of the minority of Trotskyites, the FSTMB advocated clear-cut and radical reform programmes designed to produce fundamental changes in the socio-economic and political structure of Bolivia. It was their steady support and demands which changed the 'nationalism' of the MNR into concrete and dynamic programmes, and with the progressive desertion of army and fascist elements within the party in the years after 1944, this minority labour contingent slowly came to possess almost an equal role in the party.

Meanwhile, the military régime of Villarroel, which from late March to late December 1944 ruled without the participation of the MNR, continued to exhibit a basic indifference to fundamental socio-economic reform, despite some congressional activity in these areas. It also revealed an increasing commitment to violence at all levels, especially as it continued to feel alienated from popular support. This trend was most crudely revealed late in the year in its reaction to the first open attempt at overthrowing the régime. On 19 November 1944, an anti-government coup was organized in Oruro. A completely abortive affair, the revolt was confined to Oruro alone and was easily suppressed in a few hours. The reaction of the government, however, was unprecedented. Indiscriminately selecting several leading political figures, including two congressmen and two former cabinet ministers, the government simply ordered their secret execution.

[1] Barcelli, *Medio siglo de luchas sindicales*, pp. 165–6.

Suppressing news of these executions, the government was able to keep the massacre a secret until well into the new year. But once the news was revealed, there was a strong hostile reaction from all the elements of the middle classes as well as from the radical left. Suddenly the middle classes became terrified of the government, and the press began a major attack on government tortures and brutality. A climate of intense hatred built up which progressively destroyed whatever support the régime still had.[1]

Aware of the enormity of its political miscalculation, the junta was forced to turn toward the MNR for some type of popular support, and the power-hungry party eagerly accepted a position in the government. In late December three party members, with Paz Estenssoro at their head, re-entered the government, with Paz taking over the ministry of finance.[2]

Given its continued dependence in the new government, it was inevitable that a great deal of the reform programme proposed and partially enacted by the MNR would not come to fruition. But the impetus for reform provided by the MNR, at least in the economic sphere, was also greatly blunted by the economic policy pursued by Víctor Paz Estenssoro. For Paz, who controlled government economic policy from the beginning, adopted an excessively orthodox position which was essentially detrimental to any basic reform programme. In a period of unusual wartime prosperity with its resulting higher government revenues, Paz Estenssoro concentrated exclusively on keeping a stable currency and building up a huge capital reserve fund in dollars. Thus government expenditure was constantly cut while its income rose and no concrete projects were completed. Although price control and monetary stabilization won the hearts of the

---

[1] There is a great deal of heated debate on the November massacre. Zilveti Arce, Ostria Gutiérrez, Anaya, and José Antonio Arze all accuse the MNR of direct complicity. The *movimientistas*, i.e. Peñaloza, Fellman Velarde, and Armando Arze (see his specific defence in *Los fusilamientos del 20 de noviembre de 1944 y el Movimiento Nacionalista Revolucionario* [La Paz: Talleres Gráficos Bolivianos, 1952]), all deny this involvement and put the blame solely on the RADEPA officers. Both sides fully agree, however, on the wanton nature of the tortures and killings and attest to their profound impact on the nation. One of the most detailed studies of these events will be found in Zilveti Arce, *Bajo el signo de la barbarie*, pp. 92ff.
[2] Céspedes, *El presidente colgado*, p. 188.

middle-class supporters of the MNR, and did bring down the cost of living, it completely stymied basic reforms and public works' programmes which were desperately needed by the government to meet the enormous promises of the revolutionary era.[1] In only two areas did Paz attempt major reforms. The first was a careful increase in the rates of taxes on the tin industry,[2] and the second was a perceptible shift of budgetary expenses from the economic to social expenditures, which marked a considerable break with the past. But this shift, it should be stressed, was at the expense of the programmes for economic development begun under the Peñaranda-US Aid programme.[3]

In the field of social legislation there were some important developments which, if not revolutionary transformations, at least convinced many of the popular class of the sincerity of the reformist aims of the MNR. In its support of labour, the first MNR-RADEPA cabinet in early February 1944 passed a very important 'law of union rights' (Fuero Sindical). This decree concerned itself exclusively with providing extensive protection to union leaders against arbitrary firings or compulsory work transfers.[4] In support of the miners, the government decreed a special holiday honouring mine workers on 18 December of the same year, and finally legalized a standardized annual Christmas bonus for both blue collar (obreros) and white collar (empleados) workers.[5] The Christmas bonus law (Aguinaldo), like a great deal of complementary 'labour' legislation, was designed to win the favour of both the employed middle class and the working class. Such things as guaranteed paid vacations (29 December 1944),[6] a public employees' cooperative (14 October 1944),[7] and finally a rent reduction law (January 1945)[8] all fit into this category, and together with the decline in the rate of increase in the cost of living, were greatly appreciated by the middle class.

[1] On Paz Estenssoro's economic programme see Peñaloza, *Historia del M.N.R.'* pp. 78–9, and CEPAL, *El desarrollo económico de Bolivia*, pp. 63–4.
[2] Céspedes, *El presidente colgado*, p. 189.
[3] For this budgetary shift see James W. Wilkie, 'The Finance of the Bolivian Revolution', (1968), mimeo., pp. 35–6.
[4] Abraham Maldonado, *Legislación social boliviana* (La Paz: Editorial Nacional, 1957), pp. 555–6.   [5] *Ibid*. pp. 41–2.   [6] *Ibid*. p. 561.   [7] *Ibid*. pp. 91ff.
[8] Alberto Cornejo S., *El problema social de la vivienda* (Cochabamba: Imprenta Universitaria, [1948]), pp. 95ff.

In one area, however, there was a major symbolic break-through: this was in the concern for the Indian peasant masses. Searching for support among the miners and other workers, the MNR also appealed for the first time to the Aymara and Quechuan Indians. In early May 1945, the government called together the First National Indian Congress, in which some 1,000 caciques gathered in La Paz to listen to Quechua- and Aymara-speaking government officials declaring the need to end the exploitation of centuries and integrate the Indians into national society as free men. There were also attempts to create a formal organization of Indian peasants under government auspices. While the three-day congress produced no permanent results in the latter area, the government did make use of the congress to announce several basic decrees giving a great impetus to rural education,[1] especially among the free community Indians. Even more fundamentally, however, it decreed the abolition of pongueaje for the first time in Bolivian history, an extremely revolutionary act, which if it had been carried into action, would have destroyed the classic latifundia system. In two 'supreme decrees' issued on 15 May 1945, the last day of the congress, all 'gratuitous services' pro-vided by colonos to proprietors were abolished, requiring hence-forth that all non-agricultural labour and all labour not per-formed on the owners' lands of the home estate of the pongo had now to be paid for by the landowner and freely undertaken by the colono. Nor could the landowner now lay any claim to the crops or products of the colonos' own land granted to him by the estate (article 6), except in direct purchase at current market prices. All land taxes and other government obligations were to be paid exclusively by the landowner and never by his colonos (article 7). In detailed and very sophisticated terms these decrees provided for swift government justice to arbitrate all disputes arising out of the law (article 8), though the government warned against 'political agitation' of colonos and false claims, threaten-ing them with removal from their homes for such action (article 10). The decrees also anticipated full scale agrarian reform by prohibiting non-communero, land-owning Indians from selling their lands without formal government authorization (article 13)

[1] Maldonaldo, *Legislación social*, p. 132.

and provided free government aid for Indians making claims on land (article 14). A supporting decree suppressing 'pongueaje and mitanaje' by name, also promised immediate compensation and the return to their homes of all pongos and mitanias now in service.[1]

Though the decrees themselves were never put into operation, and the government a short time later even took part in a massacre of rebellious Indian campesinos at Las Canchas,[2] the symbolic importance of this act was vital. For by this unprecedented gesture the MNR included the Indian in its growing middle-class working-class alliance and by so doing recognized a basic realignment in its entire attack on traditional Bolivian society. Henceforth the party committed itself to taking fundamental positions on land reform and the integration, political, economic and social, of the Indian into Bolivian society. By this adroit, if initially unsuccessful move, it gave the party a decidedly new revolutionary tone, which its association with the miners cemented into a radical movement in the years after the fall of this first MNR régime.

Meanwhile throughout 1945, the convention-congress proceeded to work out an elaborate constitution. Though there was considerable debate on agrarian reform and some other revolutionary proposals, the convention finally created a constitution, which was almost identical to the 1938 charter. Even the convention debates were no more advanced than those of the 1938 meetings, and revealed the still hesitant quality of the programme and ideology of the MNR. The final constitution only added the fuero sindical of February 1944 (article 126), extended the right to vote to literate women, though only in municipal elections (article 46), and extended the presidential term to six years (article 85).[3] All the other articles and sections were identical to the 1938 charter. As the leading constitutional scholar concluded in later years, the 1945 constitution 'in the strict sense of the term, is not a new fundamental charter'.[4]

---

[1] The decrees are reprinted in Flores Moncayo, *Legislación boliviana del indio*, pp. 419–25. Interestingly, much of the wording and some of the ideas of the anti-pongueaje decree were to be found in a special agrarian law written for the department of Tarija on 15 December 1944, *ibid.* pp. 414–18.

[2] Céspedes, *El presidente colgado*, p. 193.

[3] The entire text of the charter is reprinted in Trigo, *Las constituciones de Bolivia*, pp. 457–90. [4] *Ibid.* p. 131.

Without serious reform, despite the continued use of revolutionary rhetoric, it was inevitable that the popular support of the government would be eroded away. Though increases in government revenues and the temporary stabilization of prices were appreciated by the voting public, the continuous resort to indiscriminate violence by the régime created a hostile national climate.

After the Oruro massacre of the previous November, anti-government plotting continued at an ever-increasing pace. With RADEPA breaking down under the strains of governing, and the lack of any other cohesive military elements, the army itself was becoming disorganized and was increasingly ineffective in the suppression of mounting popular agitation. At the same time the MNR showed little sympathy for the radical left, the urban workers of the CSTB, or for the student movement, which were utterly hostile to the régime. Strikes by teachers were bitterly contested and the MNR instigated a full-scale assault on the university and many of its instructors.[1] The net result of this action was to force the traditional parties (the Liberals and the Republican parties) to form a common defence with the PIR and a formal anti-government *Frente Democrática Antifascista* was established by the two extremes of the political spectrum. Though the PIR was obviously sensitive to similar united front tactics of other radical Marxist parties throughout the world, there is no question that the deliberate attacks on the party by the MNR and RADEPA forced the PIR to adopt a united anti-government front in self-defence.[2]

In April 1946 bye-elections for the convention-congress were held and the MNR—with strong government support—gained a majority position in the congress, controlling some 60 per cent of the seats.[3] But this election in no way prevented the continuing anti-government pressure from reaching its peak.

[1] José Antonio Arze, *Bolivia bajo el terrorismo*, p. 29.
[2] The FDA grew out of the *Unión Democrática Antifascista* which the two Republican parties and the desperate PIR had established in May 1944. José Antonio Arze, *Bolivia bajo el terrorismo*, pp. 35–7, with original manifesto reprinted on pp. 58–67. In December 1945, these parties were joined by the Partido Liberal and the Frente Democrática Antifascista was officially established (Bonifaz, *Bolivia*, p. 167), to which the CSTB and the Federación Universitaria Boliviana later adhered. Alberto Ostria Gutiérrez, *Un pueblo en la cruz, el drama de Bolivia* (Santiago de Chile: Editorial del Pacífico, 1956), p. 96.
[3] Fellman Velarde, *Víctor Paz Estenssoro*, p. 149.

Constant acts of brutality and the inability of the military to carry through a coherent programme made revolution inevitable. When it came, interestingly enough, it came from outside the government. No military leaders defected and no troops were suborned. Rather, building on the momentum of the teachers' strike of June and July 1946, and on the university movement, the anti-fascist front succeeded in turning a mass protest movement into a revolt and on 14 July, in an unquestionably civilian controlled and led popular affair, the Villarroel government was overthrown with much bloodshed. Not since the revolution of 1930, which was very similar, had such a popular anti-government revolt occurred. With the hanging of Villarroel from a lamp post in front of the presidential palace, the MNR-RADEPA experiment was brought to a bloody climax.[1]

But the régime which replaced Villarroel was neither a return to the traditional oligarchical régimes of the past, nor was it a popular revolutionary government. It proved a strange mixture of the traditional parties tied to the dynamic and revolutionary PIR. While this alliance had been formed around a democratic anti-fascist front in exile, the alliance surprisingly held firm in the months and years following the July 1946 rebellion. It was essential for the traditional parties to have the support of the PIR to reach the newly aroused middle classes and the even more potent labour movement which had suddenly taken on major proportions. For the PIR, however, the utility of this alliance was unquestionably minimal and it paved the way for the utter destruction of the party.

Turning the government over to a civilian junta led by the president of the supreme court of La Paz, Tomás Monje Gutiérrez, the revolutionaries organized a balanced régime, giving liberals, republicans and PIR members key positions. The PIR was granted the labour ministry and both the prefectures and heads of police for Oruro and Potosí departments, which were the

---

[1] An eyewitness account of this popular revolt, which is so similar to the 1930 overthrow of Siles, is F. Priegue Romero, *La cruz de Bolivia, crónica de la revolución de Julio* (La Paz: Editorial Renacimiento, 1946). Among those hanged by the crowds was the romantic revolutionary of the 1930s, Roberto Hinojosa, who was head of the government press services. For two contrasting interpretations of the revolt see Ostria Gutiérrez, *Un pueblo en la cruz*, pp. 93ff., and Céspedes, *El presidente colgado*, pp. 205ff.

centres of the mining industry. Attempting to moderate the workers' fears, the junta proposed no major changes of MNR legislation, and at the same time deliberately hunted down all the leading RADEPA officers in the army. The resulting imprisonment of the officers was the first major civilian attack successfully carried out against the army in the post-Chaco period and had profound effect in destroying army morale as well as totally eliminating RADEPA.[1]

But dealing with the MNR was another matter entirely. Led by the most able politicians of the day, the MNR in the six years from 1946 to 1952 led a charmed and indestructible life. Reorganizing itself both publicly and clandestinely almost immediately after its overthrow, the MNR began active revolutionary plotting against the régime, as well as constant electoral pressure, despite the exiling of all its leaders. The party tried to use whatever support it still possessed in the army, and to recruit sympathetic falange military leaders, in its dozen coups between 1946 and 1952. But each revolt was deliberately destroyed by some military officer before it could fully mature and with each unsuccessful attempt it became more difficult to recruit new military support. Thus the MNR quickly began to seek its revolutionary support outside the military and the unstable FSB and began to cooperate with or coopt POR labour leaders. As the tempo of its revolts increased in 1947, 1948 and 1949 the party began to rely increasingly on general strike movements for support and the workers in their turn strongly supported the MNR with electoral votes, arms and revolts. Initially based only in the La Paz unions of factory workers (the fabriles) and Juan Lechín's POR-dominated miners, MNR leadership was able to exploit this labour on a large scale while retaining full support of its urban middle-class elements.[2]

[1] Peñaloza, *Historia del M.N.R.*, pp. 103–4, 108 ff.
[2] The most detailed analysis of these plots is contained in *ibid.* chs. 11–22. Peñaloza was for many years the in-country leader of the party and was directly responsible for several of the revolt attempts. His resulting narrative is one of the most sophisticated statements yet published on the tactics of urban revolutionary plotting in contemporary Latin America, and clearly reveals the shifts in tactics and ideology which were taking place in the so-called 'sexenio' of 1946–52. For the justifications on the POR side of its commitments to the MNR in the last years of the sexenio, see the extremely revealing article by Guillermo Lora, 'Revolution and Counter-Revolution in Bolivia, the Great Decade of Class Struggles', *Fourth International* (New York), XIII, no. 3 (May–June 1952), 89–94.

Nevertheless, the increasing importance of the worker base brought with it an increasing radicalism in the party ideology. This was especially the case with the key miners' union, the FSTMB, which throughout this six-year period included a major group of Trotskyites under the leadership of Guillermo Lora. Lora had been an observer delegate representing unemployed miners at the Third Miners' Congress which met at Llallagua-Catavi in March of 1946. By the time of the Fourth Congress at Pulacayo in November 1946, he was a voting delegate and a key member of the Llallagua delegation. Bitterly opposed by both the PIR and MNR leaders, Lora nevertheless received 40 votes to 4 in his bid to gain a seat at the congress.[1] And it was Lora and his supporters who set the tone for the entire ideological programme of the new movement.

Committed to the Trotskyite position of a 'permanent revolution', Lora proposed to the congress in his famous *Tesis de Pulacayo* that the workers had to assume the revolutionary role usually associated with the bourgeoisie, because of the essential backwardness of Bolivian capitalism. This required that the workers directly take control of the government in their own name, with the support of the peasants and some middle-class elements. Once they were in control of the apparatus of the state, they would undertake the permanent revolution of basic structures.[2]

Although this was certainly not a new idea in Bolivian radical thought, its adoption as a basic principle in the programme of the most powerful and largest national union was a revolutionary breakthrough. This was especially so since the contemporary radical ideology was dominated at the time by PIR and MNR ideologists who proclaimed an essentially middle-class reform movement.

Based upon the project presented by Lora's Llallagua delegation, the Tesis de Pulacayo became the official ideology of the FSTMB. Stating that the mine workers were the vanguard of the labouring classes, the *Tesis* put forward what Lora later called the thesis of permanent revolution. Bolivia was a backward semi-colonial economy fully exploited by international capitalism.

[1] Juan Iñiguez and Antonio Llosa, *Antitesis de Pulacayo* (La Paz: n.p., October 1950), pp. 9–12.
[2] Guillermo Lora (ed.), *Programa Obrero* (La Paz: Ediciones 'Masas', 1959), pp. 6–7, for Lora's later justifications.

Because of its backwardness, Bolivia totally lacked 'a bourgeoisie capable of liquidating the latifundia and other pre-capitalist economic forms, or of realizing national unification and liberation from the imperialist yoke'. The tasks of the 'democratic revolution' had therefore to be performed by the workers themselves, since no other instruments were available. As the workers also had to organize their own socialist revolution for basic socio-economic equality, the solution was to combine the two tasks and carry out under labour's own leadership both the democratic and socialist revolutions.[1]

In the democratic phase, the struggle had to be an attack on the mine industry and the internal capitalist structure which supported it. This meant total opposition to North American imperialism, which was especially singled out as the primary exploiting agent (Part IV) weighing upon the Bolivian masses. Rather skilfully, the *Tesis* also spoke of the fascist danger to the Bolivian working class, but cautioned against the current conservative dominated anti-fascist movements which were essentially disguised anti-labour and anti-radical positions. These latter ideas were the true fascist ones and had to be opposed. As for openly fascist groups, it proclaimed that 'the fight against fascist groups is subordinated to the struggle against imperialism and the feudal bourgeoisie. Those who, pretending to fight against fascism, surrender themselves to "democratic" feudalism and "democratic" feudal bourgeoisie, only prepare the way for the inevitable advent of a facist régime'. By this adroit and sophisticated approach, the FSTMB and its POR leaders thus rejected the united anti-fascist fronts in which the PIR had become involved, and yet did not openly endorse the MNR. Rather the *Tesis* claimed that the entire issue was irrelevant to the current scene, an analysis that was in perfect harmony with the realities of the so-called 'Sexenio' (1946–52) period.

In line with this position, it accepted the revolt of 21 July as a legitimate worker protest, but held that the PIR ministers in

[1] The thesis of Pulacayo is reprinted, *ibid.* pp. 10–30, with the above citations coming from pp. 10–11. The thesis also justified its combined revolution idea on the grounds that Bolivia's feudal élite, the latifundistas, were in fact the servitors of international capitalism and had entwined their interests with those of this foreign element.

the government were merely a front for the oligarchy and that the junta was an arch-conservative group. It claimed that the coming presidential elections were a farce, since the literacy laws excluded all Indians and a large mass of the workers. 'We workers shall not achieve power through the election box, we will achieve power by social revolution.' This was a bitter and desperate threat, and the FSTMB warned that should the present junta or a future elected government attempt to stop legitimate workers' demands, it would face violent protest.[1]

Even in its specific demands the *Tesis* was a truly radical document. It proposed as an immediate and continued policy the occupation of the mines by all workers threatened with work stoppages.[2] It demanded *co-gobierno* of the mines, with workers participating in all operations and decisions at all levels, including managerial. It decreed the immediate formation of armed worker groups, for, as it noted, 'every strike is the potential beginning of a civil war and we should be armed for this. Our object is to win, and we should never forget that the bourgeoisie has armies, police and fascist bands. It is necessary, therefore, for us to organize the first cells of the proletarian army. All the sindicatos are [thus] obliged to form armed pickets with their youngest and most combative members'.[3]

As for political tactics, it stated as a goal the formation of a united labour front, excluding all middle class participation. It also attacked the national labour federation, the CSTB, which it charged was dominated by the conservative policies of the PIR. Though direct action was the immediate and primary aim, a secondary development should be the formation in parliament of a worker bloc, but this was clearly recognized as being less important than the coming armed struggle.[4]

This was unquestionably a revolutionary stand, and one far in advance of anything contemplated by the urban middle-class leaders of the MNR. But the POR needed the support of the movimientistas to capture the government and to get the tacit support of the middle-class elements in its coming military showdown with the oligarchic régime. The MNR for its part became increasingly dependent on the militant miners as its own base in

[1] Lora, *Programa Obrero*, p. 19. [2] *Ibid.* pp. 20–2. [3] *Ibid.* p. 24. [4] *Ibid.* pp. 25–7.

the military and among the traditional parties was eroded. The result was a marriage of convenience, with Juan Lechín serving as the key broker between the two groups. Ultimately this alliance prevented the POR from breaking out beyond the confines of the mine workers' movement, and would in fact make it possible for the MNR to gain an important foothold in the movement. But the clarity and power of the POR position within the FSTMB was such that it slowly but steadily forced the MNR into an openly radical pro-labour stand, with the final commitment in the last days of the sexenio being made to the revolutionary plan for worker co-management.

Yet despite this drift toward the left, the MNR never lost its middle-class supporters. It actually increased its hold over this group through the continued undermining effects of continual inflation which disturbed these classes. The cost of living and the rates of exchange had held to a reasonably slow if steady growth in the period from 1938 to 1949, but at the beginning of 1949, the value of the boliviano began to fall at an alarming rate, matched by an equally dramatic rise in the cost of living between 1949 and 1950, as can be seen in table 2.

Table 2. *Cost of living index and exchange rates, 1938–52*

Year	Cost of living index	Exchange rate of bolivianos to US dollar
1938	100·0	30·14
1939	140·7	42·97
1940	164·3	49·30
1941	221·8	61·60
1942	287·1	71·16
1943	311·3	70·76
1944	335·1	74·65
1945	361·2	77·94
1946	418·2	82·28
1947	493·7	87·40
1948	510·6	85·36
1949	561·3	93·52
1950	762·1	125·05
1951	967·2	147·90
1952	1,170·3	176·11

Source: CEPAL, *Desarrollo económico de Bolivia*, p. 298.

Thus despite all the violence and repression and the return to conservative rule, the post-Villarroel régimes could not destroy the basis of MNR support, and by the end even the economic conditions were driving the middle class toward the leading opposition party. But this last surge of middle-class support only added a crust to the already hard core middle-class commitment.

This support was well illustrated in the first presidential elections of the new government which were held in January 1947. While the recently reunited Republican parties, again known as the Partido Unión Republicana Socialista (PURS), obtained 44,000 votes and elected Enrique Hertzog and Mamerto Urriolagoitia to the executive, Víctor Paz Estenssoro running *in absentia* from his Argentine exile still polled some 13,000 votes.[1] This was the rock base of support for the MNR which increased numerically with each passing month. In addition to its role as a major urban middle-class party, the MNR also took upon itself the task of championing every major strike movement which arose in the cities and the mines, in a brilliant campaign to obtain worker support.

In an unquestionably suicidal decision, the PIR, which had tasted power under the junta, refused to relinquish its control in the government and when its own Liberal-PIR election slate was defeated by some 400 votes in the 1947 election it decided to remain in the new government rather than taking the more logical step of withdrawing. Retaining its control over Oruro, Potosí and the ministry of labour, it played right into the hands of the oligarchy and traditional parties which proceeded to use it to destroy worker opposition.[2] With the post-war cutbacks in tin exports the major companies began mass firing of workers. This occurred at a time when the mine workers themselves were reaching a fever pitch of organizational activity and had finally installed both a powerful local union at all the major mines, and a fully functioning national confederation under the leadership of Lechín. The FSTMB thus was able to strike and protest against the brutal dismissing of workers in an effective manner and to confront the

[1] Weston, 'The Coming to Power of the MNR', p. 69n.
[2] On the error of this decision and the resulting collapse of the PIR in the sexenio see the commentary by the old PIRista and present vice-president of the party, Miguel Bonifaz, *Bolivia*, pp. 168–76.

mining companies for the first time with the need to accommodate workers' opinions.[1]

But rather than accepting mediation, the companies tried to return to their old policy of suppressing the workers by relying on the government to use force. This was the end of the PIR. Faced by a militant labour movement, intransigent mine leaders and a worsening economic situation, the PIR supported the use of government troops to suppress the workers' opposition. Just a few weeks after the 1947 presidential elections workers protesting at Catavi were overwhelmed by government troops and in the bloody struggle which followed the PIR lost its hold over the Bolivian labour movement.[2]

While the PIR was losing its control over the labour movement, the PURS was being deprived of its middle-class support. In the municipal elections of December 1947, the MNR gained control over Potosí and Santa Cruz.[3] Despite constant attempts throughout 1948 to destroy the leadership of the MNR through exiling and various internal revolts against Paz Estenssoro's leadership (first under Rafael Otazo and later under Major Taborga), the party emerged by the congressional mid-term elections of May 1949, as the second most powerful party in the nation. Its electoral victories and the resulting demonstrations caused Hertzog to resign the presidency a few days after the elections.[4]

The selection of Vice-President Mamerto Urriolagoitia as president brought little change in the situation. The PIR continued to support the régime with its presence and the PURS leadership became even more reactionary in its attempt to destroy the mine unions. In mid-May 1949, there was a major strike movement in Catavi and the government reacted by exiling Lechín, Mario Torres and other leading members of the FSTMB. News of their

---

[1] The fact that the workers and revolutionary leaders quickly labelled this mass dismissal of workers, which was far from a new experience in the cyclical industry, as the 'White Massacre', indicates the advanced stage of political awareness of the mine workers' movement. An interesting collection of documents on the FSTMB-Patiño struggle at this time is presented in Patiño Mines and Ent. Cons. (Inc.), *Los conflictos sociales en 1947* (La Paz: Editoria 'Universo', March 1948).

[2] A detailed study of this Potosí massacre and the involvement of the PIR leadership is presented in Guillermo Lora, *El stalinismo en los sindicatos* (La Paz: Ediciones 'Masas', 1963), pp. 40–68.

[3] Peñaloza, *Historia del M.N.R.*, pp. 150–1.   [4] *Ibid.* pp. 184–6.

exile caused a worker uprising in Catavi, beginning on 27 May. The use of planes, tanks and artillery soon brought the Catavi miners to heel and a delayed revolt in support of the MNR was easily suppressed by the army.[1]

In this, as in all subsequent developments, the army had finally decided on complete loyalty to the régime. With RADEPA destroyed and the MNR turning more and more toward the labour movement, the army itself became increasingly united in its fear of civilian retaliations and overthrow by the workers. Ruthless destruction became the order of the day in dealing with workers' demonstrations, and while the urban revolutionaries went largely unscathed in the multiple revolts between 1946 and 1952, the workers in La Paz and the mine fields paid a heavy price for every revolt or strike they attempted. Troops were moved into the mine fields on a massive scale, but their presence only provoked even greater violence on the part of the workers. The army was reaching the point of no return and was self-consciously uniting all its elements as the last line of defence against a mounting revolutionary movement.

This was clearly revealed in the so-called civil war of August and September, 1949. Under the leadership of Hernán Siles Zuazo, another MNR revolt was planned for 27 August. While military informants eventually caught all the plotters in La Paz before the revolt could succeed, the departmental committees were able to act and by the 28th Cochabamba, Santa Cruz, Sucre and Potosí were in rebel MNR civilian hands. The Catavi miners also rose in support and by 3 September exiled leaders of the MNR had set up a provisional government and capital at Santa Cruz. What was crucial about this exceedingly violent fighting was the largely civilian nature of the MNR revolt, with very powerful support from the miners, and the almost total unity of the army against the rebels. Time and again military units promised to remain neutral in the traditional manner when rebels seized a city, and time and again they turned on the rebels as soon as they could. Despite the desertion of a number of officers, no major regiment defected to the rebels and the fighting was an

[1] Peñaloza, *Historia del M.N.R.*, pp. 186–94; Barcelli, *Medio siglo de luchas sindicales*, pp. 209–15.

almost exclusively military *v.* civilian affair. Never before had the MNR been so completely isolated from the military and never before in the twentieth century had the military stood so firm against so initially successful a revolution.[1]

But the destruction of the revolutionary movement and the mass exiling and jailing of the MNR leaders proved of no avail. The August–September civil war of 1949 was simply a prelude to the larger and ultimately successful April revolution of 1952. By the beginning of 1950 many of the leading MNR leaders were back from exile and even attempted a party-worker revolt on 17 May 1950, when a factory workers' strike in La Paz led to an armed insurrection. Following a now familiar pattern, the government used planes and artillery to bombard the workers' district of Villa Victoria for several hours and by the 19th had destroyed the workers' protest.[2] Once again, workers and their families paid a heavy toll in loss of life, while the MNR leaders suffered only exiling and temporary imprisonment. It seems that the PURS could never bring itself to the point of deliberately liquidating the middle class *movimientistas*, but that it and the army had no such scruples about the violence involved in handling workers' revolts. Thus events were rapidly moving toward the definitive confrontation between the middle-class radical leadership of the MNR, united with the worker masses, and the oligarchy and its military dependencies, a confrontation which eventually led to full-scale revolution.

As the traditional political system was disintegrating, the social and economic tensions within Bolivian society were increasing. For Bolivia on the eve of the revolution was, paradoxically, both economically stagnant and socially advancing. By the usual social indices of urbanization and literacy Bolivia by 1950 had made great strides since 1900. From the census of 1900 to the census of 1950 the urban population (defined as those living in cities of 5,000 persons or above) rose from 14·3 per cent of the national population, to 22·8 per cent.[3] Urbanization was most rapid in the

---

[1] Peñaloza, *Historia del M.N.R.*, pp. 195–232.

[2] *Ibid.* p. 238; Barcelli, *Medio siglo de luchas sindicales*, pp. 227–31.

[3] Olen E. Leonard, *Bolivia, Land, People and Institutions* (Washington: The Scarecrow Press, 1952), p. 41; and Isidoro Alonso, *et al.*, *La iglesia en Perú y Bolivia, estructuras sociales* (Estudios socio-religiosos latino-americanos, no. 3, vol. II;

four key cities of Oruro, Cochabamba, Santa Cruz and La Paz, which had become a metropolis of over 267,000 persons. The rate of increase even in the slower growing cities was almost double that of their departments as a whole (see table 3).

Table 3. *Increases in major departmental total and departmental capital populations, 1900–50*

Department and capital city	1900	1950	Percentage increase
LA PAZ	446,500	948,446	112·4
La Paz	71,860 est.	267,000 est.	271·5
COCHABAMBA	328,200	490,455	49·4
Cochabamba	21,900	80,795	268·9
ORURO	86,100	210,260	144·2
Oruro	15,900	62,975	296·0
POTOSÍ	320,500	534,399	66·7
Potosí	20,900	43,579	108·5
CHUQUISACA	187,800	282,980	50·6
Sucre	20,900	40,128	92·0
SANTA CRUZ	202,700	286,145	41·1
Santa Cruz	18,300	42,746	133·5
Total population*	1,766,451	3,019,031	70·9

Source: Averanga Mollinedo, *Aspectos generales de la población boliviana, passim.*

* The populations of departments with unimportant cities have been excluded. Also the total populations given are the corrected total populations for both censuses.

The level of literacy and the school population also showed a significant increase. Thus between 1900 and 1950 the literate population rose from 16·6 per cent of the total population to 31·1 per cent,[1] while the student population increased over six times in size, from 22,539 in 1900 to 138,924 in 1950.[2] But the increase in literacy and school population seems to have been largely at the primary level. Of the school graduates enumerated in the census, only 128,248 had completed secondary or higher

Friburgo and Bogota: Oficina Internacional de Investigaciones Sociales de FERES, 1962), p. 159.

[1] See above, p. 168 n.

[2] *Censo de 1900*, II, Primera Parte, p. 46 and *Censo demográfico 1950*, p. 148. In 1950, 28 per cent of the 5–14 age group were attending school.

education, and this was only 7·8 per cent of the national population. The class of university students was even smaller, only 12,409 persons, and in a special university census of 1951 it was discovered that Bolivia's seven universities contained only 3,701 registered students, and in that year only 132 persons had obtained degrees.[1] Though comparable figures for 1900 are not available, it would seem that a crude estimate of the numbers of people in certain professions (see table 4) indicates that there had been an actual and severe percentage decline in the more traditional élite liberal professions, such as law and medicine, and a major increase only in such new or revitalized professions as teaching or engineering. This would seem to support the assumption that the peak of the occupational ladder was not experiencing

Table 4. *Persons in liberal professions, 1900–50*

Profession	1900	1950	Percentage change
Lawyers	1,546	1,449*	−06·0
Doctors	476	706	+48·3
Clergy	1,106	534	−50·9
Engineers	326	1,335	+309·5
Teachers	741	9,322†	+1,158·0

Source: Censo de 1900, II, Primera parte, p. 46; Censo demográfico de 1950, p. 231.

* Includes 346 persons listed as *fiscales, procuradores*, judges and magistrats all of whom probably had law degrees.

† Includes 462 university professors.

undue expansion or stress, and would tend to challenge the thesis of overproduction and underemployment of the liberal professional élite as a major cause for social discontent in pre-revolutionary Bolivian society.[2] For it would appear that although the urban, educated and literate population expanded, expansion seems to have been primarily confined to upper blue-collar and middle-rank white-collar workers; the increase in the upper professional groups was smaller and more easily absorbed into the society.

[1] Amado Canelas O., *Mito y realidad de la industrialización boliviana* (La Paz: Editorial Los Amigos del Libro, 1966), pp. 97–8. The largest single group of graduates, as was to be expected, were the lawyers, who accounted for 48 per cent of the total of graduates, with doctors and pharmacists next at 25 per cent.

[2] This is the interesting, but highly debatable thesis propounded by James M. Malloy, 'Bolivia: A Study in Revolution' (unpublished doctoral dissertation, Department of Political Science, University of Pittsburgh, 1967).

But even despite the important growth in the urban and literate population, these Bolivians were only a minority of the nation and the mass of people in 1950 were still peasant agriculturalists. Of the economically active population in the 1950 census, fully 72 per cent were engaged in agriculture and allied industries and yet this work force produced only 33 per cent of the gross national product, a factor indicating the serious economic re-tardation of this most vital of economic activities (see table 5).

Table 5. *Percentage employment of economically active population, and national product by sector, 1950*

Activity	% of economically active population	Percentage of GNP
Agriculture (including rural artisans)	72·1	32·8
Mining and extractive industries	3·2	24·4
Manufacturing	4·1	8·9
Urban artisans	4·0	4·3
Transportation	1·5	5·6
Commerce and banking	4·2	10·3
Government	3·0	4·4
Other services	7·9	9·3

Source: CEPAL, *Desarrollo económico de Bolivia,* pp. 14, 114–15, 144–6.

The incredibly low productivity of the agricultural sector is not only revealed in its share of the GNP, but is also seen in the figures of land utilization, ownership distribution and import deficiencies. It was estimated in the 1950 agricultural census that only 2 per cent of the total land area of Bolivia was under cultivation. This small percentage of cultivated lands was in turn divided into only 86,377 properties in what was unquestionably one of the most badly distorted land-ownership distribution patterns in Latin America.

Table 6 shows that 615 fincas, or 0·7 per cent of the total number of property owners, possessed 49·6 per cent of the land. If the figure of 1,000 hectares is taken as the dividing line, and this minimum would unquestionably include all fincas or lati-fundias of medium size and above, then the distortion of owner-ship is even more clearly revealed. This category of landowners (possessing 1,000 hectares or above) included only 6·3 per cent of the total number of landowners, but they accounted for 91·9 per cent of the total owned property. The reverse problem of extreme minifundismo is also easily perceived when we note that those possessing less than 1,000 hectares made up 93·7 per cent of the propertied owners, and controlled only a bare 8·1 per cent of the total land area in private hands.

Table 6. *Agricultural ownership of cultivated lands, 1950*

Size of property (in hectares)	Number of proprietors	Total owned (in hs.)	Total exploited	Exploited as % of owned
Less than 5 hectares	51,198	73,877	40,028	54·2
From 5 to 50 hectares	19,503	278,459	86,378	31·0
From 50 to 200 hectares	5,014	478,291	76,090	15·9
From 200 to 1,000 hectares	4,033	1,805,405	134,790	7·4
From 1,000 to 5,000 hectares	4,000	8,724,776	167,006	1·9
From 5,000 to 10,000 hectares	797	5,146,334	55,365	1·0
Over 10,000	615	16,233,954	85,850	0·5
Totals	85,160*	32,741,096	645,506	

Source: Oficina Nacional de Estadística y Censos, Sección Agropecuario, *Censo national agropecuario de 1950* La Paz, 1950, mimeo.

* Total number of proprietors was 86,377, with 1,217 unknown.

This gross inequality in land distribution was but one aspect of the inefficiency of Bolivian agriculture. As can be seen, the greater the size of the property, the smaller the area of land under cultivation, until the extreme is reached of 0·5 per cent utility on properties of 10,000 hectares or over, a fact which strongly supports the thesis that latifundia in Bolivia was primarily a labour control device rather than a land utilization system.[1]

Controlling land to obtain free labour for their small areas of cultivation, the latifundistas had no need to invest capital in their holdings and were scarce producers for a high-cost food market. Supplied with free labour and a guaranteed market, they

[1] This is the thesis proposed by William E. Carter, in *Aymara Communities and the Bolivian Agrarian Reform, passim.*

used only rudimentary technology and poor quality seed. The result was stagnation in Bolivian agriculture which was increasingly unable to meet the needs of Bolivia's expanding population. Thus in the period 1925–9 food imports represented 10 per cent of the total imports into the country, whereas by the period 1950–2 they had risen to 18·5 per cent of total import figures.[1]

The exporting sector of the economy presented an equally depressing picture. The vital tin industry had seriously stagnated since the Great Depression, despite short cycles of prosperity. From the late 1930s onward there was little capital investment in mining and the major mines began to run into lower quality ore veins, exhausting their richer and more easily accessible sources. Ageing plant, and declining quality of product, forced the costs of production up to levels that were rapidly becoming non-competitive, except in a time of wartime shortages.[2] In fact, neither in terms of tonnage nor of the value of the product did Bolivian mining ever achieve the peak reached in 1929 (see table 7).

The only major advance in the economy since 1930 was in the small sector of manufacturing, and then almost exclusively in light industry. During the 1930s and early 1940s there had been an important expansion in this sector, though by 1950 it still employed only 4 per cent of the economically active population and accounted for only 9 per cent of the GNP. Not only was its importance to the internal economy still minor in 1950, but it appears from almost all indicators that from sometime in the mid-1940s onward there had been a steady decline in productivity even in this sector, a decline that accelerated at an even greater pace after 1950. Thus, some six major industries (cotton and woollen goods, flour, beer, cigarettes and cement), whose employees increased from 2,727 to 4,981 between 1935 and 1950, saw an actual decline in productivity, from 3,179 bolivianos per worker (at adjusted 1955 prices) to 2,705 bolivianos, over the same period.[3]

This stagnation in the industrial sector of the economy is

---

[1] CEPAL, *Desarrollo económico de Bolivia*, p. 41, cuadro 33. If to these food imports are added primary imports for consumer industries, the respective figures of imports going to consumer consumption are 19·4 per cent in the 1925–9 period and 32 per cent in the 1950–2 period.

[2] *Ibid.* p. 44.　　　　　　　　　　　　　　　　[3] *Ibid.* p. 128, cuadro 82.

largely explained by the very low investment of capital which
resulted in ageing and largely unreplaced machinery. As a UN
study concluded after an extensive analysis of this sector, capital
input had been extremely low in the period from 1930 to 1935

Table 7. *Bolivian tin exports, 1925–50*

Year	Tonnage	Value at constant prices of 1950 (in thousands of bolivianos)
1925	32,598	66,114
1926	32,184	64,561
1927	39,972	79,823
1928	42,074	84,346
1929	47,087	94,456
1930	38,772	77,777
1931	31,637	63,464
1932	20,918	41,962
1933	14,957	30,004
1934	23,224	46,587
1935	25,408	50,968
1936	24,438	49,023
1937	25,531	51,215
1938	25,893	51,941
1939	27,648	55,462
1940	38,531	77,293
1941	42,740	85,736
1942	38,899	78,031
1943	40,959	82,164
1944	39,341	78,918
1945	43,168	86,595
1946	38,222	76,673
1947	33,777	67,756
1948	37,829	75,885
1949	34,300	68,806
1950	31,320	62,843

Source: CEPAL, *Desarrollo económico de Bolivia*, p. 12.

'and a good part of it has been used to create productive capacity
in new areas, without, at the same time, being sufficient to avoid
an effective decapitalization of certain older enterprises'. It noted
that 'the maintenance of machinery and equipment [in Bolivia]

for periods which are much longer than those judged normal in other economies, demands a permanent input of important amounts of capital in parts and replacements, in order to avoid a severe decline in productive capacity'. But the study found that the capital invested during this period was insufficient to perform all these functions, and concluded, 'as a consequence of this lack of capital investment, [there has been] an observable decline in the condition of maintenance of the machines and equipment'.[1]

To this stagnation in mining, agriculture and industry, one must add the impact of inflation. Although inflation and the decline in the value of the boliviano had become constant features of Bolivian society from the late 1930s onward, the pace of this change increased dramatically in the last three years before the revolution (see table 2).

There is little question that economic stagnation and increasingly severe inflation were taking their political toll of the previously submissive middle-class elements who had continued to support the traditional élite until almost the very end. The stagnation of mining and manufacturing may also have had its impact by the 1950s on a tightening of economic opportunity even in the previously expanding positions open to middle rank white-collar and upper blue-collar employees, though there is little direct evidence on this. It does seem evident, however, that the very rapid rise in the cost of living after 1949 and the concomitant severe decline in the value of the national currency, certainly persuaded large numbers of uncommitted elements of the middle class to openly support the increasingly revolutionary MNR, or, at the least, to adopt a position of benevolent neutrality toward the party.

With this sympathy of the middle class the MNR was able to gain enormous strength, despite the losses of the 1949 civil war, and to capture leadership of the entire revolutionary movement. This is clearly seen in the total collapse of the last possible intermediary force between outright revolution and the traditional oligarchy, the much tamed PIR. In the last months of 1949 and the early days of 1950 this once powerful party was finally destroyed. Frustrated by the constant involvement of the PIR with

[1] CEPAL, *Desarrollo económico de Bolivia*, p. 123.

the oligarchy, with its deliberate attempts to destroy the FSTMB and with the total collapse of its revolutionary position and leadership, the youth of the party decided irrevocably to destroy the party and form a new revolutionary group. Rebels within the PIR, though succeeding by late 1949 in forcing the party into official opposition, especially after the disastrous 1949 elections, failed in their attempt to change the party into an official Partido Comunista Boliviano. Under the leadership of Ricardo Anaya and Miguel Bonifaz, the radicals were defeated in the central committee and the party retained its traditional name and programme.[1] But the younger adherents finally decided to strike out on their own, and on 17 January 1950.[2] they created Bolivia's first publicly avowed Communist party. At a meeting of the PIR in the following March, fifty-one militants of the youth branch of the party accused the leadership of being tools of the oligarchy and Yankee imperialism and withdrew to support the PCB. Thereafter the PIR rapidly declined, and was temporarily dissolved in July 1952.[3]

Meanwhile by late 1950 the MNR made one last major attempt at legally overthrowing the government and prepared to run in the presidential elections of 1951. At their fifth national convention in February 1951, they selected Paz Estenssoro and Hernán Siles Zuazo as their candidates for president and vice-president.[4] The unity of the old anti-fascist alliance had finally been destroyed and even the PURS was being rocked by internal dissensions, so the MNR was able to make great headway. Instead of joining forces, the PURS and the Liberals, along with the PIR, POR and even an Aramayo-sponsored party, all ran their own separate presidential lists. The result was an electoral landslide for the MNR. Paz Estenssoro, still in exile, received some 54,000 votes in the presidential elections of 6 May, to 39,000 for the PURS candidate, 13,000 for the FSB, 6,500 for the

[1] Bonifaz, *Bolivia*, pp. 176–7.
[2] Partido Comunista de Bolivia, *Primer congreso nacional del P.C.B.*, documentos (La Paz: n.p., 5–9 April 1959), p. 92.
[3] Bonifaz, *Bolivia*, pp. 177–80. In June 1956 the PIR was re-founded under the leadership of Ricardo Anaya. For its refounding declaration see Partido de la Izquierda Revolucionaria, *P.I.R. y desarrollo nacional, soluciones para los problemas nacionales* (La Paz: Talleres Gráficos 'Gutenberg', 1961), pp. 51ff.
[4] Peñaloza, *Historia del M.N.R.* p. 241.

Aramayo-sponsored slate, 6,400 for the Liberals, with but 5,100 votes for José Antonio Arze and the completely discredited PIR.[1] Since no candidate had obtained an absolute majority, the election was to be decided in congress. But it was clear from the large margins of victory achieved by Paz, and also, by Hernán Siles Zuazo in the separate vice-presidential elections, that the party would ultimately triumph.

However, the army now decided to intervene with the consent of Urriolagoitia. On 16 May he renounced the presidency and General Ovidio Quiroga, chief of staff and one of the key military leaders in suppressing the civil war of 1949, announced that a military junta was being established under the leadership of General Hugo Ballivián. Justifying its moves on the grounds that the MNR was in league with the communists, the all-military régime annulled the elections and declared an end to civilian government. But only the PURS and the FSB gave their support to the Ballivián military régime, and the government could do little to stop a revolution that everyone now believed to be inevitable. The MNR had never been loath to take by force what it could not achieve by ballot and now that it had been deprived of a legitimate electoral victory it was only a matter of time before a revolution would occur.

At the same time the army leadership began to disintegrate. Key generals like Terrazas and Quiroga went abroad and within the government conservative and liberal military elements were alternately attempting to appease the workers or suppress their activity.[2] Thus important conciliatory gestures made by the junta throughout the rest of 1951 and early 1952 could find little support.

To this crisis in leadership and popular support, was added a miners' boycott of a purchasing agreement with the US Reconstruction Finance Corporation for Korean War tin purchases. This strike seriously weakened the government's economic position despite the undoubtedly beneficial economic effect which the war was having on the Bolivian economy. With negotiations between the US and the miners at a stand-still, workers were thrown out of jobs and a short-lived but severe depression hit the country. In February 1952, there was a hunger march in La Paz

[1] Peñaloza, *Historia del M.N.R.*, p. 248.   [2] *Ibid.* pp. 250ff.

in protest against the policies of the government and by the end of the month internal dissension within the régime had reached such proportions that the minister of government, General Seleme (then head of the carabineros), openly pledged his entire force to the coming MNR revolt. On 9 April the revolution finally began when Seleme was suddenly dismissed from the junta on charges of plotting a revolt.

The MNR acted quickly. Profiting from its experiences in the 1949 civil war, it distributed arms to civilians and workers. With the support of the carabineros the city was quickly taken. But an initially united military stand against the revolution created deep-seated fear, and Seleme and many of his military followers sought asylum in foreign embassies late on the 9th. The army's initial show of unity, however, was only temporary, for it could no longer offer any unified leadership. Key officers left their troops and went into exile and after some fierce but localized fighting the army surrendered on 11 April to the Siles régime, the majority of the leading senior officers escaping across the frontier before fighting had ended. Thus after three days of fighting, and at the cost of some 600 lives, the MNR again returned to power.[1]

But unlike the period of 1943–6, the MNR of 1952 was a newly amalgamated party of middle-class and worker elements and represented a new type of radical populist movement. Its years of revolutionary activity and skilled political manœuvring had led it to accept the revolutionary programme of the radical Marxian POR. Abandoning its traditional fascism and economic orthodoxy, it rapidly moved in the months following the revolution to a totally revolutionary position. Giving up all pretence of working with the system, the MNR now began its famous revolutionary restructuring of society under the first Paz Estenssoro presidency from 1952 to 1956.[2]

[1] The most detailed study of the plotting which led to the 1952 revolution is contained in Peñaloza, *Historia del M.N.R.*, chs. 21–2.
[2] The best survey of the immediate background and early period of the revolution is given by Robert J. Alexander, *The Bolivian National Revolution* (New Brunswick: Rutgers University Press, 1957). An interesting and perceptive eye-witness account is given by the American economist then with the UN Technical Aid Mission in Bolivia, Carter Goodrich, *The Economic Transformation of Bolivia* (Bulletin No. 34; Ithaca: New York State School of Industrial and Labor Relations, Cornell University, October 1955).

Thus began the Bolivian national revolution. Having created a powerful civilian revolutionary movement which had been bitterly opposed by the oligarchy and the army throughout the 1940s and early 1950s, the MNR leaders felt under no obligation to offer a moderate programme or compromise with any traditional institution, political or military. Soon not only the urban white and cholo classes but also the rural Indian masses were in possession of arms and the army and the national police force were completely disorganized. The aims of the party were known to all, the arms were in the hands of a militant populace, and the exiled leaders returning from abroad were not to be restrained. Thus began Latin America's most dynamic social revolution since the Mexican holocaust of 1910.

POSTSCRIPT

Now that the social revolution of the MNR has run its full course, some assessment can be made of its impact on Bolivian society. From 1952 until 1956 most of the basic legislation was passed which created an entirely new political and economic structure. To begin with a major attack was finally made on the dominant tin industry, and the big three concerns of Hochschild, Patiño and Aramayo, representing about 80 per cent of the entire tin industry, were nationalized in October 1952. In recognition of organized labour's role, the nationalized tin industry was initially established with a joint labour-government management, and an entirely new set of advanced labour decrees were passed, giving extraordinary job security to Bolivian labour.[1]

The second major economic change was the enactment of a successful land reform decree in August 1953. Without question this decree completely destroyed the pongueaje and colonato system of free labour which was at the very heart of the latifundia system.[2] Though the legalization of land titles for the peasants

---

[1] For a useful compilation of this extensive legislation, see Abraham Maldonado, *Legislación social boliviana*. For an excellent collection of documents on the events leading to the nationalization decree, the decree itself and accompanying documents see the official *El libro blanco de la independencia económica de Bolivia* (La Paz: S.P.I.C., 1952). An important book on the co-equal union-government administration, known as *control obrero*, is presented by the labour head of COMIBOL at that time, Sinforosa Cabrera R., *La burocracia estrangula a la COMIBOL* (La Paz: Editorial 'La Paz', 1960). For a detailed economic analysis of the state of the mines before and after nationalization see CEPAL, *El desarrollo económico de Bolivia*, pp. 44ff., which is largely based on the study made by the American firm of Ford Bacon and Davis, and finally the detailed work of Amado Canelas O., *Mito y realidad de la Coporación Minera de Bolivia* (La Paz: Editorial Los Amigos del Libro, 1966).

[2] Among the numerous studies on the impact of the agrarian reform, several are worth noting. A particularly perceptive survey is provided by the former president of the Consejo Nacional de la Reforma Agraria, Eduardo Arze Loureiro, 'Actitudes sociales relativas a la reforma agraria en Bolivia', *Economía y Ciencias Sociales* (Caracas), Año III, nos. 1, 2 and 3 (September 1960 to March 1961), pp. 29–40. This should be supplemented with the official government document collection, *El libro blanco de la reforma agraria* (La Paz: S.P.I.C., 1953); and with the useful legal compilation by Abraham Maldonado, *Derecho agrario. Historia-doctrina-legislación* (La Paz: Editorial Nacional, 1956).

was relatively slow, the latifundia class was literally wiped out and there were none left, at least in the heavily Indian populated areas, to exact labour tribute.[1]

In addition to these fundamental economic changes, there were also major political changes. The army was temporarily abolished and civilians, workers and peasants were all given arms and organized into militia units. The old literacy qualification was destroyed and the voting population rose from about 200,000 in the last election of 1951, to 958,000 in the first election after the electoral law was passed, or from 7 per cent to 29 per cent of the population.[2]

Finally, the inflation which had been serious before 1952, became astronomical after the revolution. Bolivia's rate of inflation between the revolution and 1956 was the highest experienced by any country at that time, and effectively wiped out much of the élite based on urban property, as well as a large portion of the traditional middle class.[3] This, together with the mass exiling of

On the actual development of the reform and its concrete impact, see Richard W. Patch, 'Social Implications of the Bolivian Agrarian Reform' (unpublished Ph.D. dissertation, Cornell University, 1956); and Antonio García, 'La reforma agraria y desarrollo social en Bolivia', *El Trimestre Económico* (Mexico), XXXI, no. 123 (July–September 1964), 339–87. For an analysis of the impact of the reform on the local indigenous community, see J. Vellard, *Civilisations des Andes, évolution des populations du haut-plateau bolivien* (Paris: Gallimard, 1963); William Carter, *Aymara Communities and the Bolivian Agrarian Reform*; Melvin Burke, 'An Analysis of the Bolivian Land Reform By Means of a Comparison Between Peruvian Haciendas and Bolivian Ex-Haciendas' (unpublished Ph.D. dissertation, Department of Economics, University of Pittsburgh, 1967). There has also been a major survey of post-reform agrarian communities carried out by the Land Tenure Center at the University of Wisconsin, under the leadership of Dwight W. Heath, which has already produced a number of as yet unpublished, but important studies. Finally two articles among many are worth noting: Madeline Barbara Leons, 'Land Reform in the Bolivian Yungas', *América Indígena*, XXVII, no. 4 (October 1967), 689–712, which discusses a vital but neglected area, and the major theoretical work of Charles J. Erasmus, 'Upper Limits of Peasantry and Agrarian Reform: Bolivia, Venezuela, and Mexico Compared', *Ethnology*, VI, no. 4 (October 1967), 349–80.

[1] As of January 1966, 263,139 titles covering 6,278,803 hectares had been distributed by the government to 173,724 families. Burke, 'An Analysis of the Bolivian Land Reform', p. 32, table 7.

[2] Henry Wells *et al.*, *Bolivian Election Factbook*, 3 July 1966 (Washington: Institute for the Comparative Study of Political Systems, Operations and Policy Research, Inc., 1966), p. 14.

[3] CEPAL, *El desarrollo económico de Bolivia*, pp. 67–8, cuadros 47 and 49; and Cornelius H. Zondag, *The Bolivian Economy, 1952–1965* (New York: Frederick A. Praeger, 1966), ch. vi.

military cadets, political figures of the old régime and frightened latifundistas, and the increased size of the government bureaucracy, opened up new channels for social mobility at an unusual rate, especially given the relative stability of the 1940s and early 1950s.

But the MNR had found that while destroying the old régime was simple, creating a new and functioning society was extremely difficult. The tin industry which it seized was a high cost, low quality, industry, with decaying capital investment, producing above world tin prices. Inflation wiped out government resources and agrarian reform initially kept large quantities of foodstuffs off the market, as peasants consumed more of their own products. The net result of this economic crisis was that the MNR leadership decided to turn to North American aid on a massive scale to support themselves in power while reconstructing the economy.

The Bolivian government astutely obtained massive assistance, despite the existence of a hard line anti-communist government in Washington, but they had to pay a heavy price for it. Among other things, the acceptance of North American aid forced the government to end the worker-middle class alliance, and to return COMIBOL, the government tin company, to orthodox management. It meant the opening up of Bolivia's oil fields to North American companies for the first time since 1938. It meant a retrenchment on some of the social welfare legislation with the return to a severely orthodox monetary policy. And finally by the late 1950s and early 1960s it meant the reinstatement of a powerful North American-trained and equipped national army as a prime guarantor of social peace.

The party itself, under the tripartite direction of Paz Estenssoro, Lechín and Siles Zuazo, was able to maintain much of the revolutionary impetus, while abandoning many of its more radical features, and until the early 1960s a delicate but operative balance was maintained within the party between right, left and centre. Unfortunately for the party, Paz Estenssoro, who held the balance between the two wings, with the very unsophisticated support of the North Americans, decided to give up his neutral position and attempted to create an outright dictatorship by serving a third term in office. The inevitable and predictable result was the unification of the two wings of the party against Paz and his successful overthrow by the American-trained army.[1] This action resulted in the destruction of the MNR. By the end of the second four-year term in 1964 the party was already divided by autonomous wings and sectors voting contrary to party discipline in congress. In the struggle over the succession and the issue of the third term, the whole labour wing finally broke with its middle-class supporters and formed a more revolutionary group. The subsequent exiling of Paz Estenssoro destroyed his own following of the middle, which left only Siles and his conservative supporters who found themselves competing fiercely with a host of new parties for middle-class support.

The actual overthrow of Paz Estenssoro had been warmly supported by Lechín and the COB (Confederación Obrera Boliviana). But what appeared to observers at the time as a possible army-labour-left coalition never took place.[2] In fact, by 1964 the army had been largely recreated in the image of the pre-1952 institution. Based on massive technical assistance from the United States, Paz Estenssoro in his last years of office had deliberately attempted to make the army into the single most powerful political and military force in the country, outweighing the civilian militias, the armed mine workers and the peasant *sindicatos*. He was eminently successful. By 1964 the army was the arbiter of national political life and easily gained office when the MNR collapsed.

The army of 1964, however, was unquestionably committed to an anti-labour and militant anti-communist position, in common with both the new and older elements in the urban middle classes. It therefore rejected labour support and rapidly aligned itself with the remains of the falange, previously uncommitted elements of the middle class (most of whom were in the MNRA or Christian democratic camps) and what remained of the traditional upper élite; i.e. private small miners, merchants, bankers

---

[1] General Barrientos, formerly head of the air force, and then the official vice-president, led the so-called 'Revolución Restaurada' on 4 November 1964, and within a few hours secured the overthrow of the tottering Paz Estenssoro régime, forcing the president into exile. *El Diario*, 5 November 1964, p. 1.

[2] The 'Revolución Restaurada' was officially endorsed by both Lechín and Siles Zuazo (*El Diario*, 5 November 1964, p. 2), and both the COB and the FSTMB endorsed the revolutionary group in the early hours of the Barrientos-Ovando régime (*ibid.* p. 5).

and the few industrialists. This new coalition deliberately destroyed the COB and FSTMB, outlawing both organizations, and at the same time froze wages in order to force the Bolivian working class to bear the brunt of economic development. This has led to bitter conflict and new government massacres of miners, massacres even more destructive of life than the famous Catavi debacle.[1]

But though the post-1964 régimes have bitterly attacked organized labour and the extreme radical elements, they have neither threatened nor destroyed in any way the most fundamental socio-economic and political reforms of the régime: land reform, nationalization of the mines and universal suffrage. Above all, they have accepted the power and involvement of the Indian peasant masses. As the November 1964 revolutionary decree announcing the new régime made quite clear, 'we adamantly assure the peasants that their land holdings will be zealously guaranteed'.[2] Furthermore, when it did put aside the new MNR constitution of 1952, it returned to the old Villarroel charter of 1945 with the 1947 modifications, in addition to 'maintaining the nationalization of the great mining enterprises, the agrarian reform, the education code and the universal vote . . . as measures necessary for the social, economic and political development of the country'.[3]

[1] In September 1965, there was a clash between the 'Rangers', an élite army unit trained by the US Special Forces, and miners at Siglo XX, with some 30 miners officially listed as killed and 100 wounded. Although the original impetus for the fighting was the arrest by the government of illegal POR mine leaders, even *El Diario* admitted the basic cause was the government's lowering of salaries and ending of all bonus payments. It appears that the government troops deliberately broke up unarmed demonstrations and there is some question as to whether air force planes and rockets were used on the miners' housing compounds. *El Diario*, 1 January 1966, segunda sección, p. 5. Apparently the 'Rangers' have been particularly brutal in recent strike repression activity and have committed numerous atrocities against workers and their families. Interview with Guillermo Lora, La Paz, 15 August 1966.
[2] *El Diario*, 5 November 1964, p. 1.
[3] *El Diario*, 6 November 1964, p. 3. Indicative of the rather important role of the campesinos in the post-1964 régime is the existence of the important Confederación de Campesinos, whose leader was the first minister of campesino affairs in the new Barrientos civilian government. *El Diario*, 7 October 1966, p. 1. The continued strength of the campesino movement, especially in the key Cochabamba valley, was well illustrated in October 1965, when a force of 3,000 armed peasants on over 100 trucks arrived uninvited in Cochabamba to protest against a meeting of the FSB in the city. The particular leader of this

The new post-revolutionary régimes thus represent an entirely new coalition of the revolutionary forces unleashed by the 1950s reform. Rejecting its rather uneasy partnership with organized labour, the middle class[1] has now aligned itself with the organized peasant groups in frank opposition to labour and the extreme left. The rejuvenated army has again returned to a powerful national political role, but as the defender of the conservative elements of the new middle class and the peasants, who have both been the prime beneficiaries of American aid and the revolutionary restructuring of society. It is in many ways reminiscent of aspects of the classical post-revolutionary alignment in France.

At the time of writing, the permanence of this new three-part coalition is still an open question, especially as the fall of the MNR has left national politics divided among a multiplicity of competing parties.[2] There is little doubt, however, that the

group, after being persuaded to leave the city, proudly announced that the campesinos possessed arms and munitions in arsenals in the key provincial cities of Sacaba, Quillacollo and Puñata, and vowed that these arms would never be surrendered or returned to anyone, because they were needed to defend the interests of the campesinos. *El Diario*, 1 January 1966, segunda sección, p. 6.

[1] The middle class was now composed of those elements which had not been destroyed by inflation: the merchants, industrialists, and small miners and a group which became known in popular terminology as *los nuevos ricos*, the members of the MNR and their supporters who grew wealthy on the US aid programmes and the vast increase in government bureaucracy.

[2] After the Barrientos overthrow, two major groups of parties emerged as the most important on the political scene. The first of these, the *Frente de la Revolución Boliviana* is a coalition of old MNR separatist parties, which had the strong support of the PRA (Walter Guevara Arze's old auténtico party), and a newly revitalized and considerably toned down PIR under the leadership of the old radical but now reformed Ricardo Anaya. Of equal strength with this government coalition movement and the PRA and PIR parties, was the unified Christian democratic movement known as the *Comunidad Democrática Cristiana* and led by the Falange Socialista Boliviana under the leadership of Mario R. Gutiérrez Gutiérrez. Apart from the FSB, the CDC included the Movimiento Popular Cristiano and the Partido Democrático Cristiano.

Outside this government coalition and its Christian democratic 'opposition' was the old left-wing party of the MNR which had been created by Lechín and his followers even before the fall of Paz Estenssoro. This was known as the PRIN, or *Partido Revolucionario de la Izquierda Nacionalista*, and was led by Juan Lechín. Farther to the left, but also in basic opposition to the ideas of the Barrientos régime, were the official Partido Comunista Boliviana and Lora's old POR, which is still strong in the mine labour movement.

As for the traditional parties, the Liberals and the PURS both attempted to revive themselves after the fall of Paz Estenssoro, but both failed to make much impact and remain largely moribund. This analysis is based on the coalitions under the Barrientos presidential régime (inaugurated in August

development of mass participation in government, which was ushered in by the national revolution, has survived the demise of the MNR and the end of the initial revolutionary stages, and has become the fundamental framework of national political life in Bolivia.

1966) see *El Diario*, 6 August 1966, p. 1; and for the first cabinet composition, *El Diario* 7 August 1966, p. 1. On the attitude of the various parties to the Barrientos régime see the interview with FSB and CDC president Mario R. Gutiérrez Gutiérrez in *El Diario*, 1 January 1967, p. 11. On the origins of these parties, see the excellent compilation of programmes and founding histories in the study by Mario Rolón Anaya. *Política y partidos en Bolivia* (La Paz: Editorial 'Juventud', 1966), a work which was designed as a companion to the earlier Cornejo compilation.

FOUNDING DATES OF MAJOR POLITICAL PARTIES

Date	Party	Notes
1883	Partido Liberal	
1884*	Partido Conservador	Extinct by 1905
1914	Partido Republicano	Title changed to Partido Republicano Socialista in 1934
1920	Partido Republicano Genuino	Founded by the salamanquista wing of the P. Republicano
1927	Partido Nacionalista	Dissolved in 1936
1934	Partido Obrero Revolucionaro	Founded in exile in Argentina
1936	Partido Socialista	Created out of old P. Nacionalista under Baldivieso. Lasted only two or three years
1937	Falange Socialista Boliviana	Founded in exile in Chile
1939	Concordancia	First of numerous coalitions combining the two Republican parties, the Liberals and various other groups. Sometimes known as the Democratic or Anti-fascist alliance in the 1940s
1940	Partido de la Izquierda Revolucionaria	Temporarily dissolved from 1952–6
1942	Movimiento Nacionalista Revolucionario	Virtually dissolved in 1964
1944	Acción Social Democrática	Made into a formal partido in 1947, since 1960 it has worked closely with FSB
1946	Partido de la Unión Republicana Socialista	Definitive amalgamation of PRS & Partido Republicano Genuino
1950	Partido Comunista de Bolivia	Formed by left wing of old PIR
1954	Partido Democrático Cristiano	Founded as P. Social Cristiano and took new title in 1964
1960	Partido Revolucionario Auténtico	Originally called MNR Auténtico, formed from right wing of MNR
1964	Partido Revolucionario de la Izquierda Nacionalista	Created by left wing of MNR

* Approximate date.

PRESIDENTS OF BOLIVIA, 1880–1952*

President	Date	Party in Power
Narciso Campero	1880–1884	
Gregorio Pacheco	1884–1888	
Aniceto Arce	1888–1892	Conservative
Mariano Baptista	1892–1896	
Severo Fernández Alonso	1896–1899	
José Manuel Pando	1899–1904	
Ismael Montes	1904–1909	
Eliodoro Villazón	1909–1913	Liberal
Ismael Montes	1913–1917	
José Gutiérrez Guerra	1917–1920	
Bautista Saavedra	1921–1925	
Felipe Guzmán (provisional)	1925–1926	
Hernando Siles	1926–1930	Republican
Junta Militar de Gobierno (provisional)	1930–1931	
Daniel Salamanca	1931–1934	
José Luis Tejada Sorzano	1934–1936	Liberal
David R. Toro (President of Junta Militar de Gobierno)	1936–1938	Military Socialist
Germán Busch	1938–1939	
Carlos Quintanilla	1939–1940	Coalition-
Enrique Peñaranda	1940–1943	Conservative
Gualberto Villarroel	1943–1946	RADEPA-MNR
Tomás Monje Gutiérrez (President of Junta Provisional de Gobierno)	1946–1947	PURS-PIR
Enrique Hertzog	1947–1949	Coalition
Mamerto Urriolagoitia	1949–1951	
Junta Militar de Gobierno	1951–1952	Military

* There were also several short-lived provisional juntas in 1880, 1899, 1920, and 1946.

GLOSSARY

Note: I have included in this glossary only those Spanish words which occur most frequently in this work, which have Bolivian meanings that differ from common Spanish usage, or which are Indian or local words known only in the Andean region. Before turning to this glossary, readers can translate for themselves a great many of the Spanish terms used in this study by remembering two simple rules. The first is that the Spanish form for designating individuals who are party members, followers of individual leaders, or supporters of an ideological position, is to add the suffix *ista* to the noun. Thus, for example, a *silista* is a supporter of Hernando Siles. Other commonly used designations are: *montista* (Ismael Montes), *patiñista* (Simón I. Patiño), *saavedrista* (Bautista Saavedra), *salamanquista* (Daniel Salamanca), *movimientista* (Movimiento Nacionalista Revolucionario), *guerrista* or *indigenista* (see below for definitions of these concepts). The second rule is that the suffix *ismo* is used like the English *ism* to designate an ideology: e.g. *nacionalismo*, *indigenismo*, etc.

alcalde: mayor of a community.

altiplano: the high plateau formed by the eastern and western ranges or *cordilleras* of the Andean mountains in Bolivia and Peru.

ayllu: a self-governing and land-owning peasant community in the Andean region. Usually used to designate such villages, and/or clan-like organizations, in the pre-Columbian period, but sometimes applied to modern communities and thus interchangeable with the word *comunidad*.

campesino: peasant.

candidatura única: phrase used to designate a multi-party slate which supports a common list of candidates for an election. Sometimes the term *fórmula única* is used as a synonym.

carabineros: the national police force.

castas: at times synonymous to *cholo* and mulatto, and at other times used to designate all racial groups inferior in status to the whites (i.e. Indians, Negroes, *cholos* and mulattoes).

caudillo: a powerful political leader with a major following.

chicha: corn alcohol usually produced by mastication. It is the primary intoxicating beverage consumed by Bolivian Indians.

chichería: a tavern which serves chicha.

cholo: a person of mixed Indian-white descent, often known as a mestizo in other parts of Latin America.

chuño: dehydrated potato flour.

colono: a landless peasant who supplies free agricultural labour on a latifundia in return for the use of usufruct land for his own crops. The system of *colono* labour is known as *colonato*. Also see *pongo*.

Glossary

comunidad: a self-governing and land-owning Indian peasant community. The *comunidad* contains three types of comunarios, or members of the community, that is: *originarios,* or original settlers of the community; *agregados,* or post-settlement arrivals who possess land; and *forasteros sin tierra,* or late arrivals who do not possess land. The latter usually sell their labour to the community.

corregidor: the official in republican Bolivia charged with administering local Indian affairs, who is almost invariably a white or *cholo.*

divisas: foreign exchange earned by exporting companies.

emboscados: a derogatory term applied to those in the Chaco War who deliberately sought safe rearguard positions.

empleados: white-collar workers paid on a weekly or monthly basis, as opposed to *obreros* who are blue-collar workers and therefore paid on a daily or piece basis.

finca: the more common Bolivian term for a large landed estate; used synonymously with *latifundia* or *hacienda.*

golpe de estado: coup d'état. Sometimes shortened to *golpe.*

gremios: artisan guilds. Also see *sindicatos.*

guerrista: from *guerra,* or war, meaning a person who believes in a strong pro-war position and is usually an extreme nationalist as well.

hispanicismo: an ideological position which is pro-white and pro-hispanic culture.

indígena: Indian.

indigenismo: an ideological position which is pro-Indian and anti-hispanic culture. A person supporting these views is an *indigenista.*

jefe fracasado: the Bolivian army used the term *jefe* to designate officers above the rank of captain and below the rank of general, and *fracasado* means a failure. Thus the phrase indicates officers of that rank who were failures, cowards, etc.

jefe supremo: supreme leader.

juventud: literally means youth, but commonly used to mean young adults and university students.

mayordomo: a manager of a large landed estate, or *finca.* It can also mean the patron of a religious festival.

oriente: the eastern lowland region of Bolivia.

patria: homeland.

patrón: the owner of a finca. Sometimes spelled *patrono,* and for a female owner the form is *patrona.*

pensadores: intellectuals who theorize about social problems.

político: professional politician.

pongo: a landless Indian peasant required to perform non-agricultural work obligations for the *patrón* and his family. The labour system is known as *pongueaje* and is always associated with *colonato.*

programa: a political plan, scheme, programme or platform.

proyecto: a proposed law, project or plan; and/or a set of political proposals.

pulpería: a general merchandise store. Almost all large companies set up such 'company stores' for their own employees.

reivindicacionalismo: irredentism.

rosca: a derogatory term used to designate the oligarchy in general, or the supportive group of lawyers and others, in particular, who acted as administrators for the ruling élite. Literally means a padded ring for carrying weights on the head.

sayañas: the plots of land used by either the *colono* or *comunario* to produce their own crops.

sindicato: a modern style industrial union.

super-estado: super-state, referring to the mining companies who were above the law.

universidades populares: institutions of free adult education.

BIBLIOGRAPHY

NEWSPAPERS

La Calle (La Paz)
El Diario (La Paz)
La Razón (La Paz)
La República (La Paz)

PRIMARY MATERIALS

Ampuero, M. L. Dick. *Organización sindicalista*. La Paz: Biblioteca Revolucionaria, 1926.

Anaya, Ricardo. *Unidos venceremos, PIR, Mensaje al pueblo boliviano*. Santiago de Chile: n.p., July–August, 1945.

Arze, José Antonio. *Bolivia bajo el terrorismo nazifascista*. Lima: Editora Peruana, November 1945.

Arze Quiroga, Eduardo (ed.). *Documentos para una historia de la guerra del Chaco, seleccionados del archivo de Daniel Salamanca*. 3 vols. La Paz: Editorial Don Bosco, 1951–60.

Ascarrunz, Moisés. *El Partido Liberal en el poder, a través de los mensajes presidenciales*. 2 vols. La Paz: Arno Hermanos, [1917].

Balcázar, Juan Manuel. *Los problemas sociales en Bolivia, una mistificación demagógica: la 'masacre' de Catavi*. La Paz: n.p., 1947.

Banco Central de Bolivia. *El Banco Central de Bolivia durante la guerra del Chaco*. La Paz: Editorial 'America', 1936.

Banco Minero de Bolivia, Sección Estadística y Estudios Económicos. *Tasas e impuestos sobre la industria minera en Bolivia*. La Paz: Imprenta 'Artística', 1941.

Blanco, Pedro Aniceto. *Monografía de la industria minera en Bolivia*. La Paz: J. Miguel Gamarra, 1910.

Bresson, André. *Bolivia, sept annés d'explorations, de voyages et de séjours dans l'Amérique australe*. Paris: Librairie Coloniale, 1886.

Bureau of the American Republics. *Bolivia*. Bulletin No. 55. Washington, 1892.

Busch, Germán. *Código del trabajo*. La Paz: Gran Editorial 'Popular', 1946.

Bustamante, Daniel S. *Programa político. Problemas de Bolivia en 1918*. La Paz: Imprenta Velarde, 1918.

Cabrera R., Sinforoso. *La burocracia estrangula a la COMIBOL*. La Paz: Editorial 'La Paz', 1960.

Canelas, Demetrio (ed.). *Documentos políticos*. [La Paz: Partido Republicano Genuino, 1938?].

Bibliography

Capriles, R., Remberto and Gastón Arduz Eguía. *El problema social en Bolivia, condiciones de vida y de trabajo.* La Paz: Editorial Fénix, 1941.

Castro, Donald S., *et al. Statistical Abstract of Latin America, 1963.* Los Angeles: Center of Latin American Studies, U.C.L.A., 1963.

Confederación Socialista Boliviana. *Programa unificado.* La Paz: n.p., 7 December 1935.

Convención Nacional de 1938. *Redactor de la Convención Nacional.* 5 vols. La Paz: Editorial 'Universo', 1938-9.

Convención Nacional. *Redactor de la H. Convención Nacional.* 4 vols. La Paz: Editorial La Paz, 1944.

Cornejo, Alberto. *El problema social de la vivienda* Cochabamba: Imprenta Universitaria, [1948].

Cornejo S., Alberto. *Programas políticos de Bolivia.* Cochabamba: Imprenta Universitaria, 1949.

Dalence, José María. *Bosquejo estadístico de Bolivia.* Chuquisaca: Imprenta de Sucre, 1851.

Departmento Nacional de Propaganda Socialista. *Informe presentado por el señor coronel Presidente de la Junta Militar Socialista de Gobierno al Ejército Nacional, de 17 de mayo a 31 de diciembre de 1936.* La Paz: Imprenta de la Intendencia General de Guerra, 1937.

Díaz Machicao, Porfirio. *La bestia emocional, autobiografía.* La Paz: Editorial 'Juventud', 1955.

Díez de Medina, Eduardo. *De un siglo al otro, memorial de un hombre público.* La Paz: Alfonso Tejerina, 1955.

Dirección General de Estadística y Censos. *Censo demográfico 1950.* La Paz: Editorial 'Argote', 1955.

Flores Moncayo, José. *Legislación boliviana del indio, recopilación, 1825-1953.* La Paz: Ministerio de Asuntos Campesinos, 1953.

Frente de Izquierda Boliviano. *¡Hacia la unidad de las izquierdas bolivianas!* Santiago de Chile: Talleres Gráficos 'Gutenberg', 1939.

Grupo Tupac Amaru. *Manifiesto, la victoria o la muerte (al pueblo boliviano: soldados, estudiantes, obreros).* N.p. [1934?].

Herndon, William Lewis and Lardner Gibbon. *Exploration of the Valley of the Amazon.* 2 vols. Washington: A.O.P. Nicholson, 1854.

Hinojosa, Roberto. *La revolución de Villazón.* La Paz: Editorial La Universal, [1944].

Humphreys, R. A. (ed.). *British Consular Reports on the Trade and Politics of Latin America, 1824-1826.* Camden Third Series, Vol. LXIII; London: Royal Historical Society, 1940.

Interview with Ricardo Anaya, La Paz, 20 August 1963.
Interview with Waldo Álvarez, La Paz, 11 October 1961.

Bibliography

Interview with Colonel Julio Díaz Argüedas, La Paz, 28 June 1961.
Interviews with Guillermo Lora, La Paz, 20 June 1963, and 15 August 1966.
Interview with Jorge Muñoz Reyes, La Paz, January 1961.
Interview with Colonel Julio A. Saavedra G., La Paz, 23 September 1961.

Lara, Jesús. *Repete, diario de un hombre que fué a la guerra del Chaco*. 2nd ed. Cochabamba: Editorial Canelas, 1938.
El libro blanco de la independencia económica de Bolivia. La Paz: S.P.I.C., 1952.
El libro blanco de la reforma agraria. La Paz: S.P.I.C., 1953.
Lora, Guillermo (ed.). *Programa obrero*. La Paz: Ediciones 'Masas', 1959.

Malagón, Javier (ed.). *Las actas de independencia de América*. Washington, D.C.: Unión Panamericana, 1955.
Maldonado, Abraham. *Derecho agrario. Historia-doctrina-legislación*. La Paz: Editorial Nacional, 1956.
Legislación social boliviana. La Paz: Editorial Nacional, 1957.
Movimiento Nacionalista Revolucionario. *Sus bases y principios de acción inmediata*. La Paz: n.p., 7 June 1942.
Víctor Paz Estenssoro y la masacre de Catavi. La Paz: MNR, Servicio de Publicidad y Orientación Popular, 1943.
Muñoz Reyes, Jorge. *La caducidad de las concesiones otorgadas a The Standard Oil Company of Bolivia*. Cuartillas informativas, No. 5; La Paz: Departamento Nacional de Propaganda Socialista, 23 March 1937.

Oficina Nacional de Inmigración, Estadística y Propaganda Geográfica. *Censo nacional de la población de la república, 1° de setiembre de 1900*. 2 vols. La Paz: José M. Gamarra, 1902–4.
Geografía de la república de Bolivia. La Paz: Ismael Argote, 1905.
Sinopsis estadística y geográfica de la república de Bolivia. 2 vols. La Paz: José M. Gamarra, 1903.
Oficina Nacional de Estadística y Censos, Sección Agropecuaria. *Censo nacional agropecuario de 1950*. La Paz, mimeo [1950?].
D'Orbigny, Alcides. *Viaje a la américa meridional*. S. Pastor, ed. and A. Cepeda trans. 4 vols. Buenos Aires: Editorial Futuro, 1945.
Ostria Gutiérrez, Alberto. *Una obra y un destino. La política internacional de Bolivia después de la guerra del Chaco*. 2nd ed. Buenos Aires: Imprenta López, 1953.

Partido Comunista de Bolivia. *Primer congreso nacional del P.C.B., documentos*. La Paz: n.p., 5–9 April 1959.
Partido de la Izquierda Revolucionaria. *Programa y estatutos del Partido de la Izquierda Revolucionaria*. La Paz: n.p., 1941.
P.I.R. y desarrollo nacional, soluciones para los problemas nacionales. La Paz: Talleres Gráficos 'Gutenberg', 1961.
Partido Liberal. *La política liberal, formulada por el jefe del partido, General Eliodoro Camacho*. Nueva ed. La Paz: Imprenta Andina, 1916.

Bibliography

Patiño Mines & Ent. Cons. (Inc.). *Los conflictos sociales en 1947.* La Paz: Editorial 'Universo', March 1948.

Primera Convención de Estudiantes Bolivianos. *Programa de principios, estatuto orgánico y reglamento de debates de la Federación Universitaria Boliviana.* Cochabamba: Publicaciones de la Federación de Estudiantes de Cochabamba, 1928.

Quiroga Ch., José Antonio. *La política interna en el primer período de la guerra (documentos producidos en el proceso para formar el gabinete de concentración nacional).* Cochabamba: Editorial 'El Imparcial', 1932.

La revolución de 'El Palmar', principales documentos jurídicos del proceso. La Paz: Editorial 'Universo', 1938.

Rolón Anaya, Mario. *Política y partidos en Bolivia.* La Paz: Editorial 'Juventud', 1966.

Romero, F. Priegue. *La cruz de Bolivia, crónica de la revolución de Julio.* La Paz: Editorial Renacimiento, 1946.

[Dr W. S. W. Rushenberger]. *Three Years in the Pacific, Including Notices of Brazil, Chile, Bolivia and Peru.* Philadelphia: Carey, Lea & Blanchard, 1834.

Saavedra, Bautista. *La democracia en nuestra historia.* La Paz: Gonzalez y Media, 1921.

Saavedra, Bautista and Edmundo Vázquez. *Manifesto programa: donde estamos y a donde debemos ir.* La Paz: Partido Republicano Socialista, 30 September 1935.

Sección de Prensa de Palacio de Gobierno. *Bajo el régimen militar socialista. ¿Hay labor gobernativa?* La Paz: Imprenta Intendencia General de Guerra, 6 August 1936.

Sotomayor Valdés, Ramón. *Estudio histórico de Bolivia bajo la administración del Jeneral D. José María de Achá...* Santiago de Chile: Imprenta Andrés Bello, 1874.

Taborga T., Alberto. *Boquerón, diario de campaña.* La Paz: Editorial Canata, 1956.

Temple, Edmond. *Travels in Various Parts of Peru, Including a Year's Residence in Potosi.* 2 vols. London: Henry Colburn & Richard Bentley, 1830.

Toro R., David. *Mi actuación en la campaña del Chaco (Picuiba).* La Paz: Editorial Renacimiento, 1941.

United States, Department of State. *Foreign Relations of the United States, Diplomatic Papers, 1939.* 5 vols. Washington: Government Printing Office, 1957.

Foreign Relations of the United States, Diplomatic Papers, 1941. 7 vols. Washington: Government Printing Office, 1963.

Bibliography

Vázquez, Edmundo. *La economía y las finanzas de Bolivia (Documentos y opiniones emitidos sobre problemas emergentes de la crisis 1929–1930)*. La Paz: Imprenta 'Atenea', 1931.
Enderecemos nuestra ruta. Buenos Aires: n.p., 1946.

Weddell, Dr H. A. *Voyage dans le nord de la Bolivie* . . . Paris: P. Bertrand, 1853.

Zalles, Juan María. *Crónicas*. Santiago de Chile: Imprenta Universitaria, 1942.

SECONDARY MATERIALS

Academia de Ciencias Económicas, Buenos Aires. *Las cláusulas económico-sociales en las constituciones de América*. 2 vols. Buenos Aires: Editorial Losada, 1947–8.
Adams, Richard N. *et al. Social Change in Latin America Today*. New York: Vintage Books, 1960.
Alcázar, Moisés. *Abel Iturralde, el centinela del petróleo*. La Paz: Editorial 'La Paz', 1944.
Crónicas parlamentarias. 2nd ed. La Paz: Talleres Gráficos Bolivianos, 1957.
Alba, Víctor. *Historia del movimiento obrero en América Latina*. Mexico: Libreros Mexicanos Unidos, 1964.
Alexander, Robert J. *The Bolivian National Revolution*. New Brunswick: Rutgers University Press, 1958.
Communism in Latin America. New Brunswick: Rutgers University Press, 1957.
Almaraz, Sergio. *Petróleo en Bolivia*. La Paz: Editorial 'Juventud', 1958.
Alonso, Isidoro, *et al. La iglesia en Perú y Bolivia, estructuras sociales*. Estudios Socio-Religioso Latino-Americanos, No. 3, Vol. II. Friburgo and Bogota: Oficina Internacional de Investigaciones Sociales de FERES, 1962.
Álvarez, Moisés. 'La organización sindical en Bolivia', *Boletín del Ministerio del Trabajo, Previsión Social y Salubridad*, No. 1 (September, 1937), pp. 35–48.
[Álvarez, Waldo]. 'Fundación de la Federación Gráfica Boliviana', *Primer Congreso Nacional de Trabajadoes Gráficos*. La Paz: Federación Gráfica Boliviana, 1952.
Álvéstegui, David. *Salamanca, su gravitación sobre el destino de Bolivia*. 3 vols. La Paz: Talleres Gráficos Bolivianos, 1957–62.
Aramayo Alzerreca, Carlos. *Saavedra, el último caudillo* (prólogo de Tristán Marof). La Paz: Editorial 'La Paz', [1941].
Arana, Oswaldo. 'La novela de la guerra del Chaco: Bolivia y Paraguay'. Unpublished doctoral dissertation, Department of Modern Languages, University of Colorado, 1963.
Argüedas, Alcides. *La dictadura y la anarquía, 1857–1864*. Barcelona: López Roberto y Cía., 1926.
Historia general de Bolivia (el proceso de la nacionalidad), 1809–1921. La Paz: Arno Hermanos, 1922.
Obras completas. 2 vols. Mexico: Aguilar, 1959.

Bibliography

Arnade, Charles W. *The Emergence of the Republic of Bolivia*. Gainesville: University of Florida Press, 1957.

Arze, Armando. *Los fusilamientos del 20 de noviembre de 1944 y el Movimiento Nacionalista Revolucionario*. La Paz: Talleres Gráficos Bolivianos, 1952.

Arze, José Antonio. *Bolivia bajo el terrorismo nazi-fascista*. Lima: Empresa Editora Peruana, 1945.

Arze Louereiro, Eduardo. 'Actitudes sociales relativas a la reforma agraria en Bolivia', *Economía y Ciencias Sociales* (Caracas), Año III, nos. 1, 2 and 3 (September 1960 to March 1961), pp. 29–40.

Averanga Mollinedo, Asthenio. *Aspectos generales de la población boliviana*. La Paz: Editorial 'Argote', 1956.

Banco Central de Bolivia. *El Banco Central de Bolivia durante la guerra del Chaco*. La Paz: Editorial 'America', 1936.

Baptista Gumucio, Mariano. *Revolución y universidad en Bolivia*. La Paz: Editorial 'Juventud', 1956.

Barcelli S., Augustin. *Medio siglo de luchas sindicales revolucionarias en Bolivia, 1905–1955*. La Paz: Editorial del Estado, 1956.

Basadre, Jorge. *Chile, Perú y Bolivia independientes*. Barcelona: Salvat Editores, 1948.

Benavides M., Julio. *Historia bancaria de Bolivia*. La Paz: Ediciones 'Arrieta', 1955.

Blanksten, George. 'Constitutions and the Structure of Power', in Harold E. Davis (ed.). *Government and Politics in Latin America*. New York: The Roland Press, 1958.

Bonifaz, Miguel. *Bolivia, frustración y destino*. Sucre: Imprenta Universitaria de Sucre, 1965.

'El problema agrario indígena en Bolivia durante la época republicana', *Revista de Estudios Jurídicos, Políticos y Sociales* (Sucre), Año VIII, no. 18 (December 1947), pp. 65–102.

Burke, Melvin. 'An Analysis of the Bolivian Land Reform By Means of a Comparison Between Peruvian Haciendas and Bolivian Ex-Haciendas'. Unpublished doctoral dissertation, Department of Economics, University of Pittsburgh, 1967.

Burr, Robert N. *By Reason or Force, Chile and the Balance of Power in South America, 1830–1905*. Berkeley: University of California Press, 1965.

Canelas Lopez, René. 'El sindicalismo y los sindicatos en Bolivia', *Revista Jurídica* (Cochabamba), Año VIII, no. 35 (June 1946), pp. 44–82.

Canelas O., Amado. *Mito y realidad de la Corporación Minera de Bolivia*. La Paz: Editorial Los Amigos del Libro, 1966.

Mito y realidad de la industrializacion boliviana. La Paz: Editorial Los Amigos del Libro, 1966.

Bibliography

Carrasco, Benigno. *Hernando Siles*. La Paz: Editorial del Estado, 1961.

Carrasco, Manuel. *Simón I. Patiño, un prócer industrial*. Paris: Jean Grassin Editeur, 1960.

Carter, William E. *Aymara Communities and the Bolivian Agrarian Reform*. University of Florida Monographs, Social Sciences No. 24. Gainesville: University of Florida Press, 1964.

Cerruto, Oscar. *Aluvión de fuego*. Santiago de Chile: Ediciones Ercilla, 1935.

Céspedes, Augusto. *El dictador suicida, 40 años de historia de Bolivia*. Santiago de Chile: Editorial Universitaria, 1956.

El presidente colgado (historia boliviana). Buenos Aires: Editorial Jorge Álvarez, 1966.

Céspedes del Castillo, Guillermo. *Lima y Buenos Aires, repercusiones económicas y políticas de la creación del virreinato del Plata*. Sevilla: Escuela de Estudios Hispano-Americanos, 1947.

Chang-Rodrígues, Eugenio. *La literatura política de González Prada, Mariátegui y Haya de la Torre*. Mexico: Andrea, 1957.

Cleven, N. Andrew N. *The Political Organization of Bolivia*. Washington: Carnegie Institute, 1940.

Colin, Michel. *Le Cuzco à la fin du xviie et au début du xviiie siècle*. Caen: Faculté des Lettres et Sciences Humaines de l'Université de Caen, 1966.

Comisión Económica para América Latina. *El desarrollo económico de Bolivia*. Análisis y Proyecciones del Desarrollo Económico, No. IV. Mexico: Naciones Unidas, Departmento de Asuntos Economicos y Sociales, 1958.

Condarco Morales, Ramiro. *Zarate, el 'Temible' Willka, historia de la rebelión indígena de 1899*. La Paz: Talleres Gráficos Bolivianos, 1966.

Cornejo S., Alberto. *El problema social de la vivienda*. Cochabamba: Imprenta Universitaria, [1948].

Costa du Rels, A. *Felix Avelino Aramayo y su época, 1846–1929*. Buenos Aires: Domingo Viau y Cía., 1942.

Crespo, Alfonso. *Santa Cruz, el cóndor indio*. Mexico: Fondo de Cultura Económica, 1944.

Dandler-Hanhart, Jorge. 'Local Group, Community and Nation: a Study of Changing Structure in Ucureña, Bolivia (1935–1952)'. Unpublished MA thesis, Department of Anthropology, University of Wisconsin, 1967.

Davis, James C. 'Toward A Theory of Revolution', *American Sociological Review*, Vol. XXVII, no. 1 (February 1962), pp. 5–19.

Di Tella, Torcuato. 'Populismo y reforma en América Latina', *Desarrollo Económico* (Buenos Aires), Vol. 4, no. 16 (April–June 1965), 391–425.

Díaz Argüedas, Julio. *Como fué derrocado el hombre símbolo (Salamanca), un capítulo de la guerra con el Paraguay*. La Paz: Fundación Universitaria 'Simón I. Patiño', 1957.

La guerra con el Paraguay, resumen histórico-biográfico 1932–1935. La Paz: Imprenta de Intendencia Central del Ejército, 1942.

Bibliography

Díaz Machicao, Porfirio. *Historia de Bolivia, Saavedra, 1920–1925.* La Paz: Alfonso Tejerina, 1954.

Historia de Bolivia, Guzmán, Siles, Blanco Galindo, 1925–1931. La Paz: Gisbert y Cía., 1955.

Historia de Bolivia, Salamanca, la guerra del Chaco, Tejada Sorzano, 1931–1936. La Paz: Gisbert y Cía., 1955.

Historia de Bolivia, Toro, Busch, Quintanilla, 1936–1940. La Paz: Editorial 'Juventud', 1957.

Historia de Bolivia, Peñaranda, 1940–1943. La Paz: Editorial 'Juventud', 1958.

Díez de Medina, Fernando. *Literatura boliviana.* Madrid: Aguilar, 1954.

Durán P., Manuel. *La reforma universitaria en Bolivia.* Oruro: Universidad Técnica de Oruro, 1961.

Elter [Luis Toro Ramallo]. *Una página de la historia de Bolivia.* Santiago de Chile: Editorial Nascimiento, 1938.

Erasmus, Charles J. 'Upper Limits of Peasantry and Agrarian Reform: Bolivia, Venezuela and Mexico Compared', *Ethnology,* Vol. vi, no. 4 (October 1967), pp. 349–80.

Fellman Velarde, José. *Víctor Paz Estenssoro: el hombre y la revolución.* 2nd ed. La Paz: E. Burillo, 1955.

Finot, Enrique. *Nueva historia de Bolivia (ensayo de interpretación sociológica).* 2nd. ed. La Paz: Gisbert y Cía., 1954.

Fitzgibbon, Russell H. 'Constitutional Developments in Latin America: A Synthesis', *American Political Science Review,* Vol. xxxix, no. 3 (June 1945), pp. 511–22.

Flores, Edmundo. 'Taraco: monografía de un latifundio del altiplano boliviano', *El Trimestre Económico* (Mexico), Vol. xxii, no. 2 (1955), pp. 209–30.

Ford, Thomas R. *Man and Land in Peru.* Gainesville: University of Florida Press, 1955.

Francovich, Guillermo. *La filosofía en Bolivia.* Buenos Aires: Editorial Losada, 1945.

El pensamiento boliviano en el siglo xx. Mexico: Fondo de Cultura Económica. 1956.

Frerking Salas, Oscar. 'Las cláusulas económico-sociales en la Constitución Política de Bolivia', Academia de Ciencias Económicas, Buenos Aires, *Las cláusulas económico-sociales,* p. 64.

Galarza, Ernest. 'Debts, Dictatorship and Revolution in Bolivia and Peru', *Foreign Policy Reports,* Vol. vii, no. 5 (13 May 1931), pp. 101–18.

García, Antonio. 'La reforma agraria y desarrollo social en Bolivia', *El Trimestre Económico* (Mexico), Vol. xxxi, no. 123 (July–September, 1964), pp. 339–87.

Germani, Gino. *Política y sociedad en una época de transición: de la sociedad tradicional a la sociedad de masas.* Buenos Aires: Editorial Paidos, 1962.

Bibliography

Gibb, George Sweet and Evelyn H. Knowlton. *History of Standard Oil Company (New Jersey): The Resurgent Years, 1911–1927.* New York: Harper & Brothers, 1956.

Gómez García, René and Rubén Darío Flores. *La banca nacional.* La Paz: Editora 'Universo', 1962.

Goodrich, Carter. *The Economic Transformation of Bolivia.* Bulletin No. 34; Ithaca: New York State School of Industrial and Labour Relations, Cornell University, October 1955.

Great Britain, Foreign Office. *Trade of Bolivia for the Year 1904.* (Diplomatic and Consular Reports, Annual Series, No. 3388.) London: His Majesty's Stationery Office, June 1905.

Greene, David G. 'Revolution and the Rationalization of Reform in Bolivia', *Inter-American Economic Affairs*, Vol. XIX, no. 3 (Winter 1965), pp. 3–26.

Guzmán, Augusto. *Baptista, biografía de un orador político.* 2nd ed.; La Paz: Editorial 'Juventud', 1957.

La novela en Bolivia. La Paz: Editorial 'Juventud', 1955.

Hanke, Lewis. *The Imperial City of Potosí.* The Hague: Nijhoff, 1956.

and Gunnar Mendoza (eds.). Bartolomé Arzáns de Orsúa y Vele. *Historia de la Villa Imperial de Potosí.* 3 vols. Providence, R. I.: Brown University Press, 1965.

Haya de la Torre, Víctor. *¿A donde va Indoamérica?* 3rd ed. Santiago de Chile: Editorial Ercilla, 1936.

Harms Espejo, Carlos. *Bolivia en sus diversas fases, principalmente económica.* Santiago de Chile: Talleres, 1922.

Ibáñez C., Donaciano. *Historia mineral de Bolivia.* Antofagasta: Imprenta Macfarlane, 1943.

Iñiguez, Juan and Antonio Llosa. *Antitesis de Pulacayo.* La Paz: n.p., October 1950.

Instituto de Investigaciones Históricas y Culturales de la Paz. *Mesa redonda sobre el problema del litoral boliviano.* La Paz: Municipalidad de La Paz, 1966.

Iundzill, Adam Dunin. *Du commerce bolivien, considérations sur l'avenir des relations entre l'Europe et la Bolivie.* Paris: G.-A. Pinard, 1856.

Jara, Álvaro. 'Dans le Pérou du XVIe siècle: La coubre de production des métaux monnayables', *Annales, E.S.C.*, Année 23, no. 3 (May–June, 1967), pp. 590–603.

Johnson, John J. *Political Change in Latin America, The Emergence of the Middle Sectores.* Stanford: Stanford University Press, 1964.

(ed.). *Continuity and Change in Latin America.* Stanford: Stanford University Press, 1964.

Bibliography

Keller, Frank Leuer. 'Finca Ingavi: A Medieval Survival on the Bolivian Alti-
plano', *Economic Geography*, Vol. xvxi (1950), pp. 37–50.
'Geography of the Lake Titicaca Basin of Bolivia, A Comparative Study of
Great Landed Estates and Highland Indian Communities'. Unpublished doc-
toral dissertation, Department of Geography, University of Maryland, 1949.
Klein, Herbert S. 'American Oil Companies in Latin America: The Bolivian
Experience', *Inter-American Economic Affairs*, Vol. xviii, no. 2 (Autumn
1964), pp. 47–72.
'The Creation of the Patiño Tin Empire', *Inter-American Economic Affairs*,
Vol. xix, no. 2 (Autumn 1965), pp. 3–23.
'The Crisis of Legitimacy and the Origins of Social Revolution: The Bolivian
Experience', *Journal of Inter-American Studies*, Vol. x, no. 1 (January 1968),
pp. 102–10.
'David Toro and the Establishment of "Military Socialism" in Bolivia',
Hispanic American Historical Review, Vol. xiv, no. 1 (February 1965),
pp. 25–52.
'Germán Busch and the Era of "Military Socialism" in Bolivia', *Hispanic
American Historical Review*, Vol. xlvii, no. 2 (May 1967), pp. 166–84.
'Social Constitutionalism in Latin America: The Bolivian Experience',
The Americas, Vol. xxii, no. 3 (January 1966), pp. 258–76.
Origenes de la Revolución Nacional Boliviana, la crisis de la generación del Chaco.
La Paz: Editorial 'Juventud', 1968.
Kling, Merle. 'Towards A Theory of Power and Political Instability in Latin
America', *Western Political Quarterly*, Vol. ix, no. 1 (March 1956), pp. 21–3.
Knorr, K. E. *Tin Under Control*. Stanford: Food Research Institute, Stanford
University Press, 1945.

Leonard, Olen E. *Bolivia, Land, People and Institutions*. Washington: The Scare-
crow Press, 1952.
Leons, Madeline Barbara. 'Land Reform in the Bolivian Yungas', *América
Indígena*, Vol. xxvii, no. 4 (October 1967), pp. 689–712.
Lipset, Seymour Martin. *Political Man, The Social Bases of Politics*. New York:
Doubleday and Co., 1963.
López, Pedro N. *Bolivia y el petróleo*. La Paz: n.p., 1922.
López Rivas, Eduardo. *Esquema de la historia económica de Bolivia*. Oruro:
Universidad Técnica de Oruro, 1955.
Lora, Guillermo. 'De grupo de propaganda, a partido de masas'. Unpublished
manuscript.
'Historia del movimiento sindical boliviano (sus tendencias políticas)'.
Unpublished manuscript.
'Revolution and Counter-Revolution in Bolivia, the Great Decade of Class
Struggles', *Fourth International* (New York), Vol. xiii, no. 3 (May–June
1952), pp. 89–94.
José Aguirre Gainsborg, fundador del POR. La Paz: Ediciones 'Masas', 1960.
El stalinismo en los sindicatos. La Paz: Ediciones 'Masas', 1963.

Bibliography

Loza, León M. *Bolivia, el petróleo y la Standard Oil Company*. Publicación no. 3 de Yacimientos Petrolíferos Fiscales Bolivianos. Sucre: Editorial 'Charcas', 1939.

Malloy, James M. 'Bolivia: A Study in Revolution'. Unpublished doctoral dissertation, Department of Political Science, University of Pittsburgh, 1967.

McBride, George McCutchen. *The Agrarian Indian Communities of Highland Bolivia*. New York: American Geographical Society, 1921.

McLeod, Murdo. 'Bolivia and its Social Literature before and after the Chaco War: a historical study of Social and Literary Revolution'. Unpublished doctoral dissertation, Department of History, University of Florida, 1962.

McQueen, Charles A. *Bolivian Public Finance*. (Trade Promotion Series, No. 6). Washington: Department of Commerce, 1925.

Marof, Tristán [Gustavo Adolfo Navarro]. *La tragedia del altiplano*. Buenos Aires: Editorial Claridad, 1934.

El peligro nazi en Bolivia. La Paz: Ediciones del Partido Socialista Obrero de Bolivia, 1941.

Marsh, Margaret Alexander. *The Bankers in Bolivia, A Study in American Foreign Investment*. New York: Vanguard Press, 1928.

Mendoza, Francisco (ed.). *La misión Kemmerer en Bolivia, proyectos e informes*. La Paz: Arnó Hermanos, 1927.

Mendoza López, Alberto. *La soberanía de Bolivia estrangulada*. La Paz: Editorial Trabajo, 1942.

Mendoza López, Vicente. *Las finanzas en Bolivia y la estrategia capitalista*. La Paz: Escuela Tip. Salesiana, 1940.

Montenegro, Carlos. *Frente al derecho del estado, el oro de la Standard Oil (el petroleo, sangre de Bolivia)*. La Paz: Editorial 'Trabajo', 1938.

Nacionalismo y coloniaje. 3rd ed. La Paz: Biblioteca Paceña—Alcaldía Municipal, 1953.

Movimiento Nacionalista Revolucionario. *El catolicismo frente al falangismo fascista*. La Paz: Publicaciones de la S.P.I.C., [1953?]

Muñoz Reyes, Jorge. *Bosquejo de geografía de Bolivia*. Rio de Janeiro: Instituto Panamericano de Geografía e Historia, 1956.

Ness, Norman T. 'The Movement of Capital into Bolivia, a backward Country'. Unpublished doctoral dissertation, Department of Economics, Harvard University, 1938.

Oddone, Jacinto. *Historia del socialismo argentina*. 2 vols. Buenos Aires: 'La Vanguardia', 1934.

Olmos, Coronel Gualberto. *Coronel Gualberto Villarroel, su vida, su martirio*. La Paz: S.P.I.C., [1953?].

Olson Jr., Mancur. 'Rapid Economic Change as a Destabilizing Force', *Journal of Economic History*, Vol. XXIII, no. 4 (December 1963), pp. 529–58.

Osborne, Harold. *Bolivia, A Land Divided*. 2nd ed. London: Royal Institute of International Affairs, 1955.

Bibliography

Ostria Gutiérrez, Alberto. *Un pueblo en la cruz, el drama de Bolivia*. Santiago de Chile: Editorial del Pacífico, 1956.
Una revolución tras los Andes. Santiago de Chile: Editorial Nascimiento, 1944.

Patch, Richard W. 'The Bolivian Falange', *American University Field Staff*, Report dated 14 May 1959.
'Social Implications of the Bolivian Agrarian Reform'. Unpublished doctoral dissertation, Department of Anthropology, Cornell University, 1956.

Paz Estenssoro, Víctor. 'El pensamiento económico en Bolivia', *El pensamiento económico latinoamericano*. Mexico: Fondo de Cultura Económico, 1945.

Peñaloza, Luis. *Historia económica de Bolivia*. 2 vols. La Paz: n.p., 1953–4.
Historia del movimiento nacionalista revolucionario, 1941–1952. La Paz: Editorial 'Juventud', 1963.

Poblete Troncoso, Moisés. *El movimiento obrero latino-americano*. Mexico: Fondo de Cultura Económica, 1946.

Prudencio Bustillo, Ignacio. *La vida y la obra de Aniceto Arce*. 2nd ed. La Paz: Fundación Universitaria 'Simón I. Patiño', 1951.

¿Quién es quién en Bolivia? Buenos Aires: Editorial Quién es quién en Bolivia, 1942.

Reyeros, Rafael. *El pongueaje, la servidumbre personal de los indios bolivianos*. La Paz: Empresa Editora 'Universo', 1949.

Rojas, Casto. *Historia financiera de Bolivia*. La Paz: Talleres Gráficos 'Marinoni', 1916.

Rosenblat, Ángel. *La población indígena y el mestizaje en América*. 2 vols. Buenos Aires: Editorial Nova, 1954.

Saavedra, Bautista. *El ayllu, estudios sociológicos*. 3rd ed. La Paz: Gisbert y Cía., 1955.

Salinas Baldivieso, Carlos A. *Historia diplomática de Bolivia*. Sucre: n.p., 1938.

Sanjines G., Alfredo. *La reforma agraria en Bolivia*. 2nd ed. rev. La Paz: Editorial Universo, 1945.

Santa Cruz Schuhkrafft, Andrés de. *Cuadros sinópticos de los gobernantes de la República de Bolivia 1825 a 1956 y de la del Perú 1820 a 1956*. La Paz: Fundación Universitaria 'Simón I. Patiño', 1956.

Schmeider, Oscar. *Geografía de América Latina*. Mexico: Fondo de Cultura Económica, 1965.

Schurz, W. L. *Bolivia, A Commercial and Industrial Handbook*. Washington: Department of Commerce, 1921.

Sétaro, Ricardo M. *Secretos de estado mayor*. Buenos Aires: Editorial Claridad, 1936.

Siles Salinas, Jorge. *La aventura y el orden, refleciones sobre la revolución boliviana*, prólogo de Roberto Prudencio. Santiago de Chile: n.p., 1956.

Bibliography

Soetbeer, Adolf. *Edelmetall-Produktion und Werthverhaltniss zwischen Gold und Silber seit der Entdeckung Amerikas bis zur Gegenwart.* Gotha: Justus Perthes, 1879.

Soria Galvamo, Rodolfo. *Últimos días del gobierno Alonso.* 2nd ed. Potosí: Imprenta Ángel Santelices, 1920.

Special Operations Research Office. *U.S. Army Handbook for Bolivia.* Washington: Foreign Area Studies Division, American University, August 1963.

Stokes, William S. 'Parliamentary Government in Latin America', *American Political Science Review*, Vol. XXXIX, no. 3 (June 1945), pp. 522–36.

Stone, Lawrence. 'Theories of Revolution', *World Politics.* Vol. XVIII, no. 2 (January 1966), pp. 159–76.

Thibodeaux, Ben H. 'An Economic Study of Agriculture in Bolivia'. Unpublished doctoral dissertation, Department of Economics, Harvard University, 1946.

Trigo, Ciro Félix. *Las constituciones de Bolivia.* Madrid: Instituto de Estudios Políticos, 1958.

Urioste, Ovidio. *La encrucijada, estudio histórico, político, sociológico y militar de la guerra del Chaco.* Cochabamba: Editorial Canelas, [1940].

La fragua, comprende la primera faz de la compaña hasta la caída de Boquerón y el abandono de Arce. [Cochabamba]: n.p. [1933].

Urquidi Morales, Arturo. *La comunidad indígena, precedentes sociológicos, vicisitudes históricos.* Cochabamba: Imprenta Universitaria, 1941.

Valencia Vega, Alipio. *Desarrollo del pensamiento político en Bolivia (bosquejo).* La Paz: Editorial. 'Trabajo', 1953.

Vázquez Machicado, Humberto, José de Mesa and Teresa Gisbert. *Manuel de historia de Bolivia.* La Paz: Gisbert y Cia., 1958.

Vellard, J. *Civilisations des Andes, évolution des populations du haut-plateau bolivien.* Paris: Gallimard, 1963.

Vergara Vicuña, Aquiles. *Bernardino Bilbao Rioja, vida y hechos.* La Paz: Imprenta Unidas, 1948.

Walle, Paul. *Bolivia, Its People and Resources.* Trans. B. Miall. New York: Charles Scribner's Sons, 1914.

Wells, Henry, *et al. Bolivia Election Factbook, July 3, 1966.* Washington: Institute for the Comparative Study of Political Systems, Operations and Policy Research, Inc., 1966.

Weston, Jr., Charles H. 'An Ideology of Modernization: The Case of the Bolivian MNR', *Journal of Inter-American Studies*, Vol. X, no. 1 (January 1968), pp. 85–101.

'The Coming to Power of the Bolivian National Revolutionary Movement'. Unpublished MA thesis, Department of Political Science, University of Chicago, 1965.

Whitaker, Arthur P. *The Huancavelica Mercury Mine*. Cambridge, Mass.: Harvard University Press, 1941.

Wilkie, James W. 'The Finance of the Bolivian Revolution'. Mimeo, 1968.

Wood, Bryce. *The Making of the Good Neighbor Policy*. New York: Columbia University Press, 1961.

Zilveti Arce, Pedro. *Bajo el signo de la barbarie*. Santiago de Chile: Editorial Orbe, 1946.

Zondag, Cornelius H. *The Bolivian Economy, 1952–1965. The Revolution and Its Aftermath*. New York: Frederick A. Praeger, 1966.

Zook, Jr., David H. *The Conduct of the Chaco War*. New York: Bookman Associates, 1960.

INDEX

'B' means Bolivia or Bolivian, 'LA' means Latin America, 'P' means *Partido*.

429

Index

433

29*

Index

Grupo de Cochabamba (RADEPA, q.v.), 370
Grupo Henri Barbusse, 204, 213
Grupo de Izquierda, 204, 211–13 passim, 236, 255, 288, 330
Grupo Oriental, 288
Grupo Orientalista, 303
Grupo (Revolucionario) Tupac Amaru, 125–6, 143–5, 194–5, 213
Guachalla, Luis Fernando, 43, 92, 135, 277
guano, 12, 16
Guaqui (town), 43, 164, 165
Guaraní offensives, 180, 181, 182
Guardia Republicana, 65, 84n.
Guevara Arze, Walter, 281, 284, 289, 290n., 296, 319; and Villarroel's government, 372, 373, 374n.
Gutiérrez Granier, Federico (financier), 222, 251, 268; minister of finance, 268–72 passim; resigns, 273; his role in cabinet, 292
Gutiérrez Guerra, José, 53, 54, 55–8, 63
Gutiérrez, José María, 151, 306
Guzmán, Augusto, 92, 264

hacendados, white, 7–8, 10, 34–5, 65, 165–8 passim
haciendas, 16in., 166
Hertzog, Dr Enrique, 221, 306, 344, 368, 374, 388, 389
Hinojosa, Roberto, 95, 109, 110, 111–21, 125
Hochschild, Mauricio, 119, 142, 257, 308, 318, 374, 403
'hombre símbolo' (Salamanca, q.v.), 127, 179, 194
Huancavelica mercury mines, 2
Huanchaca silver mines, 17–18, 35

Ichazo, Colonel (later General) Antenor, 323, 326, 328, 367, 368
immigration (of Jews), 307–8, 335
imperialism: of capitalists, 300–1, 337, 339, 364, 385; North American, 348, 351, 385; of USA, 100–1, 299–300, 399
imports, 59n., 164, 223, 347n.; of food, 164, 396
independence, Bolivian (1825), 1
Indian Congress, First National, 379; government decrees resulting from, 379–80

'Indian Problem', the (see also Indians), 70, 192, 236, 289–90, 300–1, 378
Indians (see also Indian Problem, Aymara and Quechua), 6–10, 144; exploited, 7–9; campesinos, see peasantry; colonos, see colonos; comunidades (free), 8–9, 61, 69, 73, 160, 163–7 passim, 284, 289, 290, 379; hacienda, 166; landless estate labourers, 8, 69, 161; migrate to cities, 9, 242–3; the ayllu, 67; rebel, 69, 112, 125; Saavedra and, 70; POS and, 73; integration of, 90–1, 99; FUB and, 99; votes for, 110; Siles and, 112; incited to violence, 125; and Chaco War, 155, 188, 241–2; Marof and, 192–3; had lost freedom and lands, 192; and post-war political groups, 207, 235; CSB and, 216; veterans of the war, 241–2; and sindicatos campesinos, 242; constitutional role of, 279; FIB and 330; MNR-RADEPA and, 379; and the revolution (1952), 402, 407
indigenismo and indigenista, 50, 90n., 96, 101, 144, 191, 192, 279, 339–40
industries, various, see under names of products
industry (see also agriculture and mining): light, 59, 60, 396; manufacturing, 59n., 396
inflation (see also cost of living), 218, 241, 253, 346–7, 398, 404, 492
Ingenieros, José, 98, 126
intellectuals and intelligentsia, 25–6, 29; general, 83, 91–4 passim, 98, 121, 124, 143, 167, 196, 254, 289; middle class, 93; exiled by Siles, 125; and Marxist literature, 126; demonstrations by (1931), 142; support Chaco War, 154; key, rounded up (July 1932), 154–5; in and after Chaco War, 189, 190, 197–8; CSB and, 213; radical, 236
intimidation, see violence
Iturralde, Abel, 66, 78, 82, 83
Iturralde Chinel, Fernando, 337, 347
Iturralde Chinel, Luis, 212, 217
Izquierda Boliviana (in Chile), 195, 211

Jewish immigrants, 307–8, 335, 337; defrauded, 308
Jewish imperialists, Wall Street, 337
juventud, la, 89–90

436

Index

Index

Index

radicalism, political, 95, 96, 98, 101, 121–2; and Chaco War, 190–7; in constitutional convention, 283–5
Radical party, 55; composition of, 64; in 1931 elections, 121n.
railroads (see also communications), 42–3; Pres. Arce's (Antofagasta-Altiplano), 26, 27; Argentina-Bolivia, 28; for silver and tin industries, 31; Patiño's, 35; Arica-La Paz, 42; Montes', 43; trade unions of, 61, 62, 71, 75; Saavedra's, 84; with Argentina, 84; La Paz-Buenos Aires, 84; loans for construction of, 103; open up Indian lands, 165; strikes on, 344, 349; Ostria Gutiérrez', 345
Ramírez, Domingo L., 83
Razón de Patria, see RADEPA
Razón, La (party newspaper), 34n., 52–3, 54; its alleged attacks on senate, 56; destroyed, 57; pro-Escalier, 65; and Siles, 94; closed down, 95; and communist issue ('a fabrication'), 97; and Chaco War, 170; defends Salamanca, 138; attacked by rioters in La Paz, 173; owned by C. V. Aramayo, 222; and Toro's government, 231, 252
Reconstruction Finance Corporation, 346, 400
referendum (the first in B) on constitutional amendments, 116, 117
Reforma Universitaria, 90
regionalism (see also localism), 28, 244, 303, 342
Reinaga, Fausto, 255
reivindicacionalismo and reivindicacionalista, 55, 102
República, La (party newspaper), 65, 88, 170, 238; demands Salamanca's resignation, 176; some of its staff exiled, 177; closed down, 180
Republican Era: Saavedra, 64–87; Siles, 88–113
Republican party (the original, P Union Republicana), 46–58; origin of, 46–7; its programme, 48–50; its gangs or 'clubs', 51; its newspaper (La Razón, q.v.), 52–3; and the presidency, 53; and Pando's 'assassination', 53–4; its prospects (1918), 54; and the littoral, 54–5; dissension in, 56–8; and the government, 57–8; in revolt (1920), 63; in power, 64–87; composition of,

64; factions in, 64–6, 76; and the right to strike, 65, 70–1; Saavedra and, 67; desertions from, 82; Siles and, 85–7; and P Nacionalista, 94, 105, 107; in 1931 elections, 121n.; and Tejada Sorzano, 201; and Beta Gama, 204
República Obrera Socialista, 195
'Revolución Restaurada', 406nn., 408n.
revolution, the national (April 1952), signs of and preludes to, 367–8, 391; its coming, 369–402; begins, 401–2; its impact and reforms, 403–9
revolutions, political and economic (see also violence), 25, 50, 57, 58n.; of July 1920, 63, 64, 114n.; slogans, 64; federal (1890s), 67; under Saavedra, 68; separatist (1924), 84; of 1930 (first attempt at radical social reform), 109–11, 115n., 116; of 1931, 142, 146; 17 May 1936, 225–7, 228, 238; future (pacific or violent?), 290; proletarian, 300; of May 1939, 309; of July 1946, 382, 385; Lora's, 384–5; MNR, 390, 391; of 1952, see revolution (above)
Rivera, Colonel (later General) Felipe M., 155, 182, 183, 187, 368
Riverín, Renato, 302, 304
roads (see also communications), 26, 35, 165; public and private, 285n.
Rodríguez, Colonel Ángel, 152, 183, 187
Rojas, Casto, 83, 172, 176
rojo group (of intellectuals), 25, 26
Roosevelt, President Franklin D.: his New Deal, 315
root crops, 164
Rosca (upper-class oligarchy), 34, 168, 258, 337, 339, 364
Royal Dutch Shell Group, 153, 194
rubber, 27, 28, 38, 45; boom (1890s), 33

Saavedra, Abdón S., 88, 89, 92
Saavedra, Bautista: personal details, 67–8; his opposition to Montes, 46, 58; and Republican party, q.v., 52, 54, 57; exiled, 54, 258; and Escalier, 57; leads conspiracy against Liberals, 58; in power, 64–87; dominates his party, 65; and labour, 65, 70–6; president, 66, 67; his government, 68; and the Indian problem, 70; and urban working and middle classes,

Index